Communication Research
Strategies and Sources

Communication
Research
Strategies and Sources

Seventh Edition

Rebecca B. Rubin
Kent State University

Alan M. Rubin
Kent State University

Paul M. Haridakis
Kent State University

Linda J. Piele
University of Wisconsin–Parkside

WADSWORTH
CENGAGE Learning

Australia • Brazil • Japan • Korea • Mexico • Singapore • Spain • United Kingdom • United States

WADSWORTH
CENGAGE Learning

Communication Research:
Strategies and Sources
Seventh Edition
Rebecca B. Rubin
Alan M. Rubin
Paul M. Haridakis
Linda J. Piele

Senior Publisher: Lyn Uhl

Executive Editor: Monica Eckman

Assistant Editor: Rebekah Matthews

Editorial Assistant: Colin Solan

Marketing Manager: Erin Mitchell

Marketing Coordinator: Darlene Macanan

Marketing Communications Manager: Christine Dobberpuhl

Project Manager, Editorial Production: Kristy Zamagni

Art Director: Linda Helcher

Print Buyer: Susan Carroll

Permissions Editor: Roberta Broyer

Production Service: Pre-Press PMG

Cover Designer: Grannan Graphic Design

Compositor: Pre-Press PMG

For product information
and technology assistance, contact us at **Cengage Learning Academic Resource Center, 1-800-423-0563**

For permission to use material from this text or product, submit all requests online at **cengage.com/permissions** Further permissions questions can be e-mailed to **permissionrequest@cengage.com**

Library of Congress Control Number: 2008942260

ISBN-13: 978-0-495-09588-0

ISBN-10: 0-495-09588-5

Wadsworth
20 Channel Center Street
Boston, MA 02210
USA

Cengage Learning products are represented in Canada by Nelson Education, Ltd.

To learn more about Wadsworth, visit **www.cengage.com/wadsworth.**

Purchase any of our products at your local college store or at our preferred online store **www.ichapters.com**

Printed in Canada
1 2 3 4 5 6 7 12 11 10 09

Contents

PART THREE
Communication Research Processes   195

CHAPTER 9 THE PROCESS OF COMMUNICATION RESEARCH   197

CHAPTER 10 DESIGNING THE COMMUNICATION RESEARCH PROJECT   211

CHAPTER 11 PREPARING RESEARCH PROJECTS   233

Preface

Communication Research: Strategies and Sources is designed to acquaint students with communication research and the vast array of information sources available in communication. The book describes the strategies involved in selecting, refining, and researching communication topics. It is a guide to the literature, explaining the content and utility of significant and representative research sources. It is also a communication research manual, and provides an opportunity for students to use and become familiar with communication research materials. Throughout the book, we stress the overall strategy of searching the literature for information on a particular topic.

This book provides a comprehensive overview of the necessary steps to begin communication research, and describes online and published sources that are available in or accessible through most medium-sized college and university libraries. The works that are described are used when conducting documentary, archival, or library research.

This type of research is necessary before attempting any other research methodology. Communication is a diverse discipline in which researchers are interested in many subjects. Thus, we explain the structure of the communication field and the types of research undertaken by students of communication. We focus on the basics of documentary and library research. These basics include developing and refining research questions, writing and organizing, beginning investigation of a topic, and acquiring the tools that make the research process efficient. We also describe each type of communication research source that is available for accomplishing a research goal.

This text is beneficial for students to become acquainted with the variety of available communication research resources and procedures. We introduce students to common research strategies and to sources in interpersonal, group, organizational, public, and mass communication. Because the book is designed as a supplemental text, there is a fair amount of flexibility in its use—ranging from one or two students working independently to students working on a module within a theory course or to an entire class focused on communication research. Any communication course that requires students to use the literature of the field is an appropriate vehicle for instruction in researching topics.

For example, the text is a helpful introduction to research procedures and the communication literature in fundamentals classes as well as in communication theory and research classes. It is appropriate for introductory-level classes in which it is desirable to acquaint students with the literature and research procedures of the field. In addition, instructors may select from among the many cited sources that are pertinent to their specific courses, such as Freedom of Speech, Media Law, Organizational Communication, Investigative Reporting, Interpersonal Communication, and Media Research. This book is also a useful manual to aid in research-paper writing for those working on independent studies. It is most helpful for preparing the literature reviews required in many courses and for thesis and dissertation proposals.

Students unfamiliar with a library will need general orientation instruction. The library staff will be able to clarify such matters as using the library catalog, locating periodicals and electronic media, and understanding any special location symbols used in the library.

Exercises are found at the end of each chapter. Some exercises require students to use several annotated sources. Generally, these questions hypothetically place students in a specific course and present a need to acquire information for a specific project. For example, "In your group communication class you are preparing to lead a discussion on the effects of cartoon violence on children...." These assignments lead students to important communication research sources and provide perspective on how the sources are useful in a variety of courses and situations. Questions reiterate points made in the text of the chapter and show how the sources can be used to build a comprehensive bibliography on a chosen communication topic. The book's website (see below) allows students to answer questions and e-mail answers directly to their instructors. Chapters in other sections of the book include exercises for classroom discussion.

Users of previous editions will notice major changes in the chapters devoted to searching the Internet and electronic databases. We have added artwork that depicts computer screens of some major search engines. We also have updated sources, adding new ones and eliminating older materials, and have updated several exercise questions. At the end of Chapters 1–8 we include boxed examples of student projects and explain how students have used chapter information for these projects. We have also attempted to identify more international sources and organizations, most of which are just a click away.

We have always been uncomfortable updating this text because we know that by the time it is published, important new sources or new editions will have appeared. To counter any datedness, we have developed a website for the text that contains links to sources listed in this edition, new sources and Internet sites, updated published materials, and additional information for students. This site can be accessed at **http://academic.cengage.com/communication/rubin/7e**.

Linda Piele, our steadfast colleague from library science, has decided to retire and pursue other interests. We value her expertise and contributions over the past 20+ years, yet understand her need to move into a different phase of life. Thank you, Linda, for your continued dedication to this book.

We welcome Paul Haridakis—our friend, past student, and colleague—to the project. Paul has not only taught with (and been taught by) the text, but his legal background and interest in Internet searching will benefit future developments. He also brings a fresh perspective to a subject that has changed considerably since our first edition in 1985. Once again, we thank the many students, teachers, and scholars who have helped us refine our ideas throughout our seven editions.

To the Student

We believe that students actively seek to master the available tools when learning about the field of communication. The library and the Internet contain many of these communication research tools. Our aim is to introduce these tools to you and to explain how to use them to increase your knowledge of communication. How much effort you give to this learning process will determine how much you personally gain from the process.

Overview

The book is divided into three main parts. In Part 1, we explain why and how communication research is undertaken. After surveying the field of communication in Chapter 1, we look at the research process, selecting and narrowing research topics and questions, searching the literature, and using computers to search databases and access information on computer networks.

In Part 2, we explore available types of communication research sources and reference materials. In Chapter 5 we consider general communication research sources such as subject handbooks, textbooks, encyclopedias, and annual reviews. These materials are helpful in defining subjects or topics you may wish to investigate. We examine access tools such as bibliographies, guides to the literature, indexes, and abstracts in Chapter 6. These tools are needed to locate sources and materials. In Chapters 7 and 8 we discuss more specific communication research sources, namely communication periodicals (scholarly journals and professional magazines) and information compilations (collections, statistical compendia, government publications, yearbooks, directories, dictionaries, and manuals). These periodicals and compilations are important for finding primary and factual data and for developing research projects.

In Part 3 we explain how to design and conduct research investigations and how to complete literature reviews and other projects. The first two chapters contain information about the research process and methods of conducting research. The next two chapters focus on writing projects and style. Appendix A continues the discussion of style with a guide to APA style, and Appendix B presents a glossary of terms and definitions.

Because we try to highlight a representative sample of references in each chapter, not all works important to the study of communication can be discussed at length. Numerous sources, however, are listed at the end of each chapter and are indexed at the end of the book. The sources we have selected do not constitute an exhaustive list. We chose them because they represent the many diverse areas of communication research, they are written in or translated into the English language, and they are available at many college and university libraries. We also identify specific sources of particular utility to communication researchers, such as archival and legal references available via specialized libraries.

As with any book, materials become dated, and new or revised sources become available between the time a book is written and is available for use. Visit our website **http://academic.cengage.com/communication/rubin/7e** for new and updated sources. You will undoubtedly uncover other important bibliographic tools in your literature searches. As you do, add them in the chapters and to the source index for quick future reference. Also, on the website you'll find the Internet/web sources that are listed in each chapter, so access is a click away. Bookmark the website given above for easy searching of web-based materials.

We mentioned earlier that a major goal is to introduce and explain bibliographic tools available for investigating communication topics. In so doing, we hope we accomplish a secondary goal of reducing the anxiety many students feel when researching a communication topic for the first time or when confronted with so much information they don't know where to start. We anticipate this book will be a useful starting point and reference guide and that it will assist you in learning about communication.

Helpful Hints

Students who have used earlier versions of this book have offered helpful hints. These tips make a lot of sense.

First, get to know the physical layout of the library you will be using. Find the reference section, the reserve desk, the library catalogs, and the computer stations. Discover how books and periodicals are arranged in your library. This information is usually available in printed form when you enter the library. Ask about the availability of CD-ROM databases, online databases, and accessibility of the Internet. Consult a reference librarian or staff member at an information desk if you have a question, any question. Or sign up for a library tour!

Second, become comfortable with searching the Internet. You'll be visiting many different types of databases, so knowing how to maneuver through them using your preferred browser is important. Learn how to open multiple windows, use the Back and Refresh options, and how to print both pages and frames. This will enable you to traverse the Internet efficiently.

Third, complete the exercises at the end of the chapters. Be sure to read each chapter thoroughly before trying to answer the questions. In fact, we have constructed exercises so that reading the chapter first is an enormous aid to completing the questions. Students who were looking for shortcuts to the questions in the past became frustrated. Actually, your effort will be reduced by reading the chapters before attempting to answer questions. There are no trick questions in the exercises. Each reference source you are asked to use is explained in the chapter. Read the annotations carefully. The sources that are annotated or described in detail sometimes provide clues for answering the questions. When you locate reference sources that are new to you, examine them carefully. Explore the table of contents, examine the preface and introduction, and look for an index. In so doing, the sources themselves will provide you with a more efficient method of use. If you find yourself spending more than 15 minutes on any one question, your approach to the problem may not be the best. Ask a reference librarian for advice. Also, ask for help when you cannot find a source you need. It might be shelved in a different location in the library.

Fourth, if you are working on a research paper, literature review, or research prospectus as you read this book, keep in mind the sources you examine as you develop a research topic or question. You might find it advantageous to return to the materials discussed in earlier chapters for a more thorough examination. For instance, the exercises in Part 2 sometimes ask you to look at only one volume of a multivolume work. Once you have solidified your own research topic, you might want to go back to other volumes to see whether they can lead you to additional references. Because you already will be familiar with how these sources are used, it will require little effort to check them for pertinent information. In a similar vein, if you have a clear-cut topic in mind as you progress through the chapters, do not hesitate to examine each source thoroughly as you use the guide. This will save you time in the future. You can easily compile a thorough bibliography as you proceed through the chapters of this book.

Fifth, update the references in this book whenever possible. Students in the past have found they misplace additional or updated references if they do not add them when they are first located. Update and add your new references at the end of each chapter and in the index. You may also want to augment the annotations and citations with your own notes on using the materials. In this way, the book will become an even more useful and comprehensive collection of communication research materials.

Communication Research Strategies

G ood strategy entails careful planning. Accordingly, communication research requires a comprehensive plan of action. Part 1 focuses on conventional search procedures for investigating communication topics.

In Chapter 1, we discuss the types of communication research projects students typically undertake and describe the general structure of the communication discipline. In Chapter 2, we outline search procedures and provide an orientation to library research. In Chapter 3, we explain strategies for searching computerized databases. In Chapter 4, we explain how to use the Internet for communication research and present special strategies for searching the World Wide Web.

Part 1 of the book, then, is an orientation to the process of communication research. We include end-of-chapter exercises to help you formulate a strategy—a plan of action—for completing research projects. If you are using this text in a college course, you will find it worthwhile to ask your instructor for feedback about how well you understand research strategies, based on your answers to the exercises.

Communication
Research
Strategies

chapter 1

Studying Communi...

W hy study communication? Those who do so will tell you that their work is driven by a need to know more about human interaction and the process of communication. Communication professionals develop skills for acquiring and using information throughout their professional lives. As students of communication, you need to be prepared to investigate and engage in academic and professional growth activities.

This book gives you many of the skills and resources you need for finding information to accomplish your academic and professional goals. It also introduces you to the research process, which is most helpful when the information you need isn't easy to find. Come along with us as we explore the maze of resources available to you as you conduct your research!

Research is often defined as systematic inquiry into a subject. The keyword in this definition, *systematic*, points to the need to examine topics methodically rather than to plunge haphazardly into sources. Two of our major goals in this book are to acquaint you with this step-by-step procedure of inquiry and to provide guidance for following these generally accepted principles and practices of research.

In this chapter, we explain how communication students and professionals become involved in the research process. First, we explore the profession and how the discipline is organized. This will give you an idea of the interdisciplinary nature of communication and a sense of what interests communication researchers. Then, we look at the types of projects that require systematic inquiry in the communication discipline.

THE COMMUNICATION DISCIPLINE

Communication has been defined in a variety of ways. Here, we define *communication* as a process by which people arrive at shared meanings through the interchange of messages. When people create and manage meanings and share their understanding of social reality, communication takes place. Political scientists, educators, business executives, linguists, poets, philosophers, scientists, historians, psychologists, sociologists, and anthropologists, to name some professionals, are concerned at least tangentially with communication in their specific areas of inquiry. Communication scholars, by contrast, focus on facets of the communication process. They are in fact concerned with how understanding is (or isn't) achieved and how messages influence important personal, societal, and global outcomes. Even though they use different tools for studying communication, their common interests, united focus, and complementary areas of expertise have formed a **discipline**.

Communication researchers examine the processes by which meanings are created and managed—in other words, how people structure and interpret messages and use symbols such as language in interpersonal, group, organizational, public, intercultural, and mediated contexts. Thus the breadth of communication inquiry is universal and inclusive, and the contexts in which the communication process is examined are diverse yet interrelated. It is little wonder that no other discipline of knowledge is quite as universal as communication.

Communication is a time-honored yet modern discipline. The Greek philosopher Aristotle (384–322 B.C.) devoted much thought to examining the constituent elements of *rhetoric*, or the available means of persuasion. From 1600 through the early 1900s, speech theorists focused on effective delivery of the spoken word. Early students of mass communication were intrigued by the effects of media-delivered messages. Contemporary communication researchers expanded their interests to include interpersonal, group, and organizational communication contexts and the processes that occur during communication. In examining the flow of information and the interchange of messages between individuals in a variety of contexts, researchers today probe the uses and effects of modern communication technologies in a world where people and societies are linked by instantaneous transmissions via computers and satellites.

Communication has a rich history, so rich that we cannot do justice to it here. For more information on the history of the communication discipline, consult the sources listed below.

Sources for the History of Communication

Benson, T. W. (Ed.). (1985). *Speech communication in the 20th century*. Carbondale, IL: Southern Illinois University Press.

Cohen, H. (1994). *The history of speech communication: The emergence of a discipline, 1914–1945*. Annandale, VA: National Communication Association.

Crowley, D., & Heyer, P. (Eds.). (1991). *Communication in history: Technology, culture, society* (2nd ed.). New York: Longman.

Delia, J. G. (1987). Communication research: A history. In C. R. Berger & S. H. Chaffee (Eds.), *Handbook of communication science* (pp. 20–98). Newbury Park, CA: Sage.

Rogers, E. M. (1994). *A history of communication study: A biographical approach*. New York: Free Press.

Schramm, W. (1980). The beginnings of communication study in the United States. *Communication Yearbook, 4*, 73–82.

Schramm, W. (1997). *The beginnings of communication study in America: A personal memoir*. S. H. Chaffee & E. M. Rogers (Eds.). Thousand Oaks, CA: Sage.

Schramm, W. L. (1988). *The story of human communication: Cave painting to microchip*. New York: Harper & Row.

Because communication is studied in several allied disciplines, you may sometimes find it difficult to focus on one particular research topic and to find all the available literature about that topic. And because communication is of interest in the social and behavioral sciences, the arts, and the humanities, many research sources exist in these disciplines. With so much information available, determining which sources are most pertinent becomes difficult.

For example, if you are interested in organizational communication, you will find pertinent reference materials in health education, business management, sociology, psychology, human resources, and other communication-related sources. However, the differences in vocabulary used can make understanding the works in these disciplines difficult for someone not studying in those fields. As a communication scholar, you are thus faced with learning about the communication process within a traditionally defined context while also trying to integrate knowledge from other disciplines.

Structure of the Discipline

As a result of this breadth and diversity, the communication literature includes a variety of subjects that define the field. Knowledge of these subjects will help you discover the most appropriate sources for your research. We have grouped these subjects into 10 major content categories: communication and technology, group communication, health communication, instructional communication, intercultural communication, interpersonal communication, language and symbolic codes, mass communication, organizational communication, and public communication. The study of communicators and their messages is common to all areas of communication. What differentiates one subject area from another is the focus on different settings, channels, or dominant modes of interaction.

1. *Communication and technology* is concerned with mediated communication and how people fulfill their entertainment or information needs by using technologies such as computers, cell phones, MP3 players, and digital video cameras. Scholars examine the impact of the technology on people, groups, organizations, and society. They also consider how people use technologies to enhance, complement, or substitute for face-to-face communication.

2. *Group communication* covers communication in groups of three or more persons. Researchers often study how groups emerge, accomplish their goals, and solve problems, and how group leaders function. Topics in small group communication include small group effectiveness, cohesion, conflict, group roles, team building, leadership, consensus, productivity, group culture, and social groups. In addition, family communication has evolved from group and interpersonal perspectives.

3. *Health communication* includes all aspects of illness and wellness. Communication with the disabled and ill, effectiveness of health promotion and information campaigns, communication between health care providers and patients, and the growing area of social support groups, either face-to-face or online, are topics of research interest. This fast-growing area combines interests in organizational, mass, and interpersonal communication.

4. *Instructional communication* focuses on pedagogy, media effects, and communication in the classroom. Communication pedagogy includes the study of distance learning or televised instruction, use of technology in the classroom, and methods of teaching specific communication classes. Mass media effects examines the impact of television, advertising, or film on children of various ages whereas developmental research employs theories to uncover children's growth differences and patterns. Communication in the classroom examines various student communication variables (e.g., communication apprehension, motivation to learn, and student gender differences), teacher communication behaviors (e.g., immediacy, credibility, and style), and classroom management issues (e.g., teacher power and student resistance).

5. *Intercultural and international communication* occurs in interpersonal and mediated settings. Some researchers focus on how people from different cultures communicate and form intercultural relationships, whereas others compare people's interpersonal traits, skills, or behaviors across different cultures (i.e., cross-culturally). Another main line of research compares national communication systems and examines the development of such systems and their impact on national growth and progress. Researchers interested in interpersonal, group, and mass communication come together in this subarea.

6. *Interpersonal communication* involves the study of people and their interactions or relationships. Researchers in this area study the use of verbal and nonverbal messages in developing and maintaining relationships between people. Some topics they find interesting are interpersonal competence, impression formation, spousal conflict, interpersonal attraction, relationship development, friendship, and relational communication.

7. *Language and symbolic codes* is concerned with verbal and nonverbal communication codes. When examining these codes, researchers focus on how language and nonverbal symbols are transmitted, received, and come to have meaning for people of the same or different cultures. Topics cover issues such as text or discourse, language intensity, language development in children, conversational flow, listening, proxemics, kinesics, and nonverbal immediacy.

8. *Mass communication* focuses on communication from a source or organization to many people via mediated channels such as television, radio, or newspapers under conditions of limited feedback. Those who study mass communication are concerned with how such mediated messages are formulated and received and how they affect individuals and society, as well as with media dominance and power. Mass communication researchers are often interested in media content and portrayals, media effects, history, ethics, formation of public opinion, policy and regulation, international media, and critical or textual analysis of messages.

9. *Organizational communication* is concerned with the processing and use of messages between and within organizations. It focuses on the complexities of communication in formal structures where many interpersonal and group relationships already exist. Researchers look at organizational networks, systems, conflict, negotiation, superior–subordinate relationships, training and development, and other aspects of organizational life.

10. *Public communication* covers communication in nonmediated public settings and focuses mainly on one-to-many communication. Primary topics include

rhetoric, public address, criticism, freedom of speech, persuasion, argumentation, and debate. Research focuses on speaker credibility, ethics, interpreting literature, propaganda, political campaigns, and communication education. Scholars in political communication combine public and mass communication perspectives.

These 10 subject areas are listed below, along with some terms that describe subareas of study relevant to each of the larger topics. These subareas can be useful when deciding on a research topic or locating materials in a library. Naturally, many subareas can be placed under broader headings because of the interdisciplinary and fluid nature of communication inquiry. Be sure to look at relevant handbooks (see Chapter 5) for additional subareas and topics of current interest.

Subareas of the Communication Discipline

Communication and Technology

Broadband/mobile/wireless/cellular
Computer-mediated communication
Digital information
Emerging technologies
Internet use and the World
   Wide Web
New media
Telecommunications and satellite
   systems
Visual communication design

Group Communication

Decision making
Family communication
Group dynamics
Intergenerational communication
Intergroup communication
Leadership
Problem solving

Health Communication

Communication with disabled
   and sick people
Health promotion
   and information campaigns
Physician–patient
   communication
Social support groups

Instructional Communication

Communication pedagogy
Developmental communication
Media effects on children
Teacher–student interaction

Intercultural/International Communication

Adaptation and enculturation
Comparative media systems
Cross-cultural communication
Facework and identity
Individualism–collectivism
(National) developmental
   communication

Interpersonal Communication

Conflict management
Dyadic communication
Gender and communication
Interpersonal influence
Interpersonal perception
Intrapersonal communication
Relational communication

Language and Symbolic Codes

Conversation and discourse
Linguistics, pragmatics, semiotics
Nonverbal communication
Semantics and sociolinguistics

Mass Communication

Advertising
Broadcasting and
    telecommunications
Economics of media industries
Film and cinema
Journalism
Media effects
Media ethics
Policy and regulation
Popular culture
Public relations

Organizational Communication

Business and professional
    communication
Human communication technology
Negotiation and mediation
Organizational behavior
Socialization and assimilation
Training and development

Public Communication

Argumentation
Debate
Environmental communication
Freedom of speech
Legal communication
Performance studies
Persuasion and attitude change
Political communication
Public address
Rhetorical theory and criticism

These topics illustrate how diversified the communication discipline is. Students have many available avenues of scholarship. Scholars often need to know about more than just one topic, so they conduct research on many, often overlapping, topics during their careers. This interest in multiple areas influences scholars' memberships in professional communication organizations. Members of the communication discipline often belong to several organizations or to several divisions within such organizations.

COMMUNICATION ORGANIZATIONS

Communication associations generally focus on one or more subareas of the discipline. Some are very narrow societies and seek members only in one subarea, whereas others are broad and eclectic, encouraging membership from many communication subareas. That is, some organizations exist for a specific purpose and subgroup, and others reflect the many interests of their members. Some organizations are more scholarly, whereas others are more professionally oriented. Most organizations hold annual conferences or conventions, publish materials and newsletters, and provide networking possibilities and news to their members.

Activities

Among other activities, communication associations hold annual meetings or conventions in different locations. The papers presented at these conventions represent the most current concerns of communication researchers and can be helpful in your research projects. Most associations have moved to an online version of their convention program, which allows members to examine various topics (and sometimes abstracts) of papers presented at the meeting. Students are often encouraged to attend these conferences, either to attend sessions and hear about these new developments or to present their own research studies. Both scholarly and professional associations also sponsor student organizations or groups to encourage students to become members (often with reduced annual fees).

Some convention papers are submitted to the Educational Resources Information Center (ERIC) for inclusion in the Resources in Education (RIE) system (see Chapter 6). This system places the papers in electronic data files, and researchers can access the collection. Some papers are collected in proceedings, which are published by the association or are available online or on a CD-ROM. But even if a paper is not readily available, association members can look up an author's address in an online directory (you'll need to be a member and have a password), or possibly via a World Wide Web (WWW) search you can write to an author to request a copy.

Other papers find their way into scholarly or professional journals. Paper authors submit these to the journal's editor, who then seeks advice from editorial board members on whether or not to publish the paper. Unfortunately, there could be a 2-year delay (or longer) between the time the paper is first submitted and the time it is published, given the time it takes for manuscript revisions and the printing process. It is possible to receive a copy of a convention paper by attending the convention, by writing to the author, by downloading the paper from a database, or by having paper copies made from a CD-ROM.

Newsletters and Publications

Scholarly and professional organizations publish many materials of interest to communication scholars. The National Communication Association (NCA), for example, publishes monographs, journals, tapes, books, reports, bibliographies, and a newsletter. The NCA newsletter, *Spectra*, is sent to members monthly to inform them about new developments in the field; about fellow members' promotions, grants, and new appointments; and about job openings in communication. Issues also contain reports on publications and conventions that are of interest to members. It is also available on the NCA website. NCA also manages a weekly listserv (electronic newsletter) called CRTNet, which distributes information on jobs and grants, discussion of relevant issues, and questions or requests for assistance or information.

Both the International Communication Association (ICA) and the Association for Education in Journalism and Mass Communication (AEJMC) publish general newsletters with news of issues, events, people in the field, and job listings. The Broadcast Education Association (BEA) publishes *Feedback*, its official communication of association news as well as professional essays and articles. The BEA also sends members electronic mailings. Several divisions of these four organizations also have listservs and their own newsletters, which are sent to members of those divisions. Organizations also produce online membership directories. These are helpful if you wish to contact researchers directly about their work. For more information about these professional organizations, contact the organizations directly; their Web addresses are given in the following list.

Scholarly Communication Associations Based in the U.S.

American Communication Association <http://www.americancomm.org>
Association for Education in Journalism and Mass Communication
  <http://www.aejmc.org>
Broadcast Education Association <http://www.beaweb.org>
International Communication Association <http://www.icahdq.org>
International Listening Association <http://www.listen.org>
National Communication Association <http://www.natcom.org>
World Communication Association <http://facstaff.uww.edu/wca>

Scholarly Communication Associations Based Outside the U.S.

Australian & New Zealand Communication Association <http://www.anzca.net>
Australian Speech Communication Association <http://www.
  australianspeechcommunication.com>
Canadian Communication Association <http://www.acc-cca.ca>
European Communication Research and Education Association <http://www.ecrea.eu>
International Association for Media & Communication Research
  <http://www.iamcr.org>
International Association of Language and Social Psychology <http://www.ialsp.org>
International Speech Communication Association (Formerly European Speech
  Communication Association) <http://www.isca-speech.org>
International Telecommunications Union <http://www.itu.int/net/home/index.aspx>
Pacific and Asian Communication Association <http://www.paca4u.com>
Russian Communication Association <http://www.russcomm.ru/eng/index.shtml>

Several additional organizations are affiliated with NCA and ICA. These tend to be more focused societies with a limited scope or audience. Check their home pages for additional information on membership and services for affiliate organizations, such as those listed below.

Selected NCA or ICA Affiliate Organizations

American Forensic Association <http://www.americanforensics.org>
Association for Chinese Communication Studies <http://www.uni.edu/comstudy/ACCS/
  home.html>
Chinese Communication Association <http://www.cca1.org>
Deutsche Gesellschaft für Publizistik und Kommunikationswissenschaft
  <http://www.dgpuk.de>
Korean American Communication Association <http://www.KACAnet.org>
Media Ecology Association <http://www.media-ecology.org>
National Forensic Association <http://cas.bethel.edu/dept/comm/nfa>
Religious Communication Association <http://www.americanrhetoric.com/rca>
Rhetoric Society of America <http://rhetoricsociety.org>
Society for New Communication Research <http://sncr.org/>

Types of Associations

The associations mentioned are national or international scholarly associations. We encourage graduate and undergraduate students to join those which interest them. Although most members are academic faculty and professional communicators, the associations offer special student memberships. Meetings of regional and state communication associations also provide valuable opportunities for students to attend their conferences and to present their research. There are four regional associations affiliated with the NCA. Because the executive secretaries (and thus the addresses) change often, check the associations' websites for current addresses.

Regional Scholarly Associations

Eastern Communication Association (ECA) <http://www.ecasite.org>
Central States Communication Association (CSCA) <http://www.csca-net.org>
Southern States Communication Association (SSCA) <http://www.ssca.net>
Western States Communication Association (WSCA) <http://www.westcomm.org>

Some professional organizations focus on the practical activities of their members' careers. Such organizations also distribute newsletters, hold annual conventions, and compile directories of members. They differ from the more scholarly organizations in their emphasis on information and techniques for dealing with practical problems and situations arising in practitioners' lives. Many offer scholarships and fellowships and have student chapters. Contact the following organizations for additional information.

Professional Communication Associations

Radio/TV/Film/Wireless/Satellite
Academy of Motion Picture Arts and Sciences <http://www.oscars.org>
National Association of Broadcasters <http://www.nab.org>
National Association of Television Program Executives <http://www.natpe.org>
Radio-Television News Directors Association <http://www.rtnda.org>
Satellite Broadcasting and Communications Association <http://www.sbca.com>
Society of Broadcast Engineers <http://www.sbe.org>
Society of Motion Picture and Television Engineers <http://www.smpte.org/home>
Wireless Communications Association International <http://www.wcai.com>

Newspapers/Magazines/Journalism
American Society of Newspaper Editors <http://www.asne.org>
Investigative Reporters and Editors <http://www.ire.org>
Magazine Publishers of America <http://www.magazine.org/home>
National Conference of Editorial Writers <http://www.ncew.org>
National Press Club <http://www.press.org>
National Press Photographers Association <http://www.nppa.org>
Newspaper Association of America <http://www.naa.org>
Society of Environmental Journalists <http://www.sej.org>
Society of Professional Journalists <http://www.spj.org>

PR/Marketing/Advertising
Advertising Educational Foundation <http://www.aef.com/index.html>
American Advertising Federation <http://www.aaf.org>
American Association of Advertising Agencies <http://www.aaaa.org>
American Marketing Association <http://www.marketingpower.com>
Association for Women in Communications <http://www.womcom.org>
Direct Marketing Association <http://www.the-dma.org/index.php>
International Advertising Association <http://www.iaaglobal.org>
Outdoor Advertising Association of America <http://www.oaaa.org>
Public Relations Society of America <http://www.prsa.org>

Public Speaking/Business/Education/Health/Writing
Association for Business Communication <http://www.businesscommunication.org>
Association for Educational Communications and Technology <http://www.aect.org>
Association for Media Literacy <http://www.aml.ca>
Health and Sciences Communications Association <http://www.hesca.org>
International Association of Business Communicators <http://www.iabc.com>
Media Communications Association International <http://www.mca-i.org>
National Speakers Association <http://www.nsaspeaker.org>
Speakers Platform <http://www.speaking.com>
Toastmasters International <http://www.toastmasters.org>

Last but not least, several organizations are focused on students. Some require students to demonstrate academic excellence to join whereas others welcome students from particular majors or with certain interests. Check the organizations listed below for admission requirements.

Student Associations

Lambda Pi Eta <http://www.natcom.org/nca/template2.asp?bid=21>
Public Relations Student Society of America <http://www.prssa.org>
Sigma Chi Eta <http://www.natcom.org/nca/template2.asp?bid=22>
Student Clubs <http://www.natcom.org/nca/template2.asp?bid=230020030039>

Divisions

Because of the diversity of their members' interests, major professional communication organizations have developed classifications for interest groups in the field. The National Communication Association has divisions or interest groups in, for example, applied communication, critical and cultural studies, family communication, health communication, interpersonal communication, Latina/Latino communication studies, mass communication, political communication, and rhetorical and communication theory, among other areas. For additional information about the organization, its publications, divisions, conventions, and affiliated associations, visit the association's home page at www.natcom.org. (When you see references to the SCA in publications listed in this book, keep in mind that the NCA changed its name from the Speech Communication Association [SCA] several years ago.)

The International Communication Association has similar divisions. Most subject area divisions of the ICA are reflected in earlier volumes of the *Communication Yearbook*, first published in 1977. This source, along with *Communication Abstracts*, first published in 1978 and recently made available as a computerized database, provides important access to and integration of communication knowledge. Both publications are valuable sources for those who study communication. *Communication Abstracts* is described in Chapter 6, along with *ComAbstracts, ComIndex*, and *Communication & Mass Media Complete*, other important bibliographic databases for the discipline. For additional information about the association and its divisions, conventions, and publications, visit ICA's home page at <http://www.icahdq.org.

Mass communication organizations also have specialized divisions that reflect several concerns and content areas. The Association for Education in Journalism and Mass Communication has divisions in advertising, history, law, magazine, and newspaper, for example. The Broadcast Education Association (BEA) has several divisions, including interactive media & emerging technologies, gender, international, management, and research. Be sure to examine the websites of these organizations for a complete overview of the scope of their members' interests.

COMMUNICATION RESEARCH PROJECTS

Throughout a college career, a communication student will face a wide variety of assignments requiring the use of research tools and skills:

- Compiling bibliographies
- Completing take-home exams
- Conducting audience or consumer surveys
- Conducting original research investigations
- Giving speeches or oral readings
- Investigating and writing news stories
- Leading seminars
- Preparing advertising or public relations campaigns
- Preparing debate cases or group discussions
- Writing abstracts, research reports, theses, or dissertations
- Writing television, radio, or film scripts, or critiques
- Writing term papers, seminar papers, or literature reviews

Although there are different types of student assignments or projects, many have similar characteristics. For example, projects typically have a persuasive, informative, or combined **goal**. This means the student might attempt to change the audience's mind, convince it of something, or alter its beliefs. Or the goal might be informational in nature, attempting to impart new knowledge to others through description and explanation. Sometimes, after considering available information, students need to take a stand and defend it with relevant information.

The **scope** of a project can be narrow, moderate, or broad. A narrow project is limited by time or space (e.g., a 3-minute speech or a five-page paper). A broader project might be limited by the amount of information available or be expected to include all relevant sources (e.g., a dissertation).

The **audience** can be as narrow as a college class or as broad as the general public. Often the audience is an academic one, so the language is scholarly and technical. A project with an applied focus will have a specific work group in mind. The level of language should be adjusted to that of the audience.

To complete all assignments effectively, you'll need to be familiar with the methods and materials of communication research—the tools within and outside the library that provide relevant information. You also need to know how to use these tools.

Class assignments require documenting facts and finding pertinent supporting materials. Sometimes instructors suggest you read a specific study (e.g., McCroskey and McCain's 1974 article on interpersonal attraction, Hart and Burks's 1972 essay on rhetorical sensitivity, or Horton and Wohl's 1956 discussion of parasocial interaction). How would you go about finding these works given such limited information? One way is to consult an index (see Chapter 6) to find complete bibliographic citations for journal articles.

Sometimes you will explore the scholarly literature for research on a particular idea or topic of interest. You might find a topic interesting or relevant to your life and wonder what scholars actually know about it. At other times, you will need specific facts—the current number of employees in the television or newspaper industry or the most recent decision of the Federal Trade Commission about advertising, for example. You may have to choose a method of running a meeting in a particular organization or to read articles to find out which questions are of interest and how to phrase your own questions.

ACADEMIC PURSUITS

Preparing a term paper, literature review, research study, or thesis or dissertation prospectus requires extended use of the communication literature. Often students conduct their own reseprintarch investigations by asking research questions, designing a study, and collecting and analyzing data. These projects require you to examine past research in the field to determine which important communication problems still need to be addressed and whether your research question has already been satisfactorily answered by others. They give you a solid foundation on which to build an investigation or to generate hypotheses about how communication concepts are related to one another.

For example, suppose you decide to conduct a research investigation and you conclude, after browsing through the literature, that you want to study the subject of eye contact. After reading more of the literature, you choose to examine the effect of eye contact on length of conversation during an interpersonal interaction. You will need to give a reason for proposing this study (i.e., why it is important) and make a prediction about how the variables (eye contact and length of conversation) are related. The first section of your research proposal should summarize and analyze the findings of research studies that have previously examined these variables. Then your hypotheses—educated or informed guesses about the relationships between the variables—will be the end product of your exhaustive literature search.

Sometimes you have not done enough research to allow an educated guess, so you pose a research question to guide the study. Or perhaps your method is first to observe people's eye contact when interacting with others and then to arrive at an explanation or theory about the role of eye contact in interpersonal interaction. This latter method is more *inductive* than *deductive* in nature; that is, you are reasoning from specific observations to a general principle. We will discuss different approaches to conducting a research study in Chapters 9 and 10.

PROFESSIONAL PURSUITS

The need to seek information and the importance of knowing what information is available are certainly not limited to the academic world. Communication professionals refer to such materials on a daily basis. For example:

- Film critics search past film reviews for references to particular directors.
- Public relations specialists consult directories for names and addresses of organizations.
- Television producers check current statistical sources to ascertain that a documentary is current.
- Communication consultants use abstracts and indexes to learn about new training methods.
- Advertising or media researchers search scholarly studies for relevant communication research.
- Political speechwriters examine collections of speeches and editorials for themes and issues.
- Journalists check grammatical usage or news style by consulting a wire service handbook.
- Professors keep abreast of their fields by reading professional and scholarly periodicals.

Being able to answer questions systematically and knowing what materials are available and how to find and use them are essential in any career. These materials are the tools of the trade. The projects assigned in your classes help you understand how communication researchers satisfy their need to know more about communication. Such assignments teach you systematic methods of searching for knowledge. In effect your link to the communication discipline is through your participation in scholarship.

In the examples at the end of the chapter, we present six typical assignments students complete in communication classes. In several later chapters, we'll show you how students used the information in the chapter for their projects.

SUMMARY

Communication research, like all research, must be systematic to be effective. Communication researchers study the processes through which meaning and social reality are created and managed. Researchers examine the flow of information and the interchange of messages between individuals in different contexts. Although the study of communication is broad-based and interdisciplinary, the field can be divided into several major areas of focus. Scholarly and professional communication associations publish scholarly journals and trade magazines, organize conventions and conferences, and produce materials and newsletters to keep their members informed. Students can become active in these associations while they are still in college. These associations help students and professionals accomplish their academic and professional goals. Students also complete a variety of assignments in their classes.

References

Hart, R. P., & Burks, D. M. (1972). Rhetorical sensitivity and social interaction. *Communication Monographs*, *39*, 75–91.

Horton, D., & Wohl, R. R. (1956). Mass communication and para-social interaction: Observations on intimacy at a distance. *Psychiatry*, *19*, 215–229.

McCroskey, J. C., & McCain, T. A. (1974). The measurement of interpersonal attraction. *Communication Monographs*, *41*, 261–266.

EXAMPLES

Jack is taking a basic public-speaking class. One assignment in the class is to prepare and deliver a persuasive speech. Ethics has always been a subject of interest to Jack, so pursuing a topic on communication and ethics seems worthwhile. This assignment has the following characteristics:

> GOAL: Persuasion—To take a stand and defend it
> SCOPE: Narrow
> AUDIENCE: General—College students
> SIMILAR PROJECTS: Debate case, critical essay, editorial, opinion paper

Valerie has an ongoing interest in new technologies and how they complement interpersonal communication. Recent experiences with the college's new voice mail system cause her to wonder whether this asynchronous form of communication is better than the former system. A journalism assignment to write a newspaper article about this new system provides a good opportunity to learn more about it. This assignment has the following characteristics:

> GOAL: Information—To describe and explain
> SCOPE: Narrow
> AUDIENCE: General—College students
> SIMILAR PROJECTS: Newspaper article, broadcast story,
>   documentary, magazine article, informative speech

Robin is taking an introductory communication theory class in which a variety of theories are discussed and explained. Students in the class must choose one theory and (a) write a five-page paper that explains what the theory is about and (b) lead a 10-minute discussion of the theory in class. Robin has always been interested in how we get to know others, so attribution theory seems like a good choice. This assignment has the following characteristics:

> GOAL: Information—To describe and explain
> SCOPE: Moderate
> AUDIENCE: Academic—Professor and students
> SIMILAR PROJECTS: Term paper, seminar paper, take-home exam, classroom report

Jason is a taking a graduate seminar in interpersonal and mediated communication. Students are expected to conduct a thorough review of the literature on a specific topic and to propose several possible research directions. So far, exciting topics include talk radio, portrayals of relationships on television, and parasocial interaction. Jason's first step is to find out whether these topics furnish sufficient research material to support a 20- to 25-page assignment. This assignment has the following characteristics:

> GOAL: Combined—To describe research findings with a strong thesis
> SCOPE: Limited by demands of the project
> AUDIENCE: Academic—Scholars
> SIMILAR PROJECTS: Research prospectus, senior thesis, thesis, dissertation

Kat, Rocky, and **Michelle** are taking an organizational communication class. One project is to develop a training module that can be used in any organization. The group is supposed to develop and pilot test the module in class this semester. Naturally, it takes the group quite a while to decide on a good topic, but eventually everyone decides that conflict resolution at work would be appropriate and interesting. This assignment has the following characteristics:

> GOAL: Informative/instructional—To teach others new skills
> SCOPE: Narrow, focused
> AUDIENCE: Specific and applied
> SIMILAR PROJECTS: Group discussion, campaign

Eric, Gregory, Anthony, and **Scott** are working on a research methods class project. Their goal is to conduct a research study on campus. They all are interested in how students use the Internet for maintaining interpersonal relationships with their families, so they decide to formulate some research questions and conduct a survey of students later in the semester. This assignment has the following characteristics:

> GOAL: Informative—To discover new knowledge
> SCOPE: Moderate—Focused area of investigation but requires thorough examination of literature

AUDIENCE: Academic—Professor and fellow students; possibly a
scholarly meeting
SIMILAR PROJECTS: Conducting audience or consumer surveys,
writing abstracts, research reports, theses, or dissertations

EXERCISES

1. Describe two situations in your anticipated career that require you to have knowledge of communication research. For assistance, speak to a professional in a related field and ask about communication research in that profession.
2. Identify three key terms or headings in the communication subject areas listed in this chapter that interest you. Explain how these key terms can be applied to projects you plan to complete in the near future, such as a literature review, speech, news story, group discussion, or term paper.
3. Indicate the main subject area described in this chapter with which you most closely identify at this point in your education. Find a scholarly communication organization that has a division in that area. Contact the organization for information about the division.
4. Examine some newsletters from the professional associations identified in this chapter. What issues are currently of concern to members? What functions do these newsletters serve for members?
5. Locate the home page of a professional association listed in this chapter. How is the site organized? What would you have to do to join this organization?

chapter 2

Searching the
Communication
Literature

T he process of conducting library research in communication is fairly
standard, no matter what sort of project you are attempting. Literature reviews,
research reports, thesis or dissertation prospectuses, debates, speeches, group
discussions, interviews, news editorials, and feature articles all begin the same
way. You will need to select and refine a topic, identify core concepts and
search terms, locate and read background information, decide which types of
sources support your topic, select and use appropriate databases and other
access tools, and locate and obtain the needed publications and documents. It's
a straightforward process.

Throughout this process you will need to continue to adjust your research
topic, evaluate carefully the citations and materials you retrieve, and identify
additional search terms and important authors to recycle into your searches of
print and electronic sources. Once you've assembled your sources, you might
identify some gaps in your research and head back to the library or the Internet. In fact, although the search process has starting and ending points, it can
seem at times more circular than linear. Effective research usually entails re-
cycling through some of the intermediary steps. We strongly recommend that
you document your research with careful and complete notes as you proceed.
This all takes time, but it is time well spent, and it will save you time and
frustration in the end.

Those new to conducting research frequently fall into the trap of under-
estimating the amount of time needed for doing the research. They reason that,
thanks to computers, all they need to do is pick a topic, go to the library or
access it electronically, type in the first search terms that come to mind, pull up
and print their results, and head home to write up their project. After all,

everything is online, right? Because the whole process shouldn't take more than a few hours, why not wait until a week (or a few days) before the project is due to get started on your research?

Unfortunately, everything is not online, and computers neither read minds nor evaluate the suitability of materials for a particular purpose. Finding the right, credible, quality sources takes time. Furthermore, short time frames don't allow time for adjusting topics, learning to use unfamiliar databases, refining electronic searches, asking librarians for help, recalling books that are checked out, tracking down off-the-shelf periodicals, and sending for that perfect-sounding book or article through interlibrary loan—let alone reading, evaluating, and digesting resources as the search progresses. Once home, you find that quickly compiled materials make for difficult-to-write projects. You might have found 10 or 20 sources—or whatever was needed for the assignment—but these sources just don't hang together, or they lack a clear focus. The result is anxious and frustrated students and disappointed instructors. Therefore, the time to get started on any research project is immediately after it's assigned. Instructors allow lead time for projects because they know from personal experience such time is necessary.

In this chapter we describe in some detail the steps involved in the research process. Later chapters fill out many of the concepts presented. For example, in this chapter we refer briefly to some characteristics of electronic databases and procedures for searching them, even though we won't thoroughly explain them until Chapter 3. We also refer in this chapter to different types of access tools and publications that are covered in detail in Part 2. For this reason, we suggest you read this chapter now to set the stage and then review it after you've finished reading Part 2.

To conduct library research, you'll need to have a basic familiarity with your library and its services. Many students will have gained this knowledge through library instructional programs offered to freshman classes. But if not, the following section is for you. Terms that are in **bold print** are defined in the Glossary (see Appendix B), which you may want to bookmark for quick referral as you read this section. In addition, references to books on library research processes by Bolner and Poirier (2007), Cooper and Hedges (1994), Katz (2002), and List (2002) are listed at the end of the chapter for additional reading.

BECOMING FAMILIAR WITH YOUR LIBRARY AND ITS SERVICES

Many libraries conduct drop-in orientation sessions or offer self-guided tours and handouts for new users. Take advantage of these if offered, because the information and tips you learn there will save you much confusion and frustration later.

Lacking such an orientation, the best approach when using a library new to you is simply to find the reference desk and ask a **reference librarian** some basic questions. He or she will be happy to help you find your way around and may be able to offer you instructional handouts on using the catalog and other resources. By the way, never feel reluctant to ask for such help from a librarian. That's why the reference desk is there.

Find out where the **book stacks** (library term for *bookshelves*) are located and how they are arranged. Most college and university libraries are arranged by Library of Congress (**LC**) call numbers (a mixture of letters and numbers), although a few use the Dewey Decimal System you're probably accustomed to from your school and public libraries.

Library of Congress Call Number	Book Title	Dewey Call Number
HD30.3 .G656 1998	Corporate Communications for Executive 1998	658.45 G653 C822

About all you need to know about Library of Congress call numbers is that the first one or two letters designate broad disciplines. For example, as a communication researcher, you'll find that many of the sources and tools you use fall into sections beginning with these letters:

BF	Psychology	JK	Political science
H	Social sciences (general)	K	Law
HD, HF	Business management	L	Education
HM	Sociology	P, PN	Communication

You'll also need to ask where the current and **bound periodicals** (magazines, journals, and newspapers) are housed. If a periodical is on **microfilm** or **microfiche**, is it kept in a separate location? How can you tell which periodicals the library subscribes to and where they are located? Are they arranged alphabetically by title, by call number, or by a different subject arrangement? How can you tell to which **full-text periodicals** the library subscribes? Are they available online at your institution? Where are the computer workstations that provide access to the library **catalog**, periodical indexes, reference databases that the library has licensed, and the **World Wide Web** (web)? How is the menu arranged? Will that menu also tell you about specialized databases available only on **CD-ROM** or online? Is it possible to access the electronic resource menu from other on- and off-campus locations? What sort of printing is available? Will you need a special card or password?

Almost all libraries maintain collections of reference materials (e.g., encyclopedias, handbooks, dictionaries, yearbooks, and almanacs). **Reference books**, which are designed to be consulted rather than read cover to cover, usually are part of a **noncirculating collection** (i.e., they cannot be checked out of the library). Find out where the **reference collection** is located and how these materials are identified in the catalog. Also find out how to identify those that have been made available electronically and that can be accessed via the library's website. Many libraries also have separate sections that house government documents. Find out whether these materials are listed in the main catalog and, if not, what **access tools** are available to identify and locate them. Most libraries with separate government document collections arrange materials using Superintendent of Documents (SuDocs) numbers. These numbers classify materials by the issuing agency rather than by subject.

If the library doesn't own some of the books or periodical articles you identify and they aren't available electronically through one of your library's full-text databases, you may want to order them from another library using your library's **interlibrary loan system**. Requests for such loans are usually filled out at the reference desk, the circulation desk, or the interlibrary loan department. Many libraries also allow you to file requests electronically by completing a form on their websites. Ask a librarian how to do this. The normal loan period for books is about 2 weeks. Photocopies of articles are yours to keep.

An item requested through interlibrary loan may take 2 or more weeks to arrive— this is one reason you need to begin research projects early in the semester. If you do end up short on time, you can look for an item at other local libraries. Another library in your region might own the work. You will probably be able to access the individual catalogs of other libraries in your region through the Internet. Or, perhaps, there is a state or regional **union catalog**, which lists the holdings of multiple libraries. Such catalogs can tell you whether the item is checked out or is kept in noncirculating reference collections. You can also use the Online Computer Library Center (OCLC) *WorldCat*, a national union catalog, to determine which libraries own the materials. Unfortunately, *WorldCat* cannot tell you whether the materials have been checked out. Ask at the reference desk about the availability of regional catalogs and *WorldCat*.

Interlibrary loan helps overcome one complication that can arise when the journal issue you want is at the bindery (i.e., librarians send out journal issues to be bound into hardbound volumes once all issues for a year have arrived). If you know what journal article you want (as opposed to just wanting to browse through an issue), you should be able to request a paper copy through interlibrary loan.

Library policies and procedures differ, library by library. You need to be aware of the protocols followed in the libraries you use. If a book has been checked out, some libraries will allow you to put a "hold" on it when it is returned or to recall the book from the borrower. If the catalog indicates that an item is owned but is missing from the shelf, see whether you can have it "searched." The library will notify you if the item is located. (Don't expect this to happen overnight; it can take several weeks.) Or, perhaps, your library has sorting shelves that you can peruse. Because libraries' protocols differ, inquire about specific procedures at the main information desk of your library. For basic guidelines on using research libraries, see sources in the following list.

Sources of Information on Library Research

Beasley, D. R. (2000). *Beasley's guide to library research*. Toronto: University of Toronto Press.

Mann, T. (2005). *The Oxford guide to library research*. New York: Oxford University Press.

Also, become familiar with the various features of your library's website. There will likely be a link to your library's online catalog and separate links to reference sources, databases, Internet resources, and electronic books and journals. You should be able to find information about remote access to your library from your home computer, on proxy information (whether you need your computer to prove that you are connected to the university, in order to access certain databases), and how to use the online services from off campus. Be sure to read thoroughly how to access these resources and databases and how to get help when you can't get the connection you seek.

As you go about using the library for your research and completing the exercises in this book, you will inevitably come up with additional questions. Never hesitate to ask reference librarians to help you. Some libraries have chatrooms available online for students and faculty to ask a librarian a question. They realize that libraries are somewhat complicated to use and that users will have many questions. When librarians go to an unfamiliar library, they also have to ask questions.

SEARCH STRATEGY

When you've figured out where things are, you're ready to tackle a communication research project. At this point, we're going to outline a general **search strategy** for your research topic. Although this appears as a list of steps, expect it occasionally to be a circular process. By this we mean that as you start retrieving and examining citations, bibliographies, and reading materials, you will come across additional terms and authors that can be recycled back into your search. You will find yourself looping back to repeat one or more steps. Expect to test, evaluate, and adjust. Be flexible. And know when to stop.

1. Select, narrow, and adjust your topic.
2. Identify types of sources needed.
3. Select appropriate databases and other access tools.
4. Decide what types of searches to do.
5. Formulate the search.
6. Examine the results and modify the search.
7. Evaluate and summarize information.
8. Read materials thoroughly, taking careful notes and highlighting important sections.
9. Systematically document everything.
10. Decide when to stop!

The Topic

Selecting, Narrowing, and Adjusting a Topic

Select a Topic

Often the most difficult part of the research process is selecting a topic and defining the research area. You need to identify a topic that is suitable for the project at hand and for which you will be able to find previous research. It's easy to pick a topic that is too broad, such as *interpersonal communication*. On the other hand, picking a topic that is too narrow can give you problems, too. There are no easy answers because topic selection is not a mechanical process. You can't type a few terms into the computer, for example, and expect the computer to come up with a topic. Many strategies, though, can help. One is to find an appropriate starting place.

Your starting point should be determined by your familiarity with the structure and terminology of the field. If the field is generally unfamiliar to you, you will want to step back and start with a source that can provide a comprehensive picture of the entire discipline (e.g., communication) or subfield (e.g., group communication). For your first research projects in communication, you would do well to find and browse through some general sources that will acquaint you with the various facets of communication and its terminology. Some of the sources described in Chapter 5—handbooks, textbooks, subject encyclopedias, and annual reviews—can serve this purpose.

You can get ideas for possible research topics by examining the textbooks used in your courses. Browsing handbooks and subject encyclopedias in communication and related disciplines can also help you find a topic that interests you. Specific topics can also be found in annual reviews, periodical indexes, and abstracts. **Abstracts** generally give paragraph-length summaries of research studies in articles published in scholarly and professional journals. These sources are helpful in narrowing a general topic to a specific research area because they identify subtopics or research problems that are particular to the research topic, and they list the current studies in these subtopics. Bibliographies and guides to the literature can also be used when defining and refining a problem area for investigation. These communication research sources are discussed in Chapters 5 and 6.

If your project is a debate, speech, interview, or newspaper editorial or article, you might need to find starting points that fall outside the communication literature, but the general strategy remains the same. For example, if you are thinking about giving a speech on some aspect of the social welfare system in the United States, you could start by identifying a subject encyclopedia that covers the sociology discipline. You could identify one by going to Chapter 5, where we list subject encyclopedias for communication and related disciplines, along with general search strategies for locating additional subject encyclopedias. Browse the table of contents, article titles, and the index. The purpose is to get an overview and to come up with some broad topic ideas.

A simple but effective way to find reference sources is simply to browse in the reference collection, taking advantage of its Library of Congress subject arrangement. For example, sociology materials are generally classified under HM (their **Library of Congress classification**). Go to that section of your library's reference collection and browse. You will probably find some useful subject encyclopedias and handbooks.

But let's say you want to give a speech that has something to do with bioethics, and you don't know under which section of the Library of Congress classification that would fall. Why not make a librarian's day by going to the reference desk and asking for help in locating such a source? Reference librarians know how useful these reference sources are, and their lack of extensive use by students is a continuing source of frustration for librarians.

Narrow the Topic

Once you have chosen a general topic or research problem, the next step is to narrow the topic so that you can formulate a specific research question. By constructing a specific research question, you narrow the focus of your research, and you can channel all your energies into a productive purpose. The research question also provides a theme that helps you unify disparate elements and eliminate or reduce nonproductive efforts. A specific research question sets a goal for your efforts and helps you save time. We often develop specific research questions by thinking about a topic, talking to and brainstorming with others, and, most of all, reading about the topic or research problem in the literature of the field.

For example, let's imagine that you are interested in both interpersonal communication and organizational communication and you want to investigate the interface of these two general areas. At this point, your broad topic might be "The Use of Group Discussion in Organizations." By examining some textbooks and bibliographies, you find such subtopics as group dynamics, interpersonal communication, discussion, organizational effectiveness, and so on. This will start you thinking, conversing with others, seeking out past research, and reading about the experiences of those people in organizations who must communicate with one another to solve problems or make decisions. Your initial research might cause you to ask whether these organizational professionals receive any training in group communication. At this point, you have identified a more specific research problem and can formulate a preliminary question to examine, such as "What types of training programs in group discussion do organizations provide for their management personnel?" This is a viable question that is sufficiently narrow in focus to study and discuss in a research paper. Another possible research question would be "Which type of group training program is the most effective for management personnel?"

Identify Key Concepts and Search Terms

Start by underlining the significant terms in your search question. For example:

> What types of training programs in group discussion do organizations provide for their management personnel?

Then try to identify the two or three basic concepts represented by these terms. In this example, we might identify three basic concepts:

Training programs
Group discussion
Management personnel

We drop *organizations* because it seems less critical and is probably implied in *management personnel*. Next, look for synonyms for these concepts. One way of doing this is to investigate the **subject headings** assigned to your concepts in the library catalog.

Virtually all catalogs in academic libraries use Library of Congress (often abbreviated **LC**) subject headings. These headings are an ideal place to begin the subject-headings list we recommend you maintain for your research project. (See the later section in this chapter on documenting your research.) Most computerized library catalogs provide cross-references that allow you to investigate subject headings when searching the catalog itself. For example, a subject-heading (rather than keyword) search for *management personnel* in a library catalog will get zero results. We must assume that this term is not a Library of Congress subject heading. We might guess that the appropriate subject heading is *managers*. A subject-heading search for *managers* results in this message:

MANAGERS

Search under: EXECUTIVES

In other words, *managers* is not a Library of Congress subject heading, but we do find a cross-reference, which refers us to the correct heading for this concept: *executives*. We now have these terms for this concept:

Management personnel
Managers
Executives (LC)

If we do a subject-heading search for *executives*, we find this cross-reference:

EXECUTIVES

Search also under:

GOVERNMENT EXECUTIVES
HEALTH SERVICE ADMINISTRATORS
LIBRARY ADMINISTRATORS
MIDDLE MANAGERS
SOUND RECORDING EXECUTIVES AND PRODUCERS
WOMEN EXECUTIVES

We now have still more terms to consider adding to our list. Notice that cross-references are also useful for those still seeking ideas for narrowing or broadening a search. Some topics, for example, might appropriately be narrowed to *middle managers* or *women executives*.

We include all three terms on the subject-heading list because one of the alternate terms might be used in another tool. Also, we might want to use keyword searching in some tools, in which case a list of natural language synonyms would be needed. Follow a similar process to investigate appropriate terms for each concept in your research question.

Many bibliographic databases include online thesauri that are also convenient tools for investigating subject headings. Figure 2.1 shows an entry from PsycINFO. The hierarchical arrangement provides information about broader and related headings. Options for searching include:

Search: Find records with this term as a subject heading.
Focus: Find records with this term identified as a major subject heading.
Expand: Find records with this term as a subject heading or with a subject heading of any narrower term from the thesaurus.
Expand/Focus: Find records with this term as a major subject heading or with a major subject heading of any narrower term in the thesaurus.

Notice that it is possible to enter subject headings directly from this screen. By searching under the subject heading *Group Discussion* in the PsycINFO database, you would find a **record** like the one shown in Figure 2.2. Here you can see the various subject headings that would provide additional sources on the same topic.

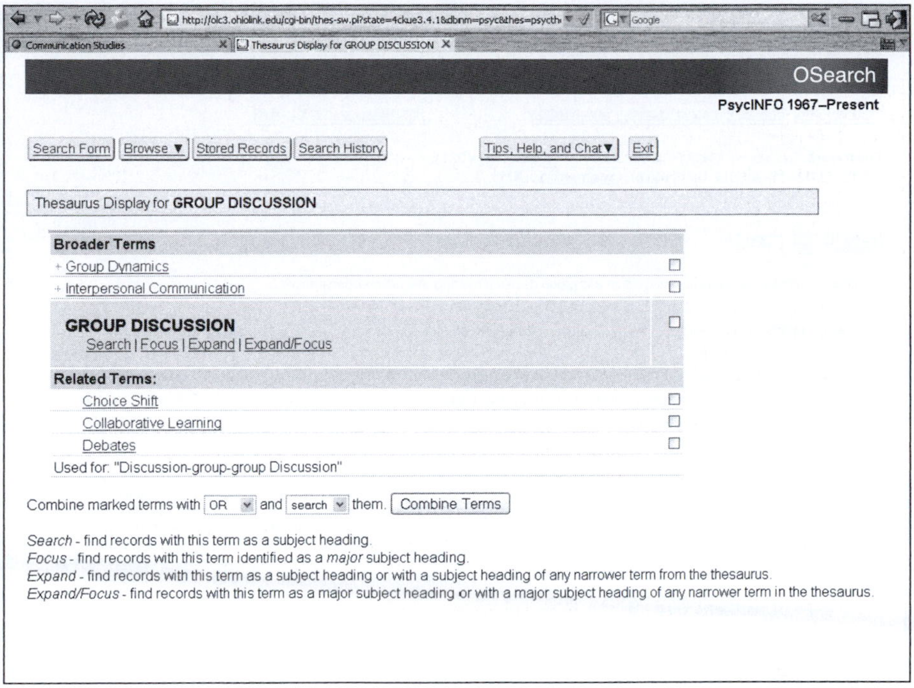

Figure 2.1 PsycINFO Thesaurus Listing

Another convenient tool for investigating subject headings (some prefer it) is the Library of Congress subject headings. The printed guide can be found in your library:

Library of Congress. (1975–). *Library of Congress subject headings*. Washington, DC: Author.

In the print version, the information listed directly below subject heading is of interest primarily to librarians who catalog library materials. Several abbreviations are used to refer library users to related headings and synonymous terms. UF, which stands for *use for*, tells the researcher that the terms listed after it are synonymous with the precise subject heading but are not Library of Congress subject headings. Thus, they will not be used in library catalogs, although they might appear in periodical indexes or abstracts. Next, related headings are listed. These are either broader terms (BT) or narrower terms (NT). The online version, found at <http://catalog.loc.gov/>, can also be used for subject searching. In addition, you can search subject headings on the Library of Congress Authorities website at <http://authorities.loc.gov/>.

Figure 2.3 shows a Library of Congress Authorities subject heading for one topic. The precise subject heading in this example is *Communication in management*. Note that there are no broader terms, but there are narrower terms. These terms

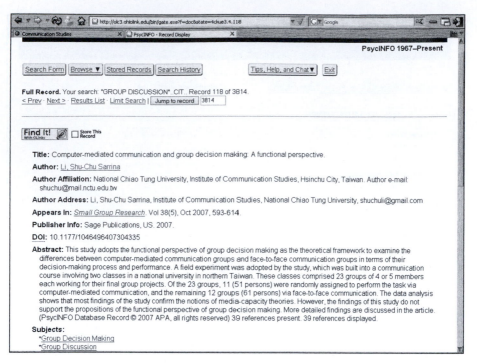

PsycINFO 1967–Present

Search Form | Browse ▼ | Stored Records | Search History | Tips, Help, and Chat ▼ | Exit

Full Record. Your search: "GROUP DISCUSSION"..CIT.. Record 118 of 3814.
< Prev · Next > · Results List · Limit Search | Jump to record 3814

Find It! With CLinks | ☐ Store This Record

Title: Computer-mediated communication and group decision making: A functional perspective.

Author: Li, Shu-Chu Sarrina

Author Affiliation: National Chiao Tung University, Institute of Communication Studies, Hsinchu City, Taiwan. Author e-mail: shuchu@mail.nctu.edu.tw

Author Address: Li, Shu-Chu Sarrina, Institute of Communication Studies, National Chiao Tung University, shuchuli@gmail.com

Appears In: *Small Group Research.* Vol 38(5), Oct 2007, 593-614.

Publisher Info: Sage Publications, US. 2007.

DOI: 10.1177/1046496407304335

Abstract: This study adopts the functional perspective of group decision making as the theoretical framework to examine the differences between computer-mediated communication groups and face-to-face communication groups in terms of their decision-making process and performance. A field experiment was adopted by the study, which was built into a communication course involving two classes in a national university in northern Taiwan. These classes comprised 23 groups of 4 or 5 members each working for their final group projects. Of the 23 groups, 11 (51 persons) were randomly assigned to perform the task via computer-mediated communication, and the remaining 12 groups (61 persons) via face-to-face communication. The data analysis shows that most findings of the study confirm the notions of media-capacity theories. However, the findings of this study do not support the propositions of the functional perspective of group decision making. More detailed findings are discussed in the article. (PsycINFO Database Record © 2007 APA, all rights reserved) 39 references present. 39 references displayed.

Subjects:
*Group Decision Making
*Group Discussion

Figure 2.2 PsycINFO Record

are Library of Congress subject headings and are used in library catalogs. Under Scope Note you would find:

> Here are entered works on the role of communication in effective management. Works on the various forms of oral and written messages used by a business in the conduct of its affairs are entered under Business communication.

By searching under the subject heading *Communication in Management* in the Library of Congress catalog at <http://catalog.loc.gov/>, you would find a record like the one shown in Figure 2.4. All subject headings under which a particular book can be searched are listed in the subject **field** at the bottom of the catalog record. It may be appropriate to search one or more of them for related sources. Consider adding them to your subject-headings list.

Note the fields included on the record: Type of Material, Personal Name (author), Main Title, Published/Created, Description, ISBN, and Call Number. Most if not all of these fields will be **access points** for searching the catalog. In other words, you will be able to search by author, title, subject, and so forth. And you might be able to limit your search to a particular library location, publication year, or format. Records may also note that books contain an index and bibliographic references. As we stress later, examining books (and other publications) that have bibliographies in

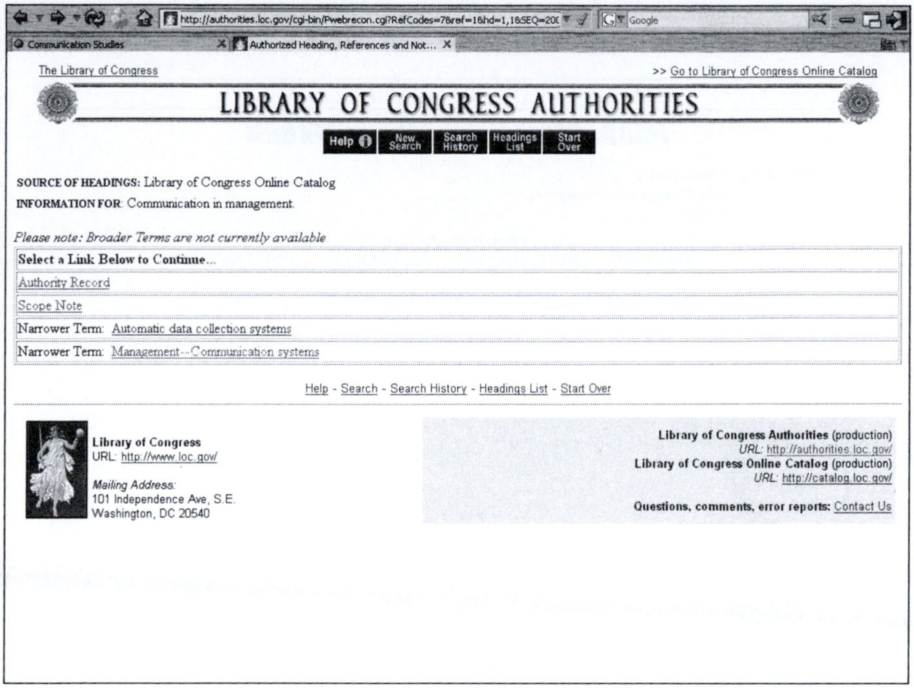

Figure 2.3 Library of Congress *Authorities* Subject Heading

order to obtain references to other useful sources is one of the most important components of an effective search strategy.

Test and Adjust the Topic

Once you have decided on a specific preliminary research question and have identified key concepts and preliminary search terms, the next step is to do some testing. You might simply select an appropriate periodical index described in Chapter 6 and try a preliminary search using the search terms you've already developed. You are trying to get an idea of the available literature related to that preliminary question. In other words, what is the status of published research and information about your topic? If the subject area is still too broad, you'll find yourself doing extraneous work and feeling uncertain about what to include. If you find it difficult to choose pertinent sources, reexamine your research question and try to limit it further. In the preceding example, for instance, you might decide to exclude government and other nonprofit organizations from consideration and to focus on commercial organizations. Naturally, you don't want to go to the other extreme and make the research question too narrow, or you will have very little information to examine.

How will you know whether your question is sufficiently narrow in focus? Your examination of the literature should tell you. If the topic is too broad, your treatment of it could be too superficial, and there will be too many sources with which to deal.

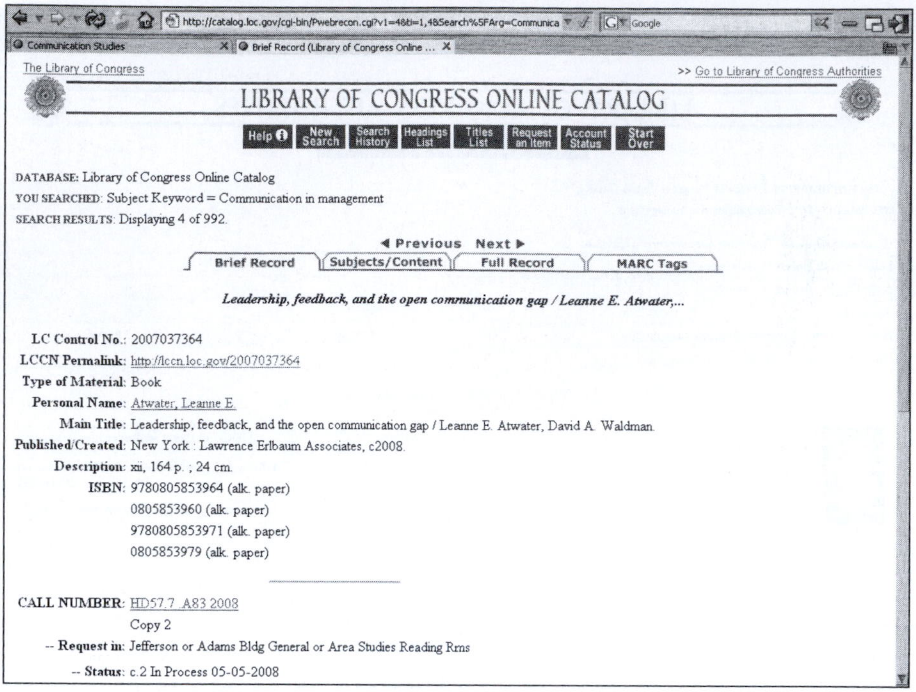

Figure 2.4 Library of Congress Subject-Heading Record

But if the topic is too narrow, the answer to the question could be obvious or insignificant.

Adjusting a question to a manageable size also depends on the scope of the task or assignment or your personal goal for the project. If you are working on a literature review or on a thesis or dissertation proposal, the amount of literature you will consult will be greater than if you are completing a 10-page research report.

This notion of adjusting a research question as the **literature search** progresses is difficult for a beginning researcher. Discussions with instructors, advisers, and librarians can be helpful in this process.

The Search

Determine Types of Sources Needed

At this point it will help you to clarify your next steps if you take some time to decide just what types of sources you need to support your topic. That is, what types of sources do you want to cite in the bibliography of your paper or other project? Naturally, the sources needed depend on the type of project you are undertaking. For example, if you are doing a paper for your communication research methods class, you'll need to cite books and journal articles written by scholars. It may also be appropriate to cite certain types of reference works (such as subject encyclopedias, handbooks, or annual reviews).

In terms of currency, you will need to include up-to-date studies, but older works can still be pertinent, as well. And you might decide that you need to cite appropriate statistical data. If you're preparing a 5-minute speech on a current topic, on the other hand, you could limit yourself to newspapers, statistical data, government documents, or magazines published within the past 2 years.

Select Appropriate Databases and Other Access Tools

Once you have clarified the types of print and online publications and other sources you need to support your topic, deciding the types of access tools needed will be relatively straightforward. As you work your way through Chapters 5 and 6, you'll learn about the scope and purpose of many electronic periodical indexes and abstracts and other access tools (including print ones). For example, if you need to identify newspaper articles, you'll use one of the newspaper indexes we describe. To locate scholarly articles in psychology, you will learn in Chapter 6 that *PsycINFO* would be an appropriate database. To find books, you would use your library's catalog and regional or national union catalogs. But you can also identify books through book-length bibliographies and through bibliographies appended to articles or other books, annual reviews, and yearbooks. You'll also learn that some periodical indexes and abstracts index books, book chapters, and book reviews.

One handy way of planning a search is to list types of sources you plan to use and the access tools you plan to search, updating these as the search progresses. We've found it useful to complete a search strategy sheet (Figure 2.5). Here you can identify the main reference sources and access tools you think will be useful for your topic. As you read through Chapters 5 and 6, you'll notice sources that are very much related to your topic and others that are not related. List the related ones on the search strategy sheet and use the sheet when you visit the library. It will also help you keep track of sources you have consulted and those that still remain.

Students can fall into the trap of relying too heavily on the access tool with which they are most comfortable, perhaps the library catalog, full-text periodical databases, or the web. Each of these tools has an important place but should be used appropriately.

The library catalog. The library catalog is the most obvious and well-known part of a library and may be the first access tool to which students turn. There are problems, however, with relying on the library catalog. Most catalogs provide detailed subject access only to books, and only to those books owned by the library. Books provide only one type of information, and the information is often dated because the lag between the time a work is written and the time it is published is often considerable. When writing a research paper, you should support material from sources with more recent information, which you usually find in journal articles.

Furthermore, libraries have to be selective about which books they purchase. No college library can own every book that has been published, so library catalogs do not truly represent all materials available to a researcher. By limiting yourself to the holdings of one library, you will miss some important sources and perhaps use sources that are not entirely relevant to the topic. Finally, the catalog does not help you judge the relative authority or relevance of books on your topic. For this reason,

Name:
Research question: What do researchers know about . . . ?
Key Concepts:
Relevant subject headings and synonymous terms:

Sources needed:
Reference books: __encyclopedias __handbooks __yearbooks
          __dictionaries __annual reviews
Books: __textbooks __by scholars __journalists __lay experts
          __series __other:
Articles: __journal __professional/trade __newspaper
          __newsmagazine __opinion/commentary __book review
          __literature review
Factual information: __statistical data __biographical data
          __case/statutory laws __administrative regulations
          __government reports __other factual information:
          __WWW pages:

  Other:

Time period: __current month/year __5 years __10 years
          __can include older items

Access tools to check:
Library catalogs:
          My library:
          Regional/national:
Guides to the literature:
Annual reviews:
Bibliographies:
Electronic periodical indexes/abstracts:
          Newspaper:
          Interdisciplinary:
          General purpose:
          Communication:
          Related disciplines:
          Citation:
          Book review:
          Government publications:
          Full-text:
Print indexes/abstracts:
Finding aids for statistics:
Directories:
WWW subject directories:
WWW search engines:

Figure 2.5 Search Strategy Sheet

a selective topical bibliography, such as those found at the end of articles in encyclopedias, handbooks, yearbooks, and textbook chapters, is often a more efficient starting place for research projects.

Full-text databases. We usually find full-text periodical databases easy to use, and the convenience of simply pushing a button to print an electronic article or send it to an e-mail address is hard to resist. These can be wonderful tools, providing quick access to periodicals to which the library doesn't subscribe. Unfortunately, we can be tempted to ignore the existence of more pertinent articles that would take a bit of effort to retrieve and copy. Relying on these tools can also cause students to forget about books as good sources of background and analysis.

The World Wide Web. The web poses similar problems. Typing a **query** into a search engine is easy; getting results of some kind is almost guaranteed, and most pages can easily be printed. Unfortunately, it has become a truism that almost anyone can put almost anything on the web. So material found here must be carefully evaluated. (You'll read more about this very important issue later in this chapter and in Chapter 3.) In addition, you'll be much more successful searching for published materials, such as journals, using the periodical indexes and abstracts licensed by libraries. However, students should plan to use the web for most projects. It is an especially appropriate source for certain types of information, such as current or recent news, government publications, and business information. The number of publications and valuable text, audio, and image archives available is growing rapidly.

Deciding What Type of Search to Do

Consider your strategy in broad terms first. With some assignments, a *general-to-specific* search strategy is most beneficial. When you know little about the topic or when the assignment involves a comprehensive overview of the literature, it is best to begin with general sources such as encyclopedias, annual reviews, and handbooks (see Part 2). Next, move to bibliographies, guides, and periodical indexes and abstracts. Then, complete the literature search by examining the original journal articles, books, or media. With this search strategy, you limit the topic as you continue through the search, rather like the strategy used in searching **computerized databases** (see Chapter 3).

Keywords are combined to enlarge the search (e.g., adding *radio* to *television* to find out more about the broadcast media). Keywords are separated to limit the number of sources you will find (e.g., removing *radio* from the descriptors examined).

In other situations, you may find it advantageous to use a *specific-to-general* search strategy. For example, if you have found a key reference or article, you will want to enlarge the search beyond that one reference. Again, periodical indexes, especially those with abstracts and bibliographies, provide additional information. **Citation indexes** are particularly helpful in locating related studies. (These are all discussed in Chapter 6.)

Sooner or later you will need to confront the capabilities of the electronic databases available to you. Most databases offer a variety of access points. You can choose to search by subject heading, keyword, author, or title, at a minimum. In some databases, subject searching is facilitated by an excellent online **thesaurus** (i.e., an organized list of subject headings, also known as **descriptors**), making it easy to identify and use appropriate subject headings. In this case, subject searching is generally the option of choice. Other databases might have such poorly designed subject-heading listings that they encourage searchers to start with keyword searches. A popular and effective strategy is to start with a keyword search, examine the subject field of the pertinent records retrieved, and select appropriate subject headings. Then redo the search as a subject search. Of course, you might need to do a keyword search if your topic is unusual or not used as a subject heading. At this juncture, subject searching on the web is limited to a keyword search.

You will want to do an author search if you've identified a prominent author who writes on your topic. Maybe you need to do a title search because someone gave you a title to an article, but you don't know what journal it's in or when it was published. If you are looking for something very specific, you will want to use a database that allows you to search the full text of articles or books. Often you will find a combination of search types to be most successful. When you first connect to a database, you will see what your options are.

Formulate Searches

In Chapter 3 you will learn how to put together the subject headings and terms on your subject-headings list to construct effective searches, most often using the **operators** AND, OR, and NOT. Because database **interfaces** differ from one another and change rapidly, concentrate on learning the concepts of database searching. Students who are familiar with these will have little difficulty adjusting systematically to the rapidly changing information environment, particularly if they learn to use the Help function available for each database.

Examine the Results and Modify the Search

Once you have a list of articles, take a good look at the items and decide whether they will help you with your project. It would be surprising if you did a perfect search on your first attempt, but you can probably find a few items that are at least close to what you are seeking. Look carefully at the records that look promising. What you are looking for are additional access points: subject headings, keywords, and key authors. Using this information, reformulate your search query to narrow or broaden the search or just to improve its focus. Repeat this process until you are satisfied that you have retrieved all the most appropriate records for your topic.

Evaluate Citations Retrieved, Selecting Items Worth Retrieving

Students are often too quick to hit the Print button at this point. Don't print a bunch of citations before you have taken the time to do some preliminary evaluation. You can tell quite a bit about a source just from its record. (Be sure to look at the item's full record, not just its brief record.) First, is the item really on topic? The fact that a keyword you typed appears someplace in the record is no guarantee of this. Read the abstract carefully and examine the subject headings assigned. Do you need scholarly articles? You can make some determination about whether an article is scholarly in nature from the journal title as well as from the article title. (Scholarly articles tend to be long and explicit; they sometimes include a colon followed by a subtitle.) Other clues to look for include article length, publication date, and publisher. You'll find other things to look for in the *Evaluate the Sources* section following.

Now is the time to get your hands on the actual articles, book chapters, books, and other sources. In most cases you will need to check the library catalog to see whether the library owns the book or subscribes to the journal, magazine, or newspaper in question. If it's a periodical article, be sure to look in the catalog for the title of the periodical (not the title of the article).

If the library does not have what you need, there are other options. First, check with a librarian to make sure the periodical in question is not available electronically in full text. (Some full-text periodicals might not be listed in the library catalog.) Full-text articles present a variety of delivery options (e-mail, cut and paste, different file formats, and the like), which we explore in Chapter 3. **Document delivery services**, which deliver articles—for a fee—via fax, are also a viable option. And, of course, you can usually order what you need from another library in your region using your library's interlibrary loan service.

Examine Bibliographies for Additional Leads

As you retrieve published works, be sure to examine the bibliographies or reference lists. They can provide you with additional access points to search. Let's say the bibliography lists what appear to be some key books on your topic. Does your library own any of them? Does it own other books by the same authors? If you find entries in the catalog, what subject headings have been assigned to them? Do these subject headings fit your topic? Following up with a subject search on these headings will help you find more recent books on the topic.

The Results

Evaluating and Summarizing Information

Scholarship is not of uniform quality. Some research studies and books are of greater substance than others. Not all authors engage in flawless research. The scholar who is conducting a literature review is expected to know and to evaluate the quality of the work in addition to summarizing the findings. To evaluate a scholarly journal article, you must understand the research process and its conventions. We discuss these in Chapter 9. Rules guide research investigations, and breaking these rules can result in research of lower quality. By conducting a systematic review process, most scholarly journals prevent publication of articles that have major or serious flaws. Occasionally, though, dubious practices are not uncovered or are overlooked in the review process and result in published articles that cause one to question the validity of the findings. As beginning scholars in the communication discipline, you need to learn about research conventions and rules and be able to evaluate research articles and books with a critical eye.

Evaluate the Sources

Just because a book has been published and acquired by a library or an article has been published in a scholarly journal doesn't mean it is a quality source. Many complex factors determine a book's or an article's worth or quality. Here are some suggested ways for judging quality. Note that some of these criteria are relevant for Internet sources as well; we discuss Internet materials more specifically in Chapter 4.

Examine the book's front matter. The Preface and Introduction should indicate why the work was written. Is the purpose to inform, interpret, explain, or share new discoveries? Also determine the intended level of audience (e.g., high school students, college seniors, other researchers). Books such as textbooks that are intended as **secondary sources**—ones that summarize previously reported research or contain opinion essays—might help you understand the field better but may not be works you would want to cite in a literature review.

Literature reviews should contain findings from **primary sources** (scholarly books and journal articles). Sometimes, authors of journal articles intend to summarize published literature in an area or to comment on that literature. Such articles mostly serve the purpose of a secondary source, yet they can contain new conclusions or a research agenda that you'd want to cite. Journal articles that are primary sources seek to add new knowledge or insights.

However, all primary research is not of even quality. Sometimes the author's purpose is to test or to develop a new theory or research procedure. If such research is published in a top-tier national or international journal in the discipline (see Chapter 7), it is likely to be highly regarded, even if the theory is controversial. At other times, an author's purpose might be (a) to replicate previous studies looking for similar or contrasting results, (b) to revise or to adapt a scale or other research measure, or (c) to test a small aspect of an existing theory. These studies are important and well-regarded but will typically fall below the level of research that breaks new ground about theory and measurement. The purpose of the article or book, then, can tell you the scope of the study and its potential value.

Critique the methodology and data. The methodology should be clearly detailed. The **data** should be accurate. The work that went into producing the study should be apparent. Also determine how recent the research is. Have environmental or social conditions changed since the data were collected in a way that might cause you to question the results? Sometimes you are not expert enough to critique a work's validity and reliability. If not, consult reviews for others' opinions about books. Book reviews, too, are of uneven quality, but there might be agreement among several reviews about the book you're evaluating. Another indicator of quality is whether the book or article has received an award from a national association. Directories or association websites can contain this information.

Explore the author's background and qualifications. Try to check the author's publication track record. What else has the author written in the area? Who else has cited his or her writings in their own work? Authors should be experts in the area, and their qualifications should tell you whether they are. If their qualifications are not printed in the book, look them up in relevant directories to see whether they belong to national professional organizations and what their work affiliation is. If authors are in the communication discipline, you can examine their research records in *ComIndex*, in the printed *Index to Journals in Communication*, or in *Communication & Mass Media Complete* (see Chapter 6). You can search a convention program online to identify their current research interest. Or you can look in *Social Sciences Citation Index* or *Arts and Humanities Citation Index* to see who else has cited their research (see Chapter 6).

Investigate the reputation of the publisher. National and international journals with high rejection rates tend to publish consistently high-quality articles. Readers can generally trust editorial boards and editors to scrutinize the articles before publication. Regional journals are also respected, although often below the level of the national or international journal. State and local journals and those with lower rates of rejection often have somewhat lower standards and publish articles that can have some minor flaws or are of interest to a more specific population. Book publishing companies also have reputations. Some have editors and editorial boards in charge of reviewing texts or scholarly books for possible publication; these tend to have higher standards. At the other end of the continuum are publishers who are paid by authors to publish their work. These vanity presses might publish books of lower quality.

Examine the back matter. A book that contains an **index** can be used as a reference source. If it lacks an index, the use of the book is limited. The footnotes and bibliography indicate the breadth and depth of research that went into the book and the author's authoritative knowledge of the field. It is possible, though, that innovators do not have many works to cite or are restricted to citing their own work because of the recentness of the topic. If few original books and articles are cited or if major works in the field are not mentioned, there is reason to question the value of the book as a reputable source. Also, expect some works cited in the bibliography to be 1 or 2 years older than the copyright date of the book itself. For instance, this edition of this book was completed in late 2008, but because of the publication process the copyright date is 2010. We have included, however, sources that were available through late 2008. Had we not included recent sources, you could suspect that we haven't done our homework. Visit this book's home page for updated sources.

Read Materials Thoroughly

Some articles and books are easier to read than others. Historical, critical, and qualitative research reports (see Chapters 9 and 10 for explanations of these research forms) typically contain verbal descriptions of findings; the results are presented in everyday language or common communication jargon. Empirical research relying on observation, surveys, or experimentation often contains statistical data and tables, which students frequently skip over when reading. If you are not familiar with statistics, this may be the only way you can read the article. Here are some pointers, though, for reading a research article, chapter, or book:

- *Look at the title*. Often the main features can be identified from the title. Also take a look at who the authors are and what their backgrounds are.

- *Read the abstract* (if provided). The abstract gives you a short synopsis of the work and prepares you to read it.
- *Read the introductory material and review of research.* This tells you why the study was done and what prior research led to this present research project. This is a good time to create new bibliography records for important sources that you might have missed.
- *Read the method section.* Here you will find how the study was actually performed, who was involved in it, and what instruments or techniques were used. This section will reveal the soundness of the empirical choices made by the authors.
- *Read the results.* This is the meat of the research article. Most of your notes about this research report will come from this section because it contains the actual findings. Look at the tables and figures to see what was found. If the results contain numbers and statistics that you can't understand, read past the numbers to the conclusions drawn by the authors. Don't give up!
- *Read the discussion.* The authors typically summarize the results in less technical terms here. Authors sometimes overstate the importance of the findings, but some journal editors temper these exaggerations. Try to identify the most important findings in the study, the meaning or implications of these findings, and the limitations of the study. Authors also offer good ideas for future research projects.
- *Scan the bibliography* for sources that might be useful but which you have not yet encountered.

Careful reading of research takes energy and concentration. The reading is much more difficult and time-consuming than textbook prose, and you should be prepared for it. Keep a communication, statistics, or general dictionary handy so you can look up terms you don't understand (see Chapter 8).

Take Careful Notes

New scholars sometimes find it difficult to take notes on what they read, either because the material contains too much information or because they are unfamiliar with the techniques of abstracting. Abstracting helps you synthesize the information you read and distinguish the most important parts of the article, book, or chapter. In effect, abstracting helps you become more critical of what you read because it forces you to understand the research thoroughly. We explain some basic steps involved in abstracting in Chapter 11. For additional guidance, consult the following source:

Cremmins, E. T. (1996). *The art of abstracting* (2nd ed.). Arlington, VA: Information Resources Press.

When taking notes from books or research articles, be sure to summarize the materials in your own words, or you might fall prey to inadvertent plagiarism. If you summarize the material in your own words, you will be certain that what you write later will be your own words, not those of the original author. If you find that certain passages are so well stated that you couldn't do justice to them yourself, copy the direct quote (using quotation marks) and the page number for future reference in a footnote or bibliographic citation. But as a rule of thumb, try to understand what the author is saying and then translate it into your own words.

Scholars who take careful notes during the literature search can proceed to the writing stage without having to reexamine sources already read. When preparing the bibliography, you will find that entering these citations on index cards or into a bibliography management program is helpful.

Documenting the Search Process

Library or **documentary research** is much easier to conduct if it is done systematically. Disorganized researchers find that they waste much time searching for and consulting sources that were previously located but forgotten. You can simplify the organizing effort in any research project if you construct bibliography records, prepare a subject-headings list, and keep a search record.

Keep Bibliographic Records

A **bibliography record** holds complete information for each source examined. It lists a complete and accurate citation as well as where the source is found. It should include a summary of the pertinent contents of the source. Bibliography records serve three major purposes:

1. They furnish a complete and current record of sources for later use in compiling a bibliography or citing references.
2. They eliminate the practice of repeating or retracing steps by allowing recently located sources to be checked against what was previously examined.
3. They provide a record of needed sources that have yet to be retrieved in the research process.

If you produce this manually, we suggest using cards instead of notebook paper because the former are handy, sturdy, and easy to organize and alphabetize. Figure 2.6 shows an example of a bibliography card.

Note-taking programs are also available for desktop and notebook computers, and students with these resources will find them useful for preparing bibliography records. Students beginning extensive research projects might want to invest in **bibliography-management programs**, such as EndNote, Reference Manager, RefWorks, and ProCite. These time-saving tools, which can be set up to accept citations downloaded directly from a growing number of periodical indexes, offer the ultimate in convenience. Once installed, they work as an integral part of standard word processing programs. Stored citations can be formatted automatically to print in standard bibliographic styles, including APA, MLA, and Chicago.

People have found a variety of note-taking styles useful for summarizing what they have read. You should use the system that works best for you. We suggest you use a citation format similar to the one shown in Figure 2.6. This is a modification of the style used by the American Psychological Association (APA), which is explained later in this book. This modified style for the bibliography record begins with full information on the author(s), the year (and month) of publication, and the title of the article. Then, the publication name, volume number (both underlined or italicized), and inclusive page numbers follow. This modification is necessary because, although

Papacharissi, Zizi, & Rubin, Alan M. (Spring 2000). Predictors of Internet use. *Journal of Broadcasting & Electronic Media, 44,* 175–196.
Internet uses and gratifications study. RQs: (1) What are people's motives for using the Internet? (2) How do antecedents relate to motives for using the Internet? (3) How do Internet antecedents, perceptions, and motives predict outcomes of using the Internet?
Survey sample: 279 college students who use the Internet, 58.8% women. Measured Internet motives, antecedents (contextual age, unwillingness to communicate), perceptions (social presence), use, affinity, and satisfaction.

[Card 1 of 2]

Papacharissi & Rubin. (2000). JOBEM.
Findings: RQ1: Five Internet motive factors: interpersonal utility, pass time, information seeking, convenience, and entertainment. RQ2: "those who found interpersonal communication to be less rewarding and were anxious when communicating with others... used the Internet for interpersonal utility" (p. 188). RQ3: information & entertainment motives pos. predicted email use; life satisfaction neg. predicted & info. motives pos. predicted Internet affinity; interpersonal reward and info. motives pos. predicted Internet satisfaction.
Discussion: Findings "support the informative and interactive capabilities of the Internet" (p. 191). The Internet is a functional alternative forthose "for whom other channels were not as available or rewarding" (p. 191).

[Card 2 of 2]

Figure 2.6 Bibliography Card

the APA style does not require authors' first names or the journal issue (if each issue does not begin with page 1), some other bibliographic styles do. By including this information here you can save much time in the future should you use the information in a project requiring a different style or if you need to use a masculine or feminine pronoun to refer to the author's work.

The *Publication Manual of the American Psychological Association* details bibliography form and provides a quick reference guide for writing style, editorial style, preparing and submitting manuscripts, and proofreading. Communication researchers often use it when they prepare final versions of papers. You should, however, use one style during the entire research process. It is unnecessarily time-consuming to convert bibliographic references written in one format to another format for the paper. Learning a style early can save time in the future.

We use the APA format throughout this book because it is used in most major communication journals. With the exception of the style used on the bibliography record in Figure 2.6, you should be able to use our citations as guides for your own bibliographic citations.

Students often find photocopying or printing full-text articles preferable to sitting in the library and taking notes. Keep in mind, though, that this practice is costly and time-consuming. Often you scan a newly discovered article first to see whether it is relevant to your topic and to make some initial judgment about the article's worth. This means you are preparing yourself to take notes on a bibliography record, but you stop short. Later, you'll have to reread the article and repeat this preparatory process. Also, by stopping at this point and filing the photocopy of the article for later use, you are not making full use of the article's reference list for other places to search. Finally, by photocopying everything, you tend to put off reading the articles until just before writing, so writing is delayed and hurried. By reading articles and taking notes immediately, you're ready to organize and write once you have found all sources. So, you might be tempted to photocopy or print everything but doing so can add extra time and costs to the search and writing processes.

Maintain a List of Subject Headings

You should develop a subject-headings list and keep it current throughout the research process. Include in this list all possible headings and synonyms related to the topic that you will use when consulting the library catalog, bibliographies, and periodical indexes and abstracts. For example, information on the topic *Audiovisual Aids* can be found under many headings (Figure 2.7). The more topical categories you include in the subject-headings list, the more likely you will find most of the possible references to that topic.

Use Search Records

When undertaking lengthy research projects, it is wise to note all sources you have consulted to prevent redoing research work or missing valuable sources. Search records indicate which access tools or sources (indexes, abstracts, bibliographies, and so forth) you have already examined and what portions of these sources you inspected. Index cards are convenient for this purpose, although search records can also be entered in notebook computers. You should prepare a general search record for quick reference (Figure 2.8), which lists all sources you have examined. Use another record, which includes relevant subject headings and dates searched, for each source (Figure 2.9).

AUDIOVISUAL AIDS

Film	Television
Multimedia	Visual aids
Recordings	Graphics
Radio	Photography
Educational media	Instructional media

Figure 2.7 Subject-Heading List

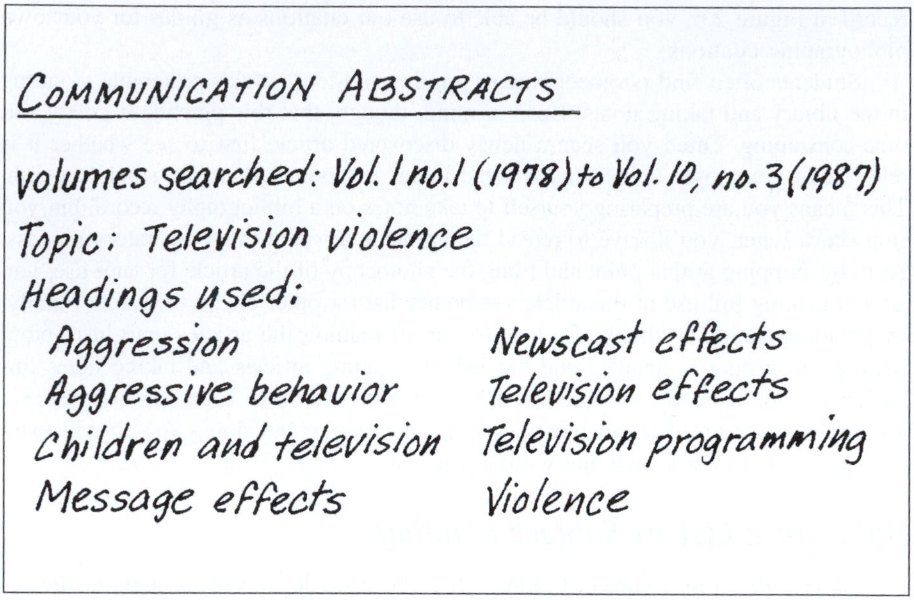

COMMUNICATION ABSTRACTS

volumes searched: Vol. 1 no.1 (1978) to Vol. 10, no. 3 (1987)
Topic: Television violence
Headings used:
  Aggression   Newscast effects
  Aggressive behavior   Television effects
  Children and television   Television programming
  Message effects   Violence

Figure 2.8 General Search Record Card

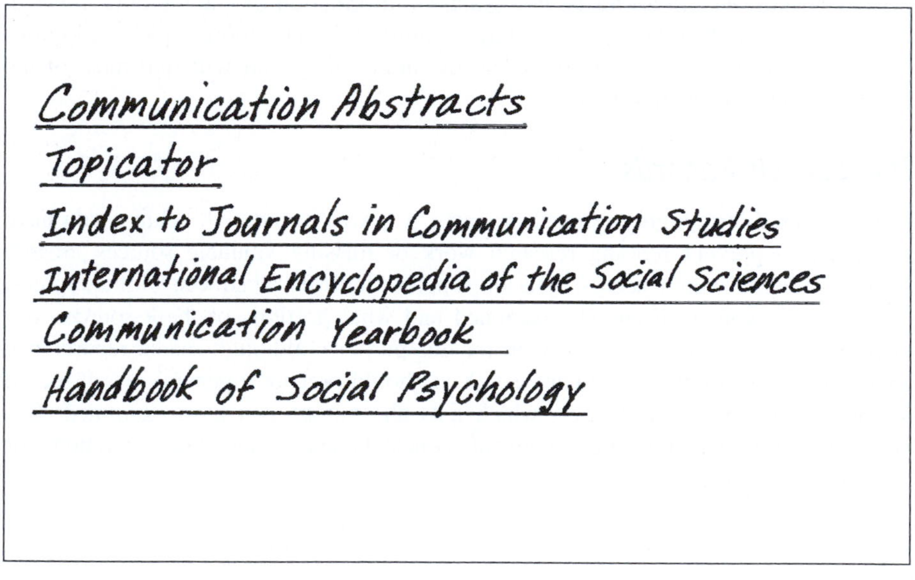

Communication Abstracts
Topicator
Index to Journals in Communication Studies
International Encyclopedia of the Social Sciences
Communication Yearbook
Handbook of Social Psychology

Figure 2.9 Search Record Card

Tips on Searching the Literature

Keep in mind three main points when searching the literature. First, don't let your-self get bogged down. Read completely only those articles that are relevant and note other interesting articles for future reading. It is sometimes tempting to browse through a multitude of new sources, but all you will be doing is delaying the inevitable task of pursuing your research.

Second, don't entertain the illusion that you can exhaust all possible sources related to your topic. It is of course important to be as thorough as possible. It is also important to start your research early. Remember, some sources will not be in the library, so you will need to order them through an interlibrary loan. You will never find all possible references, though, so you must set a research stopping point and at that time start writing. You will learn to realize that you've exhausted all the pertinent, available sources when newly found bibliographies list sources you've already seen and have nothing new for you to examine.

Third, remember to practice good note-taking skills when you are conducting your library research. To take notes on the content of the material, you will need to abstract, or condense, what you read. Windows Notepad offers an opportunity to take notes while reading online material. You will also need to have a complete and accurate bibliographic citation (one that is legibly written). We summarize proper format for bibliographic citations in Appendix A, "APA Style Basics." You may want to refer to that section as you proceed through this book.

Writing

We emphasize throughout this book how essential it is that you thoroughly examine the literature before you start the writing process. That means all library work should be done before you begin to write. As you pursue your search, find a topic that is interesting and related to the project. Through exploratory reading of general sources, narrow the topic to a manageable size.

One or more research questions should emerge at this point. These questions will guide the rest of the literature search, your evaluation of what you read, and the writing process. After exhausting all relevant sources, you will need to consider how best to organize the materials you've found into a meaningful review of the literature. Even if your research goal is something other than a research paper (e.g., a speech, group discussion, broadcast script, debate case, feature article, seminar, critique, review, or exam), the process is similar. You will need to make sense of the information, organize it into a coherent pattern, and select the best method of presentation. To do this, you must keep your specific research question and the goal of your research endeavor clearly in mind.

Develop an Outline

Complete an initial outline at this time to help decide which specific sources to examine. An outline organizes the subtopics or subthemes found in the literature and guides the arguments you will make in your review. Once you have found all the materials you need, expand and develop your original outline. Always check your outline along the way to ensure it conforms to the thesis statement or research questions. Word processing programs often include a handy outlining function that is worth trying.

Edit

Write from the outline. Then set the written review aside for a day or two before editing and revising it into final form. We suggest you also set this final form aside for another day or two, then edit again. Once the final copy is typed, proofread it carefully for typographic errors. Don't rely on your word processing program to find all spelling and grammatical errors. Details on writing, proofreading the parts of the literature review, and summarizing strategies are found in Chapters 11 and 12 and in Roth's (1999) manual. Be sure to take a look at these chapters before you begin writing.

SUMMARY

The success of your research relies on how well you define your topic and your awareness of the many possible sources of information. Research about topics is necessary for most assignments that communication students encounter and for many tasks communication professionals face in their daily routines. Being able to identify a research topic and to clarify specific questions for investigation are essential skills for all communication researchers. These skills simplify the research process by providing an efficient, organized direction.

Selecting a topic and defining the research problem are often the most difficult parts of searching the literature. Once a topic is chosen and a specific research question is formulated, a researcher concentrates on finding and reviewing the available literature related to that preliminary question. Often the topic must be adjusted (i.e., narrowed or broadened) during the search process. Lists of citations retrieved should be carefully reviewed to make sure the most appropriate terms are being used. Particular care should be placed on effectively using the subject headings or descriptors available for each database searched.

Researchers must be familiar with the library and understand the workings of the library catalog, interlibrary loan, and systematic procedures for library searching. These procedures include bibliography records, subject-headings lists, and search records. Tips for conducting a literature search include reading only relevant materials, setting a stopping point for the search, and practicing good note-taking strategies such as abstracting. Researchers also must understand and evaluate what they read before they begin writing.

In general, researchers must be organized and approach library or documentary research tasks systematically. Not only does having a search plan save time and energy, but it also results in a better, more coherent product.

References

Beasley, D. R. (2000). *Beasley's guide to library research*. Toronto: University of Toronto Press.

Bolner, M. S., & Poirier, G. A. (2007). *The research process: Books and beyond* (4th ed.). Dubuque, IA: Kendall/Hunt.

Cooper, H., & Hedges, L. V. (Eds.). (1994). *The handbook of research synthesis*. New York: Russell Sage Foundation.

Cremmins, E. T. (1996). *The art of abstracting* (2nd ed.). Arlington, VA: Information Resources Press.

Katz, W. A. (2002). *Introduction to reference work* (8th ed., 2 vols.). Boston: McGraw-Hill.

List, C. (2002). *Introduction to information research* (2nd ed.). Dubuque, IA: Kendall/ Hunt.

Mann, T. (2005). *The Oxford guide to library research* (3rd ed.). New York: Oxford University Press.

Roth, A. J. (1999). *The research paper: Process, form, and content* (8th ed.). Belmont, CA: Wadsworth.

U.S. Library of Congress. (1975–). *Library of Congress subject headings*. Washington, DC: Author.

EXAMPLES

Jack's topic, "Ethics," is too broad for a 5-minute persuasive speech. By talking about the topic, thinking about why the topic was interesting in the first place, and looking at some general references, Jack finds ways to narrow the topic. He locates subtopics dealing with ghost-writing, and, because this is a speech class, this direction seems promising. One first step is to check the Library of Congress subject-headings list for related topics. When logging onto the Library of Congress site, Jack chooses *Library Catalogs* and then *Basic Search* to find the subject headings. When he types *ghostwriting* to allow for the various forms of the term as a subject and uses *Subject Browse* to see what possible subject terms exist, 11 relevant subject headings appear. Among them are:

> *Ghostwriter* (television program)
> Women Ghostwriters
> Authors Ghostwriting
> Speechwriting

Valerie's news article assignment on the new campus voice-mail system is sufficiently narrow. A chance exists, though, that even with the best search she will find few sources because of the multiple terms that have been used in the literature. A good first step is to start identifying all those possible keywords: *voice mail, v-mail, answering machines,* and *telephone information systems.* Valerie must also consider which type of reference materials would be most worthwhile. The following are relevant: professional and trade journals, newspapers, newsmagazines, websites, periodical indexes, statistics, and interviews with relevant people. Only sources published within the past 5 years are relevant.

Robin's communication theory paper on attribution is proving to be a nightmare. She decided to test the topic and selected a periodical index, *PsycINFO,* to see how many articles were published during the 1990s. Searching for the term *attribution* in the subject-heading (descriptor) field results in 5,811 hits. A similar search for *interpersonal interaction* resulted in 5,916 hits. Combining these terms and looking at only those focusing on humans and written in English from 1990 to 1999 resulted in 50 hits. Because this is a communication class, adding the term *communication* (in a title or abstract) reduced the number to six hits. If these were supplemented with books, chapters, or annual review materials, this number might be reasonable. Broadening the search to 1980–1999 adds four additional sources. So the keywords to use are *attribution*, *interpersonal interaction*, and *communication*.

Jason's literature review on parasocial interaction seems to be one that can be handled in 20–25 pages, or so the databases suggest. To identify other access tools that will result in relevant literature, Jason uses a general-to-specific strategy by reading through Chapters 5–8 of this book and picking out relevant sources. But a specific-to-general strategy is also possible because everyone seems to cite Horton and Wohl's article (see the citation at the end of Chapter 1) as the origination of the term. By using the *Social Sciences Citation Index* (described in Chapter 6), Jason double-checks that all literature has been found.

Kat, **Rocky**, and **Michelle** are tossing around ideas about their training module on conflict resolution. After identifying several keywords, they decide to divide the labor and each search different sources. They promise to keep full search records to share with one another so all can be assured the sources were searched as expected. Kat takes the online research databases and library catalogs and also plans a full Internet search, including relevant search engines and communication metasites. Rocky uses directories to find organizational consultants to interview. And Michelle scans professional and trade journals for references to training programs.

Eric, Gregory, Anthony, and **Scott** start searching databases for previously published research on their topics. Each takes a different database and looks for relevant descriptors and keywords for the main terms. Then they find articles that are relevant for their study and start taking notes on them. By comparing their findings, they determine how comprehensive their searches of the literature actually were. The articles, then, give them more information on what is important about the topic and what types of questions have not yet been answered.

EXERCISES

1. Choose an area of communication that you identified as being of interest to you in Chapter 1 and describe a general research topic you would like to pursue further.
2. Formulate three specific research questions about this general research topic.
3. Complete a search strategy sheet for one of these three research questions. Examine each of these general sources and complete bibliography records for

each source you find. The bibliography should include a sufficient number of sources to support a 20–page research report. The bibliography should be listed on index cards or in computer records and entries should follow the style used in this chapter.

4. As your bibliography progresses, complete the following additional records:
   a. Subject-headings/keyword list. Keep a record on an index card or computer record of all headings and keywords that pertain to your topic.
   b. Search records. Keep both a general record, listing by title all sources used, plus an individual record for each finding tool (e.g., index or abstract), using the format in this chapter.

5. Answer the following questions as a way of tracking your literature search progress.

Topic

- Have you selected a topic? What is it?
- Does it need to be narrowed? What is the narrowed topic?
- How can you adjust the topic to one that is manageable? What is the topic now?

Search

- Have you selected a search strategy appropriate for this topic? Which one is best? Have you completed your search-strategy sheet?
- Have you toured the library? Do you know how to use the library catalog? Do you know how to order material through interlibrary loan? Do you know where reference materials, government documents, and statistical materials are located?
- Have you set up a system for searching the literature? Do you have a bibliography card or computer record system developed? Do you have a subject-headings list? Do you have search records for each reference source? Do you have a general search record for all sources?

Results

- Have you evaluated the sources you plan to use? Are they reliable? Have you read the materials carefully?
- Are your notes in your own words? Did you use quotation marks around materials you had to quote, and did you record the page numbers for these quotes?

Writing

- Are you ready to write? What is the thesis of the work? Have you constructed an outline? What are its main points or divisions?
- After you wrote, did you revise the paper two or three times to make sure it made sense? Did you edit the manuscript and proofread carefully for typographical errors and misspellings?

6. Narrow a topic by completing the following steps:
   a. Pick a broad topic in which you are interested.
      Topic: _____
   b. What is a research question you might pose about this topic?
      Question: _____?
      _____
   c. Now identify two or three key concepts in your question.
      _____
      _____
   d. Provide synonyms for each of the concepts you identified.
      _____

   For help in finding synonyms, (1) identify and consult a reference source that provides an overview of the discipline or general subject and (2) test your concepts and terms in the library catalog or a periodical index.
   Reference source I used. _____
   I tested it in: _____
   e. Now reformulate your question using the information you have gained. Your reformulated question should use some of the new terms you identified and should be narrower and more focused.
      New question: _____?

chapter 3

Using Computers to Search Electronic Databases

M ost of the access tools that you will use in communication research—especially library catalogs and periodical indexes—will be available only as electronic **databases**. Catalogs and indexes are bibliographic databases, one of the types of databases that we discuss in this chapter. You will also need to search other types of databases: directories, statistical sources, and the full text of books, newspapers, journals, and other periodicals. The World Wide Web itself can be thought of as a database—either one large database or several smaller, more specialized databases.

A researcher who is reluctant to use computers to find information or who does not know how to do so effectively will be severely handicapped. Fortunately, learning to search databases well simply involves learning some basic concepts and standard searching procedures you can then apply to many different situations. The search interfaces used by different database **vendors** usually offer only slight variations of these concepts and procedures. In this chapter we introduce you to the different types of computerized databases and explain the process and concepts for searching them.

DIFFERING ENVIRONMENTS

The electronic environment you find on your campus might vary considerably from that at another university. This is partly because technology has provided libraries with many options. For example, libraries are able to select different versions of standard databases from a variety of vendors. Each database has a different search interface, covers different time periods, and can include other features such as the full text of articles cited. So a database you search in one library can look quite different when you search it in a library across town.

Another result is that you might locate a citation to an article that is, unbeknownst to you, available full-text through a different database. To help you connect to that full-text article, libraries have developed special lists and other means to help you track it down, but this can all seem a bit complicated. Fortunately, database vendors are working with libraries to develop the capability to link directly from article citations in one database to full-text articles in different databases. This development is taking place over a period of years, and libraries vary their method used and the pace of implementation.

Users may become confused by all these options, but they need not be. Libraries usually provide a browser-based menu that serves as a gateway to the electronic databases provided, no matter what their origin or format. From this menu you should be able to determine which periodicals the library subscribes to, either in print or electronically, and to access the electronic versions. If you have questions, ask a reference librarian for assistance. Librarians can help you find out what electronic sources are available and how you can access and use them effectively.

VARIETIES OF COMPUTERIZED DATABASES

A **database** is information stored in such a way that it can be retrieved. Catalogs and periodical indexes—in fact, all the reference sources discussed in this book—are examples of databases. They are organized so that you can easily find what you're looking for. A **computerized database** is simply information stored electronically, to be retrieved via a computer. Such databases greatly increase the flexibility for retrieving information.

Databases can be categorized broadly in many different ways. One way is to think of them as either bibliographic, directory, or source databases. Many combine aspects of these types. Furthermore, it is important to distinguish between electronic *databases*, which are fully searchable, and electronic *publications* whose text can be retrieved but not searched electronically. Many resources now available are a combination of the two.

Bibliographic Databases

Bibliographic databases consist of **citations** to published literature, often with **abstracts**, or short summaries. They correspond to print periodical indexes and abstracts. Computerized library catalogs are also examples of bibliographic databases. At the conclusion of their search, users of these databases will usually still need to locate the actual publications cited, although many periodical indexes do now include online (or link to) the full text of at least some of the publications they cite.

Most of the periodical indexes and abstracts described in Part 2 were initially print publications that are now available online as bibliographic databases. Those of major interest to communication researchers are *ERIC* (Educational Resources Information Center), the computerized equivalent of the printed indexes *Resources in Education* and *Current Index to Journals in Education*; *PsycINFO* (*Psychological*

Abstracts); *Sociological Abstracts*; *Wilson Business Abstracts* (*Business Periodicals Index*); *Social Sciences Abstracts* (*Social Sciences Index*); *Humanities Abstracts* (*Humanities Index*); and *Education Abstracts* (*Education Index*). Most of these databases correspond closely to their print counterparts in scope and journal coverage. A major difference, however, is the number of years available for retrospective searching. Just a few databases were available online before the 1970s, and the coverage of most starts after 1980. Fortunately, many online indexes have started to add retrospective coverage.

Other bibliographic databases do not correspond to any printed index and are available only in computerized form. These, too, require library subscriptions. Useful examples for communication researchers are *ComAbstracts* (CIOS), which indexes and abstracts more than 100 journals in communication; *Communication & Mass Media Complete* (EBSCOhost), which provides cover-to-cover coverage of 440 journals, selective coverage of 200 others, and full text coverage of over 300 of these; and *Communication Abstracts* (Sage), which indexes over 100 journals and provides coverage across the communication discipline. Other examples include *JSTOR* (JSTOR) and *Business Source Complete* (EBSCOhost), which index and abstract periodical literature in business and management, making them particularly useful for those in organizational communication. More interdisciplinary, comprehensive indexes include *Psychology and Behavioral Sciences Collection* (EBSCOhost), *WorldCat* (OCLC, Online Computer Libraries Center), and *Academic Search Complete* (EBSCOhost). These and other bibliographic databases are described in detail in Chapter 6.

Directory Databases

Directory databases, also called *referral databases*, correspond to printed directories and contain references to organizations, people, grants, archives, research projects, and so on. Although some directory databases contain summaries or abstracts, researchers most often use these databases to locate a primary information source. A directory database of possible interest to communication researchers is the *Encyclopedia of Associations*.

Source Databases

In contrast, **source databases** contain such complete information that after consulting them you may not need to continue the search for information. This category includes statistical, full-text, image, and multimedia databases.

Statistical databases consist primarily of statistical or other numeric data and are somewhat equivalent to statistical compendia such as yearbooks and **almanacs**. They can also contain some textual information. Many libraries received 1990 census data as statistical databases on CD-ROMs produced by the U.S. Bureau of the Census. Data from the 2000 census are largely distributed through the web. The searching **protocols** for statistical databases allow the user to create, correlate, and retrieve personally defined sets of data that would take many hours to assemble from printed publications. Many statistical sources available on the web are not true databases in the sense that web data cannot be manipulated. Statistical compendia are often published online simply as text documents, in which the data are consulted in tabular form, much as one would view the pages of a printed volume.

Full-text databases contain the complete text of publications such as journals, newspapers, wire service stories, court decisions, encyclopedias, almanacs, and other books. In true full-text databases, every word of the entire text can be searched interactively online. For example, if a person's name, hometown, street address, or occupation appeared as incidental information in a newspaper article, the article could be retrieved by searching for any of those words or phrases. This capability distinguishes full-text databases from electronic publications available merely for online perusal. Be warned, however, that the term *full text* is used loosely and can be applied to one or both types of products. *Contemporary Authors* (Gale, part of Cengage Learning; http://www.contemporarywriters.com/authors/) is an example of an extensive series of print reference volumes now available and searchable full-text through the web. Full-text searching capability in this database allows one, for example, to identify authors with a particular first name, those who were born in a certain town or country, those who graduated from a particular university, and so on.

Image databases consist of graphic images, such as photographs, representations of works of art, and textual material. Textual material available in this manner is simply a reproduction of the printed page and cannot be searched interactively. Many periodicals are available as part of image databases. In fact, many periodical indexes now offer the option of viewing articles either as text alone (often referred to as *html*) or as an image (often referred to as **PDF**, or portable document format). *Full-image* textual databases store documents in file formats that require special helper applications for viewing (e.g., Adobe Acrobat for viewing PDF files). In contrast, *full-text* publications available on the web are usually webpages written in the standard web language, html. An example of such an index available in many university libraries is *Academic Search Complete*, from EBSCOhost. An advantage of viewing the image of an article is that, in contrast to the text-only version, it includes illustrations and photographs as they appeared in the printed publication. The pagination will also be identical, which makes it possible to cite them more precisely.

The web is a rich repository of many other types of image databases. Photographs, manuscripts, representations of artworks, illustrations, and other images have been collected and are searchable on their website of origin. Some can be searched through specialized search engines.

Multimedia databases include, in addition to text and graphics, audio and video components. Many multimedia databases are now available through the web, including important collections of broadcasting archives (discussed in Chapter 8). We discuss each type of database in Part 2. The *Gale Directory of Online, Portable, and Internet Databases* (Cengage Learning/Gale) attempts to list comprehensively those available commercially online, on CD-ROM, and in other formats. Many web-based databases are listed in web subject directories. We discuss these in Chapter 4.

HOW TO SEARCH COMPUTERIZED DATABASES

Computerized databases can be deceptively easy to search. When novice searchers type the first topical word or phrase that occurs to them into a bibliographic database and retrieve citations to articles on their topics, they might be satisfied with the results. They may not realize, however, that they have failed to identify many other, sometimes more appropriate, articles. Or they spend hours browsing through hundreds of citations, not realizing that they could easily have narrowed their search and obtained more manageable results. Such problems tend to be compounded when using search engines to search the web.

In this section we describe some basic features of search systems. Mastering these concepts will help you search effectively, making your searches as precise or as comprehensive as you wish. Of course, it will be necessary to combine this general information with specific information about the features of the databases you are searching. Fortunately, such specific information is readily available. Most databases include online tutorials and ample Help screens. Such tutorials are well worth the small amount of time that it takes to go through them. Once you understand the concepts of searching computerized databases, you can more easily understand and use the Help screens provided by online sources.

STANDARD SEARCH FEATURES

The search features that we describe next are so widely used that they can be considered standard. Their implementation varies from one system to another, but the concepts involved remain the same.

Controlled Vocabulary Versus Keyword Searching

Most databases allow a user to enter **search statements** simply by typing in words or phrases. The system then retrieves those citations whose records contain the words or phrases entered. The citations retrieved find matches in almost any field: title, journal title, abstract, or subject heading. Searching in this way, using everyday language, is searching by **keyword**.

Keyword searching, also called **free-text searching**, is often effective in locating citations on a topic, but it does have drawbacks. First, because language is imprecise, it is likely that at least some records retrieved will match the words entered but will not actually be on the topic intended. At the same time, the searcher can miss several citations on the topic that did not happen to contain the term used. Perhaps the citation contained a synonym instead.

For these reasons, almost all bibliographic databases have established a **controlled vocabulary** that is used in a systematic way to describe the subject of articles and books. Subject terms (called subject headings or descriptors) are assigned to each record and are listed in the subject (or descriptor) field for each item. The example in Figure 3.1 is a record from the *Psychology and Behavioral Sciences Collection* database, using the EBSCOhost system. Notice that nine subject terms were assigned to this article.

If we had done a keyword search for the term *attribution* in *Psychology and Behavioral Sciences Collection*, we would have retrieved the record in Figure 3.1, because this term occurs in the record in one or more fields, in this case the abstract

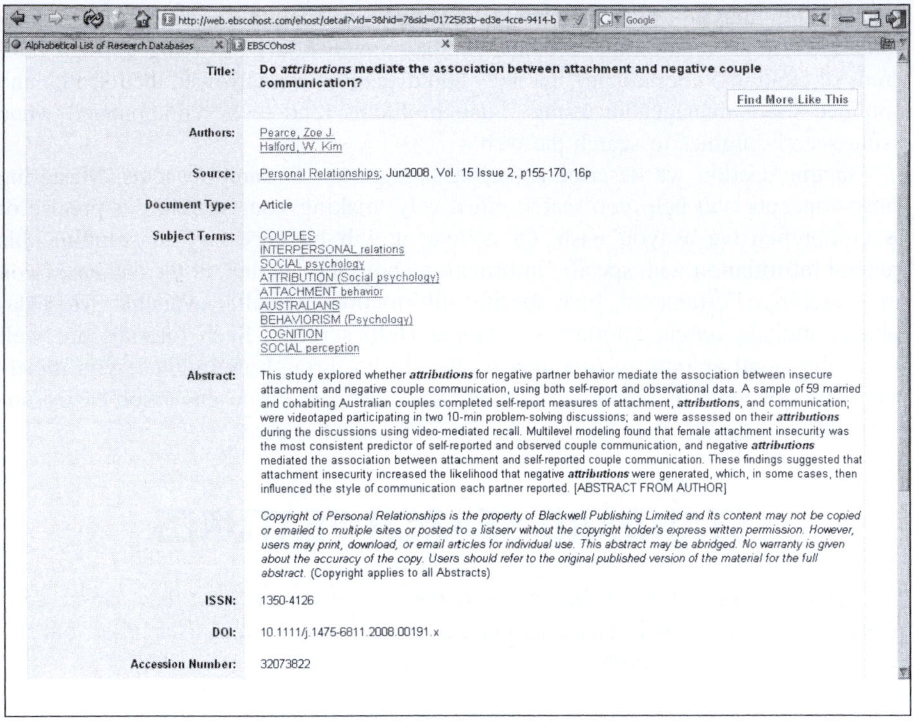

http://web.ebscohost.com/ehost/detail?vid=3&hid=7&sid=0172583b-ed3e-4cce-9414-b

Alphabetical List of Research Databases | EBSCOhost

Title: Do *attributions* mediate the association between attachment and negative couple communication?

Find More Like This

Authors: Pearce, Zoe J.
Halford, W. Kim

Source: Personal Relationships; Jun2008, Vol. 15 Issue 2, p155-170, 16p

Document Type: Article

Subject Terms: COUPLES
INTERPERSONAL relations
SOCIAL psychology
ATTRIBUTION (Social psychology)
ATTACHMENT behavior
AUSTRALIANS
BEHAVIORISM (Psychology)
COGNITION
SOCIAL perception

Abstract: This study explored whether ***attributions*** for negative partner behavior mediate the association between insecure attachment and negative couple communication, using both self-report and observational data. A sample of 59 married and cohabiting Australian couples completed self-report measures of attachment, ***attributions***, and communication; were videotaped participating in two 10-min problem-solving discussions; and were assessed on their ***attributions*** during the discussions using video-mediated recall. Multilevel modeling found that female attachment insecurity was the most consistent predictor of self-reported and observed couple communication, and negative ***attributions*** mediated the association between attachment and self-reported couple communication. These findings suggested that attachment insecurity increased the likelihood that negative ***attributions*** were generated, which, in some cases, then influenced the style of communication each partner reported. [ABSTRACT FROM AUTHOR]

Copyright of Personal Relationships is the property of Blackwell Publishing Limited and its content may not be copied or emailed to multiple sites or posted to a listserv without the copyright holder's express written permission. However, users may print, download, or email articles for individual use. This abstract may be abridged. No warranty is given about the accuracy of the copy. Users should refer to the original published version of the material for the full abstract. (Copyright applies to all Abstracts)

ISSN: 1350-4126

DOI: 10.1111/j.1475-6811.2008.00191.x

Accession Number: 32073822

Figure 3.1 *A Psychology and Behavioral Sciences Collection* Record

field and the subject field. If we had specified that we wanted to do a subject search, our search would have been limited to the subject field. In this case we would have retrieved the record with either method.

You are probably familiar with the concept of a controlled vocabulary and the use of subject headings because their use is essential for all printed indexes and catalogs. And you are probably familiar with the **Library of Congress subject headings**, which are used in almost all college and university library catalogs and are described in Chapter 2. **Database producers** usually publish a list of the subject headings or descriptors used in a particular database (often called a **thesaurus**). Knapp (2000) has published a volume that contains most common thesaurus terms. Even better, many products have incorporated this thesaurus into their search system. Thus, when searching these databases, it is possible to query the online thesaurus to determine whether a particular term is a subject heading. The online thesaurus allows the user to move easily between cross-references, and terms can be selected and entered directly from the screen. The most common mistake that new searchers make is to ignore a database's controlled vocabulary, relying exclusively on keyword searching. Figure 3.2 is a sample entry from the online *ERIC* thesaurus.

Of course, some concepts are so new that they have not yet been incorporated into the controlled vocabulary, so keywords must be used. As they gain experience, searchers will find that it is effective to use both keywords and subject headings. In

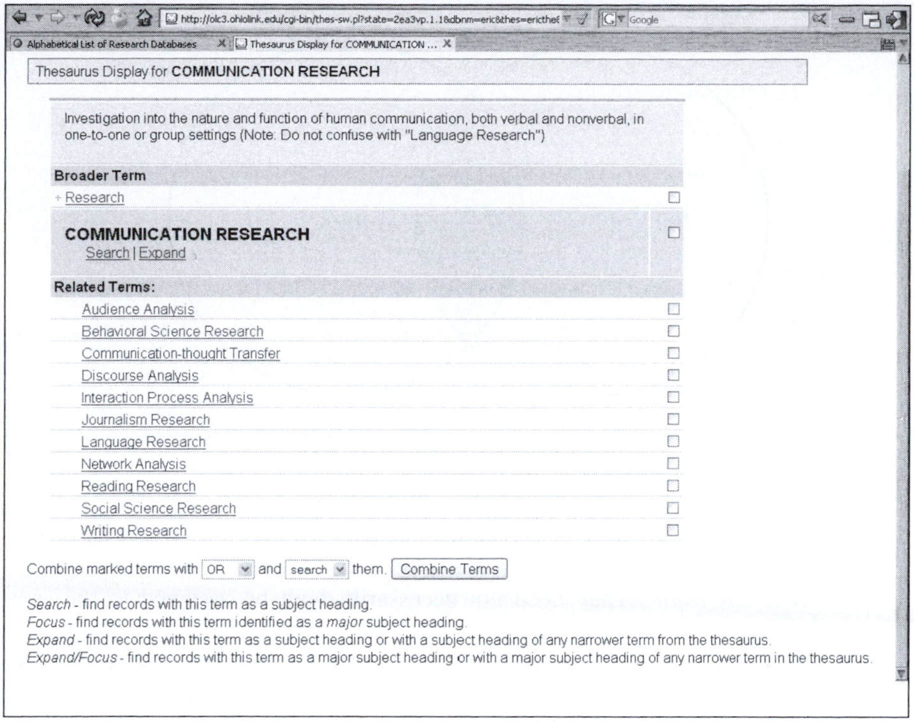

Figure 3.2 ERIC Thesaurus Entry

fact, a common and often effective strategy is to start by doing a keyword search, then to review the displayed citations. If you find citations on your topic, the subject headings assigned to that record are usually an excellent source of headings that can be entered to make the search more effective. Locating subject headings in this way is sometimes called *lateral* or *sideways searching*, and search systems are usually designed to facilitate it. In web-based search systems, subject headings assigned to records are usually links that can be searched simply by clicking on them. This is the case in the example record shown in Figure 3.1.

Boolean Operators

Operators are special terms that allow searchers to connect or combine words and concepts. The most widely used operators—AND, OR, and NOT—are sometimes called **logical**, or **Boolean**, **operators**.

> **AND** The *AND* operator retrieves only those citations that include all the combined search terms. In Figure 3.3, *television AND radio* include terms contained in bibliographic records that the computer is searching. The computer is asked to AND the sets of records together. The shaded area represents those records that the computer is asked to retrieve. It includes only those records in which *both* words, *television* and *radio*, appear.

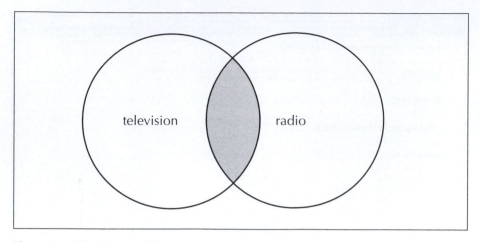

Figure 3.3 Television AND Radio

> **OR** When we *OR* the sets of records together (Figure 3.4), we get all records
> to which at least one of these descriptors has been assigned—either *televi-*
> *sion OR radio*. They need not necessarily both be assigned to the same
> document. Thus many more records will be found with the OR operator
> than with the AND operator. This operator is generally used to combine
> synonyms, related terms, alternate spellings, and acronyms.
>
> **NOT** (sometimes called AND NOT or BUT NOT) The *NOT* operator excludes
> a particular term from your search results. For example, *television NOT*
> *radio* (Figure 3.5) excludes all records that include the term *radio*. This
> operator is used much less often than AND and OR, and it should be used
> with care. In the example in Figure 3.5, we could be excluding desirable
> articles that contain valuable information on television simply because they
> also mention radio.

In conducting searches, we often group together with the OR operator all synonyms and related terms that represent each separate concept we wish to search.

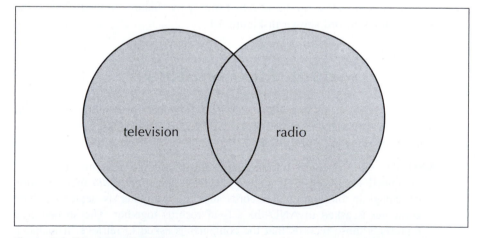

Figure 3.4 Television OR Radio

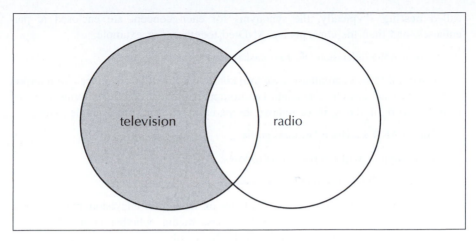

Figure 3.5 Television NOT Radio

The resulting sets of records, which tend to be large, are then AND-ed together to produce a much smaller set. Simply stated: *Synonyms are OR-ed, then the resulting sets, representing concepts, are AND-ed.* Using a form such as the one in Figure 3.6 when preparing a search can clarify the relationships between *concepts* and *terms*.

Nesting with Parentheses

When searches are entered into a search system, parentheses are used to indicate how we want to group the terms we have selected. Grouping the terms in this way is

		CONCEPT 1	AND	CONCEPT 2	AND	CONCEPT 3
s						
y						
n		OR		OR		OR
o						
n						
y		OR		OR		OR
m						
s						

Topic:_____

Figure 3.6 Search Preparation Form

called **nesting**. Typically, the synonyms for each concept are enclosed in parentheses, and then the concepts are AND-ed together. For example:

women AND (television OR mass media)

If we fail to use parentheses, we lose control of how the computer will interpret and process our search statement. The computer simply combines terms in order from left to right. Thus, if we remove the parentheses from the example given:

women AND television OR mass media

the computer will interpret it as follows:

(women AND television) OR mass media

We would retrieve some relevant articles on women in television, but we would also retrieve all of the articles related to mass media, whether or not they were related to women. Figure 3.7 should clarify this result.

Search systems for web-based databases often include guided search screens that allow us to enter terms in separate search boxes and specify which operator (AND, OR, or NOT) should be used to combine them. This saves us from having to use parentheses, but it can make it difficult to specify the order in which we want the terms to be processed. One way of getting around this is to enter all the synonyms for each concept in a single search box, connected with OR. Then make sure that AND will combine the results of the search boxes. See the example in Figure 3.8.

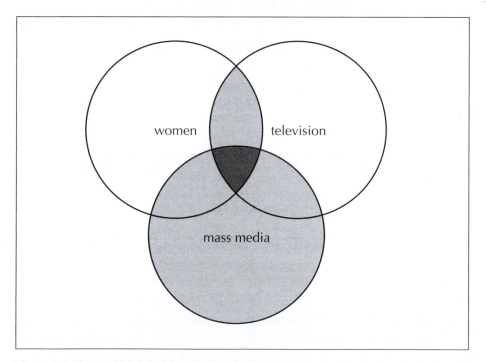

Figure 3.7 Women AND Television OR Mass Media

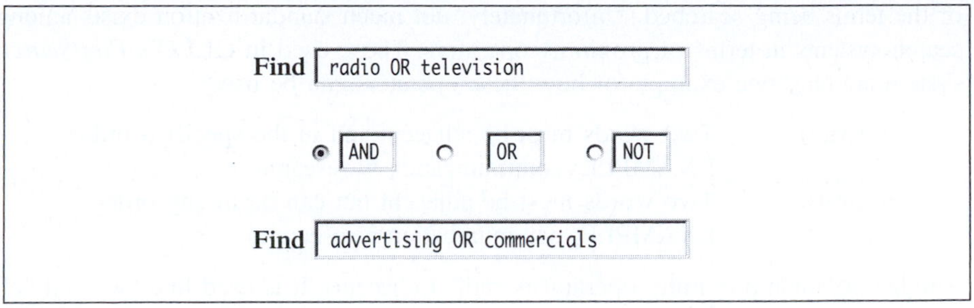

Figure 3.8 AND OR NOT

Alternatives to Boolean Operators

Some search systems use Boolean concepts without resorting to the operators AND, OR, or NOT. For example, you might enter search terms into a search box and then be asked to specify whether you wish to search for:

- "all of the words" or "must contain the words" (each equivalent to AND)
- "any of the words" or "can contain the words" or "at least one of the words" (each equivalent to OR)
- "must not contain the words" or "should not contain the words" or "without the words" (each equivalent to NOT)

Another popular alternative is to use symbols (+ and −) in place of AND and NOT. These are sometimes called **implied Boolean symbols**. The plus symbol (+) is placed in front of terms that must be *included*, and the minus symbol (−) is used to *exclude* terms. Thus, "+" is somewhat equivalent to AND, and "−" to NOT. If you want to retrieve articles (or websites) that deal with radio commercials exclusively, for example, you might enter this search:

+ radio + commercials − television

Notice that, to be retrieved by this search, records must contain *both* the words *radio* and *commercials*, but any records that also happen to include the word *television* will be eliminated. As with the NOT operator, use extreme caution when using "−".

What is less clear to many searchers is that *no* symbol—that is, simply a space— means something, too. For most search engines a space between two search terms now *implies* AND. That is the case for the search engine *Google*, for example. In a few others it implies OR, which was actually the standard practice in earlier search engines. This default will make a big difference in your results, so consult the Help function of the system you are using to determine how spaces are interpreted.

Proximity Operators

Other operators frequently available for use with search systems are called **proximity operators**. These operators allow the searcher to specify the physical proximity of the terms being searched. Unfortunately, not much standardization exists among search systems in terms of proximity operators. Those used in OCLC's *FirstSearch* system are only one example of how these operators can be used:

w (with):   Two words must be adjacent and in the specified order.
              EXAMPLE: communication w research
n (near):   Two words must be adjacent but can be in any order.
              EXAMPLE: communication n research

Another common proximity operator is "adj" (adjacent). It is used like "w" and "n" to indicate that two terms must be immediately adjacent. Often it is possible to specify that two terms must be separated by no more than a specified number of words. Thus, *television n3 commercials* would retrieve records in which these two words were close but not immediately adjacent. To determine which, if any, proximity operators are available in a particular database and how they are defined, you must check the online Help function. In another database, for example, *with* might mean that the two terms must be in the same sentence, and *near* might mean that they must be in the same paragraph.

Phrase Searching

You will often want to search for a phrase rather than for a single word. The search systems for most bibliographic databases assume that two adjacent words constitute a phrase. For example, if you enter the words *television commercials* in a search box, you will normally retrieve records in which those two words appear together and in that order. An increasingly common way of forcing a phrase search is to enclose the phrase in quotes: "television commercials". This method of phrase searching is the common practice in web search engines. It is coming into practice in search systems for bibliographic databases as well.

Field-Specific Searching

The information in each database record is organized in fields (author, title, subject headings, and so on). The fields available and the terms used to designate them vary from one database to another. Some databases include many fields with a great deal of information that can be used by the searcher to narrow and broaden searches. To search most effectively, searchers should familiarize themselves with the fields used in the database they are searching. Often this requires seeking help via the Help screens for the *database* itself (e.g., *PsycINFO*) rather than the Help screens for the vendor or *search system* (e.g., FirstSearch, ProQuest, EBSCOhost, SilverPlatter).

The record in Figure 3.9 from the *ERIC* database via EBSCOhost illustrates the relatively wide variety of fields available in this database. Notice that this *ERIC* record is for a journalism article using the same keyword (*attribution*) as that shown in Figure 3.1 as it appeared in the *Psychology and Behavioral Science Collection* database. Compare the fields available and the descriptors assigned by each database. Notice that *ERIC* has a special category of controlled vocabulary, called

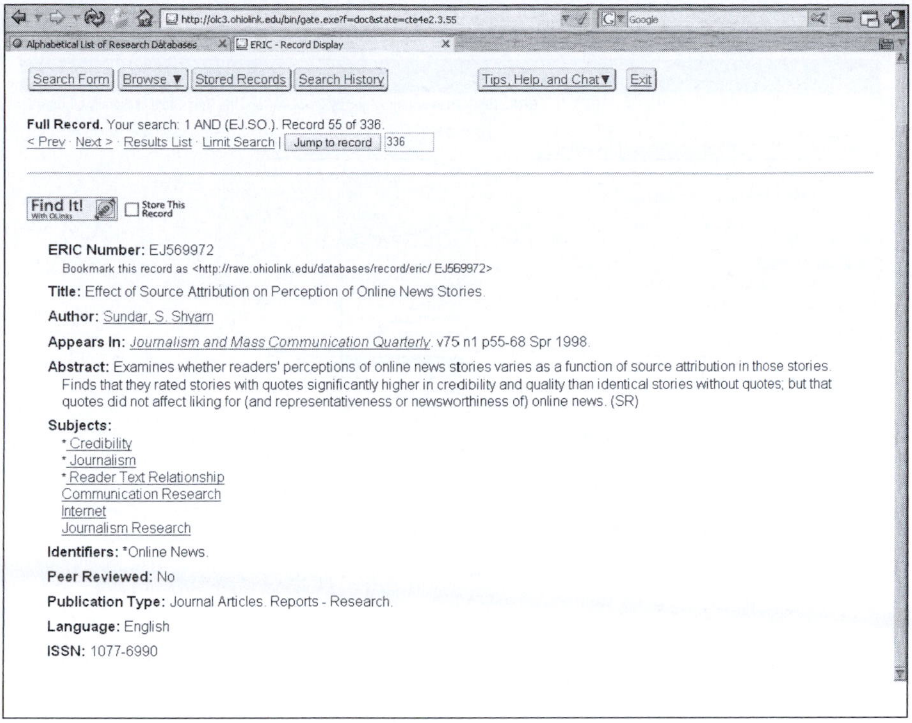

Figure 3.9 An ERIC Record Via EBSCOhost

identifiers. Identifiers are not listed in the *ERIC* thesaurus but are highly specific subjects that are useful for subject retrieval.

ERIC also has two classes of descriptors: major (used for the primary focus) and minor (used for peripheral subject areas). Major descriptors in EBSCOhost are those preceded by an asterisk. Notice that the broad term *Communication Research* is assigned as a minor descriptor to this record. Because this descriptor is assigned fairly consistently by *ERIC* indexers, you can use it to narrow searches to the literature of this discipline. (See Figure 3.2 to see how the *ERIC* thesaurus can help you identify related terms to consider.) *ERIC* has document type, year, and language fields; you can restrict your search to certain types of documents, publications in a particular language, and items published in a specified year or range of years.

Many bibliographic databases allow you to specify the field or fields to be searched. This offers many possible access points and a great deal of flexibility. For example, you can elect to search only the title field, only subject headings (descriptors), a combination of title-abstracts-descriptors, and so on. Furthermore, in some search systems you can specify whether you want to search the descriptor field using specific descriptors or by *keyword*. The difference can be significant. If you specify that you wish to search the term *television* as a descriptor in the descriptors field of *ERIC*; for instance, you would retrieve only records to which the descriptor *television* had been assigned. If, however, you searched *television* as a keyword in the descriptors field, you would retrieve all records in which *television* appeared as

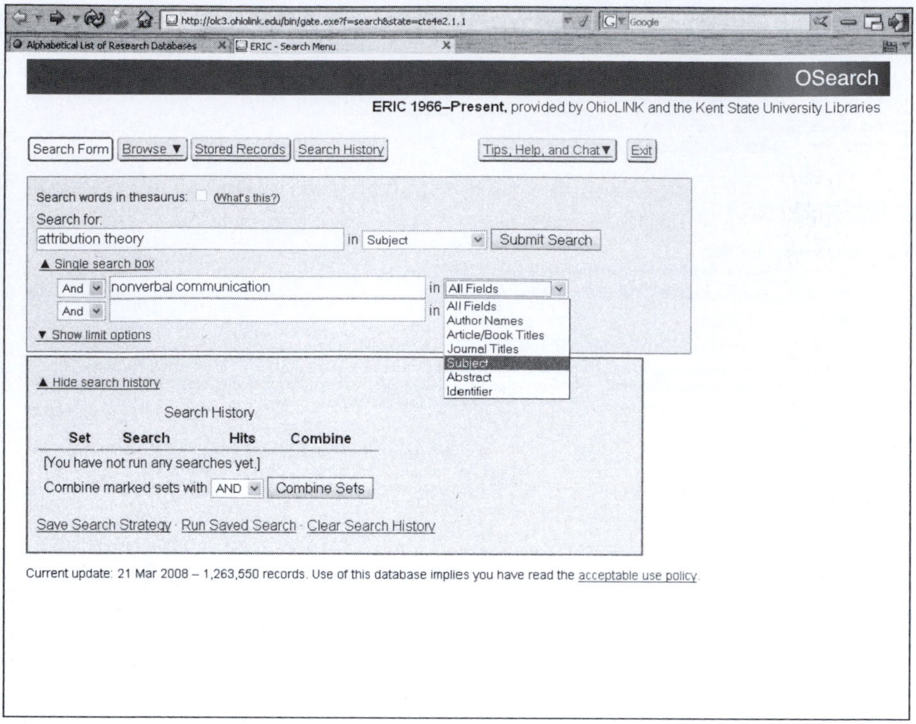

Figure 3.10 An ERIC Search Screen

part of a descriptor, including these: *television commercials, television curriculum, television research, television surveys,* and *television viewing.* Which way you elect to go—keyword or exact descriptor—will depend on what you are looking for and whether you wish to broaden or narrow your search.

Web-based search interfaces typically offer guided search screens that facilitate field-specific searching. Figure 3.10 shows what this type of screen would look like for an *attribution* AND *nonverbal communication* subject term search.

Truncation

When entering keyword terms, you may find that you want to enter several words that have the same root (e.g., *adolescent, adolescents, adolescence*). It is possible to do this simply by typing each word connected with the OR operator, but it is a bit faster to truncate (shorten) the word to its root. Most search systems allow you to use a symbol to indicate that you wish to truncate a word. Here are some examples: adolescen*, adolescen?, adolescen$. Check Help screens to see which truncation symbol a particular database uses.

Of course, you must use truncation with caution. If you truncate a root too short, you will retrieve many irrelevant terms. For example, *auto* would retrieve not only *auto, automobile*, and *automotive*, but also *automatic, autobiography*, and so on. It is almost always a good idea to use truncation to search for both the singular and plural form of terms.

Browsing Word and Phrase Indexes

Many databases have an **index** feature that allows you to **browse** and select terms from an alphabetized list of words and phrases contained in the database as a whole or, more often, in a particular field. Searching the names of authors in bibliographic databases is often particularly troublesome for researchers, due to variations in first names and initials. Using the Index feature to browse the author field will solve this problem and is highly recommended. You can also use this feature to browse and select subject headings, a useful practice if the database doesn't offer an online thesaurus. If the search system allows you to browse all words in the database, you'll easily be able to pick out alternate forms of keywords (*adolescents, adolescence*, and so on). Keyword indexes are usually as is: Don't be surprised when you find typos and misspellings.

Creating and Reusing Sets

As you enter search terms into some search systems, the results are displayed on the screen in numbered **sets** of records, or **hits**. For example, if you have separately entered the terms *television, children*, and *violence*, the results displayed might look something like this:

set 1	6709	TELEVISION
set 2	2171	VIOLENCE
set 3	54547	CHILDREN

It is then possible to refer to these sets by set numbers and to combine them using AND, OR, and NOT operators. For example, if we AND-ed the preceding sets, we would receive the following result:

| set 4 | 95 | #1 and #2 and #3 |

The resulting set, #4, could then be modified and combined with other sets, as desired. We might, for example, limit set #4 to English-language books and journal articles published since 1990.

Other search systems might take you directly to a display of brief records rather than to a listing of sets. Often these systems offer a History feature that allows you to review sets already created and to combine them in various ways using Boolean operators. Of course, sets can also be created using parentheses to group terms connected by operators, as they are entered:

(sex bias OR sex stereotypes) AND (television OR TV)

This search will give us only listings of records in which the terms *sex bias* or *sex stereotypes* appear that also mention *television* or *TV*.

SEARCH STRATEGIES: BOOLEAN SEARCHING

A well-designed **search strategy** will use several of these search options to search efficiently and effectively. Start by investigating the controlled vocabulary to see whether there are descriptors for your concepts. If you have several from which to choose, pick the most specific available, enter them as search statements, and appropriately combine them with AND and OR operators. Then review the results. Depending on your objective, you might be able to stop here. If you retrieve too few citations, you will need to broaden your search. If you locate too many, you will want to narrow it. In either case, you have many options.

To narrow a search:

■ Use the AND operator to add additional concepts, one at a time.
■ Use field-specific search statements and the AND operator to limit your search (e.g., by year, language, age groups, publication type). Many systems offer advanced search screens that make it easy to limit searches in this way.
■ Consult the thesaurus and choose a more specific descriptor.

To broaden a search:

■ Consult the thesaurus and choose a broader search descriptor.
■ Use the OR operator to add synonyms.
■ Reduce the number of concepts that are AND-ed.

As you attempt to refine your search, take full advantage of the interactive nature of computerized searching systems. By examining the records you retrieve together with the assigned descriptors, you can determine whether you should drop or add search terms to achieve either a more precise or a more complete set of results.

To illustrate these strategies, we'll again search the *ERIC* database, via EBS-COhost, to find reports dealing with the effects of television on children. This database includes records from 1966. Naturally if we were to do a comprehensive search on this topic, we would need to search other communication databases and the social sciences as well. If we followed our own advice, we would start by using *ERIC*'s thesaurus feature to investigate possible descriptors. To make this search closer to the way many students, researchers, and librarians actually behave, however, we'll plunge in with a keyword search statement. We enter our search statement on the initial search screen:

television AND children [all fields]

The result is 4,019 records retrieved.

Wow! We don't want to look through over 4,000 records, so it's time to narrow this search. One way to do so is to restrict the terms we used, *television* AND *children*, to the subject field. By limiting our search to the subject field, we should eliminate items that are only peripherally related to the topic.

television AND children [subject]

The result is 1,564 records retrieved.

That's better, but it's still far too many citations to browse through. Perhaps we can narrow one of the descriptors. Let's look at some of the records we retrieved to find one that's right on the topic and then see which descriptors were assigned to it. After examining several records, we decide that the descriptor *television viewing* comes closest to our intent. We also notice that *children* is itself a descriptor, but that a narrower term, such as *kindergarten children*, is often assigned to a record instead. If we continue to search simply with the term *children*, we'll retrieve both the broader and the narrower terms, which seems appropriate for now. So we enter:

television viewing AND children [subject]

The result is 916 records retrieved.

More progress, but it looks as though this topic was just too broadly conceived to begin with. It's time to do some serious thinking about how to narrow it. We look for a way to search the *ERIC* thesaurus and find some ways to limit the search. We could:

- Add another concept (*academic achievement* or *violence* are two possibilities).
- Narrow the *children* concept by restricting it to *young children*.

Here are the results of each option:

television viewing AND children AND academic achievement [subject]

Results: 30

television viewing AND young children in [subject]

Results: 131

television viewing AND children AND violence [subject]

Results: 92

The first result is puzzling: Only 30 records were retrieved for our search *television viewing AND children AND academic achievement*. There must be more published on that topic in the education literature. Looking at our search, we realize that the term *children* is somewhat redundant in a search that includes the term *academic achievement*. It may seem odd, but this term would not automatically be assigned to every publication that relates to children, so including it unnecessarily restricts our results. Let's take it out. When we do so, our search retrieves 131 records. That sounds better, but we would have to examine some records to decide for sure. We'll let you decide which of these narrowed options you would choose.

As you can see, there are many different ways to proceed in virtually every search. Furthermore, at any point you could opt to limit your search by language, year, or document type. Limiting an *ERIC* search to *Journal Articles since 1995* would be particularly useful if you were looking for more recent research studies; this results in 23 hits.

Natural Language Searching

Natural language searching is the basic search option for some search engines. It is an option for an increasing number of bibliographic search systems as well.

In a **natural language** mode, searchers are encouraged simply to type in words and phrases that resemble spoken language. Note that some systems require you to put the phrase you're searching in quotation marks. The system interprets what we enter and retrieves what often seems like an impossibly large set of results, ranked by **relevance** (see below). Such an approach is a departure from the Boolean methods usually used to search bibliographic databases, which involve a much more structured approach. In fact, a natural language query entered in a standard bibliographic search system may retrieve no records at all. A Boolean search system takes everything entered literally, so it can't cope with extraneous words (*is, what, where, be, interested, find, related to*, and so on). The most flexible natural language search systems, on the other hand, just ignore what they can't use and attempt to interpret what is entered.

Which system is better? The answer depends on many factors. It seems that both systems can work well, and one type of searching might be better than another in particular situations. For comprehensive results, it's advantageous to try both. For many topics, relevant results will be retrieved with both approaches, with surprisingly little overlap. The most important thing is to be aware of which type of system you are using and to adjust your search methods accordingly.

Searching the World Wide Web

Many of the strategies and tools traditionally used to search bibliographic databases are also applicable to searching the web. We have already discussed the basic tools. Boolean operators, adjacency operators, and truncation can be used in most search engines, often on their Advanced Search screens. Implied Boolean operators (+, −) and phrase searching using double quotes have become standard features of search engines. But the web differs in important ways from bibliographic databases. Different approaches are called for; we discuss these in Chapter 4.

SORTING YOUR RESULTS

Many search systems now offer options for sorting your results. Such options can include sorting by author, journal, date, or *relevance*. Many factors can be used to determine relevance. Where in a record do the search terms appear (for instance, in the title, descriptors, abstract, full text)? How many of the terms appear in the record or document? How frequently? How close are the terms to one another? A ranking algorithm particular to each search system takes the answers to these and many other questions into account and, in a somewhat mysterious way, comes up with a ranked listing. The items at the top of the list should, in theory, be highly relevant, whereas those at the bottom might include only one of the search terms. Sorting by relevance is often most appropriate when you have used a natural language search option.

USING YOUR SEARCH RESULTS

The final product of most searches is a printed list of sources. If the databases you've searched have included full-text documents, you have probably printed several of these. You have a couple of other options as well. The first is to e-mail the results to yourself. Most web-based search systems allow this.

Another option is to save the results to the computer's hard drive or to a jump drive. The search systems of some vendors now allow you to store searches right on the system for retrieval at a later session. My EBSCOhost is an example of such a feature. If you have an appropriate bibliography-management program, such as EndNote, ProCite, or Reference Manager, you can export the citations you've retrieved in a format that allows you to add them to others you've previously entered in your database. The RefWorks bibliography-manager system is web-based, allowing the user to access it from any location. It is available by individual subscription, although some campuses make it available through a site license.

A bibliography-management program should allow you to add not only your own descriptors and notes to individual records but also to sort your records, selectively retrieve and print them, use them with a word processing program, and so on. Of course, such **downloading** practices do raise questions of copyright, and database vendors and producers have varying policies about downloading, which you should explore. It also raises the possibility of plagiarism, either from the original article or from the abstract. These abstracts are written by others and are copyrighted, so you cannot use sections of the abstract without using quotation marks and citing the abstract as the source.

Citing abstracts in this manner, though, is not typically done. The abstract itself is incomplete and merely provides a summary of someone else's interpretation of the original publication. In other words, the abstract should help you identify a publication as being relevant to your project, but you then must locate and read the actual publication (e.g., journal article) if you are going to use it in your own literature review or research project.

As with other search aids, then, the final step in using a bibliographic database is to retrieve the actual documents. After exploring the resources of your library to determine which publications are readily available, either in print or online, you will probably want to use your library's interlibrary loan service to obtain any other sources you need that your library does not have. Many records for journals will include a special number, called an ISSN (International Standard Serial Number). This number can help your library staff quickly identify and retrieve the document you need. Citations can also provide other useful numbers. Ask the interlibrary loan staff which numbers to include on your request.

Another convenient avenue for retrieving materials is available for those library users fortunate to live in states that have created statewide online systems. These allow users access to the **online catalogs** of all or most of that state's college and university libraries as well as to various periodical databases. These systems can allow users to initiate transactions online to borrow materials from other libraries, thus eliminating the need to fill out interlibrary loan request cards. Often materials can be delivered using these systems in a matter of days. At the very least, your library probably allows you to place interlibrary requests online by completing a form on the library's website. If you're not sure how to take advantage of these electronic options, be sure to ask a reference librarian.

Many database producers and distributors offer an additional service to help you secure publications not owned by your library. Called **document delivery services**, they allow you to order publications online for delivery by fax or through the mail.

Ingenta, ERIC, and many of the **Online Computer Library Center's** (OCLC) First-Search databases provide such document delivery services. The fees charged for such services, which include a copyright fee, can often be charged to a credit card. Before paying a fee for such services, though, be sure to check with your library. It may well be able to supply the publications you are looking for through its own interlibrary networks.

MEDIATED SEARCHING

Although most libraries now make a wide variety of electronic databases available to their users to search on their own at computers within and outside the library, access to some specialized databases may be available only through such vendors as DIALOG on a pay-per-search basis. Using these databases often requires special training, so they are made available through a mediated **online search service**. In this situation you would relay your needs to the librarian searcher, who would enter your request, discuss the results with you, revise the request, and so on. Typically, users make an appointment with a librarian to discuss their search topics and are present when the librarian performs the search. Students can be asked to pay some or all of the online fees associated with such searches. If you have questions about the availability of additional computerized databases, ask a reference librarian about this service. And if you have questions about searching in general, check Mann's (2005) library research guide.

SUMMARY

Methods used by communication professionals to conduct documentary research are changing rapidly. Using computer-based sources has become essential. Many necessary tools for communication research are available only in electronic formats and through electronic networks. A computerized database stores information on a magnetic or optical storage medium so that the information can be retrieved via a computer. Databases can be classified as bibliographic, directory, statistical, or source.

To use computerized databases effectively, researchers must understand basic searching concepts and acquire skill in using controlled vocabularies, keywords, field-specific searching, word and phrase indexes, and logical and proximity operators. They should understand the differences between Boolean searching and natural language searching and be able to use them both for comprehensive retrieval.

Documentation should be used to gain familiarity with the structure of databases and the features of search systems. Online Help screens and tutorials are usually available. A few minutes spent exploring such documentation will save time in the long run and will help you retrieve more relevant search results.

In general, the most effective search strategy is to start with the most specific descriptors available, examine the results, and add search statements to broaden or narrow the search as necessary. To narrow a search, add additional concepts, one at a time, using the AND operator. You can also limit search results by publication year, language, document type, and so on. To broaden a search, use a less specific descriptor and/or add synonymous terms using the OR operator. Computer databases help researchers identify pertinent publications, but the actual document must then be located and fully examined before it is used in a research project.

References

Knapp, S. D. (2000). *The contemporary thesaurus of search terms and synonyms: A guide for natural language computer searching* (2nd ed.). Phoenix, AZ: Oryx.

Mann, T. (2005). *The Oxford guide to library research* (3rd ed.). New York: Oxford University Press.

EXAMPLES

Jack is preparing for database searching. The best strategy seems to AND the term *ethics* with a group of speech terms: *speech, speaking, speechwriting, speechwriters*, *ghostwriting*, and *collaboration* (these latter terms will be OR-ed together). Some terms could be truncated to simplify things and to make sure he doesn't miss anything (e.g., speech*, ghostwrit*, ethic*).

Valerie's initial investigation of voice mail tells her that the two words must be considered together as a phrase because *voice* or *mail* produces too many bad hits. The topic, being relatively new, might allow her to search selectively in the literature of the past 10–15 years.

Robin has now read several summary articles about attribution, and the term seems to be used consistently in the literature. Because many articles point to Heider as the originator of the term, this information might come in handy when she needs to narrow the term in upcoming searches.

Jason's paper on parasocial interaction will be using the upcoming access tools and databases extensively. Because the word is spelled in different ways, Jason makes a note of the variations found: *para-social* and *parasocial*. Also, references to the first use of the term by Horton and Wohl in 1956 will be important when searching the journal indexes.

Kat, Rocky, and **Michelle's** training idea in the area of conflict resolution results in too many different terms for conflict: *fighting, arguing, conflict management, conflict resolution, disagreements*, and so on. They keep a running list of these and make a note to use a thesaurus whenever they can in searching databases to identify the relevant subject headings or descriptors for each.

Eric, Anthony, Gregory, and **Scott** have been investigating various databases to research their topic, "How do students use the Internet for maintaining interpersonal relationships with their families?" Because this could be a very extensive topic to search, they decide to search for the terms as keywords or phrases and to AND together *Internet, interpersonal relationship*, and *family* in *PsycINFO*. First, however, they find that OR-ing together the following terms produces a much richer set for the *family* construct: *mother, father, family, parent, grandparent, siblings, brother, and sister*. This produces a list of five articles, which contain all three elements.

EXERCISES

1. When a descriptor is not available for your topic and keywords must be used, take care to find all possible alternative phrasings and spellings. For each of the following concepts, make a list of at least 10 synonymous keywords or phrases: *role playing, executives, news media, press interviews, minorities*, and *gender*.

2. In your research paper, you want to investigate the relationship among communication styles of teachers, gender or ethnic background of students, and student performance. You have decided to limit your research to middle schools. You have entered a number of terms and now have the following sets:

#1	minorities	#10	gender differences
#2	educational performance	#11	student performance
#3	teachers	#12	middle schools
#4	blacks	#13	ethnic groups
#5	styles	#14	males
#6	females	#15	African Americans
#7	Native Americans	#16	Mexican Americans
#8	junior high school	#17	academic achievement
#9	Hispanics	#18	Asian Americans

Assuming that you wish to use all these terms in your search, write a single search statement that will incorporate all of them. Use set numbers to refer to each term, combining sets as appropriate with AND and OR operators. Use parentheses to group terms, for example: (#1 OR #2 OR #7), (#6 OR #8), and (#11 AND #15).

If you retrieve too many citations, how could you narrow this search? If you retrieve too few citations, how could you broaden it?

3. Now plan searches for the topic in Exercise 2 in each of the following databases: *PsycINFO, ERIC*, and *Sociological Abstracts*. Use the thesaurus for each database to identify relevant descriptors and list search statements in the order in which you would enter them.

4. Try one or more versions of the search statement you developed in Exercise 3 in a comprehensive, interdisciplinary periodical database licensed by your library. Examine the first 10 records you retrieve and adjust your search accordingly. How did you change your search statement? Compare the results you retrieved with your previous results.

5. Complete the Search Preparation Form shown in Figure 3.6 for your topic.

chapter 4

Using the Internet for Communication Research

Increasingly, the resources used for communication research are stored on computers. In fact, most of the access tools (such as catalogs and periodical indexes), a large number of periodicals, and selected reference sources described in this book have made the transition from print to electronic format and are residing in various computers. But they would lead an isolated existence without the Internet, or net. The **Internet** can be thought of as the communication utility that connects all those computers that store all those resources.

The **World Wide Web** (web) is the interface that allows us practically seamless access to it all. You'll carry out much of your research seated at a computer using a web browser to search periodical indexes, consult reference works, and read periodical articles. Even nonreference books are becoming accessible through web browsers. You'll use the same web browser to search library catalogs and various types of **websites**. These changes reflect a fundamental shift in the role of the library. Instead of simply being repositories of materials they own, libraries have become gateways to information resources available electronically.

Some dangers lurk in this convenience and integration. One is that students can fail to differentiate among the types of resources they are using and to value them appropriately. An article in a scholarly journal can physically resemble a document put up on a homegrown website, and you will use similar search procedures to find both. At a basic level they're both on the web. In this situation your ability to evaluate the quality of resources and the necessity of doing so becomes more critical than ever. Also dangerous is the tendency to get ahead of reality by concluding that all information is on the Internet. Wishful thinking doesn't make it so, and acting under this false assumption will lead you to miss whole categories of information.

All these developments started in a remarkably undirected way. About 35 years ago, researchers wanting to share data thought it would be useful to connect their networks. The government financed the project and from this the Internet grew. All sorts of resources on computers came to be shared over the Internet, but the systems and commands necessary to do so were not particularly friendly or easy to use. The web more or less solved the problem. Developed by Tim Berners-Lee at CERN, the European Laboratory for Particle Physics, the web provided a way to access many different types of resources through one interface. The World Wide Web refers to that collection of resources.

One web innovation was to use hypertext to link resources. **Hypertext** is simply regular text that includes connections, or **hyperlinks**, within the text to other documents. Thus hypertext documents allow you to move from one document to another by selecting links. Besides text, a link can also be an icon. Links can connect to other types of media, including images, video, and sound recordings. Because of the promise of this new technology for sharing information, many text resources were converted into **HTML** (hypertext markup language) format to be readily accessible through the web. Webpages are written in this relatively simple format, although they can include links to documents formatted in more sophisticated ways to resemble, for example, the actual printed pages of a journal article.

It is important to understand that no one person or organization is in charge of the Internet. In other words, no one started this enterprise by first devising an overall organizational structure, and no one exerts overall control of what is made available in terms of content, quality, or format. Anyone can publish a **webpage**, and anyone does. The result is a collection that includes both valuable gems and worthless fakes, and everything in between. Quality control is established only at the level of a particular resource or site. Therefore, we stress that an important task of all researchers is to evaluate web resources to determine which have such quality control and can claim credibility. We include in this chapter a section on the special challenges posed by evaluating web resources.

RESEARCH AND THE WORLD WIDE WEB

Many traditional types of scholarly, research-oriented resources are accessible through the web. These include library catalogs, periodical indexes and abstracts, scholarly journals, government publications, bibliographies, dictionaries, encyclopedias, almanacs, directories, statistical compendia, and other types of reference works. Even books are increasingly available online for reading and searching. Many, though by no means all, of these types of resources are available to researchers only through licensing arrangements made by their libraries.

In addition, there is a vast and somewhat hard to define category: other types of websites. Many are of potential interest to communication researchers. Important categories include:

■ Collections of primary sources (print, audio, video, and images), including important electronic archives of political speeches, press releases, and historical documents. Transcripts and video archives of many news broadcasts are available, for example. We identify several of these in Chapter 8.

- Research so recent that it has not yet been formally published (or even evaluated for possible publication).
- News and current events.
- Information about popular culture.
- General reference material of all types.
- Biographical information about scholars and other communication professionals, maintained on personal or professional home pages.
- Statistical information from many sources. The U.S. Census Bureau, for example, now issues most census reports on the web rather than in print.
- Publications issued by nongovernment agencies, including everything from brochures to research reports.
- Educational sites. There seems to be a tutorial for everyone, no matter what the level or topic. There are several examples: tutorials on such topics as how to do library research; how to write a research paper; how to write an **annotation**; how not to plagiarize; how to give an effective speech or presentation; how to cite sources in APA-, MLA-, or Chicago-style format; how to search the web; how to find statistical information; and how to use a certain database.
- Departments of communication at universities around the world. These websites include information about programs and faculty as well as links to other communication-related sites.
- Professional associations. Many associations try to make themselves useful to members by including listings of employment opportunities, research bibliographies, convention activities, and links to research-related sites in the field. See Chapter 1 for a listing of communication associations with web addresses.
- Online communities. The web is of course not only a repository of information but also a communication medium. Communication researchers often find electronic discussion groups in their fields of interest to be useful.
- The web as a broadcast medium. You can, for example, view the nightly news on the websites of news organizations, either in real time or at your convenience. Other websites (e.g., YouTube) permit you to share videos with other users by e-mailing a link to the video or uploading the video to the site.

GAINING ACCESS TO THE INTERNET

Students normally access the Internet at home or through workstations in the library, computer labs, or residence halls. On virtually all campuses you'll be able to find a workstation with a browser installed that will allow you to access resources on the web. To use your institution's e-mail system, it's necessary to obtain an e-mail account on a university computer. If you don't already have an account, ask at your computer center for information about getting one. Even if you have been using a different e-mail system, you will normally want to establish an e-mail account through your university as well. It may, for example, be needed to access online library resources from home or other off-campus locations.

From off campus, you currently have two options. One is to access the Internet by dialing into your e-mail account from off campus, using a personal computer equipped with **communications software** and a **modem** (many of which are wireless today). To access the web, you'll need to do so through a connection that is somewhat specific to your institution. Your computer center can provide directions. Connecting to the Internet through the university can offer a significant advantage to researchers. When you attempt to connect to periodical indexes and other databases that your library has licensed, database vendors will often automatically recognize authorized users and permit access to databases. (They will recognize the university's **Internet protocol**, or **IP address**.) You also can access the Internet via a local or national Internet service provider (ISP) or through commercial online services such as *America Online* or *Earthlink*. Many of these services now offer the advantage of high-speed, or broadband, access.

Internet Addresses

When you get an e-mail account, your Internet address will look something like those of the authors of this book:

Rebecca Rubin:	rrubin@kent.edu
Alan Rubin:	arubin@kent.edu
Paul Haridakis:	pharidak@kent.edu
Linda Piele:	pielel@uwp.edu

The symbol @ (*at*) is used to separate the name of an individual (on the left) from his or her **domain** (to the right). In the first three cases shown, the domain, **kent.edu**, refers to a mainframe computer at Kent State University. In the fourth case, the domain is a computer at the University of Wisconsin–Parkside. You'll use addresses like these to send electronic mail to other people.

Each website also has an address, as does each page (or file) on that site. Web addresses are called **uniform resource locators** (or URLs). Published references to Internet resources supply their URLs, and these addresses must be included in APA citations. The URLs of the websites of the institutions just mentioned, for example, are

<http://www.kent.edu>
<http://www.uwp.edu>

Breaking down this address into its component parts, we have:

http://	**hypertext transfer protocol**, which is the WWW protocol
www	host computer name
kent	second-level domain name
edu	top-level domain name

Taken together **<www.kent.edu>**, this is the address of the **server** (computer) on which the various files for the university's main website reside. Often there are additional campus servers that link to the main server.

The following domain name extensions (or top-level domains) are among those most commonly used. Extensions, such as .com, provide useful information about various Internet addresses. You are most likely to encounter these extensions:

com	commercial sites (companies or corporations) in the United States
edu	educational sites in the United States
gov	government institutions

mil   military sites in the United States
net   an administrative site for a network
org   nonprofit organizations that don't fit elsewhere

The following is an example that's a bit more complicated: the URL for the website for this textbook. Notice that this website resides on a different server:

<http://academic.cengage.com/communication/rubin/7e>

The additional components tell your browser the complete path to a particular server and file:

<academic.cengage.com>	server (host computer name, second-level domain, top-level)
communication	directory name
rubin	subdirectory name
7e	file name

Another piece of general information that you can glean from an Internet address is the country of origin. Each country has been assigned a two-letter code. For example, **.fr** refers to France, **.it** to Italy, **.ch** to Switzerland, **.ca** to Canada, **.de** to Germany, and **.us** to the United States. If there is no country designation, the location is the United States. In fact, **.us** is used within the United States to designate governmental websites not covered by **.gov**.

You may also see addresses, termed *IP addresses*, that are entirely numerical. These addresses, which consist of four numbers connected by dots, are assigned to each machine on the Internet. A typical IP address is 137.113.10.35. Actually, each Internet domain address has a corresponding IP address, which is how the address is transmitted over the Internet.

Browser Basics

When you access the web you do so through a browser. Popular examples include Mozilla's Firefox and Microsoft's Internet Explorer. A **browser** is a computer program that enables you to use your computer to view and capture web documents, taking advantage of hypertext links, images, sound, motion, and other features. To take full advantage of multimedia, a browser will need to have additional programs installed, called *plug-ins* or *helper applications*. These develop and change rapidly, so you'll need to refer to current information to find out about them. The websites maintained by your browser are often the best sources of information about plug-ins. These websites can be accessed through links provided in your browser's Help function. A helper application frequently used to access textual information, Adobe Acrobat, was described in Chapter 3.

Browsers regularly incorporate additional functions and features and have become powerful tools. We use browsers to handle our e-mail, to participate in Usenet newsgroups (discussed later in this chapter), to participate in real-time meetings, to compose text in HTML, and to listen to the radio or watch a movie. To take full advantage of these capabilities, seek out training opportunities at your university for these web applications.

To use a browser as an access tool for research, however, you need to perform only a few tasks. Learning how to do the following will enable you to carry out research effectively and efficiently. If you like to figure out things by yourself, the browser's Help function may suffice. Or go through the list with a net-savvy friend. You should be able to:

- Type in a URL to go directly to a website.
- Use the Back button to go to the previous page visited.
- Use the Stop button to stop a slow page from loading.
- Reload a page that was not completely retrieved the first time.
- Adjust the font size of text. (Sometimes the default size will be either too small or too large for comfortable viewing or efficient printing.)
- Adjust the colors of a page. (They may be impossible or uncomfortable to view or print.)
- Use the Find in Page feature to locate a term or phrase in a web document. This is particularly useful when viewing full-text journal articles and other long documents.
- Print entire documents or only specified pages.
- Use the Print Preview feature to help you see the page layout for a long document, allowing you to determine which pages you want to print.
- Send a webpage or a webpage address to your e-mail account.
- Use the Cut and Paste feature to save URLs, article titles you wish to paste into a search box, and the like. You should also be able to cut and paste to a word processor.
- Use the Search History feature to go back to sites visited previously.
- Maintain personal lists of Favorites or Bookmarks (websites you may want to visit again).

Troubleshooting

As you use the web, you are sure to encounter the frustrating problem of links that do not work. You might get an error message that the server housing that resource is down or that the URL doesn't exist. Servers do go down, sometimes for a short period and sometimes for longer. In this case, you have no choice but to try again later.

The nonexistent URL could indicate one of several things. First, it can mean simply that the network is busy. Often you will be successful on your second or third attempts. Second, if you typed it in directly, check your typing. Make sure that each space and character is correct. URLs are case sensitive, so use lowercase unless part of the address you are typing is in uppercase. If you are working from an online source, cut and paste the URL instead of typing it in. Finally, if mistyping is not the problem, consider other possibilities. Is this the type of site that is likely to be short-lived or transient? Is it conceivable that the individual maintaining the site simply decided to remove it? Or would it have been located on the type of server that would seem to be more stable, perhaps one sponsored by a university, government agency, organization, or company?

If you determine that you're probably dealing with an *address change* rather than a page *disappearance*, there are some simple things to try. First, attempt to go to the home of the site: the university, agency, organization, or company **home page**. Lacking a link to take you there, you could simply work from the URL that is displayed, erasing the file name and successive directories, stopping just before each forward slash (/) until you reach the server name itself. At one of these stopping places you can often locate what you are looking for by using a directory or a site-based search engine. If this approach fails, try searching for the page using a web search engine (discussed following), using the title of the site plus any additional information you have.

Finding Resources on the World Wide Web

Many of the most important research resources you will use on the web will be licensed by your library for the use of students and faculty at your university. Most libraries list the periodical indexes, collections of full-text periodicals, reference works, directories, and statistical sources they provide on a webpage linked to their home page. Often these listings are arranged by broad subjects. Of course, they can also be listed in the library catalog. These are the primary tools you will use as you pursue most of the steps in the search strategy presented in Chapter 2. When you are ready to go beyond these sources to see what is available on assorted websites, you'll turn to web directories and search engines.

Web Directories

Web directories are subject listings, sometimes annotated, of selected websites. *Yahoo!* is the most familiar example of such a directory. You will find web directories variously titled as virtual libraries, webliographies, gateways, clearinghouses, subject directories or guides, metaindexes, and metasites. They vary in quality, currency, and comprehensiveness. Most web directories are arranged hierarchically by broad subject and are searched by browsing, although larger sites usually include the ability to search them by keyword. Some web directories are highly selective whereas others (such as *Yahoo!*), list just about any website or information that is available. Use selective web directories to find recommended sites, still at a broad level.

Besides general purpose, comprehensive directories such as *Yahoo!*, specialized web directories, often maintained by academic departments or by professional associations, service academic fields. They could be initiated and maintained by a single person in the field. Several useful web directories are available for the communication field. Browsing these is a good way to get a feel for the types of assorted web resources available to communication researchers. The URLs listed were current as of mid-2008 but may well have changed. If so, use the troubleshooting tips described earlier in this chapter to locate them.

University of Iowa. (Oct. 6, 2003). *Links to communication studies resources.* (Available: <http://www.uiowa.edu/commstud/resources>; Retrieved June 4, 2008)

■ This comprehensive site, based at the University of Iowa Department of Communication Studies, lists websites under these categories: Advertising, Cultural Studies, Digital Media, Film Studies, Gender and Race, General Communication Education, Health and Science, Interpersonal and Small Group, Journalism and Mass Communication, Media Studies,

Political Communication, Rhetorical Studies, Social Science Resources, Visual Communication, and Speeches and Speechmakers. Included is an annotated list of "Listservs Related to Communication and Media."

Communication Institute for Online Scholarship (CIOS). *ComWeb MegaSearch* (n.d.). (Available: <http://www.cios.org>; Retrieved June 4, 2008)

■   Anyone can search this site, but the links will not be active for the ComWeb Mega-Search unless your institution is an affiliate of CIOS or unless you subscribe to the service. If so, the site provides full-text searches for webpages on more than 350 communication, journalism, speech, and rhetoric-related departmental websites and resources. This directory is accessed by keyword searches rather than by browsing hierarchical directories.

University of Wales. (1995–). *MCS*. (Available: <http://www.aber.ac.uk/media/index.html>;
   Retrieved June 4, 2008)

■   This site originates from the University of Wales. Admitting to a British focus, it covers global resources as well. The site is well-organized and updated. Resources are listed under broad categories that include Active Interpretation, Gender, Ethnicity, IT and Telecoms, News Media, Advertising, Media Education, Textual Analysis, Film Studies, Media Influence, Active Interpretation, TV and Radio, Pop Music/Youth, Visual Image, and the Written and Spoken Word. This site's search capability allows you to search either the directory entries or the full text of documents.

Additional web directories are devoted to subfields of communication. Examples include *Douglass: Archives of American Public Address* **<http://douglassarchives .org/>** and *Advertising World: The Ultimate Marketing Communications Directory* **<http://advertising.utexas.edu/world/>**. One well-organized example of such a more narrowly focused directory is *CMC Information Sources*.

December, J. (1996–). *CMC information sources*. (Available: <http://www.december.com/cmc/info/>; Retrieved June 4, 2008)

■   This annotated list, sometimes known as the *December List*, provides links to information sources about computer-mediated communication. Its focus is on "CMC technology, use, and study, with an emphasis on Internet-based CMC."

Many other specialized web directories for communication and related areas can be identified through the web directories described here.

Communication researchers should also be aware of major interdisciplinary web directories. The best of these are selective, well-organized, and searchable. Annotations are evaluative, and sites are often rated. They can save researchers much time. The communication field often gets significant coverage in these tools. These directories will also help you identify the best sites in related disciplines and will point you in the direction of the best sites for research using a particular type of source such as government and statistical sites.

University of California, Riverside, Library. (1994–). *Infomine: Scholarly Internet resource collections*. (Available: <http://infomine.ucr.edu>; Retrieved June 4, 2008)

■   Librarians from the University of California and several other university libraries in the United States participate in selecting, annotating, and indexing university-level databases, web directories, textbooks, conference proceedings, and journals. The directory is both searchable by keyword and browsable. As of 2008, the site indexed more than 32,000 resources with over 100,000 links.

Librarians' Index to the Internet, lii.org. (1996–). (Available: <http://lii.org>; Retrieved June 4, 2008)

■   The motto of this directory, "Information You Can Trust," is indicative of its high degree of selectivity. It also gets high marks for organization and maintenance. Library of Congress subject headings are assigned to each resource, which enhances its search capabilities. Its more than 12,000 web resources are selected for their usefulness to public libraries, but it can also be very useful in an academic setting. The directory can be either browsed or searched by keyword.

The WWW virtual library. (1994–). (Available: <http://vlib.org/>; Retrieved June 4, 2008)

■   *The WWW Virtual Library* is one of the oldest and most respected subject directories on the web. This directory consists of individual subject collections, many of which are maintained at universities throughout the world.

Other selective, annotated, searchable web directories are also useful for research purposes. *Academic Info* **<http://www.academicinfo.net/>** includes a rich collection of sites. (Don't be distracted by the sponsored listings, which provide financial support.) *About.com* is another comprehensive directory **<http://www.about.com/>**. Its pages, which are selected and maintained by individuals, can be uneven, but many have a scholarly focus. Thousands of more specialized directories can be great starting places for a research topic. As you search the web keep your eyes open for titles that include terms such as *subject directory, subject guide, virtual library, metaindex, metasite, and webliography. Yahoo!* uses the category *web directories*, which can be searched using that phrase (in quotes) and then browsed by the different categories retrieved to find directories for many subjects.

Search Engines

Search engines are access tools that allow keyword searching of many websites. Many comprehensive search engines are available, and new ones appear regularly. As of 2008 the most popular search engine was *Google*. Others worth using include *AltaVista* (advanced search) **<http://www.altavista.com/>**, *Ask.com* **<www.ask.com>**, and *AllTheWeb* (advanced search) **<www.alltheweb.com>**.

Google's popularity is well-deserved. It indexes significantly more web pages than other search engines and searchers come to rely on it for quick, successful searches. *Google* also gets kudos for innovative features such as its news search, which allows the user to search current news from more than 4,500 online news sources worldwide. Its image database is outstanding and easy to search, and its newsgroup search provides a simple way to participate in and search the archives of newsgroups (discussed later in this chapter). *Google Scholar* **<http://scholar.google.com/>** is another feature that permits you, at times, to search for articles published in scholarly journals. However, it is not as complete as many scholarly databases available through university libraries and should not be used to replace the databases described in Chapter 3. Studies show that it pays to use more than one search engine because there is not as much overlap between them as one might expect. Search engines take different approaches to indexing websites, searching them, and ranking them, so they will often produce quite different results.

Metasearch engines attempt to facilitate this process by making it possible to run a search through multiple search engines at one time. They offer a good place to start a search, to test the waters, and to get a feeling for what is available on a topic. Meta-search engines are best searched with simple search syntax and a limited number of terms. If necessary, you can follow up with more complex searches using the syntax of a particular search engine. Popular metasearch engines include *Vivisimo* **<http://www. vivisimo.com>**, *Ixquick* **<www.ixquick.com>**, and *SurfWax* **<www.surfwax.com>**.

Be aware that there's a lot of material on the web that search engines can't identify, at least at the level of individual documents. This part of the web is often called the *Invisible Web* or *Deep Web*. For example, search engines cannot search web databases, including the web catalogs of libraries, as well as databases licensed by libraries. Databases, including archival collections, must be searched using an internal search system. At the website of the *Christian Science Monitor*, for example, you can find archives for the newspaper that extend back to 1980. Although these are freely available, they can be retrieved only by searching the database at that site. There are thousands of such databases available on the web, but you must often make an effort to find them. Many are listed in three of the web directories described previously (*Librarians' Index to the Internet, Infomine*, and *AcademicInfo*). *Yahoo!* also lists them in its directory using the term *databases*. You can look for databases using most search engines by combining a subject term with the term *databases*. For example, to find a database of radio stations, you could enter this search in *Google*:

radio stations database

The search engine field is extremely competitive, with strong pressure to improve their effectiveness and efficiency. These tools have a daunting task. Each search engine must visit each site on the web to create and regularly update its own version of a web database, containing millions of sites. Then it must attempt to devise an easy-to-use and effective search system that will be able to identify and retrieve any document in its database rapidly, all without benefit of human indexing. We should not be surprised when the search engine does not distinguish between a fifth-grade report on climate change and a study written by a panel of geologists. Because of the difficulties involved, it takes more preparation and ingenuity to search the web effectively than it does to search other databases. However, many of the principles involved are similar.

Understanding how search engines work will help produce a more effective search. Each search engine starts by creating its own version of a web database. This process is usually carried out automatically, using *robots* and *spiders* that search the web automatically to build the database specified by a particular search engine. For example, some search engines index only certain parts of a web page whereas others index the entire page. Some index images, such as photographs, in more useful ways. Others strive for comprehensiveness and include many more documents than others. When deciding which engine to search, you should take these characteristics into account. It's also important to realize that the database you are searching is not the web as it exists at the moment. It's the version created at an earlier moment (days or weeks earlier), when the spiders and robots last made their rounds. Of course, no human indexer is involved in the process of building these databases, and a controlled vocabulary is not available (although webpage creators themselves can include keywords as metatags to help retrieval). Keyword searching is required, so the liberal use of synonyms pays off.

Many search engines create records with the equivalent of the fields we have seen in bibliographic database records. Fields typically include title (the official page title that appears at the top of your browser), domain (edu, com, gov, e.g.), and other parts of the URL (host, file names, directories). Some search engines allow field-specific searching, which can be helpful in narrowing results. The advanced search screens of search engines often offer search options that can be useful in special situations. For example, they can make it easy to determine which webpages link to a particular page. This can be handy when attempting to evaluate web documents. They also facilitate field-specific searching, the searching of particular sites or domains, limiting results to particular formats, and so on.

Until recent years, all search engines sorted results by their **relevancy**, as determined by the search engine. Many factors were used (and still are used by many search engines and other database search software) to determine relevancy. Where does the search term appear (title, body, URL, and the like)? How many of the terms in the search statement appear in the document? How often do they appear? How close are they to one another? A ranking algorithm (particular to each search engine) takes the answers to these and many other questions into account and, in a somewhat mysterious way, produces a ranked listing. The items at the top of the list should, in theory, be highly relevant, whereas those at the bottom might include only one of the search terms.

Search engines that still use this method are now thought of as *first generation* systems. *Second generation* search engines, exemplified by *Google*, go outside the document itself to measure off-the-page factors that determine ranking. *Google*, for example, keeps track of how many other webpages it ranks highly link to each of the pages it indexes—in a sense, how popular each page is among popular webpages—and it ranks results accordingly. Web searchers generally find that they are more successful when they use second generation search engines, which include all those described.

Those using search engines are often dismayed when they retrieve a huge number of results, but this is normal and should not be considered problematic. It's assumed that only the results near the top will be of interest. The searcher's challenge is to ensure not just that documents be retrieved, but that those most wanted appear near the top of the list. These tips can help:

- Use several synonyms (including variant spellings) for the most important concept.
- Enter the most important concepts first. They are weighted more heavily than terms at the end of a statement.
- Use terms specific to your topic. If possible, include unique terms (distinctive names, abbreviations, acronyms).
- Avoid broad terms.
- Enclose phrases in double quotes.
- In general, use lowercase, although using the uppercase of proper nouns can be helpful in some search engines.
- Truncate terms only when the search engine offers this option; check first!

- Use the implied Boolean operators ($+$, $-$) to indicate terms and phrases that must be included or excluded. *Google* uses the minus ($-$) but not the plus (which is implied between adjacent terms).
- Look at the search engine's Help screens to determine how it treats adjacent words. *Google* assumes a Boolean AND between adjacent words, which is a standard but not universal practice. Often you will get the same results by using the Boolean alternative, the plus sign ($+$).

  Google: television violence
  Other search engines: television + violence

- Use Boolean operators (AND, OR, NOT) and parentheses when possible, often from an advanced search option. As usual, use OR to combine synonyms but use AND to combine concepts. (Some search engines allow Boolean operators; others do not.) *Google* allows the use of OR (must be capitalized) between two words (but not between phrases).
- Advanced search screens offer many useful options. Try out the different options so that you'll be able to use them as needed.
- Be prepared to enter several versions of a search. For example, when searching names in *Google*, it will pay to enter your search in each of the following ways:

  "Jane Smith"
  Jane Smith
  "Jane * Smith"

The bottom line is that search engines vary a great deal. They offer different features and capabilities. To use them most effectively, it pays to look at their documentation and become aware of their peculiarities. Fortunately, websites are available that attempt to do that for you. Going to one of these sites can help you decide which search engines to use for a particular purpose and alert you to particular syntax used by each. One academic site that keeps track of and presents the features of most popular search engines is maintained at the University of California, Berkeley Teaching Library **<http://www.lib.berkeley.edu/TeachingLib/Guides/Internet/FindInfo.html>**.

COMMUNICATING ON THE INTERNET
E-Mail

You probably send mail to people, groups, and organizations—perhaps even to yourself—using the **e-mail** system that your college or university provides. You'll find it necessary to use e-mail for various research-related activities, such as subscribing to electronic discussion groups or retrieving documents from periodical indexes. You can e-mail these documents to yourself.

Electronic Discussion Groups and Blogs

Another important way researchers use e-mail is to participate in electronic discussion groups. You might want to join a group because you have an ongoing interest in the topic being discussed. Or, perhaps, you have a research project that would benefit from locating an expert in the field and getting some advice. Although discussion groups can be used for this purpose, you should be forewarned that a blatant request for information needed for a classroom project, if the information is readily available elsewhere, will seldom be successful. But it is often possible to search the archives of discussion groups, allowing you to see what information might have been shared about a particular topic. Electronic discussion groups are of two distinct types: e-mail discussion lists (often called *listservs*) and Usenet newsgroups.

Because it was the software first used for this purpose, **listserv** has become the generic term for electronic discussion lists that share messages through e-mail. Many lists continue to use listserv, but you might also come across discussion lists using other software programs, such as ListProc or Majordomo. The commands for using these programs are similar.

These programs facilitate the sharing of e-mail messages among members by automatically forwarding to the entire mailing list any message addressed to the group. Messages are received by group members in their individual mail boxes, at their home e-mail sites. Such a system facilitates ongoing discussion of research and professional topics of common interest. Listservs have become a popular way to share information in many fields. The list software also makes it simple to join or resign from groups.

Listservs are available for most communication fields. A listing of many can be found on the web directory maintained at the University of Iowa's Department of Communication Studies: **<http://www.uiowa.edu/commstud/resources>**. Let's say you browse the listservs at the University of Iowa and decide to participate in POPCULTURE-L, "a list devoted to the study of popular culture." This address is listed: **listserv@list.ufl.edu**

Use this address to subscribe to the group. Once you do so, you'll be sent instructions, together with a second address that you will use to send messages to the group as a whole. It's very important not to confuse the two addresses if you want to avoid clogging the mailboxes of your new electronic colleagues with extraneous and annoying messages.

To subscribe, you would send an e-mail message to the listserv address:

listserv@list.ufl.edu

Leave the subject line blank. Type a one-line message, as follows:

SUBSCRIBE POPCULTURE-L

This model can be used to subscribe to most listservs. You'll quickly receive a message welcoming you to the group, describing its operation, and giving you instructions for, among other things, canceling your subscription. It's important to save this message because you may decide at some point that this group is not for you or that you want to suspend your subscription during a vacation period. Naturally, all messages about your subscription should be sent to the listserv address, not to the group address. The instructions will also tell you how to search the group's archives, if available.

Communication Research and Theory Network (CRTNET) is a communication listserv, which is moderated at the National Communication Association (NCA). A list like this should be of interest to students in the field. If you would like to subscribe, you'd send a message like the one described to **listserv@list.psu.edu.** CRTNET provides discussions of issues relevant to all aspects of communication. It also includes announcements posted from the NCA, job listings, and texts of recent political speeches. To contribute to the list, you would send e-mail to **crtnet@natcom.org.**

In addition to listservs, blogs have become a popular source of discussion and debate on an array of topics, including those related to communication. A **blog**, originally a shortened variation of the term *weblog*, can be maintained by an individual, corporation, media organization, or other entity. Most are arranged around a particular topic, subject matter, or theme. Many invite comments and discussion by readers in an interactive environment, with individual entries routinely arranged in reverse chronological order. Some blogs also provide links to other websites related to the subject to which the blog is devoted.

If you are interested in finding a blog related to a particular topic or issue, there are various websites available that help users locate blogs (e.g., **<www.blogged.com>** and **<www.blogsearch.google.com>**). Generally, these sites can be searched by topic. For quick reference, particular predetermined categories (e.g., entertainment, technology, shopping, sports) might be listed. Remember, though, these blogs are purely the opinion of the *blogger* and those who choose to reply; they should not be used in traditional research studies.

Usenet Newsgroups

Newsgroups are discussion groups on **Usenet**, a network of thousands of groups available on most campus networks. Instead of receiving e-mail in your mailbox, you use special software to read and participate in the newsgroups. Unlike listservs, you do not need to subscribe actively to a newsgroup. The current messages of all groups are available for anyone to read, so you can check what is going on in any group at any time. Students might select a few groups that they read regularly or irregularly. Those newsgroups then automatically come up whenever they access the **newsreader** software.

Although many newsgroups are strictly recreational in nature, others serve professional and scholarly purposes. In fact, some listservs are also available as Usenet newsgroups, providing an alternative and convenient method for participating. (Some people prefer to access listservs through Usenet to avoid dealing with an overabundance of messages in their e-mail boxes.)

Many discussion groups have developed FAQs (i.e., frequently asked questions), a compilation of questions that newcomers and visitors to the group often pose. Sometimes a group effort, they include useful information on the group topic and can become used by a wider audience. Newcomers to newsgroups are expected to read a group's FAQs before actively participating (it's considered bad form to ask a group a question that is answered on its FAQ). One website, **<http://www.faqs. org>**, seeks to compile and maintain a comprehensive list of discussion group FAQs.

Newsgroup messages usually stay on a university system for only a few days. But archives exist, and some search engines, including *Google Groups*, offer the option of searching these. In fact, you might find newsgroup messages popping up unexpectedly among your results when you use a search engine. *Google*'s newsgroup archives extend back to 1981. *Google Groups* allows you to post messages to newsgroups as well as to read them.

The need to evaluate information sources critically is important in this venue, especially when dealing with information gathered in Usenet newsgroups. Listservs tend to be associated with academic institutions, and participants often include scholars and professionals. Topics discussed are often scholarly and professional. Newsgroups, on the other hand, cover topics that range far beyond academe, and the expertise of participants varies widely. As always, try to establish the author's credentials and point of view, check the validity of facts, and look for underlying assumptions.

CIOS/Comserve

Comserve is an online service of the Communication Institute for Online Scholarship (CIOS). It provides access to news services (position announcements, new books, news, new research), electronic journals, syllabi, bibliographies, research articles, and hotlines (electronic discussion groups in the many different areas of the discipline). Communication scholars join hotlines to discuss issues relevant to many specialty interests, including: computer-mediated, family, gender, health, intercultural, interpersonal, mass, organizational, and political communication; history; magazine journalism; philosophy; research methods; rhetoric; speech disorders; and speech education. Students can join ComGrads, a hotline for students to exchange ideas about graduate school, teaching, and research.

Students attending universities that are affiliates of CIOS can download an unlimited number of files and join as many hotlines as they wish, whereas students at nonaffiliated universities and the general public have limited access. If the university is an affiliate, students, faculty, and others connected to the university can conduct global searches of CIOS/Comserve's Journal Indexes and do searches in the resource library.

CIOS/Comserve is an important electronic service, one designed especially for communication scholars. You can access it at **<http://www.cios.org>**. It's a way to become involved in the discipline, to see what topics are of interest to faculty and fellow students, and to search the communication literature.

EVALUATING INTERNET SOURCES

Our ability to find information quickly on the web sometimes leads us to forget that our goal is not just *some* information but the *best* information. We can easily forget to slow down enough to evaluate carefully what we find and to make sure it meets our needs. As we discussed earlier, evaluation is important in a self-publishing medium such as the web. Some websites are managed by an expert or group of experts, others by laypersons or amateurs. The latter can be appropriate for some purposes, but we need to distinguish, for example, between a research paper written by a university professor and a term paper submitted for a class project by an undergraduate student.

Of course, evaluating sources has always been an important part of doing research. We discussed criteria for evaluating traditional sources in Chapter 2. Many of the points addressed there apply equally to the evaluation of websites. In fact, if the source you are using on the web is a traditional print source that has simply changed format, the criteria suggested in Chapter 2 should be used to evaluate it. A scholarly journal that appears in print and electronic forms is no different on the web than in print format. Often, however, websites prompt us to give a new twist to standard evaluation criteria. Along with much information and websites of top quality, there is enough propaganda, disinformation, and misinformation on the Internet that it pays to develop the suspicious side of your nature. So think of evaluating web resources as an opportunity to develop your critical thinking skills as you play the role of editor that much of the web lacks. Be prepared to relegate a good portion of what you find to your virtual reject pile. Learn to ask questions such as the ones in the following section when you review a website for research purposes.

Author's Authority

The author or authors can be a person or a group, but in either case you're looking for credibility and accountability.

■ Is the author or responsible group readily identifiable?
You wouldn't consider an anonymously published book to be a suitable source for a research project, and you should be similarly skeptical of anonymous webpages. Credible sources assume accountability for what they have written.

■ Can you determine the author's background and credentials from the webpage (or by following a link from the page)?
If not, you should be extremely skeptical.

■ Is information provided to enable you to contact the author or responsible group?
Be suspicious of any webpage that doesn't provide contact information that can be used to investigate its credibility. This information should include an address and telephone number, not just an e-mail address.

■ Does the author have a degree and experience relevant to the topic?
Education and degrees mean much less once an author gets outside his or her field. If the author is outside his or her specialty, you will need to look for other types of relevant qualifications.

■ Does the author have a publication record, and is it relevant?
When evaluating an item that purports to be scholarship, you would expect that at least some articles within this record have been published in peer-reviewed journals.

■ If there is a bibliography, does it include authors you have identified elsewhere as authorities in the field?

■ Is the author affiliated with a particular institution?
If you're looking for scholarly items, you would expect the author to be affiliated with a research institution, for example. If this isn't the case, it raises a question for you to investigate.

■ What do others (especially people you recognize as authorities) have to say about this author?
You can use a web search engine to see what other webpages reveal. You will be looking for positive mention from authorities you recognize as being credible. Names of individuals and organizations can also quickly be checked in a comprehensive, interdisciplinary periodical index, described in Chapter 6. If an initial search doesn't turn up anything, search the full text of articles as well. The name

might even turn up in a search of the archives of Usenet newsgroups, described earlier in this chapter.

■ How did you find this document?
If you linked to this document from a source with well-established authority, that is in itself a recommendation. Official webpages of academic and scholarly organizations and selective web directories, such as *Infomine* or *Librarian's Index of the Internet*, would qualify here, but unselective directories, such as *Yahoo!*, would not.

■ What other documents or websites link to this document?
You can determine this by using a search engine (see the section on search engines earlier in this chapter). You should be looking for links from authoritative websites, external to the document at hand.

Publisher's Authority

In the print world, publishers work hard to establish their credibility. By being selective in what they publish, they engender a degree of trust that their publications uphold established standards. In the web world, the entity comparable to a print publisher is the server on which a web document resides.

■ What entity (corporation, government agency, nonprofit organization, institution) owns this server?
This information should be readily apparent by looking at the page headings and footers. Official websites make their accountability apparent.

■ Is there a link to its home page?
Lacking such a link, you can shorten the URL from its end, directory by directory, to attempt to find a sponsoring organization, but your suspicion level should be elevated. This should not be necessary for credible sources.

■ Can you easily contact the site's webmaster from this document?
Again, you're trying to establish the bona fides of this document and server.

■ What type of domain does the server have (org, edu, gov, us, mil, com, net, international)? Is this consistent with the type of organization sponsoring it?
One would expect, for example, a page purporting to be sponsored by a government entity in the United States to have one of the following domains: gov, mil, or us. If this is not the case, you could suspect this is a fraudulent site.

■ Is the topic of the web document you are looking at something that you would expect to find on this server and in this domain? Is it consistent with the purpose of the server?

■ What do you know about the organization sponsoring the server? What type of web documents would you expect to find on such a server?
You probably would not, for example, expect to find a research study on a company web server. If you did, it would raise questions you should address when assessing its credibility.

■ What is the relationship between the author and the publisher (the entity that owns or sponsors the server)?
Attempt to determine whether the author's contribution is made within the context of his or her professional duties and expertise or whether the relationship is more casual.

- Does the item reside in a personal account rather than being part of an official website?

  Examine the URL, looking for a personal name, usually in the format, user id, in the URL. For example: **www.uwp.edu/~piele/**. A percent sign (%), the words *members, users,* or *people* also signal personal pages.

Objectivity and Bias

A less inflammatory term for bias is *point of view*. Somehow it's easier for us to acknowledge that we share a particular point of view than to confess to being biased. Whatever you choose to call it, you should assume it's there in everything you read. Your job is to detect it. This doesn't mean that a source that is less than objective is unusable for a research project. It does mean that your instructor will expect you to have detected the bias, to acknowledge it in your own analysis, and to use the item to support your own conclusions appropriately.

- Should you assume the material is presented from a particular point of view, given the author's background, the sponsor, or other evidence? Is it trying to sell you something?

  We take for granted that material on a company's website describing a product will lack balance and objectivity, for example. It's trying to sell us something. Learn to ask yourself what other types of organizations are trying to sell. An obvious example would be reading about a political candidate on the opposition's website. Again, we would take for granted that the information presented will be carefully selected to support a particular point of view—in other words, it will be biased. The web is the home of many advocacy groups whose purpose is to sell particular ideas to promote a point of view. In the case of some organizations, the bias may be less obvious. For example, much that looks like scholarship is published by think tanks, many of which have an underlying philosophical agenda. Learning to detect the bias in such circumstances is more difficult, but we need to attempt to do so.

- Is the tone objective, analytical, and reflective? Or is it emotional or subjective? Emotional, subjective material should raise a red flag.

- Are conclusions clearly supported by evidence?

  We all have opinions, but we don't expect to convince others without assembling relevant facts from credible sources. This is why blog sources are not trustworthy.

- Does the presentation feel balanced?

  The author should identify points that are less well-supported by his or her evidence. Then she or he should attempt to represent other points of view fairly.

- Is there a bibliography and/or list of other websites?

  Lack of such documentation raises all sorts of questions. There may well be projects for which scholarly sources are not necessary, but make sure this is one of those times before using such a source.

- If the documentation includes websites, do the links work?

- Are the references in the bibliography complete? You should be given enough information to be able to track down the sources easily.

- Does the bibliography include sources that support only a particular point of view?

To be considered balanced the bibliography should include publications and links to external websites that allow you to compare the author's conclusions with contrary ones.

Accuracy

How much time you need to spend verifying facts and data depends on answers to the previous questions. In the case of a document from an unknown author on an unfamiliar server whose credibility is not readily apparent, verifying the details becomes imperative.

- Does the page use facts and figures you can verify? Do these agree with information you've already learned?
  Seek to verify facts independently, using reliable sources.
- Are sources provided for all data?
  The source of all statistical data should be clearly identified and dated.
- If this document purports to be original research, is the methodology used to gather the data clearly explained? Is it valid and reliable? Can it be replicated?
- Are conclusions consistent with other materials you've gathered, particularly with conclusions of specialists in the field?

Currency

Currency is more important for some topics than for others. Think about which aspects of your research require current information.

- When was the site last updated?
  There should be a date of when the site was created or last updated, often found at the bottom of the page.
- Is this date recent enough to include important new developments in this field?
- If a bibliography is provided, are items in it reasonably current?
- Given what you've learned, does this source meet your needs? Does it meet your requirements for authority, objectivity, currency, level of scholarship, and accuracy? How difficult is it to make the case that this is a good source for your research?

ETHICAL ISSUES

Websites are so easily accessed and inviting that we sometimes get the mistaken impression that documents found there can be freely used. They can be, up to a point. The authors have placed them there to be consulted by a wide audience. Whether or not webpages include an explicit copyright notice, however, they are copyrighted and can be used only to the extent allowed by *fair use* provisions of the copyright law. Documents and multimedia obtained through the web should be treated with the same respect as books or journal articles. Anything you quote or paraphrase must be properly attributed with a standard citation. Anything else is plagiarism. Appendix A includes examples of APA format for citing Internet resources.

Downloading documents is something you will naturally want to do because it is so much more convenient than photocopying. You might then be tempted simply to copy and paste material into your project, with the intention of paraphrasing and citing later. If you follow this practice, you run the risk of making a mistake and forgetting exactly which are your words and which are someone else's. Or you could lose track of which quotation comes from which source. To avoid this problem, anticipate it. Develop a system to keep track of your sources. Any time you paste something in, change the font or the font size. Or convert it to all caps. Devise an abbreviation for each publication (e.g., the first four letters of the author's name and first four letters of the title), and put this in front of each piece of text you paste.

The same caution applies to images and multimedia files. Downloading a portion of a speech, for example, to use as an audio or visual aid in your own speech might constitute fair use as an educational aid. But downloading several speeches and then selling that CD would surely violate fair-use principles.

SUMMARY

The Internet is a network of networks connecting computers worldwide. The World Wide Web functions as an interface to the Internet facilitating access to materials in electronic format. Traditional library access tools, selected reference sources, and large numbers of periodicals are now accessed through a web browser, and libraries serve as gateways to all types of web-based resources.

You need to differentiate among types of web-based resources. Asking evaluative questions about resources encountered is particularly important in the case of assorted websites. Quality control on the Internet can be exercised only at the local level, so you must take responsibility for checking the authority of website authors and sponsors and the validity of factual information. You must learn to detect unsupported assumptions and to be cognizant of points of view and possible bias.

Many valuable sources of potential interest to researchers are available on a wide assortment of websites. Collections of primary sources (print, audio, video images), government publications, statistical data, news, and current events are particularly important for researchers.

Researchers find materials on the Internet by browsing web directories (for broad subjects), using search engines (for specific topics), and taking part in electronic discussion groups. Discussion groups are of two types: e-mail discussion lists, to which one subscribes, and Usenet newsgroups, which one can access and read with few formalities.

Using search engines to search the web poses special challenges. Search engines vary in terms of search features, size, speed, comprehensiveness, indexing, and methods used to rank results. More sophisticated search strategies can often be employed via advanced search screens. Most searches should be run in more than one search engine. Searchers should be aware of the Invisible, or Deep, Web and develop strategies to take advantage of resources found there. Information gathered on the web must be evaluated for author and publisher authority, objectivity, accuracy, and currency.

Almost all web documents are copyrighted and must not be used without acknowledgment. The presence or absence of a copyright notice is irrelevant. The speed and ease with which material can be accessed and downloaded requires us to make special efforts to evaluate sources and information, to avoid plagiarism, and to read carefully and think critically about the sources we use.

SELECTED SOURCES

Barker, J. (2008). *Finding information on the Internet: A tutorial.* Retrieved June 4, 2008, from <http://web.lib.berkeley.edu/TeachingLib/Guides/Internet/FindInfo.html>.

Calashain, T., & Dornfest, R. (2003). *Google hacks: 100 industrial-strength tips & tools.* Sebastopol, CA: O'Reilly.

Gale Guide to Internet Databases. (1995–). Farmington Hills, MI: Gale Research.

Hock, R. (2007). *The extreme searcher's Internet handbook: A guide for the serious searcher* (2nd ed.). Medford, NJ: CyberAge Books.

Kaye, B. K., & Medoff, N. J. (2001). *The World Wide Web: A mass communication perspective* (2001 update ed.). Mountain View, CA: Mayfield.

Mintz, A. P. (2002). *Web of deception: Misinformation on the Internet.* Medford, NJ: CyberAge Books.

Notess, G. R. (2000–). *Search engine showdown: The user's guide to web searching.* Retrieved June 4, 2008, from <http://searchengineshowdown.com/>.

Schlein, A. M. (2006). *Find it online: The complete guide to online research* (4th ed.). Tempe, AZ: Facts on Demand Press.

Sharkey, J. (2007). Evaluating Internet sources & sites: A tutorial. Retrieved June 4, 2008, from <http://web.lib.purdue.edu/ugrl/staff/sharkey/interneteval/>.

Sherman, C., & Price, G. (2001). *The invisible web: Uncovering information sources search engines can't see.* Medford, NJ: CyberAge Books.

Tensen, B. L. (2007). *Research strategies for a digital age* (2nd ed.). Boston: Thomson/Wadsworth.

EXAMPLES

Jack's topic is starting to take shape. He decides to check whether the Internet has any information available on this topic. But rather than type this term into a search engine (and come up with more hits than he could manage), he visits the University of Iowa's Communication Studies' Links to Resources for possible sites. The site **<http://douglassarchives.org/>** leads him to the text of many different speakers on various issues. After looking through some of these, he wonders whether the speakers actually wrote the speeches themselves or whether someone else did. This direction seems promising, especially because his instructor stressed that his speech must be original and *not* written by anyone else.

Valerie's interest in voice mail is a prime candidate for the Internet. She chooses *Librarian's Index to the Internet* and enters *voice mail* as a phrase. Results indicate one category for *voice mail system*. It includes only one item, but it's about a project called *Community Voice Mail* that deals with providing voice mail for the homeless. She then moves to *Yahoo!* where she finds mostly voice mail companies, some of which explain their products and services. This provides a little background information. By doing an advanced search and limiting it to the Society and Culture category, she finds three sites that demonstrate the breadth of this topic. One deals with the homeless, another with a teen chat company, and the third with something called *telephone cramming*, in which charges for extra telephone services are fraudulently billed.

Robin's interest in interpersonal communication and attribution is starting to take shape. Because her college is an affiliate of CIOS, she checks to see whether its database has any information on attribution theory. At CIOS she searches the demonstration indexes, specifically *Human Communication Research*. She retrieves four articles and their abstracts. They provide a little more information on the topic.

Jason's topic of parasocial interaction, being a mass communication topic, might be searchable in *Links to Communication Studies Resources*. After looking at the Journalism and Mass Communication page (no references to *parasocial*) and the Radio, TV, and Media page (no way to search it), Jason turns to General Resources and decides that a better way to approach this is to look at one of the professional organization's sites. At the National Communication Association, he uses its search engine and finds five references to *parasocial*. One of these provides some interesting background information.

Kat, Rocky, and **Michelle**, for their conflict-resolution training program, decide to see whether there are relevant sites in *Infomine*. They search the phrase *conflict-resolution training* and find an entry for Mediate.com, which advertises books and training videos. They decide to look into renting videos instead of purchasing them.

Eric, Anthony, Gregory, and **Scott** decide to do some preliminary research on their topic by asking students in a *Yahoo!* chatroom to talk about how they maintain relationships with others via the Internet. They set up focus group discussions and record the chat for later use.

EXERCISES

1. Go to the link for the Communication Studies Resources website <http://www.uiowa.edu/commstud/resources/>. Under the category *General*, find a link to Cultural Studies Central. Explore that page. Who is the webmaster? What are the webmaster's credentials for maintaining a website in this subject area?

2. Use a search engine to find two webpages related to your topic. Referring to the section on evaluating web resources in this chapter, write a paragraph evaluating each site.

3. You have heard there are useful FAQs about digital cameras. To find these FAQs you use the Usenet FAQ Archives **<http://www.faqs.org>**. Go to *Other-FAQs* and select the link to the digital cameras site. What level of resolution is necessary for putting photos on your website?

4. Go to the Communication–Internet Skills page on the Libraries website at Kent State University **<http://www.library.kent.edu/page/10899/>** and find the Electronic Communication section. Review the main features of bulletin boards, newsgroups, e-mail, and listservs. Try some of the tutorials to improve your skills.

5. What type of resources relevant to your topic might be available on websites? Think in terms of particular organizations, types of organizations, people, programs, government reports, archival materials, and so on. Make a list of terms you could use in a search engine to retrieve web documents. Select two individual search engines and one metasearch engine. Using the advanced search screen, search your topic in all three engines, adjusting your search strategy. What was your initial search statement? What was your final search statement? Compare the results you retrieved from the three search engines.

part two

Communication Research Sources

I n this part of the book, we identify current important and useful communication and communication-related sources available in print or electronically. In the next four chapters, we discuss a variety of general and specific research sources. We describe handbooks, textbooks, encyclopedias, and annual reviews in Chapter 5. These are useful for defining, refining, and developing a research topic. The bibliographies, guides, and indexes described in Chapter 6 can help further develop the research topic or question. In Chapter 7 we discuss the periodical literature of communication: scholarly journals and professional or trade magazines. The articles found in these publications present current conceptual and practical knowledge. Finally, in Chapter 8 we describe specific factual information sources such as collections, statistical sources, government publications, yearbooks, directories, dictionaries, and manuals.

In each chapter we annotate several sources. We consider these to be some of the more important, useful, or representative sources of the type discussed. The end-of-chapter exercises refer you to some of these sources and ask you to use them. Clues to their use are found in the annotations or in the questions themselves.

The annotated sources certainly do not constitute the totality of sources of that genre. Many additional and valuable sources are listed at the end of each chapter and on our home page. Several of these can help you select, refine, and develop an interesting research topic and project. Add new sources in the book margins and at the ends of chapters when you find especially useful ones. You'll then be able to refer to these sources whenever you undertake a research project in the future.

chapter 5

General Sources

I n the preceding chapters you've become acquainted with the multifaceted nature of communication and with systematic research search strategies used to address communication topics. Now it's time to examine more closely the various communication sources that are available in or accessible from most college and university libraries.

You may be working on a literature review or research project yet have not fully identified a specific topic or research question. To gain an understanding of topics that others find interesting or relevant, browse through some general sources; this can help you formulate or develop your own research topic. If you already know the topic you wish to investigate, these general reference works often have useful bibliographies that can lead you to sources specifically related to your research question.

After you examine these sources, list them in bibliography and search records (see Chapter 2) as a reminder that you've already searched them for references to pertinent materials. As we have stressed, this action can save much time, especially because so many sources are potentially valuable to your research goal.

Like many other disciplines, communication is a rapidly evolving field. New research results, new applications, and changes in professional practices often make it difficult to grasp the state of generally accepted knowledge in a given field. Even the vocabulary keeps changing. To alleviate this problem, authorities in all disciplines create handbooks, subject encyclopedias, and subject dictionaries. These sources summarize generally accepted findings or practices in a field at a particular time. In so doing, they provide a useful reference point when you begin researching a subject area.

HANDBOOKS

The term **handbook** is often used to categorize two distinct publications. One type, a manual, is a compact book of facts. We discuss manuals in

Chapter 8 when we deal with other compilations of information. The other type of handbook, the scholarly or subject handbook, is more general in nature and helps orient students of communication to current issues and topics.

Scholarly handbooks provide a comprehensive summary of past research and thematic viewpoints in a particular discipline. They are generally broad-based and treat a great number of topics. It is difficult for the editors of these volumes to keep them current because of the breadth of topics covered and the delays in publication time. Thus handbooks soon become outdated, although they provide important background information about knowledge and development of many relevant topics.

Although they must also always look for other sources to give perspective on new developments, one handbook outside the discipline that communication researchers find valuable for background information is:

> Gilbert, D. T., Fiske, S. T., & Lindzey, G. (Eds.). (1998). *The handbook of social psychology* (4th ed., 2 vols.). Boston: McGraw-Hill.
>
> ■ Two volumes contain independent articles (each with a lengthy bibliography) summarizing the state of the art in social psychological theory and research. Volume 1 provides a historical perspective, explains theories and models of social psychology (e.g., attitude change, motivation, child development, and gender), and reviews research methods, including attitude measurement, quantitative methods, experimentation, survey methods, and data analysis.
>
> Volume 2 contains articles on altruism, aggression, small groups, language use and social behavior, personality, attraction, intergroup relations, organizations, social influence and conformity, health behavior, social movements, psychology and law, opinion and politics, and cultural psychology. Indexes appear at the end of each volume.

Similar handbooks concentrate on more specific content areas. Sometimes these handbooks are one-time works. Others may be revised and reissued. One useful handbook examines organizational communication:

> Jablin, F. M., & Putnam, L. L. (Eds.). (2000). *The new handbook of organizational communication: Advances in theory, research, and methods.* Thousand Oaks, CA: Sage.
>
> ■ This handbook offers a multidisciplinary view of organizational communication issues, contexts, structures, and processes. The 21 chapters cover such topics as communication technologies, culture, networks, collaborative work, leadership, identity, conflict, decision making, assimilation, and power. There are also chapters on quantitative and qualitative research and interaction analysis.

Another handbook updates theory and research in persuasion. It contains perspectives on interpersonal, small group, media, and campaign communication.

> Dillard, J. P., & Pfau, M. (Eds.). (2002). *The persuasion handbook: Developments in theory and practice.* Thousand Oaks, CA: Sage.
>
> ■ This handbook contains 34 essays that summarize theory and research in persuasion. It begins with a section on basic issues and then moves to nine important theories. This section is followed by ones that address affect, message features, contexts, persuasion campaigns, and media. A summary of final thoughts by the editors follows. Each essay contains a series of references.

Other handbooks have been developed for different areas of the discipline. One handbook examines dimensions of intercultural communication:

> Gudykunst, W. B., & Mody, B. (Eds.). (2002). *Handbook of international and intercultural communication* (2nd ed.). Thousand Oaks, CA: Sage.
>
> ■ Communication specialists, psychologists, and anthropologists review the state of research in international and intercultural communication. They attempt to provide a framework for future work in the field. The essays provide overviews and address processes, effects, and contexts. An index provides access to subjects and authors.

Another communication handbook provides an overview of group communication:

> Frey, L. R. (Ed.), Gouran, D. S., & Poole, M. S. (Assoc. Eds.). (1999). *The handbook of group communication theory and research*. Thousand Oaks, CA: Sage.
>
> ■ Communication specialists and researchers review the state of research in group communication. They seek to provide a framework for future work in the field. The essays are arranged in six sections: Foundations, Individuals and Group Communication, Task and Relational Group Communication, Group Communication Processes, Group Communication Facilitation, and Contexts and Application. An index provides access to subjects and authors.

Another handbook is a revised edition of a specialized handbook in interpersonal communication:

> Knapp, M. L., & Daly, J. A. (Eds.). (2002). *Handbook of interpersonal communication* (3rd ed.). Thousand Oaks, CA: Sage.
>
> ■ This handbook summarizes the development and state of theory and research in interpersonal communication. The authors discuss approaches to basic issues in studying interpersonal communication, fundamental units, processes and functions, and contexts. Chapters cover such topics as language, communicator characteristics, nonverbal signals, power, influence, competence, and communication in work, social, health, and family contexts. Each essay contains a lengthy list of references.

Communication researchers, especially those in organizational communication, advertising, and public relations, often find business subject handbooks useful. These usually offer a practical, rather than scholarly, approach to their subjects. Although they may lack extensive bibliographies, their concise explanations of accepted practices, procedures, and concepts in a given area are useful when you start a research paper or other communication project. Among the handbooks available in marketing, advertising, and public relations is:

> Heath, R. L., & Vasquez, G. (Eds.). (2001). *Handbook of public relations*. Thousand Oaks, CA: Sage.
>
> ■ This handbook describes different aspects of public relations, the work of public relations professionals, the global nature of public relations, and a variety of communication concerns. Topics include relationship building, crisis communication, strategic planning, conflict resolution, social responsibility, ethics, corporate communication, managing community relationships, sports information, media effects, new technologies, and international public relations. Bibliographic references and an index are provided.

As you might note, Sage has been a leader in publishing communication handbooks. Their recent handbook series illustrates this point:

SAGE Handbook of Advertising
SAGE Handbook of Conflict Communication: Integrating theory, research, and practice
SAGE Handbook of Film Studies
SAGE Handbook of Gender and Communication
SAGE Handbook of Media Studies
SAGE Handbook of Nonverbal Communication
SAGE Handbook of Organizational Discourse
SAGE Handbook of Organization Studies
SAGE Handbook of Performance Studies
SAGE Handbook of Political Advertising
SAGE Handbook of Public Opinion Research

We list other scholarly and subject handbooks from communication and related disciplines at the end of this chapter. These handbooks are valuable for selecting and refining research topics. Their content also provides specific information for developing a literature review, seminar or research paper, or prospectus.

BOOKS

Students of communication use various types of books when researching communication processes. **Edited books** are similar to handbooks and annual reviews but often are not quite as inclusive and extensive. The editors solicit chapters from experts or knowledgeable writers in a particular area. **Monographs** are books the author has written in entirety. Both edited books and monographs are considered scholarly because they define or extend the discipline through their work. The authors have credentials to write about a particular topic, and the references and footnotes indicate a great deal of effort and research has gone into the work.

Textbooks are handy aids when defining and refining research questions. They seek to survey information about a field of study and to present the fundamentals of a subject in an easy-to-understand manner. Some textbooks are edited collections of writings in a subject area and are similar to handbooks. In fact, it is sometimes not an easy task to distinguish some textbooks from scholarly handbooks. At times, instructors may use handbooks as class texts.

In basic textbooks the authors offer a brief summary of existing knowledge and their conclusions about the essential points derived from communication theory and research in that area. The bibliographies at the ends of chapters are useful for locating other books and articles on the subject. However, these bibliographies are often limited in scope. As with all printed materials, when using textbooks keep in mind the gap between the time the book is written and the time it is printed. As secondary sources, it is best to use textbooks to acquire an overview or general orientation to a topic and to gather a few reference sources. Several communication books are listed at the end of this chapter. The list is selective and by no means represents the many communication books published each year.

A newer phenomenon is the **e-book**. Text is downloaded into an electronic display and readers page-through the text as they would with a printed book. Besides classics such as the Bible and various dictionaries, many other books are available in electronic format. It is an increasingly popular format for textbooks as well. Your library can point you to search engines (with which they've contracted) to find such materials. Some of the more popular ones are NetLibrary, Electronic Reference Books (ABC-CLIO), Books24x7, Safari Tech Books Online, and Oxford Reference Core Online. Oxford is a particularly useful site for dictionaries and encyclopedias. Check out their websites at **<http://www.oxfordscholarship.com>** and **<http://www.oxfordreference.com>**.

ENCYCLOPEDIAS

Encyclopedias are all-embracing compilations of information that provide a multifaceted approach to a subject. The essays within encyclopedias generally have bibliographies that can be used to find other general sources about a topic. These bibliographies may also identify specific sources that give background on narrower aspects of the topic. It may not be too helpful, though, to consult general encyclopedias like the *Encyclopaedia Britannica* or *Wikipedia* **<http://en.wikipedia.org/wiki/Main_Page>** unless you initially know very little about your topic.

Subject encyclopedias contain overview articles on what is known about topics in a specific discipline. The newest communication subject encyclopedia, published in 2008, promises to be a useful source for years to come:

Donsbach, W. E. (Ed.). (2008). *International encyclopedia of communication*. (12 vols.). Malden, MA: Wiley-Blackwell.

■ This encyclopedia contains over 1,300 original essays in 29 editorial areas of communication. Major areas include media, technology, developmental, educational/instructional, gender, information, intercultural, international, interpersonal, journalism, organizational, political, rhetorical, strategic (public relations and advertising), and visual communication. Articles are illustrated and include bibliographies of general works for further reference. A comprehensive index lists concepts, terms, names, and titles.

This volume is jointly published with the International Communication Association. An international editorial board and over 1,000 authors from 47 countries contributed entries ranging from relatively specific topics (e.g., "China Central Television Channel 9") to very broad ones (e.g., "Communication as a Field and a Discipline"). Online access and searching is available for those who purchase it. More information can be found at **<http://www.communicationencyclopedia.com>**.

A useful and relatively recent encyclopedia of the broader social and behavioral sciences provides coverage of topics relevant to the study of communication:

Smelser, N. J., & Baltes, P. B. (Eds.). (2001). *International encyclopedia of the social & behavioral sciences*. (25 vols.). New York: Elsevier.

■ More than 4,000 authors cover hundreds of topics in the social and behavioral sciences. Communication students will find some of the following topics relevant to their interests: Family and Generations, Gender Studies, Global/International Studies, Health, Industrial and Organizational Psychology, Information Science and Technology, Language, Linguistics, Management, and Organization and Management.

Most pertinent to communication are the Social Psychology and Media topic areas. Social Psychology includes articles about attitude formation and change, attribution, decision making, nonverbal communication, person perception, and verbal communication. The Media area contains articles on media effects, advertising and marketing, effects and audiences, journalism, popular culture, semiotics, and legal issues. Libraries that own the bound version of the encyclopedia can provide access to the online abstracts for their patrons.

A **legal encyclopedia** is another type of subject encyclopedia. It is a useful source when you are researching topics of communication law, freedom of speech, and debate. Legal encyclopedias are typically written in narrative form and are nonevaluative in approach. They best serve as case finders and starting points in searching the law. They generally include a statement of the applicable law, citations to appropriate cases, and analytical and subject indexes. Good encyclopedias also have frequent supplements.

The two principal legal encyclopedias of national scope are *Corpus Juris Secundum* and *American Jurisprudence Second* (second series). If your campus has access to the *Westlaw Campus* legal search system, you may be able to gain online access to *American Jurisprudence Second*. State and local legal encyclopedias are also available.

When first reading the literature of an academic discipline, you will encounter a whole new language. The words may be familiar, but many times the meanings are different. Although we discuss most dictionaries in Chapter 8 as largely information manuals, a **subject dictionary** is an abbreviated type of subject encyclopedia. Subject dictionaries can help clarify your understanding of new or unique terms and lead to important references.

ANNUAL REVIEWS AND SERIES

Besides handbooks and encyclopedias, other general sources will help you find information or define a research question more clearly. Communication, like many other disciplines, is experiencing a surge in research activity. This expansion is so rapid that keeping abreast of what others in the various specialty areas are researching is difficult. **Annual reviews** provide yearly summaries of current research activities. They are useful for selecting and refining a research topic or question, finding information and sources, and updating bibliographies. Because some of the sources cited in annual reviews can be outside your usual reading area, reading annual reviews helps to broaden your search strategy.

Annual reviews, then, are vehicles for gauging the level of research activity in various areas of communication. They also update research and are helpful later in the research process when you're looking for recent information and bibliographic citations.

Some annual reviews provide updates of current research and thinking in several content areas. Others focus on one particular content area that changes each year. One annual review of the former type is *Communication Yearbook*. It contains current research and writings in several related content areas.

Communication Yearbook. (1977–). Malden, MA: Blackwell.

■ This annual review is an official publication of the International Communication Association (ICA). Volumes before 1988 presented two different types of articles: reviews and commentaries, covering general communication topics, and selected studies, including research papers in each subfield (e.g., interpersonal, organizational, and mass communication). These papers were competitively selected and presented at the annual meeting of the ICA. Early editions also included yearly overviews of developments within the subfields. From 1988 to 1994 the *Yearbook* offered original essays and commentaries reflecting conceptual developments across the communication discipline. Starting in 1995 the *Yearbook* refocused to feature reviews of the literature.

Such reviews and research studies contain valuable bibliographic sources. Examine the table of contents to determine the broader chapter topics and use the subject index at the back to locate references to narrower topics. There also is an index by author.

Another annual review focuses on information systems, communication uses and effects, and control of communication and information:

Progress in Communication Sciences. (1979–2001). Stamford, CT: Ablex.

■ Each annual volume contained 7 to 10 review essays on topics in most subareas of communication. Over the years, essays have focused on broadcast regulation, grapevines, communication networks, children's television, political campaigns, nonverbal communication, communication competence, gender, statistics, telecommunications, persuasion, intercultural communication, ethnography, and many other topics too numerous to list here. Each volume has a subject and author index. Although the series ceased in 2001, the volumes contain useful historical perspective on important communication topics.

Series examine new topics each year, focus on research related to those specific subjects, and often have different titles. The articles in each volume are reports of original research or theoretical pieces. Sage Publications published a series (which it called an *annual review*) of communication research. These volumes are helpful in identifying research topics, finding information, providing background and perspective, and broadening your search strategy.

Sage Annual Reviews of Communication Research, which ceased publication in 1994, contained many useful volumes. Topics ranged from mass and political communication to persuasion and interpersonal and nonverbal communication. More recent volumes focused on media audiences, critical perspectives on narrative, negotiation, culture, information campaigns, and message effects.

Other series that contain helpful reference sources are listed at the end of this chapter. Several of these series, including *Sage Annual Reviews of Communication Research, Media and Society, LEA's Communication Series*, and the *SUNY Series in Communication Studies*, are known as publishers' series. This means volumes in the series have different titles and may not appear regularly. Because many libraries list these works only by the title of the individual volumes and not by the series title, identifying and locating the specific volumes that make up a particular series can be difficult. If you wish to find individual works in a series, check *WorldCat* (see Chapter 6) for series titles.

Handbooks, textbooks, encyclopedias, and annual reviews and series, then, provide a general understanding of the communication field as well as specific interests, concerns, and methodologies of communication researchers. They are most helpful when identifying a specific area within communication of interest for a seminar or term paper, literature review, or research prospectus. In many instances, handbooks, yearbooks, and annual reviews also serve as vehicles for widening a search strategy and locating additional and, in some cases, recent sources about a chosen communication topic.

SUMMARY

General sources are useful when trying to identify a topic for a research project or paper. The articles, chapters, and review essays found in these sources provide an overview of what others in the discipline find interesting and worthy of study. They also contain references to major works that can get you started on your project. Dictionaries help you keep up with the changing vocabulary, nuances of various subjects with which you're not familiar, and meanings of new words you run into in your reading.

Handbooks, as discussed in this chapter, provide a comprehensive summary of past research and themes in the literature of the field. Even though they become outdated, they're useful as background reading and provide perspective on topics. Edited books and monographs contain original research reports as well as reviews of literature. Textbooks, on the other hand, refer to the most important studies in an easy-to-understand fashion; they're a good starting place to find a topic of interest.

Encyclopedias are also written in an easy-to-understand manner, often providing definitions and selected sources for further reading. Legal encyclopedias and subject dictionaries are two additional reference sources that serve the same function.

Annual reviews provide yearly summaries of research on a particular topic. Series are similar in that they appear periodically, and usually each volume has a different title.

These general sources, then, help scholars new to a particular research area obtain a realistic picture of the scope of an area and the dimensions into which it is divided. This is important because often you don't know how broad a topic is until you're halfway through your search. By looking at general sources, your search becomes much more economical and satisfying.

SELECTED SOURCES

Handbooks

Andersen, P. A., & Guerrero, L. K. (Eds.). (2007). *Handbook of communication and emotion: Research, theory, application, and contexts.* Amsterdam: Elsevier.

Berger, C. R., & Chaffee, S. H. (Eds.). (1987). *Handbook of communication science.* Newbury Park, CA: Sage.

Christ, W. G. (Ed.). (2005). *Assessing communication education: A handbook for media, speech, and theatre educators* (2nd ed.). Mahwah, NJ: Erlbaum.

Clegg, S. R., Hardy, C., Nord, W. R., & Lawrence, T. (Eds.). (2006). *The SAGE handbook of organization studies* (2nd ed). Thousand Oaks, CA: Sage.

Dillard, J. P., & Pfau, M. (Eds.). (2002). *The persuasion handbook: Developments in theory and practice.* Thousand Oaks, CA: Sage.

Donald, J., & Renov, M. (Eds.). (2008). *The SAGE handbook of film studies.* Los Angeles: Sage.

Donsbach, W., & Traugott, M. W. (Eds.). (2008). *The SAGE handbook of public opinion research.* Los Angeles: Sage.

Dow, B. J., & Wood, J. T. (Eds.). (2006). *The SAGE handbook of gender and communication*. Thousand Oaks, CA: Sage.

Downing, J. (Ed.). (2004). *The SAGE handbook of media studies*. Thousand Oaks, CA: Sage.

Fine, M. A., & Harvey, J. H. (Eds.). (2006). *Handbook of divorce and relationship dissolution*. Mahwah, NJ: Erlbaum.

Frey, L. R. (Ed.), Gouran, D. S., & Poole, M. S. (Assoc. Eds.). (1999). *The handbook of group communication theory and research*. Thousand Oaks, CA: Sage.

Gilbert, D. T., Fiske, S. T., & Lindzey, G. (Eds.). (1998). *The handbook of social psychology* (4th ed., 2-vols.). Boston: McGraw-Hill.

Grant, D., Hardy, C., Oswick, C., & Putnam, L. (Eds.). (2004). *The SAGE handbook of organizational discourse*. Thousand Oaks, CA: Sage.

Greene, J. O., & Burleson, B. R. (Eds.). (2003). *Handbook of communication and social interaction skills*. Mahwah, NJ: Erlbaum.

Gudykunst, W. B., & Mody, B. (Eds.). (2002). *Handbook of international and intercultural communication* (2nd ed.). Thousand Oaks, CA: Sage.

Hardt, H. (Ed.). (2001). *Social theories of the press: Constituents of communication research, 1840s to 1920s*. Lanham, UK: Rowman & Littlefield.

Hargie, O. (Ed.). (2006). *The handbook of communication skills* (3rd ed.). London: Routledge.

Hogg, M. A., & Cooper, J. (Eds.). (2003). *The SAGE handbook of social psychology*. Thousand Oaks, CA: Sage.

Jablin, F. M., & Putnam, L. L. (Eds.). (2000). *The new handbook of organizational communication: Advances in theory, research, and methods*. Thousand Oaks, CA: Sage.

Jonassen, D. H. (Ed.). (2004). *Handbook of research for educational communications and technology* (2nd ed.). Mahwah, NJ: Erlbaum.

Kaid, L. L. (Ed.). (2004). *Handbook of political communication research*. Mahwah, NJ: Erlbaum.

Kaid, L. L., & Holtz-Bacha, C. (Eds.). (2006). *The SAGE handbook of political advertising*. Thousand Oaks, CA: Sage.

Knapp, M. L., & Daly, J. A. (Eds.). (2002). *Handbook of interpersonal communication* (3rd ed.). Thousand Oaks, CA: Sage.

Kruglanski, A. W., & Higgins, E. T. (Eds.). (2007). *Social psychology: Handbook of basic principles* (2nd ed.). New York: Guilford Press.

Landis, D., & Bennett, J. M. (Eds.). (2004). *Handbook of intercultural training* (3rd ed.). Thousand Oaks, CA: Sage.

Lievrouw, L., & Livingstone, S. (Eds.). (2002). *Handbook of new media: Social shaping and consequences of ICTs*. Thousand Oaks, CA: Sage.

Madison, D. S., & Hamera, J. (Eds.). (2006). *The SAGE handbook of performance studies*. Thousand Oaks, CA: Sage.

Manusov, V. L., & Patterson, M. L. (Eds.). (2006). The *SAGE handbook of nonverbal communication*. Thousand Oaks, CA: Sage.

Miller, J. L., & Eimas, P. D. (Eds.). (2007). *Speech, language, and communication* (2nd ed.). Amsterdam: Elsevier.

Nussbaum, J. F., & Coupland, J. (Eds.). (2004). *Handbook of communication and aging research* (2nd ed.). Mahwah, NJ: Erlbaum.

Oetzel, J. G., & Ting-Toomey, S. (Eds.). (2006). *The SAGE handbook of conflict communication: Integrating theory, research, and practice.* Thousand Oaks, CA: Sage.

Raney, A. A., & Bryant, J. (Eds.). (2006). *Handbook of sports and media.* Mahwah, NJ: Erlbaum.

Robinson, W. P., & Giles, H. (Eds.). (2001). *The new handbook of language and social psychology.* Chichester, UK: Wiley.

Singer, D. G., & Singer, J. L. (Eds.). (2001). *Handbook of children and the media.* Thousand Oaks, CA: Sage.

Sriramesh, K., & Verčič, D. (Eds.). (2003). *The global public relations handbook: Theory, research, and practice.* Mahwah, NJ: Erlbaum.

Swanson, D. L., & Nimmo, D. D. (Eds.). (1990). *New directions in political communication: A resource book.* Newbury Park, CA: Sage.

Swanson, J. L. (Ed.). (2005–2006). *First amendment law handbook.* Eagan, MN: Thomson/West.

Tellis, G. J., & Ambler, T. (Eds.). (2007). *The SAGE handbook of advertising.* Los Angeles: Sage.

Thompson, T. L., Dorsey, A., Miller, K., & Parrott, R. (Eds.). (2003). *Handbook of health communication.* Mahwah, NJ: Erlbaum.

Turner, L. H., & West, R. (2006). *Family communication sourcebook.* Thousand Oaks, CA: Sage.

Vangelisti, A. L. (Ed.). (2003). *Handbook of family communication.* Mahwah, NJ: Erlbaum.

Vangelisti, A. L., Daly, J. A., & Friedrich, G. W. (Eds.). (1999). *Teaching communication: Theory, research, and methods* (2nd ed.). Mahwah, NJ: Erlbaum.

Vangelisti, A. L., & Perlman, D. (Eds.). (2006). *The Cambridge handbook of personal relationships.* New York: Cambridge University Press.

Weiner, I. B., Freedheim, D. K., Schinka, J. A., & Velicer, W. F. (Eds.). (2003). *Handbook of psychology* (12 vols.). New York: Wiley.

Textbooks

Alexander, A., Owers, J., Carveth, R., Hollifield, C. A., & Greco, A. N. (Eds.). (2004). *Media economics: Theory and practice* (3rd ed.). Mahwah, NJ: Erlbaum.

Beebe, S. A., & Masterson, J. T. (2006). *Communicating in small groups: Principles and practices* (8th ed.). Boston: Pearson/Allyn and Bacon.

Bryant, J., & Oliver, M. B. (Eds.). (2008). *Media effects: Advances in theory and research* (3rd ed.). New York: Routledge/Taylor and Francis.

Carter, T. B., Franklin, M. A., & Wright, J. B. (2003). *The first amendment and the fifth estate: Regulation of electronic mass media* (6th ed.). New York: Foundation Press.

Carter, T. B., Franklin, M. A., & Wright, J. B. (2005). *The first amendment and the fourth estate: The law of mass media* (9th ed.). New York: Foundation Press.

Christians, C. G. (2005). *Media ethics: Cases and moral reasoning* (7th ed.). Boston: Pearson/Allyn and Bacon.

Dindia, K., & Canary, D. J. (2006). *Sex differences and similarities in communication.* Mahwah, NJ: Erlbaum.

Eastman, S. T., & Ferguson, D. A. (Eds.). (2006). *Media programming: Strategies and practices* (7th ed.). Belmont, CA: Thomson/Wadsworth.

Foss, S. K., Foss, K. A., & Trapp, R. (2002). *Contemporary perspectives on rhetoric* (3rd ed.). Prospect Heights, IL: Waveland Press.

Frey, L. R. (Ed.). (2002). *New directions in group communication.* Thousand Oaks, CA: Sage.

Gudykunst, W. B., & Kim, Y. Y. (2003). *Communicating with strangers: An approach to intercultural communication* (4th ed.). Boston: McGraw-Hill.

Harris, R. J. (2004). *A cognitive psychology of mass communication* (4th ed.). Mahwah, NJ: Erlbaum.

Head, S. W., Spann, T., & McGregor, M. A. (2001). *Broadcasting in America: A survey of electronic media* (9th ed.). Boston: Houghton Mifflin.

Hecht, M. L., Jackson, R. L., II, & Ribeau, S. A. (2003). *African American communication: Exploring identity and culture* (2nd ed.). Mahwah, NJ: Erlbaum.

Howard, P. N., & Jones, S. (Eds.). (2004). *Society online: The Internet in context.* Thousand Oaks, CA: Sage.

Infante, D. A., Rancer, A. S., & Womack, D. F. (2003). *Building communication theory* (4th ed.). Prospect Heights, IL: Waveland Press.

Jamieson, K. H., & Campbell, K. K. (2006). *The interplay of influence: News, advertising, politics, and the mass media* (6th ed.). Belmont, CA: Thomson/Wadsworth.

Jandt, F. E. (2007). *An introduction to intercultural communication: Identities in a global community* (7th ed.). Thousand Oaks, CA: Sage.

Krolokke, C., & Sorensen, A. S. (2006). *Gender communication theories and analyses: From silence to performance.* Thousand Oaks, CA: Sage.

Littlejohn, S. W., & Foss, K. A. (2008). *Theories of human communication* (9th ed.). Belmont, CA: Thomson/Wadsworth.

Lustig, M. W., & Koester, J. (2006). *Intercultural competence: Interpersonal communication across cultures* (5th ed.). Boston: Pearson/Allyn and Bacon.

Middleton, K., & Lee, W. E. (2008). *The law of public communication* (7th ed.). Boston: Pearson/Allyn and Bacon.

Newsom, D., Turk, J. V., & Kruckeberg, D. (2007). *This is PR: The realities of public relations* (9th ed.). Belmont, CA: Wadsworth/Thomson Learning.

O'Keefe, D. J. (2002). *Persuasion: Theory and research* (2nd ed.). Thousand Oaks, CA: Sage.

Papa, M. J., Daniels, T. D., & Spiker, B. K. (2008). *Organizational communication: Perspectives and trends.* Los Angeles: Sage.

Perloff, R. M. (2008). *The dynamics of persuasion: Communication and attitudes in the 21st century* (3rd ed.). New York: Erlbaum.

Perse, E. M. (2001). *Media effects and society.* Mahwah, NJ: Erlbaum.

Rogers, E. M. (2003). *Diffusion of innovations* (5th ed.). New York: Free Press.

Schumann, D. W., & Thorson, E. (2007). *Internet advertising: Theory and research* (Rev. ed.). Mahwah, NJ: Erlbaum.

Segrin, C., & Flora, J. (2005). *Family communication.* Mahwah, NJ: Erlbaum.

Severin, W. J., & Tankard, J. W. (2001). *Communication theories: Origins, methods, and uses in the mass media* (5th ed.). New York: Addison Wesley Longman.

Stempel, G. H., III., Weaver, D. H., & Wilhoit, G. C. (Eds.). (2003). *Mass communication research and theory.* Boston: Allyn and Bacon.

Sterling, C. H., & Kittross, J. M. (2002). *Stay tuned: A history of American broadcasting* (3rd ed.). Mahwah, NJ: Erlbaum.

Stewart, C. J., Smith, C. A., & Denton, R. E., Jr. (2007). *Persuasion and social movements* (5th ed.). Long Grove, IL: Waveland Press.

Tedford, T. L., Herbeck, D., & Haiman, F. S. (2005). *Freedom of speech in the United States* (5th ed.). State College, PA: Strata.

Teeter, D. L., & Loving, B. (2001). *Law of mass communications* (10th ed.). New York: Foundation Press.

Trent, J. S., & Friedenberg, R. V. (2008). *Political campaign communication: Principles and practices* (6th ed.). Lanham, MD: Rowman & Littlefield.

Van Evra, J. P. (2004). *Television and child development* (3rd ed.). Mahwah, NJ: Erlbaum.

Wolvin, A. D. (2009). *Listening and human communication: 21st Century perspectives*. New York: Blackwell.

Wood, J. T. (2008). *Gendered lives: Communication, gender, and culture* (8th ed.). Belmont, CA: Thomson/Wadsworth.

Encyclopedias

American Jurisprudence Second (82 vols.). (1962–). Rochester, NY: Lawyers Cooperative. (Available online via *Westlaw campus*.)

Amey, L., & Rasmussen, R. K. (1997). *Censorship* (3 vols.). Pasadena, CA: Salem Press.

Barnouw, E. (Ed.). (1989). *International encyclopedia of communications* (4 vols.). New York: Oxford University Press.

Bidgoli, H. (Ed.). (2003). *The Internet encyclopedia* (3 vols.). Hoboken, NJ: Wiley.

Borgatta, E. F., & Montgomery, R. J. V. (Eds.). (2000). *Encyclopedia of sociology* (2nd ed., 5 vols.). New York: Macmillan Reference.

Bouissac, P. R. (Ed.). (1998). *Encyclopedia of semiotics*. New York: Oxford University Press.

Byrne, J. H. (Ed.). (2003). *Learning and memory* (2nd ed.). New York: Macmillan Reference.

Cole, R. (Ed.). (1998). *The encyclopedia of propaganda* (3 vols). Armonk, NY: Sharpe Reference.

Cooper, C. L., Argyris, C., & Starbuck, W. H. (2005). *The Blackwell encyclopedia of management* (2nd ed., 12 vols.). Malden, MA: Blackwell Business.

Corpus Juris Secundum (100 vols.). (1936–). St. Paul: West.

Craighead, W. E., & Nemeroff, C. B. (Eds.). (2001). *The Corsini encyclopedia of psychology and behavioral science* (3rd ed., 4 vols.). New York: Wiley.

Donsbach, W. E. (Ed.). (2008). *International encyclopedia of communication* (12 vols.). Malden, MA: Wiley-Blackwell.

Encyclopaedia Britannica Online. (1996). Chicago: Encyclopaedia Britannica. (Available: http://www.britannica.com.)

Findlay, M. S. (1998). *Language and communication: A cross-cultural encyclopedia*. Santa Barbara, CA: ABC-CLIO.

Forest, J. J. F., & Kinser, K. (2002). *Higher education in the United States: An encyclopedia* (2 vols.). Santa Barbara, CA: ABC-CLIO.

Gardner, R., & Shortelle, D. (1997). *From talking drums to the Internet: An encyclopedia of communications technology*. Santa Barbara, CA: ABC-CLIO.

Guthrie, J. W. (2003). *Encyclopedia of education* (2nd ed., 8 vols.). New York: Macmillan Reference.

Helms, M. M. (Ed.). (2005). *Encyclopedia of management* (5th ed.). Detroit: Thomson/Gale.

Johnston, D. H. (Ed.). (2003). *Encyclopedia of international media and communications* (4 vols.). San Diego, CA: Academic Press.

Jones, S. (Ed.). (2003). *Encyclopedia of new media*. Thousand Oaks, CA: Sage.

Kazdin, A. E. (Ed.). (2000). *Encyclopedia of psychology* (8 vols.). Washington, DC: American Psychological Association.

Kennedy, D. (Ed.). (2003). *Oxford encyclopedia of theatre & performance* (2 vols.). New York: Oxford University Press.

Kuper, A., & Kuper, J. (Eds.). (2003). *The social science encyclopedia* (3rd ed.). New York: Routledge.

Lackmann, R. W. (2003). *The encyclopedia of 20th-century American television*. New York: Checkmark Books.

Lewis, R. (1997). *Communication: Print, images, sounds, and the computer* (Rev. ed.). New York: Macmillan Reference.

Malonis, J. A. (Ed.). (2000). *Encyclopedia of business* (2nd ed., 2 vois.). Detroit: Gale Group.

Manstead, A. S. R., & Hewstone, M. (1999). *The Blackwell encyclopedia of social psychology*. Oxford, UK: Blackwell.

McDonough, J., & Egolf, K. (Eds.). (2003). *The advertising age encyclopedia of advertising* (3 vols.). New York: Fitzroy Dearborn.

Miller, D. (2004). *The Blackwell encyclopedia of political thought*. Oxford, UK: Blackwell.

Muller, N. J. (2000). *Desktop encyclopedia of telecommunications* (2nd ed.). New York: McGraw-Hill.

Murray, M. D. (1999). *Encyclopedia of television news*. Phoenix: Oryx Press.

Nadel, L. (Ed.). (2003). *Encyclopedia of cognitive science* (4 vols.). London: Nature Publishing Group.

Newcomb, H. (Ed.). (2004). *Encyclopedia of television* (2nd ed., 4 vols.). New York: Routledge.

Pearson, R. E., & Simpson, P. (2001). *Critical dictionary of film and television theory*. London: Routledge.

Pendergast, T., & Perdergast, S. (2000). *St. James encyclopedia of popular culture* (5 vols.). Detroit: St. James Press.

Schement, J. R. (Ed.). (2002). *Encyclopedia of communication and information* (3 vols.). New York: Macmillan Reference.

Sloane, T. O. (Ed.). (2001). *Encyclopedia of rhetoric*. Oxford: Oxford University Press.

Smelser, N. J., & Baltes, P. B. (Eds.). (2001). *International encyclopedia of the social & behavioral sciences* (25 vols.). New York: Elsevier. (Available: http://www.sciencedirect.com/science/referenceworks/0080430767.)

Sterling, C. H. (1998). *Focal encyclopedia of electronic media*. Woburn, MA: Butterworth Heinemann.

Sterling, C. H. (Ed.). (2003). *Encyclopedia of radio* (3 vols.). New York: Routledge.

Sterling, C. H., & Keith, M. (Eds.). (2004). *The museum of broadcast communications encyclopedia of radio* (3 vols.). New York: Fitzroy Dearborn.

Vaughn, S. L. (Ed.). (2007). *Encyclopedia of American journalism* (3 vols.). New York: Routledge.

Warner, M., & Kotter, J. P. (Eds.). (2002). *International encyclopedia of business and management* (2nd ed., 8 vols.). London: Thomson Learning.

Watson, J., & Hill, A. (2006). *Dictionary of media and communication studies* (7th ed.). London: Hodder Arnold.

Annual Reviews

Advances in Experimental Social Psychology. (1964–). San Diego: Academic Press.

Advances in the Study of Behavior. (1965–). San Diego: Academic Press.

Annual Review of Anthropology. (1972–). Palo Alto, CA: Annual Reviews.

Annual Review of Applied Linguistics. (1980–). New York: Cambridge University Press.

Annual Review of Information Science and Technology. (1966–). Medford, NJ: Learned Information.

Annual Review of Psychology. (1950–). Palo Alto, CA: Annual Reviews.

Annual Review of Sociology. (1975–). Palo Alto, CA: Annual Reviews.

Communication Yearbook. (1977–). New York: Blackwell.

Free Speech Yearbook. (1961–). Washington, DC: National Communication Association.

German Communication Yearbook. (1999–). Cresskill, NJ: Hampton Press.

International and Intercultural Communication Annual. (1974–). Washington, DC: National Communication Association.

Progress in Communication Sciences. (1979–2001). Norwood, NJ: Ablex.

Research in Consumer Behavior. (1985–). Greenwich, CT: JAI Press.

Syntax and Semantics. (1972–). San Diego: Academic Press.

Series

Advances in Communication and Culture. (2000–). Stamford, CT: Ablex.

Advances in Discourse Processes. (1977–). Stamford, CT: Ablex.

Advances in Semiotics. (1976–). Bloomington: Indiana University Press.

Communication and Human Values. (1988–). Thousand Oaks, CA: Sage.

Communication & Information. (1992–). New Brunswick, NJ: Transaction Press.

Communication Series. (1992–). Cresskill, NJ: Hampton Press.

Critical Studies in Communication. (1992–). Boulder, CO: Westview.

International Topics in Media. (2000–). Ames: Iowa State University Press.

LEA's Communication Series. (1985–). Mahwah, NJ: Erlbaum.

Media Culture & Society. (1987–). Thousand Oaks, CA: Sage.

A Rhetorical History of the United States. (1994–). East Lansing: Michigan State University Press.

Sage Annual Reviews of Communication Research. (1972–1994). Thousand Oaks, CA: Sage.

Studies in Rhetoric/Communication. (1984–). Columbia: University of South Carolina Press.

SUNY Series in Communication Studies. (1998–). Albany: State University of New York Press.

SUNY Series in Computer-Mediated Communication. (1996–). Albany: State University of New York Press.

EXAMPLES

Jack decides to check out the meaning of the term *ghostwriting* by looking in *Wikipedia*. The short definition of *ghostwriter* found here wasn't much help. So, he also checks *New Directions in Political Communication: A Resource Book* for additional information. The index leads Jack to a discussion of political speeches of presidents, but it doesn't help much with specifics on ghostwriting.

Valerie's topic, voice mail, is new and specialized, so many of the general sources will not be useful. In looking through the encyclopedia list at the end of this chapter, however, one recent volume seems possible, *From Talking Drums to the Internet: An Encyclopedia of Communications Technology*. This volume is not in Valerie's library, so she orders it via interlibrary loan. She also looks the term up in the *International Encyclopedia of Communication*, but there is no listing for *voice mail*, only for *personal communication via CMC*. This provides some background information on mediated interpersonal communication.

Robin hits the jackpot in the *International Encyclopedia of Communication* for her attribution theory topic. There's a lengthy essay on attribution processes. Because this topic is an interpersonal one, several other sources are pertinent here: *Handbook of Communication Science, Handbook of Interpersonal Communication*, and *The Handbook of Social Psychology*. These sources will provide more than enough information for the class report. The index to volume 1 of *The Handbook of Social Psychology*, for instance, leads Robin to a three-page summary of attribution theory and its origins.

Jason's parasocial interaction topic receives only brief treatment in some textbooks or handbooks, but there is one volume of *Sage Annual Reviews of Communication Research* (Vol. 16, *Advancing Communication Science: Merging Mass and Interpersonal Processes*) that might be useful. Unfortunately, the volume lacks an index, and the table of contents doesn't contain listings that would be helpful. This topic is better approached through indexes (see Chapter 6).

Kat, Rocky, and **Michelle** look for handbooks on organizational conflict and find *The New Handbook of Organizational Communication*, Vol. 20 of the *Sage Annual Reviews* (Communication and Negotiation), *The Handbook of Group Communication Theory and Research*, and *The Handbook of Organization Studies*. They divide the labor, and each looks for relevant sources. *The New Handbook of Organizational Communication* has some relevant sections.

Eric, Anthony, Gregory, and **Scott** choose several handbooks on their topic—*The Handbook of Interpersonal Communication, The Handbook of Communication and Social Interaction Skills,* and *The Handbook of Family Communication*—and find several chapters in each that pertain to their topic. Relationship maintenance seems to be an important topic in the field, so these handbooks provide perspective on how researchers approach the topic and how they study it. Some of the references point out key individuals who work in this area, so the searching of the databases can be more direct and focused.

EXERCISES

1. For your group communication class, you have decided to write a report on some aspect of group conformity, but you still need to narrow your topic further. To get some background on research that has been done on various aspects of this subject, you consult *The Handbook of Group Communication Theory and Research.* Turning to the chapter that looks most promising (Chapter 11), you find a reference to a publication by Allen.
   a. On which page does the first reference to this article appear?
   b. By referring to the bibliography at the end of this essay, in which edited book do you find the piece?
2. You are a member of a small group in your organizational communication class that must plan a presentation on the culture within organizations. Your group decides to focus on organizational culture and turns to Jablin and Putnam's *The New Handbook of Organizational Communication* to find out more about it. In which chapter would this topic be explained for you?
3. To begin a research paper on propaganda, you consult a subject encyclopedia covering all the social sciences, the *International Encyclopedia of Communication,* to find an introductory essay. You find that an essay is devoted to this topic.
   a. In which volume and on which page does the essay begin?
   b. What is the title of the first book in the bibliography at the end of the essay?
4. You are preparing for a classroom discussion on social control and obedience in the workplace. You decide to examine one publisher's series described in this chapter, *Sage Annual Reviews of Communication Research,* for a survey of research in this area. It appears that one volume might be most appropriate for your topic.
   a. What is the title of the article in this volume that seems most closely related to your topic?

b. An essay by Bormann in 1983 is mentioned in this article. On which page is the first reference to this study found in the article?

c. In which book was the Bormann essay originally published?

5. You're doing a literature review in your advanced interpersonal communication class on interpersonal communication competence. One handbook, *The Handbook of Interpersonal Communication*, has a chapter that relates to your topic.

a. On which page does the chapter begin?

b. As you read through the chapter, what are three components of most definitions of *competence?*

6. Identify some situations in which a researcher would consult an edited textbook when doing communication research.

7. Browse through recent volumes of *Communication Yearbook*. What themes are prevalent? What questions are researchers asking?

8. List five articles from the *International Encyclopedia of Communication* you find interesting. Skim through each and identify five potential research topics you'd like to pursue. Choose one of these for a literature review.

9. Identify sources you discovered in this chapter that would be helpful in searching a communication topic and list them on your search strategy sheet.

chapter 6

Access Tools

The general sources identified in Chapter 5 should have helped you develop a precise research topic. Do not be concerned, though, if you find that you need to reword or refine the topic as your research progresses. This is normal. The more you learn about the topic, the more precisely you can state the research question. At this point our example topic, "The Use of Media in Organizations," could be narrowed to a research question: "What types of public interview training programs do organizations provide for their management personnel?" It is likely that we would once again alter this question, if only slightly, as we continue our search for more sources of information.

In this chapter we focus on three types of tools that provide access to information sources: bibliographies, guides, and indexes. If you are writing a research paper and have already found a bibliography pertinent to your topic in a handbook or annual review, you are well on the way to identifying sources to consult for more information on the topic. If you have not yet found a bibliography, this chapter should lead you to helpful ones. At this juncture in your research, you will want to start using your library's catalog to determine which books listed in the bibliographies you have found are owned by the library. You also will want to locate items published after these bibliographies were compiled. Note that following this search strategy means that your first approach to the library catalog is by the authors or titles of works you have already identified rather than by subject.

Besides books, you have probably identified periodical articles as a type of information source you need to obtain. Do you need articles in scholarly journals, trade or professional journals, newsmagazines, or newspapers? Perhaps you want to find reviews of the books you've already located. At this point you've probably already identified some relevant articles through careful review of bibliographies, but you'll no doubt need more. Are websites and webpages appropriate for your topic? If you've done a web search, you might have already stumbled across periodical articles that seem pertinent.

You need to evaluate these carefully to assess their quality. They, too, might include references to other periodical articles.

In this chapter we explain the different types of periodical indexes available and how they can help you identify particular types of articles. We describe access tools devoted to communication journals and those for related disciplines, general and interdisciplinary tools, and media indexes. We also cover a special type of tool, citation indexes, in which the primary access point is a *cited author* rather than a subject heading or keyword. Most periodical indexes are now available online, so you will get a lot of practice using the electronic search strategies from Chapter 3. In Chapter 8 we examine sources such as media indexes and government publications and concentrate on specialized access tools—those dealing with collections and archives of original media sources (such as newspapers, television, and film) and documents of the U.S. government.

Not all research topics, of course, benefit from including the sources found using the specialized **finding tools** for media and government sources. For example, there are few government publications on "Eye Contact in Initial Interactions." However, research on other topics, such as "The Effect of Television Violence on Children" or "The Impact of Government Regulation on the Operation of Cable Television," are incomplete without these specialized sources.

Once you have examined and used the sources listed in this chapter, you will have a fairly comprehensive list of sources (books, articles, and so on) to consult in the research process and to consider including in the bibliography of a research paper.

BIBLIOGRAPHIES

The idea of a **bibliography** as a list of citations to sources needs little introduction, particularly if you are currently compiling such a list. Your final product will probably fit the definition of a **selective topical bibliography**. This is a carefully chosen list of materials on a given topic. Like many (but by no means all) bibliographies, yours will include several types of sources, such as books, periodical articles, websites, and government documents, which you have identified using many types of references. Because each of your citations will include complete bibliographic information, another researcher will be able to use and build upon the work you do.

You will want to use bibliographies to take advantage of the work others have already done in selecting and compiling sources relevant to your topic. As we saw in Chapter 2, tracking down the leads provided by bibliographies to find additional sources is a crucial research strategy. Other authors might even have provided the additional service of annotating their bibliographies—that is, giving a brief summary of the content of the article or book and possibly commenting on its quality. Here is a relatively recent **annotated bibliography**:

Sterling, C. H., & Shiers, G. (2000). *History of telecommunications technology: An annotated bibliography*. Lanham, MD: Scarecrow.

■ This annotated bibliography contains more than 2,500 entries concerning the history of technology in communication over the past 175 years. Chapters focus on serials, company histories, biographies, television, newer technologies, and so on. Extensive name and title indexes help users find specific sources of interest.

Selective topical bibliographies, such as those compiled for research papers and literature reviews, are often appended bibliographies—that is, they are attached to the end of an article, chapter, book, or web document. The bibliographies found in encyclopedias, handbooks, and yearbooks also are examples of **appended bibliographies**. Such bibliographies in other publications can be more difficult to find, but the *Bibliographic Index* does provide a systematic and efficient way of locating both appended and book-length bibliographies. Check your library to see whether it subscribes to either the online or print version of this useful index.

Some book-length bibliographies are similar to appended bibliographies in that they are topical (devoted to one specific topic, such as nonverbal communication), whereas others are general. A **general bibliography**, such as the following one, can be more useful at the beginning of the search process, when you are still choosing and narrowing a topic.

Blum, E., & Wilhoit, F. (1990). *Mass media bibliography: An annotated, selected list of books and journals for reference and research* (3rd ed.). Urbana: University of Illinois Press.

■   This annotated bibliography of 2,100 sources in mass communication serves as a reference tool for locating research materials. The entries identify mass communication sources on such topics as theory, structure, economics, and effects. Annotated entries are arranged according to media: general (two or more media); broadcast (radio and television); print (newspapers, books, and periodicals); film; and advertising and public relations. The source includes lists of mass communication bibliographies, annuals, journals, and indexes. There are author-title and subject indexes that refer users to entry numbers.

Many valuable general book-length and topical bibliographies are published for communication researchers. A listing of several bibliographies, which represent a variety of subject areas and have been published within the past 15 or so years, is at the end of this chapter.

The bibliographies described thus far are known as **retrospective bibliographies**. This means they appear at a particular point in time and are not updated. The type of bibliography that appears in *The Handbook of Social Psychology* (Gilbert et al., 1998), for example, includes sources (such as books, research articles, and government documents) that have appeared since the topic was first investigated. Retrospective bibliographies, then, lend historical perspective to the research area.

In contrast, **current bibliographies** are published regularly—monthly, **semiannually**, or yearly. Each issue lists books and sometimes articles that have been published since the previous issue. Current bibliographies lead you to contemporary investigations and writings. Not many current bibliographies are published specifically for communication, although bibliographies appended to **review articles** on regularly recurring topics in the annual editions of *Communication Yearbook* sometimes fulfill this function. One useful current annotated bibliography, which is published **quarterly**, is the following:

Communication Booknotes Quarterly: CBQ. (1998–). Mahwah, NJ: Erlbaum.

■   This quarterly is an annotated bibliography of new works in mass communication, telecommunications, and the information industry. Each issue describes more than 100 books, periodicals, reports, government documents, and reference sources from the United States and abroad. Coverage includes books and publishing, public relations, cable television, international media, journalism history and law, ethics, motion pictures, political communication, popular culture, health communication, radio, television programming and impact, television production and aesthetics, Internet and technology, and women and communication. Editors and contributors also annotate sources from other countries and regions, and provide review essays about related works. The publication was titled *Mass Media Booknotes* from 1969 to 1981 and *Communication Booknotes* from 1982 to 1997. The final issue each year includes author and cumulative annual indexes. An online version is available by subscription from **<http://www.tandf.co.uk/journals/HCBQ>.**

Communication researchers working in some subject areas may find it useful to check the current bibliographies of related disciplines, such as business, political science, philosophy, sociology, and psychology. A listing of some of these is provided at the end of the chapter.

Locating satisfactory bibliographies on a topic can sometimes be difficult. An option available in this case is to seek out the most comprehensive of bibliographies—those of national libraries. The Library of Congress attempts to collect copies of all significant publications available in the United States. It contributes its cataloging records to a national **union catalog**, *WorldCat*, maintained by **Online Computer Library Center (OCLC)** and available through its FirstSearch collection of databases. Besides the records contributed by the Library of Congress, *WorldCat* includes cataloging records from most academic and public libraries in the United States. Searching *WorldCat* is an effective way of updating information sources you have located in retrospective bibliographies, such as Blum and Wilhoit's (1990) *Mass Media Bibliography*.

Ask a reference librarian to find out what type of access the library provides to this and other large union catalogs. Keep in mind, though, when using comprehensive bibliographies, that works are included not because they are necessarily authoritative or important but simply because they exist. Before going to some trouble (using interlibrary loan, e.g.) to obtain a copy of a book you have identified through this catalog, it would be wise to find more information about it and to determine its relative worth (see Chapter 2). Look carefully at the subject headings assigned to the book in *WorldCat* or other catalogs to see whether it's really pertinent to your topic. Be sure that you have looked at the *full*, not merely the *brief* record for the item. If you do so, you might find that the catalog includes the book's table of contents, as is often the case for books published in recent years. Do a web search to see whether you can find the publisher's description of the book and, often, its table of contents. Finally, look for a review of the book, using an appropriate periodical index.

GUIDES TO THE LITERATURE

One particularly useful type of bibliography is called a *guide*. **Guides to the literature** are broad bibliographies made up primarily of reference works and periodicals available in a given subject field or fields. Many guides also list and describe organizations that can lead you to sources of information outside of libraries. Guides describe the basic organization of the field's literature and the processes and techniques of literature searches peculiar to that field. Thus they can orient you to the literature of fields with which you are not familiar.

As you become acquainted with different types of reference works and their uses, you will probably realize at some point in a literature search that you need a particular type of reference work—a dictionary of statistics or an annual review of psychology, for example. A guide to the literature can often help you identify such a source. The following is a general guide that covers the literature of many subject fields:

Kieft, R. H. (2008). *Guide to reference* (12th ed.). Chicago: American Library Association.

■ This source helps locate a listing and evaluation of reference works. The reference works are arranged under broad headings: General Reference Works, Humanities, Social Science, History and Area Studies, and Pure and Applied Sciences. Within each of these groups, the listings are broken down by narrower subject fields and by type of publication (such as bibliography or dictionary). An index provides access by title, author, and subject. An online edition of this source, *Guide to Reference*, is available for individual or institutional subscription.

The following guide is a good introduction to the literature of the social sciences:

Herron, N. L. (Ed.). (2002). *The social sciences: A cross-disciplinary guide to selected sources* (3rd ed.). Englewood, CO: Libraries Unlimited. (Available through *NetLibrary*)

■ One chapter of this guide is devoted to the general reference literature of the social sciences and one chapter to statistics and demography. Each of the remaining 12 chapters covers the literature of a particular discipline (including communication). Other disciplines covered are political science, economics and business, history, law and legal issues, anthropology, sociology, education, psychology, and geography. Essays on the nature of each discipline and its literature introduce each chapter, followed by fully annotated listings of reference works.

If you're trying to find topics for speeches, Congressional Quarterly publishes a weekly guide to topics of interest:

CQ Researcher. (1992–). Washington, DC: Congressional Quarterly.

■ In each issue, this guide identifies a topic of national concern faced in the United States. The issue is thoroughly discussed, background is provided, the current situation is explained, and a bibliography of sources is provided. These are published weekly and are compiled in a loose-leaf binder with an annual bound **accumulation**. Cumulative indexes cover the five most recent years. It is also available online in many libraries. Check in the reference area of the library or in the library's list of online resources.

Other guides deal with a specific field of study. For example, Cates's (2004) *Journalism: A Guide to the Reference Literature* identifies sources and writing methods helpful for those conducting research in journalism. In addition, the following work has several uses, one of which is to serve as a guide to research in mass communication:

Sterling, C. H., Bracken, J. K., & Hill, S. M. (1997). *Mass communications research resources: An annotated guide.* Mahwah, NJ: Erlbaum.

■ This guide presents selected publications and research sources in mass communication. Its 10 chapters describe bibliographic and selected secondary resources in general reference areas, such as bibliographies, dictionaries, databases, indexes, and abstracts; history, including archives and libraries; technology, such as patents and technical standards; industry and economics, including associations, organizations, and annual reports; content, such as secondary resources; research and audiences, including research organizations and media education; policy and regulation, including government sources and policy; international arenas, such as international satellites and United Nations agencies; periodicals, including international and legal sources; and audiovisual resources, including technology, and industry and economics. Two appendixes describe how to find library materials and how to read Library of Congress subject headings.

And the following guide promises to be useful for students planning a career in organizational communication or business.

Belanger, S. E. (2005). *Business and technical communication: An annotated guide to sources, skills, and samples*. Westport, CT: Praeger.

■ This guide provides both academic and practical sources for business communicators. Chapter 1 contains research guides, bibliographies, dictionaries, encyclopedias, directories, handbooks, and quotations. Chapter 2 lists research resources such as abstracts, indexes, electronic databases, periodicals, newsletters, and websites. Chapter 3 details information sources such as associations, hotlines, research institutions, and government agency addresses. Chapter 4 overviews written and oral communication skills. Examples of written models are in Chapter 5 (e.g., annual reports, brochures, cover letters, manuals, newsletters, résumés) and oral models are in Chapter 6 (e.g., interview tips, telephone skills, listening, conducting meetings, public speaking). Name, title, and subject indexes are provided.

This work and a few of the other guides available for disciplines related to communication are listed at the end of this chapter.

Legal Research Guides

Legal research poses some interesting complexities to communication students. Students of debate, media policy and regulation, freedom of speech, and conflict, among others, often need to consult legal literature in their research endeavors. Just as the field of communication is constantly changing, so are the everyday legal decisions that affect the operations of communication organizations, the expression of ideas in a society, and the formulation of public policy.

Like the literature of other fields, the legal literature consists of primary sources, secondary sources, and finding tools. Primary sources include legislative statutes, court decisions, executive orders, administrative agency decisions and rules, and treaties. These are the enforceable rules of a society. Secondary sources include legal textbooks, dictionaries, and encyclopedias (some of which we listed at the end of Chapter 5). They also include commentaries, periodicals, restatements, and document sourcebooks. Their purpose is to describe and explain the law. Finding tools ease access to the many legal statutes and court decisions. Bibliographies, citators (i.e., citation indexes for legal cases), computerized search services such as LEXIS and Westlaw, indexes, law digests, loose-leaf services (see Chapter 8), and legal research guides provide the means of locating primary sources.

Although further explanation of legal research is beyond our scope, there are several legal research guides you can consult. These guides focus on primary, secondary, and finding-tool sources. They describe the legal process and legal research procedures as well as standard legal and citation forms. They often include identification of legal abbreviations and a glossary of legal terms. They serve not only as guides to the literature but also as manuals for conducting legal research. Several of these guides are listed at the end of this chapter. One especially useful legal research guide is:

> Mersky, R. M., Dunn, D. J., & Jacobstein, J. M. (2002). *Fundamentals of legal research* (8th ed.). New York: Foundation Press.

> ■ This guide accomplishes three purposes. First, it explains the legal process and research procedures. Second, it details primary sources (such as federal court decisions, federal legislation, and administrative law), secondary sources (such as legal periodicals and legal encyclopedias), and finding tools (such as court report digests, annotated law reports, loose-leaf services, and citators). Third, it describes international law, English legal research, federal tax research, and computers in legal research. Among the appendixes are a glossary of legal abbreviations, state guides to legal research, state reports, and coverage of the national reporter system. There is a subject-source index.

Finding Additional Bibliographies and Guides

We list many book-length bibliographies and literature guides at the end of this chapter, and new ones appear each year. You can search for these using library catalogs and *WorldCat*. The Library of Congress (LC) subject heading *bibliography* is usually assigned as part of the subject heading for both bibliographies and guides to the literature. Sometimes the subject heading *reference books* is also assigned. For example, these LC subject headings were assigned to *Journalism: A Guide to the Reference Literature*:

> Journalism–Bibliography
> Reference books–Journalism

You also can do keyword searches combining *bibliography* AND/OR *reference books* with broad subject areas or narrower topical terms. For example:

> communication AND bibliography
> mass media AND reference books
> telecommunications AND bibliography
> radio AND bibliography
> television violence AND bibliography

If the catalog you are using allows you to restrict terms to particular fields (as *WorldCat* does), try restricting the search for *bibliography* to the subject headings field. As always, examine the subject headings of any records retrieved to find additional access points (more specific or broader subject headings, authors, and so on). If you sort them by descending date, you'll be sure to find the most recent ones.

Bibliographies on the World Wide Web

Scholars and students frequently "publish" bibliographies on the web. Although they vary in length and quality and must be evaluated carefully (see Chapters 2 and 3), some can be very useful. Identifying them can be difficult. One place to look is on websites maintained by associations, journals, and academic institutions. For example, the website maintained by the Poynter Institute <**http://www.poynter.org/**> includes bibliographies on several broad journalism-related topics, including broadcast journalism, politics and the press, media ethics, new media, presidential debates, and many others. Some attempt is made to update them. The website also provides links to other journalism-related websites.

Search engines also can be used to find bibliographies rather easily, using the following method. Assuming you've already found several good citations, start by selecting one that appears to be substantial. Ideally, the author is one you've already identified as important, and the article should have a distinctive title. Longer titles will work better than shorter ones. Enter the article title in the search box, enclosing it in quotes. If you've chosen well, you are likely to get some hits for documents that cite the article. There's a good chance they include a bibliography that is at least peripherally related to the topic. Of course, you can use the same technique to search any full-text database in which the text of articles is searchable.

PERIODICAL INDEXES

The primary purpose of **periodical indexes** is to provide access to articles in journals, magazines, and newspapers. A few include other types of publications as well, such as government reports, dissertations, and book chapters.

Though many began publication in print format, most periodical indexes are now available online. The electronic versions of these tools incorporate many features and conveniences that greatly increase their efficiency, scope, and power. They usually offer the searcher at least these standard access points: subject heading, keyword, author, article title, and periodical title. Thus, although you will most often search indexes by subject or keyword, indexes offer other options that often come in handy. In addition, most searches can be limited by publication year and language. Many now allow you to limit results to *peer-reviewed* or scholarly journals, a particularly useful feature when searching comprehensive indexes that include several types of periodicals. Of course, fewer access points are available for printed indexes, most of which can be searched only by subject and author.

Records in these databases typically include these fields: author, title, subject headings, periodical title, volume, date of publication, and page numbers. Periodical indexes also usually include abstracts, or summaries, of each article, allowing you to see whether the original source is relevant to the topic. A few online periodical indexes even offer bibliographies of articles they include, making it possible to find related articles, and sometimes link to the full text in HTML format or downloadable as a PDF file.

We now include in the category *periodical indexes* many access tools that started off as **abstracting services** or, simply, **abstracts**. In the not-too-distant past, periodical indexes did not provide summaries, and one had to turn to abstracting services to find these. Now the distinction between the two types of tools has faded. Most abstracting services useful for communication researchers are now available on the Internet.

Abstracts provide a valuable service. By supplying condensed versions of articles, they allow you to find relevant sources efficiently. It is important, though, not to rely on abstracts at the expense of the original works. The original sources contain essential information about the research problem, procedures, findings, and conclusions. You need to read and review these fully, especially if you are going to list these sources in bibliographies, literature reviews, and research reports.

As mentioned above, an increasing number of periodical indexes are moving beyond abstracts to include the full text of a significant portion of the articles indexed. Such **full-text databases** can be a real boon to the researcher, providing the ultimate in convenience. But *full text* can mean several different things. It often means that the article text can be easily viewed and printed, using your browser's Print function, but that accompanying graphics (such as photographs, illustrations, charts, and graphs) will be missing. Furthermore, page numbers will not be available for citing particular passages. If the graphics are included, the databases are said to be **full-image** (or **image databases**). Viewing and printing full-image database searches can be a bit more complicated, often requiring Adobe Acrobat or another such computer program. Some databases offer you a choice of format: full text or full image (sometimes called PDF format). The full-image format will provide a replica of the article as it appeared in print format; photographs or graphs will be included, and the page numbers will be available for citing quotations.

The full-text articles included in periodical databases may or may not be searchable. In other words, if you're searching a full-text searchable database and you enter the search term *asynchronous*, you will retrieve any article that includes that term anywhere in the article, even if it is not included in the subject headings, abstract, or title. This capability can come in handy on those occasions when you want to find articles that mention something too obscure to be included as a subject heading or mentioned in an abstract.

There are differences among a database, a database producer, a database interface, and a database vendor. For example, if your instructor asks you to report on which databases you used in your research, you don't want to give the name of the vendor or its interface rather than the name of the database. When you are looking for a particular database, you shouldn't be confused by the prominently displayed name of the vendor or the search interface.

Some companies produce databases, some develop a proprietary search interface and distribute (or vend) databases, and some do both. Databases are often distributed by multiple vendors. In Table 6.1 we identify some vendors, interfaces, databases, and producers. This is not meant to be a comprehensive listing of vendors, but it does include many of those you're likely to come across. You should assume that the details (interface names, database names, who offers what) will change from year to year.

What difference does this make to you? You may become accustomed to and prefer a particular vendor's search interface. This might lead you to seek out databases from that vendor. But, because libraries have to limit the number of vendors they use, you will probably have limited choices. In any case, you should be a knowledgeable consumer and focus on the quality and characteristics of the

Table 6.1 Some Database Vendors

Vendor	Interface	Sample Databases	Database Producer
Ovid/SilverPlatter	WebSPIRS	*PsycINFO*	American Psychological Association (APA)
		ERIC	ERIC
OCLC (Online Computer Library Center)	FirstSearch	*ABI Inform*	ProQuest
		PsycINFO	APA
		Social Sciences Abstracts	H. W. Wilson
		ERIC	*ERIC*
		Sociological Abstracts	Sociological Abstracts/CSA
EBSCO	EBSCOhost	*Academic Search Complete*	EBSCO
		Communication & Mass Media Complete	EBSCO
		Psychology & Behavioral Sciences Complete	EBSCO
		Educational Research Complete	EBSCO
ProQuest	ProQuest Direct	*ABI/Inform Complete*	ProQuest
		Proquest Research Library	ProQuest
Gale/Cengage	InfoTrac	*Expanded Academic ASAP*	Gale/Cengage
H. W. Wilson	WilsonWeb	*Social Sciences Full Text*	H. W. Wilson
		Humanities Full Text	H. W. Wilson
CSA (Cambridge Scientific Abstracts	Illumina	*CSA/Sociological Abstracts*	Sociological Abstracts/CSA
		Communication	Sage
		AbstractsPAIS International	CSA

underlying database rather than the vendor and the names they have chosen to market their products.

Notice that many of the statements we've made are qualified by terms such as *many*, *most*, and *usually*. Databases differ, and you need to be aware of these differences in order to select the right database for the job. For starters, you need to know the subject area, type of periodicals indexed, and time period.

There are several questions to consider when choosing a database. For example, if you're looking for something recent, how often is the database updated? What access points are available? In what ways can searches be limited? Does the database index primarily scholarly journals, trade publications, popular magazines, or a mixture of all three? Can you limit your results to peer-reviewed journals? Does the search interface offer other useful special features? If you're looking for something that is extremely specific, you will want to select a database with searchable full text.

As you search, learn to evaluate the subject headings used in different databases critically. Some have excellent specific subject headings and assign them consistently. Others use broad subject headings with little apparent consistency. Consider how many headings are assigned to each record. Some databases don't add subject headings at all, so you'll need to develop complete lists of synonyms. These factors must be taken into account as you decide how to formulate your search. Don't use a cookie-cutter approach. A search that works well in one database should be adjusted when you search another database. One source helpful for selecting terms to use when searching communication literature is:

> Knapp, S. D. (2000). *The contemporary thesaurus of search terms and synonyms: A guide for natural language computer searching* (2nd ed.). Phoenix: Oryx Press.

As you search and retrieve items, remember that you're going to be following through on these parts of the search strategy outlined in Chapter 2:

- Examine and evaluate the citations retrieved.
- Identify additional access points (keywords, subject headings, authors, titles) and reformulate search queries to narrow, broaden, or improve focus, as needed.
- Evaluate citations retrieved, selecting items worth retrieving.
- Examine bibliographies for additional leads.

Discipline-Based Periodical Indexes

Indexes devoted to the periodical literature of specific disciplines are often more useful for research papers and literature reviews because they list the articles published in the scholarly journals read by professionals in that field. Unfortunately, no one index covers all communication and communication-related journals, but several indexes can be used together to obtain broad coverage of the field. Fortunately, since the last edition of this book, much progress has been made in providing online access to these indexes.

One online periodical index, *ComAbstracts*, is produced by the Communication Institute for Online Scholarship (CIOS). It is available to users from member institutions.

> Communiction Institute for Online Scholarship (CIOS). (1990–). *ComAbstracts*. Albany, NY: Author.
>
> - Available through CIOS membership is access to *ComAbstracts*, a web-based database that indexes and provides abstracts for more than 55,000 articles in over 70 communication journals. It can be searched by word, phrase, or author. Subject keywords are added to each record. This feature, together with keyword searching of abstracts, greatly improves its retrieval capabilities. *ComAbstracts* is updated on a continuous basis with both older and current material. Coverage for most journals starts in the 1980s. Detailed information on this important database can be found at: **<http://www.cios.org/www/aboutcomabstracts.htm>**.

A newer database provides more comprehensive coverage of communication and related journals.

> EBSCO. (2004–). *Communication & Mass Media Complete (CMMC)*. Ipswich, MA: Author.

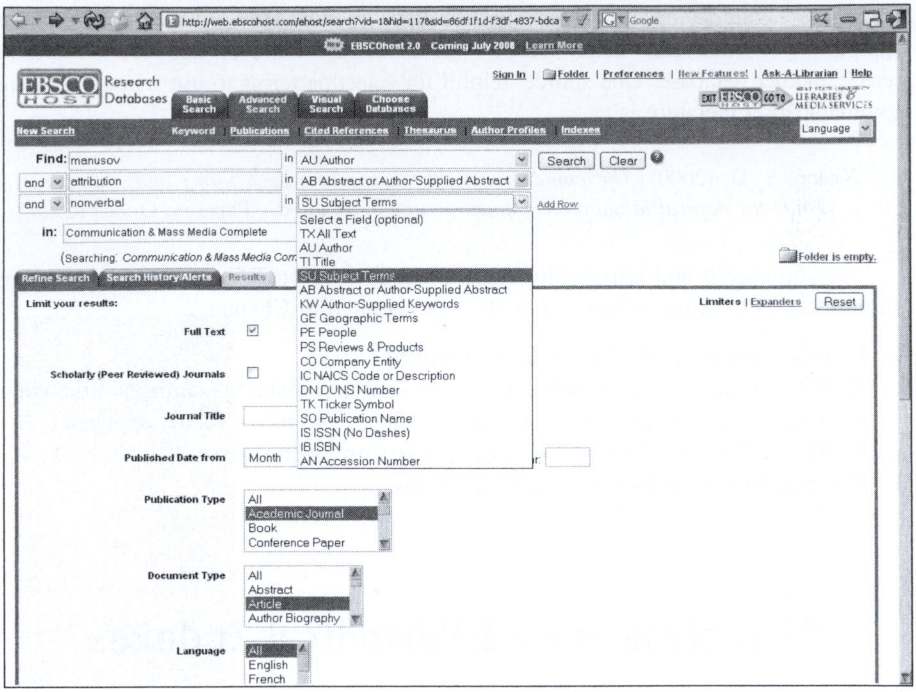

Figure 6.1 CMMC Search Screen

■ This database incorporates two former indexes: *CommSearch*, a CD-ROM database published by the National Communication Association, and *Mass Media Articles Index*, formerly produced by Pennsylvania State University. As part of *CommSearch*, the *Index to Journals in Communication Studies Through 1995*, long a favorite print resource for researchers in the field, is also incorporated. Coverage of many additional journals has been added, bringing the total to more than 285 journals indexed and abstracted in their entirety. Articles from about 100 other journals are indexed and abstracted when they are relevant to the communication field. This database includes the full text of more than 160 of the journals indexed. Monographs, conference proceedings, working papers and other types of publications also are indexed. National Communication Association members can access this free of charge through the *members* area of the NCA website, and many libraries subscribe to EBSCOhost, which includes this database.

As seen in Figure 6.1, you can search for several terms at once. You can search by the author's last name, by keyword, title, and by subject. You can even limit the results to English language academic journal articles, for example. As you can see at the bottom of the figure, two academic journal articles appeared in the results, and both were available as PDF full-text files.

Since its initial publication in 1978, *Communication Abstract*s has been the most widely used abstracting source in the field. Most major communication journals, related periodicals of allied fields, and many communication books are represented in these volumes. Now available online, it is much easier to search.

Sage Publications. (1978–). *Communication Abstracts*. Thousand Oaks, CA: Author.

■ This source comprehensively inspects the worldwide literature of communication and abstracts selected communication-related articles from over 160 periodicals, as well as relevant monographs, books, and research reports. *Communication Abstracts* includes paragraph-length summaries of journal articles and books, usually within the last year. More recent articles may need to be located in the journals, themselves.

Abstracts are listed alphabetically by the author's last name, and a complete subject guide is included in each issue. Among the many subjects covered are advertising, attitudes, broadcasting, broadcast regulation, communication technology, communication theory, consumer behavior, economic issues, group communication, health communication, information processing, intercultural communication, interpersonal communication, law, media effects, national development, news, organizational communication, political communication, public opinion, research methods, speech communication, and telecommunications.

Communication Abstracts is published six times per year, in February, April, June, August, October, and December, with an annual bound accumulation. Cumulative subject and author indexes for each year appear in the December issue. It has recently become available as a searchable database through Cambridge Scientific Abstracts. Additionally, ProQuest and CSA Illumina web-based information systems provide online access to it as a full-text journal, where it can be searched by keyword. Figure 6.2 contains the results of the same search we demonstrated in Figure 6.1. Note the additional reference found.

Note that the search screen examples we're providing might change over time. Often they're redesigned to add new features or ways to access the searching tools. Don't be too surprised if your screen isn't exactly like the ones we captured in mid-2008 as we wrote this book.

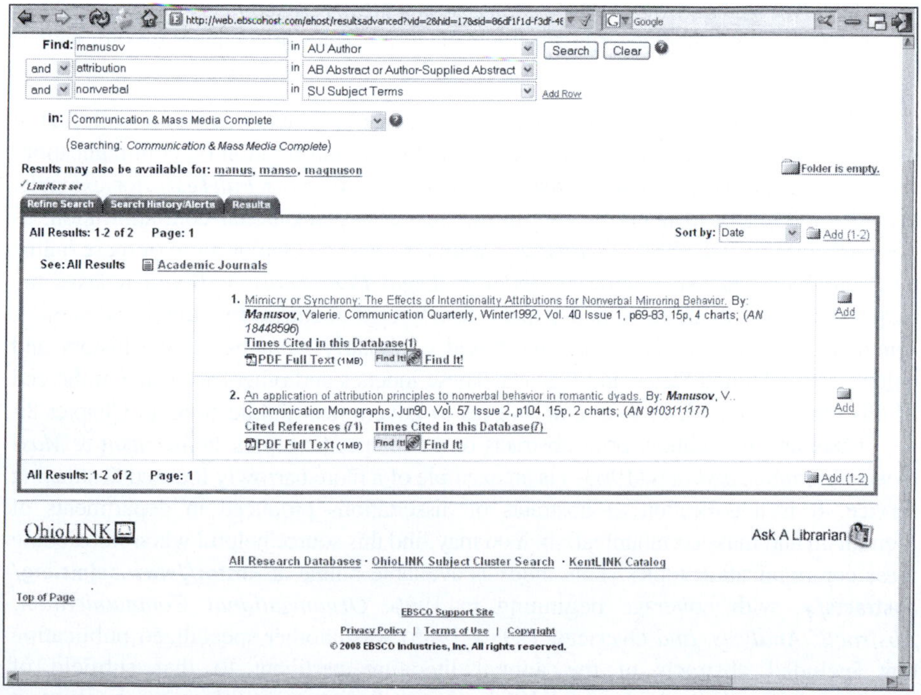

Figure 6.2 Communication Abstracts Search

Because communication is an interdisciplinary field, you should also use indexes and abstracts that concentrate on the journals of other disciplines but selectively include several communication journals. For example, *Journal of Communication* and the *Journal of Broadcasting & Electronic Media* have been referenced in both *Humanities Abstracts* and *Social Sciences Abstracts*, whereas *Communication Quarterly* and *Communication Research* have been covered by *Social Sciences Abstracts* and the *Quarterly Journal of Speech* by *Humanities Abstracts*. Researchers in psychology and sociology often publish communication-related articles, so inspection of these databases is also essential sources for communication researchers.

Communication researchers interested in education and related areas often turn to *ERIC*, a database produced with the aid of the Educational Resources Information Center (ERIC). It is available directly at **<http://www.eric.ed.gov/>** or can be accessed through OCLC's FirstSearch system, CSA's IDS system, or EBSCOHost.

Educational Resources Information Center. (1969–). *ERIC*. Washington, DC: Author.

■ *ERIC* covers journals (more than 800 periodicals) as well as documents and reports. *ERIC*'s coverage of a particular journal is often selective rather than cover to cover. The *ERIC* thesaurus includes many terms specific to communication studies. The descriptor *communication research* is used fairly consistently by *ERIC* for reports of research in the communication field, so if the initial search is too broad, adding this phrase to the search can be helpful. *ERIC* documents include research and project reports, bibliographies, books, curriculum materials, conference papers, and other materials. The number of journal articles and documents that are available full text vary from one database vendor to another. Conference papers can be ordered online for a minimal cost. *ERIC* contains the *Resources in Education* and *Current Index to Journals in Education* databases, both of which ceased in 2001. The online *ERIC* database, available at **<http://eric.ed.gov/>**, began in 2004. Before this time, libraries subscribed to periodical updates of computer files for patrons to use.

Many additional discipline-specific indexes are available, and you will find it useful to consult indexes from other fields that provide information on communication-related topics. Wilson *Business Abstracts* (or *Wilson Business FullText*), for example, provides references to many articles in the area of organizational communication, as does *ABI/Inform* and EBSCO's *Business Source Complete*. One or more of these online tools are found in many libraries. *Index to Legal Periodicals & Books* indexes the major legal journals in this country and a few foreign countries by author and subject. *America, History and Life* covers the world's scholarly literature on the history and culture of the United States and Canada. These indexes and others are listed at the end of this chapter. We identify several indexes to government publications in Chapter 8.

There are, in addition, print abstracts on more specific topics. *Journalism & Mass Communication Abstracts* (1963–) is an example of a more narrowly focused abstracting service. It is a collection of abstracts of dissertations produced in departments of journalism and mass communication. You may find this source helpful when researching mass communication topics. This index is available online at **<http://www.aejmc.org/abstracts/>**, with coverage beginning in 1996. *Organizational Communication: Abstracts, Analysis, and Overview* (1976–1985) was another specialized publication that included abstracts of the annual literature pertinent to that subfield of communication through the mid-1980s, but it isn't as useful today because it hasn't been updated and isn't available online. Other specialized abstracts are noted in the list at the end of the chapter.

General and Interdisciplinary Periodical Indexes

Most libraries subscribe to a comprehensive, interdisciplinary index. (Few libraries can afford more than one, and they are similar in coverage.) At present, several companies compete in producing these indexes: ProQuest , EBSCO, Gale Group (InfoTrac), and H. W. Wilson. In a competitive marketplace, the indexes these companies supply tend to be repackaged and renamed with some frequency. In 2008, four databases of this type that were found in the library included: *Academic Search Complete* (EBSCO: EBSCOhost), *Expanded Academic ASAP* (Gale Group: InfoTrac), *ProQuest General Reference* (ProQuest: ProQuest Direct), and *Wilson Omnifile Full Text Mega Edition* (H. W. Wilson: WilsonWeb).

These indexes provide access to a wide range of general interest magazines and scholarly journals. They cover business, education, social sciences, humanities, medicine, and general science, as well as a few newspapers. Most index more than 3,000 periodicals. All provide abstracts and—for half or more of the periodicals indexed—the full-text or full-image articles. The full text is optionally searchable. The availability of full text and, sometimes, full image and their ease of use make these very convenient and popular tools. *LexisNexis Academic*, another widely available interdisciplinary index, includes fewer scholarly journals but many more newspapers, law reviews, and trade journals; all sources are full text.

Media Indexes

Media indexes help you find newspaper materials, specific media sources, and reviews. Newspapers and media such as films and videotapes can provide communication students with useful information for research endeavors. They also serve as important working tools for communication professionals. Because these tools provide access to media collections (e.g., newspaper articles or television broadcasts), we discuss these fully in Chapter 8, along with the collections they access.

Book Review Indexes

Besides listing articles, many periodical indexes—including most of those discussed in this chapter—perform another service by referencing book reviews. Reviews appearing in the scholarly and professional journals covered by these and similar indexes are useful sources when you need to determine how scholars and other communication professionals have evaluated a particular work. One new online source containing reviews of Internet-related books is the *New Book Reviews in Cyberculture Studies*, available at **<http://www.com.washington.edu/rccs/booklist.asp/>**.

You can find reviews of works of a more general or popular nature by using indexes that consist entirely of listings of book reviews, such as *Book Review Digest* or

Book Review Index (both are available in print, online, and on CD-ROM). Several other indexes of this type are listed at the end of the chapter. Not to be overlooked as a good source of reviews of both general and scholarly books are such interdisciplinary indexes as *ProQuest General Reference, Academic Search, Expanded Academic Index*, and *Wilson Omnifile*.

Citation Indexes

We've already discussed the valuable role bibliographies play in research and their importance in a systematic search strategy. Often, our best leads come when we examine the bibliographies found at the end of journal articles, books, book chapters, annual reviews, encyclopedias, and other reference books. This is where authors acknowledge their debt to prior research, helping you identify key authors and works. One disadvantage of bibliographies, of course, is that the items cited necessarily have an older publication date. Thus, we must find the latest research using book catalogs and periodical indexes. To do so, we first need to determine the right subject heading and keyword searches. This process can be inexact, to say the least. Citation indexes provide an alternative way to do this updating that is in many ways more precise, direct, and effective.

Citation indexes compile the **cited references** from journal articles and selected books. When you use a citation index, you look up a reference to *a work that you know* to find articles *that have cited it*. For example, when researching political advertising you will find the following citation, which seems dated, in many bibliographies:

> Sears, D. O., & Freedman, J. L. (1967). Selective exposure to information: A critical review. *Public Opinion Quarterly, 31*, 194–213.

You look at the article and wonder what more recent information on the topic is available. It is likely that more current articles in this area will cite this work, so you consult a citation index under the first author's last name (Sears, D. O.). Here you find quite a few specific citations to this work, including:

> Kennamer, J. D. (1990). Self-serving biases in perceiving the opinions of others: Implications for the spiral of silence. *Communication Research, 17*, 393–404.

You determine that this is also an important work on your topic, so you look it up in the citation index to see where it has in turn been cited, and so on. This process can be quite productive in identifying works that are closely related to a topic.

The Institute for Scientific Information (ISI) publishes three citation indexes that cover most communication literature: *Arts & Humanities Citation Index, Social Sciences Citation Index*, and *Science Citation Index*. These are all accessible in ISI's *Web of Science*.

> Institute for Scientific Information. (1975–). *Arts & Humanities Citation Index.* Philadelphia: Author
> Institute for Scientific Information. (1956–). *Social Sciences Citation Index.* Philadelphia: Author.

Institute for Scientific Information. (1961–). *Science Citation Index*. Philadelphia: Author.

■ These multidisciplinary indexes cover the journal literature of the sciences, social sciences, and the arts and humanities. The *Social Sciences Citation Index* covers more than 1,700 journals and the *Arts & Humanities Citation Index* covers more than 1,100; these two are most useful for communication students. ISI citation databases are known collectively as *ISI Web of Science*, which may be the way they are identified in your library's listing of electronic databases.

Citations in the print version of these indexes are searched in an abbreviated format. For example, to search for the article just mentioned by J. D. Kennamer in *Communication Research*, you would enter *KENNAMER JD* as the cited author and *COMMUN RES* as the cited work. Journal abbreviations can be looked up online at the point of entry, so there is no need to be intimidated by this level of abbreviation. If you are using the print indexes, excellent instructions are available on the inside cover of each volume. In the online version, extensive help is also available.

FULL-TEXT DOCUMENTS IN COMMUNICATION

Most full-text documents (scholarly journal articles) in communication can be found in one of three databases, all of which are controlled by publishers who sell or contract subscriptions. *Communication & Mass Media Complete*, which is published by EBSCO, contains links to full-text articles, available in either HTML or PDF format (which requires a download of the Adobe Reader prior to use). Members of the National Communication Association can enter the EBSCO site and search for journal articles in the NCA journals and others they've contracted for. Then it's just a matter of downloading the PDF file for your own copy of the article.

The second database available from CIOS, or Communication Institute for Online Scholarship, not only allows searching, but links to the full text are available as well. Most of the articles are in PDF files, allowing the reader to see all tables, figures, and text as originally published.

The third database—*Sage Full-Text Collection*—contains more than a dozen journals published by Sage. Several of these are central to the communication discipline: *Communication Research, European Journal of Communication*, and *Management Communication Quarterly*. Others are also relevant but newer and with more limited circulations.

Communication researchers will find these tools to be useful for a full range of projects, from a short speech to a substantial research study. Most index a fair number of core communication journals, which can include full-text articles in communication journals to which your library does not otherwise subscribe. Their interdisciplinary nature makes them particularly worthwhile. Because these tools include popular as well as scholarly periodicals, students must distinguish among them to select sources appropriate for projects (see Chapter 7). Check to see whether the index you are using has the capability of limiting search results to journals that are **peer reviewed**, one of the characteristics of quality scholarly journals. (Articles in peer-reviewed journals when being considered for publication are evaluated by scholars in the field.)

Communication researchers looking for an interdisciplinary approach that is even more comprehensive should be aware of *Ingenta*, a periodical index and document delivery service that can be searched free of charge <**http://www.ingentaconnect.com/**>. Based on the tables of contents of periodicals, it is an example of a particular type of periodical index, a **table-of-contents service**.

> *Ingenta.* (1988–). Cambridge, MA: Ingenta.
>
> ■ This index covers more than 28,000 periodical titles. The table of contents of each journal issue can be displayed. Access points are keyword, author name, and journal title. There are real limitations. No subject headings are added, and there are no abstracts, unless they happen to appear in the table of contents. Thus, keyword searching does not generally provide an effective subject approach. However, *Ingenta* covers communication journals comprehensively and is searchable by author. Ingenta also offers a *journal alerting service* (or *current awareness service*) and, for a fee, will provide the full text of articles either online or via fax or e-mail. Before paying for this service, check with your library to see whether it can provide the article to you free of charge. Some libraries have site licenses for the journal-alerting service. This index was formerly known as *CARL UnCover*.

ArticleFirst, produced by OCLC, is another index based on the tables of contents of periodicals. It covers approximately 12,000 periodical titles.

SUMMARY

Bibliographies, guides, and indexes are tools that help provide access to additional information sources. Annotated bibliographies not only lead you to the sources but provide a summary of the content and often a comment about the worth of the source. Guides often sort the sources into different types, such as reference materials, periodicals, monographs, and so on. And indexes list basic reference information about periodicals, bibliographies, and book reviews. The ability to search indexes has become a critical research skill. Listed below are some additional access tools; where dates are listed for online sources, the date reflects the range of coverage rather than the date the website was created.

References

Blum, E., & Wilhoit, F. (1990). *Mass media bibliography: An annotated, selected list of books and journals for reference and research* (3rd ed.). Urbana: University of Illinois Press.

Cates, J. A. (2004). *Journalism: A guide to the reference literature* (3rd ed.). Englewood, CO: Libraries Unlimited.

Gilbert, D. T., Fiske, S. T., & Lindzey, G. (Eds.). (1998). *The handbook of social psychology* (4th ed., 2 vols.). Boston: McGraw-Hill.

Knapp, S. D. (2000). *The contemporary thesaurus of search terms and synonyms: A guide for natural language computer searching* (2nd ed.). Phoenix: Oryx Press.

SELECTED SOURCES

*Available Online

Bibliographies

Alred, G. J. (1997). *The St. Martin's bibliography of business and technical communication*. New York: St. Martin's.

Bibliographic Index. (1984–). New York: H. W. Wilson.

Catalog of Current Law Titles, Annual. (1991–). Buffalo, NY: Hein.

Communication Booknotes. (1969–1997). Washington, DC: Center for Telecommunications Studies, George Washington University.

Communication Booknotes Quarterly. (1998–). Mahwah, NJ: Erlbaum.

Greenberg, G. S. (1996). *Tabloid journalism: An annotated bibliography of English language sources*. Westport, CT: Greenwood Press.

Lent, J. A. (1999). *Women and mass communications in the 1990's: An international annotated bibliography*. Westport, CT: Greenwood Press.

Martin, J. B. (2002). *Mass media: A bibliography with indexes*. Hauppauge, NY: Nova Science.

National Union Catalog. (1953–2002). *N.U.C. books*. Washington, DC: Library of Congress. (Replaced by the Library of Congress Online Catalog; available: http://catalog.loc.gov/)

Nordquist, J. (2001). *Gender and racial images/stereotypes in the mass media: A bibliography*. Santa Cruz, CA: Reference and research services.

Northwest Regional Educational Laboratory. (1998). *Bibliography of assessment alternatives: Oral communication*. Portland, OR: Author.

Public Relations Society of America. (1996). *Bibliography for public relations professionals*. New York: Author.

Shiers, G. (1997). *Early television: A bibliographic guide to 1940*. New York: Garland.

WorldCat. (1978–). Dublin, OH: Online Computer Library Center.

Guides to the Literature

Aby, S. H., Nalan, J., & Fielding, L. (2005). *Sociology: A guide to reference and information sources* (3rd ed.). Westport, CT: Libraries Unlimited.

Asante, C. E. (1997). *Press freedom and development: A research guide and selected bibliography*. Westport, CT: Greenwood Press.

Awe, S. C. (1997). *ARBA guide to subject encyclopedias and dictionaries* (2nd ed.). Englewood, CO: Libraries Unlimited. (Available through *NetLibrary*)

Balay, R., Carrington, V. F., & Martin, M. S. (1996). *Guide to reference books* (11th ed.). Chicago: American Library Association.

Belanger, S. E. (2005). *Business and technical communication: An annotated guide to sources, skills, and samples*. Westport, CT: Praeger.

Bracken, J. K., & Sterling, C. H. (1995). *Telecommunications research resources: An annotated guide*. Mahwah, NJ: Erlbaum.

Cabott, J. H. (2001). *Human psychology: Index of new information with authors, subjects, research categories, and references*. Washington, DC: Abbe.

Cates, J. A. (2004). *Journalism: A guide to the reference literature* (3rd ed.). Westport, CT: Libraries Unlimited.

Chandler, Y. J. (2001). *Neal-Schuman guide to finding legal and regulatory information on the Internet* (2nd ed.). New York: Neal-Schuman.

*Dyer, C. (Ed.). (2002). *The Iowa guide: Scholarly journals in mass communication and related fields* (10th ed.). Iowa City: University of Iowa. (Available: http://fm.iowa.uiowa.edu/fmi/xsl/iowaguide/search.xsl)

Elias, S., Levinkind, S., & Stim, R. (2005). *Legal research: How to find and understand the law* (13th ed.). Berkeley, CA: Nolo.

Herron, N. L. (2002). *The social sciences: A cross-disciplinary guide to selected sources* (3rd ed.). Englewood, CO: Libraries Unlimited. (Available through *NetLibrary*)

Hoffman, F. W. (1995). *American popular culture: A guide to the reference literature*. Englewood, CO: Libraries Unlimited. (Available through *NetLibrary*)

Kelly, P. T. (1999). *Television violence: A guide to the literature* (2nd ed.). Commack, NY: Nova Science.

Martin, F. S., & Goehlert, R. (1996). *How to research Congress*. Washington, DC: Congressional Quarterly.

Mersky, R. M., Dunn, D. J., & Jacobstein, J. M. (2002). *Fundamentals of legal research* (8th ed.). New York: Foundation Press.

Morgan, J. (1996). *Film researcher's handbook: A guide to sources in North America, South America, Asia, Australasia and Africa*. New York: Routledge.

Moss, R. W., & Strauss, D. W. (2004). *Strauss's handbook of business information: A guide for librarians, students, and researchers* (2nd ed.). Westport, CT: Libraries Unlimited.

Reed, J. G., & Baxter, P. M. (2003). *Library use: Handbook for psychology*. Washington, DC: American Psychological Association.

Sterling, C. H., Bracken, J. K., & Hill, S. M. (1998). *Mass communications research resources: An annotated guide*. Mahwah, NJ: Erlbaum.

Walford, A. J. (Ed.). (2005). *The new Walford guide to reference resources*. London: Facet Publishing.

Ward, J., & Hansen, K. A. (1997). *Search strategies in mass communication* (3rd ed.). New York: Longman.

Wick, R. L., & Mood, T. A. (1998). *ARBA guide to biographical resources, 1986–1997*. Englewood, CO: Libraries Unlimited. (Available through *NetLibrary*)

Online Periodical Indexes and Abstracts

ABI/Inform Global. ProQuest.
Academic Search Complete. EBSCO.
Alt-PressWatch. ProQuest/Softline Information.
America, History and Life. ABC-CLIO.
American Humanities Index. EBSCO.
ArticleFirst. Online Computer Library Center (OCLC).
Arts & Humanities Citation Index. Institute for Scientific Information. (Available through *ISI Web of Science*)
ASHA. American Speech-Language-Hearing Association.
Book Review Digest. H. W. Wilson. (Available through Wilson Web)

Business Index ASAP. Gale Group.
Business Source Complete. EBSCO.
ComAbstracts. Communication Institute for Online Scholarship.
Communication Abstracts.: Sage/Cambridge Scientific Abstracts.
Communication & Mass Media Complete (CMMC). EBSCO.
Communication Studies: A SAGE Full-text Collection. Sage.
Computer Database. Thomson Gale.
CQ Researcher. Congressional Quarterly.
Dissertation Abstracts. University of Michigan, ProQuest.
Education Research Complete. EBSCO.
ERIC. Educational Resources Information Center.
Factiva. Dow Jones & Reuters.
Family Studies Abstracts. EBSCO.
Film & Television Literature Index with Full Text. EBSCO.
Gender Studies Database. EBSCO.
Gender Watch. ProQuest Information and Learning/Softline.
Global NewsBank. NewsBank.
Government Periodicals Universe. LexisNexis/Congressional Information Service.
Historical Abstracts. EBSCO.
Humanities Abstracts. New York: H. W. Wilson.
Humanities International Index. EBSCO.
Index to Legal Periodicals and Books. H. W. Wilson. (Available through *Wilson Omnifile Full Text Mega Edition*)
InfoTrac LegalTrac. Gale Group/InfoTrac.
InfoTrac OneFile. Gale Group.
Ingenta. Ingenta. (Formerly *Carl UnCover*)
International Abstracts of Human Resources. IAHR. (Formerly *Personnel Management Abstracts*)
ISI Web of Science. Institute for Scientific Information. (Contains *Arts-& Humanities Citation Index, Science Citation Index*, and *Social Sciences Citation Index*)
Journalism & Mass Communication Abstracts: M.A., M.S., Ph.D. Theses in Journalism and Mass Communication. Association for Education in Journalism and Mass Communication.
Legaltrac database. Information Access.
Lexis/Nexis Academic. Lexis/Nexis.
Library, Information Science & Technology Abstracts with Full Text. EBSCO.
Linguistics and Language Behavior Abstracts. Sociological Abstracts/Cambridge Scientific Abstracts.
PAIS International. OCLC Public Affairs Information Service. (*PAIS International in Print* formed from merger of *PAIS Bulletin* and *PAIS Foreign Language Index*)
Periodical Contents Index. OCLC.
Philosopher's Index. Ovid Technologies.
ProQuest. ProQuest Information and Learning.
PsycINFO. American Psychological Association.
Psychology & Behavioral Sciences Collection. EBSCO.
Public Administration Abstracts. EBSCO.
Readers' Guide to Periodical Literature. H. W. Wilson.

Resources in Education. Government Printing Office. (Included in the *ERIC* database)

Sage Public Administration Abstracts. Sage.

Science Citation Index. Institute for Scientific Information. (Included in *ISI Web of Science*)

Social Sciences Citation Index. Institute for Scientific Information. (Included in *ISI Web of Science*)

Social Sciences Full Text. H. W. Wilson.

SocINDEX with Full Text. EBSCO.

Sociological Abstracts. Sociological Abstracts/Cambridge Scientific Abstracts.

WilsonBusiness. H. W. Wilson.

Wilson Omnifile Full Text Mega Edition. H. W. Wilson. (Combines *Readers' Guide to Periodical Literature, General Science Abstracts, Wilson Social Science Abstracts, Humanities Abstracts*, and others)

Women's Studies International. EBSCO. (Formerly *Women's Resources International*; includes *Women's Studies Abstracts*)

EXAMPLES

Jack decides to use *ComAbstracts* to find articles on ghostwriting. By entering the term *ghost*, he finds several relevant articles.

Valerie decides it's time to look at some newspaper abstracts to find other reporters' stories on voice mail. *Factiva* seems a fairly general and far-reaching source, so that is a good place to start. This search reveals several recent articles on this phenomenon. She also decides to use *LexisNexis Academic*. Both include major papers such as the *New York Times*, but *LexisNexis* includes a wider array of smaller newspapers and other periodicals.

Robin has now read several summary articles about attribution. Because the term originated in psychology, she decides to search the *PsycINFO* database. Looking only in the past 5 years for English-language peer-reviewed journal articles about humans, Robin finds there are more than 1,000 articles focused on this topic. So she combines (*AND*) the results with a search focused on the subject *communication*; this reduces the search to two items. She e-mails herself the search results along with the abstracts so that she can make an informed decision about which articles to read.

Jason's discovery that the term *parasocial interaction* was coined by Horton and Wohl in 1956 allows for a *Social Sciences Citation Index* search. By entering the relevant information about this original article, Jason can identify the citations of all articles that cited this original piece. This is especially fruitful for tracing research in this area over the years. Other relevant indexes and abstracts to search for this topic are *PsycINFO, Sociological Abstracts*, and *Communication & Mass Media*

Complete. By searching all these, Jason should have the many articles needed for a thorough literature review of parasocial interaction.

Kat, **Rocky**, and **Michelle's** training program will undoubtedly benefit from the use of educational media. They consult the *NICEM AV Database* from the National Information Center for Educational Media and find several conflict-oriented videos. Kat and Rocky volunteer to find some reviews and then preview those that are most appropriate.

Scott, **Anthony**, **Gregory**, and **Eric** decide to look in electronic abstracts and collections. Scott chooses *PsychINFO* and finds 7 articles with *email* in the title, 2 with *e-mail*, and 209 with *family*, but none of these articles has both *e-mail* and *family*. Greg looks in CIOS's *ComAbstracts* and finds one article on e-mail and family. Anthony examines the *Communication & Mass Media Complete* database and finds 2 articles with both terms but decides to expand the search to the full text of the article; this results in 82 possible articles. And Eric looks at Sage's *Communication Abstracts* and finds 42 possible articles on *e-mail/email* and *family*. The abstracts help pare down this list to the most relevant.

EXERCISES

1. You are not having much luck with your literature search and notice that the few articles you have managed to find on your topic have appeared in journals in allied disciplines, mostly sociology. You turn to a guide to the literature of the social sciences, *The Social Sciences: A Cross-Disciplinary Guide to Selected Sources*, to identify sources in that discipline that can help you in your search. Use the subject index to:
   a. Find the entry number of the first literature guide listed under this discipline.
   b. Give the title of this guide.

2. By using the bibliographies of subject encyclopedias and other standard texts, you have found several references to a 1972 article by M. E. McCombs and D. Shaw published in *Public Opinion Quarterly*. It appears to be a key piece of research on your topic. Unfortunately, this study is several years old. To identify research done at a later time that you hope will update the article, you turn to the online version of the *Social Sciences Citation Index*.
   a. Who is the author of the last article listed that cites your key article?
   b. In what journal and year did this appear?
   c. What is the title of this article?

3. You are doing research on interpersonal communication. Subject bibliographies have been useful, but you wish to find other sources for your literature search. To find summaries of research on your topic, you are now using *Communication Abstracts*. Search for *interpersonal communication*.
   a. How many entries did you find?
   b. This appears quite broad. Try AND-ing the results with *trust*. How many entries result from this?

4. When doing research for a term paper in your intercultural communication class, you have been fortunate to find plenty of background information on your topic, multicultural training, but nothing on research done in this area since 1990. Because you feel the topic of interviewing is likely to be of interest to educators, you believe online searching of *ERIC* would be a good finding tool.
   a. Turning first to the online thesaurus, what descriptors do you find used for your topic? In other words, to what descriptors are you referred? Choose the first one.
   b. Search the database from 1990 to the present. How many sources did you find?
   c. E-mail the results to your e-mail account.
5. Complete your search strategy sheet by adding sources from this chapter that will help lead you to primary sources. Have your instructor check your list before you begin examining each source for your topic.
6. Examine issues of *Communication & Mass Media Index* in class and read some of the abstracts. Is your topic area a keyword? If not, which keywords lead you to articles in this area?
7. List the steps necessary for searching *ComAbstracts*, selecting articles and determining whether your library provides access to them, either in print or electronically. Try locating sources for your topic.

chapter 7

Communication Periodicals

In previous chapters we identified important books for researching communication topics and suggested how a book might be judged a standard or viable work. We've also described the tools used to identify periodical articles. In this chapter we focus on the periodicals containing these original research reports, articles on communication industry practices, and other original information.

We first discuss the major scholarly journals in communication. We describe the content and publisher of each journal. Any research study, literature review, or prospectus in communication typically references several articles in these journals. Articles found in professional and trade magazines are less scholarly in nature in that they are usually not original research studies. These periodicals contain data on industry trends along with industry news, opinion, and thought essays. They allow industry professionals to keep abreast of developments in their field. They contain useful information for communication students. For example, we can turn to them to find out about organizational management-training programs for dealing with the media.

Periodicals are publications with distinctive titles that are published on a regular basis. Communication periodicals are useful when researching any communication topic. Examine these sources during the research process and consider including them in research paper assignments. Be aware of their potential value in the future. In many careers, knowledge of these sources provides a means of networking and gives professionals a deeper understanding of the issues and research in the field.

SCHOLARLY JOURNALS

Scholarly journals are the major vehicles for reporting current studies conducted by academic and professional researchers. These journals are usually edited and published by a learned society, a professional association, an academic institution, or a commercial publishing firm. The **articles** are written by specialists and usually are critically evaluated by other scholars before being accepted for publication. They often represent well-designed, important, and current research efforts. A scholarly journal article can examine a topic that has not yet been studied and may never be treated in a book-length publication, or it can contain new information about a subject that has been researched and reported in the past. Many of these journals have webpages that contain submission information and often the tables of contents for past issues.

Although editorial practices differ, scholarly journals primarily publish unsolicited reports of research endeavors. This means that the researcher conducts an investigation and submits the report or manuscript to a journal editor. The editor then sends the manuscript, typically for a blind review, to other communication researchers who are specialists in a given area. Thus the quality of unsolicited research articles is scrutinized before publication, and reviewers of the work are usually unaware of the author's identity. Articles that withstand this review process are generally rewritten once or twice before publication. Such revised manuscripts are often reviewed again before a publication decision.

Most quality journals have a rather hefty manuscript rejection rate. Sometimes scholarly journal editors solicit specific articles or opinion pieces from communication scholars. Editorial board members might also review these solicited pieces to ensure their quality. Book reviews, notices of other publications, bibliographies, and general news about the field may also appear. But scholarly journals concentrate on publishing original theory and research articles.

As you examine scholarly journal articles, you will note that they are fairly standardized, especially the quantitative research articles. Quantitative studies begin with an introductory section analyzing past research about a conceptual issue or problem. This introduction includes a summary of previous related research, an explanation of gaps or contradictions found in studying the problem, a rationale for the significance of addressing the research problem, and the positing of research hypotheses or questions. The second section details the method of the investigation and how the information was observed or collected. It includes a description of the people, objects, or events studied. For survey research or experimental studies, for example, it contains a summary of sample size, sample selection, and devices used to measure the variables. Next, the results of the analysis are presented along with other findings. In quantitative research, this section describes the application of appropriate statistical tests to interpret the collected data. Finally, the last section presents a discussion of the meaning or implications of the results, the limitations of the study, and the directions for future research about the problem.

Qualitative studies, on the other hand, do not have a standard format. Case studies often follow a problem or issue chronologically, from beginning to end. Rhetorical criticism pieces often present the theoretical approach first and then apply it to a relevant situation or communication event. Qualitative researchers might present observations of behavior or an examination of selected content (such as newspaper stories) and then explain regularities or idiosyncrasies in that behavior or content.

A several-sentence summary or paragraph-length *abstract* is usually found at the beginning of each article or in the journal's table of contents. These brief abstracts are often the basis of the synopses published in sources such as *Communication Abstracts*. They can be helpful in determining the article's utility for your own research project.

The references cited in footnotes or in the bibliography at the end of each article are usually the most up-to-date sources of material for that area of study at the time the article was written. Thus both the content of the article and the references cited are valuable research aids. It is important to emphasize, though, that there are varying periods of delay between the time the research study is initially conducted, when it is submitted for publication consideration, when it is revised, when it is eventually accepted for publication, and when the journal issue that contains the report is finally published. This lag time is often 2 years or even longer. Electronic journals have eliminated some of this lag.

An annotated list of some of the scholarly journals used by communication students and researchers follows. These journals represent a selection of several major national and international scholarly journals in communication.

Communication Education. (1952–). Washington, DC: National Communication Association.

■ This quarterly journal publishes research and pedagogy articles about elementary, secondary, and higher education, primarily in instructional communication settings. It has occasionally included reports that focus on organizational training or mass communication instruction. Earlier volumes contained sections on innovative instructional practices, ERIC reports on specific communication topics, and reviews of print and nonprint resources for educators. Volumes contain reviews of books and other resources. *Communication Education* (formerly *Speech Teacher*) is published in January, April, July, and October, and an annual index appears in the October issue.

Communication Monographs. (1934–). Washington, DC: National Communication Association.

■ *Communication Monographs* publishes research reports and new theories about the processes of communication in several contexts. Typically, the journal contains quantitative empirical research articles focusing on message, source, and receiver variables in interpersonal, group, organizational, and public communication. It is published quarterly in March, June, September, and December. An annual index appears in the year's final issue. (Volumes 1 through 42 were published under the title *Speech Monographs*)

Communication Research. (1974–). Newbury Park, CA: Sage.

■ This bimonthly journal focuses on models that explain communication processes and outcomes. Published articles report research in mass, international, political, organizational, and interpersonal communication. Some articles integrate interdisciplinary interests in human communication. There also are research and book-review essays. *Communication Research* is published in February, April, June, August, October, and December. Two issues each year have been devoted to different themes. A yearly cumulative author index appears in the December issue.

Critical Studies in Media Communication. (1984–). Washington, DC: National Communication Association.

■ *Critical Studies* publishes theoretical and critical essays in several areas: the evolution, economics, and organization of mass media systems; the form and structure of media content; the relationship between culture and media; models of media processes;

and media criticism. There have been review and criticism, and booknotes sections. The journal is published quarterly in March, June, September, and December. A yearly cumulative article index appears in the December issue. This journal was formerly published as *Critical Studies in Mass Communication*.

Human Communication Research. (1974–). Washington, DC: International Communication Association.

■ *HCR* offers a behavioral science approach to the study of human communication. Articles report original research, offer new methodological approaches, synthesize research literature, and present new theoretical perspectives on human interaction. The journal publishes research in interpersonal, organizational, and mass communication as well as in methodology, information systems, and persuasion. Early volumes contained state-of-the-art pieces and a colloquy section presenting alternative ways of looking at communication issues. This quarterly journal is published in the fall, winter, spring, and summer. An annual index appears in the summer issue.

Journal of Broadcasting & Electronic Media. (1956/1957–). Washington, DC: Broadcast Education Association.

■ This quarterly journal, formerly the *Journal of Broadcasting*, publishes research articles about communication and the electronic media. Subject matter includes audience and media effects research, communication policy and regulation, new technologies, broadcast history, international communication, media criticism, media content and programming, and economics. It also contains brief reports of research and book reviews. The journal is published in the winter, spring, summer, and fall, and yearly author and title indexes appear in the fall issue.

Journal of Communication. (1952–). Washington, DC: International Communication Association.

■ This quarterly journal focuses on the interdisciplinary study of communication theory, practice, and policy. Articles concentrate on communication mass media processes and the societal impact of communication. Also included are book reviews and review essays. The journal returned to being a publication of the International Communication Association in 1992. It is published in winter, spring, summer, and autumn. Title and author indexes appear annually in the autumn issue.

Journalism & Mass Communication Quarterly. (1924–). Columbia, SC: Association for Education in Journalism and Mass Communication.

■ This journal, formerly *Journalism Quarterly* (also known as *JQ*), focuses on research in journalism and mass communication. Articles report on the conduct of news, mass media effects, international communication, historical treatments of issues, and social and legal dimensions of the media. Brief research reports, book reviews, mass communication bibliographies, and annual convention summaries also have been included. It is published quarterly in the spring, summer, autumn, and winter.

Quarterly Journal of Speech. (1915–). Washington, DC: National Communication Association.

■ *QJS* is the oldest journal in speech communication. Articles are generally historical or critical in nature, with an emphasis on rhetorical theory and criticism. The goal of the journal is to broaden awareness and understanding of speech communication from a humanistic viewpoint. Book review and forum sections are included. The journal is published in February, May, August, and November. (Volumes 1–3 were published under the title *Quarterly Journal of Public Speaking*, and Volumes 4–13 were titled *Quarterly Journal of Speech Education*)

Several other journals are also frequently consulted by communication researchers. Among these are journals published by different communication associations, such as:

Communication and Critical/Cultural Studies (National Communication Association)

Communication Theory (International Communication Association)

Journal of Applied Communication Research (National Communication Association)

Journal of International and Intercultural Communication (National Communication Association)

Journal of Intercultural Communication Research (World Communication Association)

Journal of Radio & Audio Media (Broadcast Education Association)

Journalism & Mass Communication Educator (Association for Education in Journalism and Mass Communication)

Journalism & Mass Communication Monographs (Association for Education in Journalism and Mass Communication)

Text and Performance Quarterly (National Communication Association)

Some journals are published by divisions of communication associations, such as *Mass Communication and Society, Newspaper Research Journal*, and *Communication Law and Policy*, which are published by divisions (i.e., interest groups) of the Association for Education in Journalism and Mass Communication.

Besides the journals of several state associations, seven journals are published quarterly by four regional communication associations:

Communication Quarterly (Eastern Communication Association)

Communication Reports (Western States Communication Association)

Communication Research Reports (Eastern Communication Association)

Communication Studies (Central States Communication Association)

Qualitative Research Reports in Communication (Eastern Communication Association)

Southern Communication Journal (Southern States Communication Association)

Western Journal of Communication (Western States Communication Association)

Several electronic journals also have begun in recent years. The *Journal of Computer-Mediated Communication*, the *American Communication Journal, Communication Teacher*, and the *Electronic Journal of Communication* publish articles of interest to communication scholars and practitioners. Several new journals are just starting up, and we expect to see more of these emerging in the future. In assessing the quality of electronic journals, consider the editor, editorial board, and review process (e.g., whether the journal uses a blind review process), the journal's acceptance rate, the quality of the articles, and the reputation of the authors.

Besides these scholarly communication journals, there are several interdisciplinary journals—such as *Political Communication, Media Psychology, Health Communication, Management Communication Quarterly*, and the *American Behavioral Scientist*—and journals from related disciplines—such as *Public Opinion Quarterly*, the *Journal of Conflict Resolution*, and the *Journal of Personality and Social Psychology*—that you might find useful.

A list of scholarly journals appears at the end of this chapter. Consult your library's catalog or serials list to determine whether these scholarly journals are available. Descriptions of many of these journals can be found in the following:

> LaGuardia, C., Katz, W. A., & Katz, L. S. (2002). *Magazines for libraries* (11th ed.). New Providence, NJ: Bowker.

In addition, copies of the tables of contents of scholarly journals are often available on the journal's, association's, or publisher's home page or in the following:

> *Current Contents: Social and Behavioral Sciences.* (1961–). Philadelphia: Institute for Scientific Information.
>
> ■ This is a weekly publication of more than 1,300 tables of contents. Each issue has a keyword subject index, author index, address directory, and publishers' addresses. Volumes related to the arts and humanities are also available.

An online table of contents service such as Ingenta, described in Chapter 6, might be more convenient: **<http://www.ingenta.com/>**. By using this service you can browse recent issues, ones that might not yet be indexed or abstracted.

PROFESSIONAL AND TRADE MAGAZINES

Professional and **trade magazines** are often important sources of information and insight in the communication field. They are used to lend perspective to practical applications of communication theory and research or to detail the issues, events, and trends facing the communication industry. Generally, research reports are not the mainstay of professional and trade magazines, although the results of a study can sometimes be encapsulated. These publications emphasize news of events, issues, and innovations in the field.

For example, trade publications publish articles on new audio and video technologies, advertising campaigns, marketing and management strategies, communication and corporate training programs in industry, public relations cases and techniques, and in-house organizational publications. In addition, they often present news about people in the industry, upcoming professional events, and employment opportunities. Most offer electronic versions, and subscriptions are possible through their websites. Check the home pages of the organizations or publications for current news.

The following four publications are often consulted by students looking for information related to the professions of advertising, broadcasting, journalism, and public relations.

> *Advertising Age.* (1930–). Chicago: Crain Communications. (Available: http://adage.com)
>
> ■ This weekly magazine provides an extended review of news related to advertising and marketing. The publication has included several segments: summaries of current news about advertisers, syndicators, agencies, and products; interactive media and technology reports; news about advertising professionals and businesses; analyses of media and marketing issues; data about products, market shares, and companies; viewpoints and letters to the editor; special reports on advertising and marketing; classified advertising; and an index of marketing and media companies.

Broadcasting & Cable. (1931–). New York: Cahners. (Available: http://www.broad castingcable.com)

- This weekly trade publication offers broadcast industry news and special in-depth reports on major issues and developments in radio, television, and cable. Regular departments include broadcast and cable news, programming, government actions, technology, business, people, editorials, and special reports. Online tools are also available to search archives, classified, events, statistical research, and industry links.

Columbia Journalism Review. (1962–). New York: Columbia University, Graduate School of Journalism. (Available: http://www.cjr.org)

- This bimonthly magazine critically assesses the performance of the press. Articles focus on news professionals, journalistic practices, the media, press treatment of politics and contemporary issues, press news from around the world, and the operation of news organizations. Current issues and events in journalism are chronicled, and websites are highlighted. The website's resources section also includes a Who owns what? guide to media ownership, language corner, and CJR study guides.

Public Relations Strategist. (1995–). New York: Public Relations Society of America. (Available: http://www.prsa.org/_Publications/magazines/strategist.asp)

- This quarterly magazine focuses on issues and trends for public relations practitioners. Features include interviews with public relations CEOs discussing public relations in organizations and articles on research, strategies, and issues. Articles have addressed feminism, alternative media, crisis public relations, getting the message across, moral reasoning, and corporate values.

Additional professional and trade magazines related to communication are listed in the *Selected Sources* that follow. The articles in these publications are often indexed in the comprehensive, interdisciplinary indexes discussed in Chapter 6 (*Academic Search, Academic Index, Periodical Abstracts*). In listings we include earlier titles of scholarly journals in parentheses.

SUMMARY

Communication periodicals contain the most up-to-date information about the communication discipline. Two main types of periodicals are scholarly journals and professional and trade magazines. Scholarly journals contain original research reports, review essays, and theoretical pieces. They are edited by scholars who accept only the best of the research submitted, and the manuscripts undergo scrutiny by a board of reviewers who are experts in the field. Professional and trade magazines emphasize the current status of the discipline, with articles about issues, events, and trends facing the profession or industry. News about professionals, new technologies, upcoming events or meetings, and successes of various campaigns or marketing efforts are often given as well. These publications are important to the professional lives of scholars and professionals in communication.

In the list of journals that appears below, former titles are given in parentheses. Also, because many journals are published by both scholarly associations and publishers (which often change), we list only the association's name if the journal is linked to a professional association. If the journal is published only by a publishing company, we provide the name of the publisher. Because many journals are available both in print and online, consult the organization or publisher for subscription possibilities.

SELECTED SOURCES

Scholarly Journals

Communication

Argumentation and Advocacy (*Journal of the American Forensic Association*). (1964–). American Forensic Association.

Asian Communication Research. (2004–). Korean Society for Journalism and Communication Studies.

Asian Journal of Communication. (1990–). Asian Media Information and Communication Centre.

Australian Journal of Communication. (1982–). Communication Institute.

Chinese Journal of Communication. (2008–). Routledge.

Communication and Critical/Cultural Studies. (2004–). National Communication Association.

Communication and Medicine. (2004–). Mouton De Gruyter.

Communication Education (*Speech Teacher*). (1952–). National Communication Association.

Communication Methods and Measures. (2007–). Taylor & Francis.

Communication Monographs (*Speech Monographs*). (1934–). National Communication Association.

Communication Quarterly (*Today's Speech*). (1953–). Eastern Communication Association.

Communication Reports. (1988–). Western States Communication Association.

Communication Research. (1974–). Sage.

Communication Research Reports. (1984–). Eastern Communication Association.

Communication Review. (1998–). Taylor & Francis.

Communication Studies (*Central States Speech Journal*). (1949–). Central States Communication Association.

Communication Theory. (1991–). International Communication Association.

Communications: The European Journal of Communication Research. (1998–). Mouton de Gruyter.

Environmental Communication: A Journal of Nature and Culture. (2007–). Routledge.

European Journal of Communication. (1986–). Sage.

European Journal of Communication Research. (2008–). Mouton De Gruyter.

Health Communication. (1989–). Taylor & Francis.

Howard Journal of Communications. (1988–). Howard University.

Human Communication Research. (1974–). International Communication Association.

International Journal of Listening (*Journal of the International Listening Association*). (1987–). International Listening Association.

Journal of Applied Communication Research. (1973–). National Communication Association.

Journal of Asian Pacific Communication. (1991–). John Benjamins.

Journal of Communication. (1951–). International Communication Association.

Journal of Communication and Religion (Religious Communication Today). (1978). Religious National Communication Association.

Journal of Communication Inquiry. (1977–). Sage.

Journal of Communication Studies. (2008–). Marquette Books.

Journal of Family Communication. (2001–). Taylor & Francis.

Journal of Global Communication. (2008–). Marquette Books.

Journal of Health Communication. (1996–). Taylor & Francis.

Journal of Intercultural Communication Research (World Communication, Communication). (1972–). World Communication Association.

Journal of International and Intercultural Communication. (2008–). National Communication Association.

Journal of International Communication. (1994–). International Association for Media & Communication Research, International Communication Section.

Journal of the Association for Communication Administration (Bulletin of the Association for Communication Administration, ACA Bulletin, Bulletin of the Association of Departments and Administrators in Speech Communication). (1972–2001). Association for Communication Administration.

National Forensic Journal. (1983–). National Forensic Association.

Philosophy and Rhetoric. (1968–). Pennsylvania State University Press.

Political Communication (Political Communication and Persuasion). (1980–). International Communication Association and American Political Science Association, Political Communication Divisions.

Qualitative Research Reports in Communication. (1999–). Eastern Communication Association.

Quarterly Journal of Speech (Quarterly Journal of Public Speaking, Quarterly Journal of Speech Education). (1915–). National Communication Association.

Rhetoric & Public Affairs. (1998–). Michigan State University Press.

Rhetoric Review. (1982–). Erlbaum.

Rhetoric Society Quarterly. (1971–). Rhetoric Society of America.

Russian Journal of Communication (2008–). Marquette Books.

Southern Communication Journal (Southern Speech Communication Journal, Southern Speech Journal). (1935–). Southern States Communication Association.

Western Journal of Communication (Western Journal of Speech Communication, Western Speech Communication, Western Speech). (1937–). Western States Communication Association.

Women's Studies in Communication (ORWAC Bulletin: Women's Studies in Communication). (1977–). Organization for Research on Women and Communication.

Information

Information, Communication & Society. (1998–). Routledge.

Information Economics and Policy. (1983–). International Telecommunications Society.

The Information Society. (1985–). Taylor & Francis.

Science Communication (Knowledge). (1979–). Sage.

Mass Communication

American Journal of Media Psychology. (2008–). Marquette Books.

American Journalism. (1983–). American Journalism Historians Association.

Asian Journal of Communication. (1990–). Asian Mass Communication Research and Information Centre.

Canadian Journal of Communication (Media Probe). (1974–). University of Calgary, Program in Communication Studies. (Available: http://www.cjc-online.ca/)

Cinema Journal. (1966–). Society for Cinema Studies.

Communication Law and Policy. (1996–). Association for Education in Journalism and Mass Communication, Law and Policy Division.

Communications and the Law. (1979–). Rothman.

Continuum: Journal of Media & Cultural Studies (1987–). Cultural Studies Association of Australia.

Critical Studies in Media Communication (Critical Studies in Mass Communication). (1984–). National Communication Association.

Educational Technology Research and Development (Educational Communication and Technology Journal). (1953–). Association for Educational Communications and Technology.

Electronic News. (2007–). Association for Education in Journalism and Mass Communication, Radio-Television Journalism Division.

Equid Novi: African Journalism Studies (1980–). Institute for Media Analysis in South Africa.

Federal Communications Law Journal (Federal Communications Bar Journal). (1937–). Federal Communications Bar Association.

Feminist Media Studies. (2001–). Routledge.

Film History. (1987–). Taylor & Francis.

Film Journal International (Film Journal). (1934–). Sunshine Group.

Film Quarterly (Quarterly of Film, Radio, and Television). (1945–). University of California Press.

Games and culture: A Journal of Interactive Media. (2006–), Sage.

Gazette. (1955–). Sage.

Hastings Communications and Entertainment Law Journal (COMM/ENT: A Journal of Communications and Entertainment Law). (1977–). University of California, San Francisco, Hastings College of Law.

Historical Journal of Film, Radio and Television. (1981–). International Association for Media and History.

International Journal of Media Management. (1999–). Institute for Media and Communication Mangagement.

International Journal of Public Opinion Research. (1989–). World Association for Public Opinion Research.

Journal of Broadcasting & Electronic Media (Journal of Broadcasting). (1956/1957–). Broadcast Education Association.

Journal of Children and the Media. (2007–). Routledge.

Journal of Film and Video. (1949–). University Film and Video Association.

Journal of Health and Mass Communication (2008–). Marquette Books.

Journal of Mass Media Ethics. (1985–). Taylor & Francis.

Journal of Media and Religion. (2002–). Taylor & Francis.

Journal of Media Economics. (1988–). Taylor & Francis.

Journal of Media Law & Ethics. (2008–). Marquette Books.

Journal of Media Sociology. (2008–). Marquette Books.

Journal of Popular Culture. (1967–). Bowling Green State University.

Journal of Popular Film & Television (Journal of Popular Film). (1972–). Bowling Green State University.

Journal of Radio & Audio Media (Journal of Radio Studies). (1992–). Broadcast Education Association.

Journal of Visual Culture. (2002–). Sage.

Journalism: Theory, Practice and Criticism. (2000–). Sage.

Journalism & Mass Communication Educator. (1946–). Association for Education in Journalism and Mass Communication.

Journalism & Mass Communication Monographs. (1966–). Association for Education in Journalism and Mass Communication.

Journalism & Mass Communication Quarterly. (1924–). Association for Education in Journalism and Mass Communication.

Journalism History. (1974–). California State University Foundation.

Journalism Studies. (2000–). Routledge.

Mass Communication & Society (Mass Comm Review). (1973–). Association for Education in Journalism and Mass Communication, Mass Communication & Society Division.

Media, Culture & Society. (1979–). Sage.

Media History. (1994–). Taylor & Francis.

Media Psychology. (1999–). Taylor & Francis.

New Media & Society. (1999). Sage.

Newspaper Research Journal. (1979–). Association for Education in Journalism and Mass Communication, Newspaper Division.

Nordicom Review of Nordic Research on Media & Communication. (1981–). Nordic Documentation Center for Mass Communication Research.

Popular Communication. (2003–). Taylor & Francis.

Public Opinion Quarterly. (1937–). American Association for Public Opinion Research.

Quarterly Review of Film and Video (Quarterly Review of Film Studies). (1976–). Harwood Academic Publishers.

Telecommunications Policy. (1976–). Butterworth Scientific.

Television & New Media. (2000–). Sage.

Visual Communication Quarterly. (1994–). Association for Education in Journalism and Mass Communication, Visual Communication Division.

Speech, Language, and Nonverbal Communication

American Journal of Speech-Language Pathology. (1991–). American Speech-Language-Hearing Association.

American Speech. (1925–). American Dialect Society.

Applied Psycholinguistics. (1980–). Cambridge University Press.

Critical Discourse Studies. (2004–). Routledge.

Discourse & Society. (1990–). Sage.

Discourse Processes. (1978–). Society for Text and Discourse.

Discourse Studies. (1999–). Sage.

ETC.: A Review of General Semantics. (1943–). International Society for General Semantics.

Human Development. (1958–). Karger.

International Journal of American Linguistics. (1917–). Linguistics Society of America.

Journal of Communication Disorders. (1967–). Elsevier.

Journal of Consumer Psychology. (1991–). Elsevier.

Journal of English Linguistics. (1972–). Sage.

Journal of Language and Social Psychology. (1982–). Sage.

Journal of Linguistics. (1965–). Linguistic Association of Great Britain.

Journal of Memory and Language (*Journal of Verbal Learning and Verbal Behavior*). (1962–). Academic Press.

Journal of Nonverbal Behavior (*Environmental Psychology and Nonverbal Behavior*). (1976–). Human Sciences Press.

Journal of Psycholinguistic Research. (1971–). Springer.

Journal of Sociolinguistics. (1997–). Blackwell.

Journal of Speech, Language, and Hearing Research (*Journal of Speech and Hearing Research*). (1958–). American Speech-Language-Hearing Association.

Language & Communication. (1981–). Pergamon Press.

Research on Language and Social Interaction. (1968–). Taylor & Francis.

Semiotica. (1969–). International Association for Semiotic Studies.

Space and Culture. (1998–). Sage.

Text and Performance Quarterly (*Literature in Performance*). (1980–). National Communication Association.

Visual Communication. (2002–). Sage.

Written Communication. (1984–). Sage.

Advertising, Business, Marketing, and Public Relations

Academy of Management Journal. (1957–). Academy of Management.

Academy of Management Review. (1976–). Academy of Management.

Administrative Science Quarterly. (1956–). Cornell University.

Business Communication Quarterly (*Bulletin of the Association for Business Communication, ABCA Bulletin, ABWA Bulletin*). (1936–). Association for Business Communication.

Industrial & Labor Relations Review. (1947–). Cornell University.

International Journal of Advertising. (1983–). Advertising Association.

International Journal of Strategic Communication (2007–). Routledge.

Journal of Advertising. (1972–). American Academy of Advertising.

Journal of Advertising History. (1977–). History of Advertising Trust.

Journal of Advertising Research. (1960–). Advertising Research Foundation.

Journal of Business. (1927–). University of Chicago Press.

Journal of Business and Technical Communication (*Iowa State Journal of Business and Technical Communication*). (1987–). Sage.

Journal of Business Communication. (1963–). American Business Communication Association.

Journal of Communication Management. (1996–). Henry Stewart Publications.

Journal of Consumer Research. (1974–). University of California, Los Angeles, American Association for Public Opinion Research.

Journal of Current Issues and Research in Advertising (*Current Issues and Research in Advertising*). (1978–). CtC Press.

Journal of Marketing. (1936–). American Marketing Association.

Journal of Marketing Research. (1964–). American Marketing Association.

Journal of Public Relations Research (*Public Relations Research Annual*). (1989–). Association for Education in Journalism and Mass Communication, Public Relations Division.

Management Communication Quarterly. (1987–). Sage.

Organization. (1994–). Sage.

Organizational Behavior and Human Decision Processes (*Organizational Behavior and Human Performance*). (1966–). Academic Press.

Personnel Psychology. (1948–). Personnel Psychology.

Public Relations Quarterly (*Quarterly Review of Public Relations*). (1955–). American Public Relations Association.

Public Relations Review. (1975–). Foundation for Public Relations Research and Education.

Psychology, Sociology, and Social Psychology

American Behavioral Scientist. (1957–). Sage.

American Journal of Psychology. (1887–). University of Illinois Press.

American Journal of Sociology. (1895–). University of Chicago Press.

American Sociological Review. (1936–). American Sociological Association.

Child Development. (1930–). Society for Research in Child Development.

Cognitive Psychology. (1970–). Academic Press.

Cultural Studies. (1987–). Routledge.

Developmental Psychology. (1969–). American Psychological Association.

Family Relations (*Family Coordinator*). (1952–). National Council on Family Relations.

Gender & Society. (1987–). Sociologists for Women in Society.

Group & Organization Management (*Group & Organization Studies*). (1976–). Eastern Academy of Management.

Human Organization (*Applied Anthropology*). (1941–). Society for Applied Anthropology.

International Journal of Intercultural Relations. (1977–). Society for Intercultural Education, Training, and Research.

Journal of Applied Psychology. (1917–). American Psychological Association.

Journal of Applied Social Psychology. (1971–). Winston.

Journal of Consumer Psychology. (1991–). Society for Consumer Psychology.

Journal of Cross-Cultural Psychology. (1970–). International Association for Cross-Cultural Psychology.

Journal of Educational Psychology. (1910–). American Psychological Association.

Journal of Experimental Social Psychology. (1965–). Academic Press.

Journal of Humanistic Psychology. (1961–). Association for Humanistic Psychology.

Journal of Marriage and the Family (*Living, Marriage and Family Living*). (1939–). National Council on Family Relations.

Journal of Personality (*Character and Personality*). (1932–). Duke University Press.

Journal of Personality and Social Psychology (*Journal of Abnormal and Social Psychology, Journal of Abnormal Psychology*). (1906–). American Psychological Association.

Journal of Personality Assessment (*Journal of Projective Techniques & Personality Assessment*). (1936–). Society for Personality Assessment.

Journal of Research in Personality (*Journal of Experimental Research in Personality*). (1965–). Academic Press.

Journal of Sex Research. (1965–). Society for the Scientific Study of Sex.

Journal of Social and Personal Relationships. (1984–). International Association for Relationship Research.

Personal Relationships. (1994–). International Society for the Study of Personal Relationships.

Personality & Social Psychology Bulletin. (1974–). Society for Personality and Social Psychology.

Small Group Research (*Small Group Behavior, International Journal of Small Group Research*). (1970–). Sage.

Social Forces. (1922–). Southern Sociological Society.

Social Psychology Quarterly (*Sociometry*). (1937–). American Sociological Association.

Symbolic Interaction. (1977–). Society for the Study of Symbolic Interaction.

History and Political Science

American Historical Review. (1895–). American Historical Association.

American Journal of Political Science (*Midwest Journal of Political Science*). (1957–). Midwest Political Science Association.

American Political Science Review. (1906–). American Political Science Association.

American Politics Quarterly. (1973–). Sage.

American Politics Research. (1973–). Sage.

Comparative Political Studies. (1968–). Sage.

Comparative Politics. (1968–). CUNY Political Science Program.

Harvard International Journal of Press/Politics. (1996–). Center on the Press, Politics, and Public Policy.

Journal of American History. (1914–). Organization of American Historians.

Journal of Conflict Resolution (*Conflict Resolution*). (1957–). Peace Science Society.

Journal of Politics. (1939–). Southern Political Science Association.

Journal of Social Issues. (1945–). Society for the Psychological Study of Social Issues.

Political Behavior. (1979–). Plenum.

Political Science Quarterly. (1886–). Academy of Political Science.

Professional and Trade Periodicals

Advertising Age. (1930–). Crain Communications. (Available: http://adage.com)

Adweek. (1979–). Adweek.

American Cinematographer. (1920–). American Society of Cinematographers.

American Editor: Bulletin of the American Society of Newspaper Editors. (1970–). American Society of Newspaper Editors.

American Journalism Review (Washington Journalism Review). (1977–). University of Maryland, College of Journalism.

Applied Environmental Education and Communication (2002–). Routledge.

Audio-Visual Communications. (1967–). United Business Publications.

Billboard. (1894–). Billboard.

BPME Image. (1985–). Broadcast Promotion and Marketing Executives.

Broadcast Management/Engineering. (1965–). Mactier.

Broadcasting & Cable. (1931–). Cahners. (Available: http://www.broadcastingcable.com)

Broadcasting and the Law. (1970–). L & S Publications.

Business Horizons. (1958–). Indiana University, Graduate School of Business.

Columbia Journalism Review. (1962–). Columbia University, Graduate School of Journalism.

Communication Teacher (1987–). Routledge.

Corporate Television: The Official Magazine of the International Television Association. (1986–). International Television Association.

Daily Variety. (1933–). Daily Variety.

Editor & Publisher. (1901–). Editor & Publisher.

Educational Technology. (1966–). Educational News Service.

Electronic Media. (1982–). Crain Communications.

Feedback. (1959–). Broadcast Education Association. (Available: http://beaweb.org)

Film Comment. (1962–). Film Society of Lincoln Center.

Folio: The Magazine for Magazine Management. (1972–). Merket Publications.

Harvard Business Review. (1922–). Harvard University, Graduate School of Business Administration.

Hollywood Reporter. (1930–). HR Industries.

Inside PR. (1990–). Editorial Media Marketing International.

Journal of Technical Writing and Communication. (1971–). Baywood.

Journalism Practice. (2007–). Routledge.

Marketing News. (1967–). American Marketing Association.

Media & Methods (Teachers Guide to Media & Methods; Educators Guide to Media & Methods). (1964–). North America Publishing.

Mediaweek (Marketing & Media Decisions, Media Decisions). (1966–). A/S/M Communications.

Presstime. (1979–). American Newspaper Publishers Association.

Public Communication Review. (1981–). Boston University, School of Public Communication.

Public Relations Journal. (1945–). Public Relations Society of America.

Publishers Weekly. (1873–). R. R. Bowker.

Quill. (1912–). Society of Professional Journalists.

RTNDA Communicator. (1946–). Radio-Television News Directors Association.
Sight and Sound. (1932–). British Film Institute.
Technical Communication. (1954–). Society for Technical Communication.
Technical Communication Quarterly. (1991–). Routledge.
Television Quarterly. (1962–). National Academy of Television Arts and Sciences.
Television/Radio Age. (1953–). Television Editorial Corporation.
Variety. (1905–). Variety.
Writer's Digest. (1920–). Writer's Digest.

Electronic Journals

(Available only Online)

Advertising & Society Review. (2000–). (Register at: http://www.aef.com/aef.asr
.html)
American Communication Journal. (1997–). (Available: http://www.acjournal.org)
Counterblast. (2001–). (Available: http://www.nyu.edu/pubs/counterblast/)
Electronic Journal of Communication. (1990–). (Available: http://www.cios.org/
www/ejcmain.htm)
Intermundo. (2001–). (Available: http://www.stephweb.com/forum)
Interpersonal Computing and Technology Journal. (1993–1999). (Available: http://
jan.ucc.nau.edu/,ipct-j/)
Journal of Computer-Mediated Communication. (1995–). (Available: http://www.
jcmc.indiana.edu)
Liminalities: A Journal of Performance Studies. (2005–). (Available: http://
liminalities.net/)
Review of Communication. (2003–). (Available from Taylor & Francis to NCA
members by subscription)

EXAMPLES

Jack, in searching the indexes identified in Chapter 6, has found
several journal articles on the ghostwriting topic. By reading articles
such as the following, Jack finds the issues start falling into place.

Bormann, E. G. (1961). Ethics of ghostwritten speeches. *Quarterly Journal of
Speech, 47,* 262–267.

Valerie has found a reference to an electronic journal, *Journal of
Computer-Mediated Communication,* which might contain articles
related to voice mail. She finds the site, searches for *voice mail,* and
finds several articles that contain these keywords.

Robin has now collected enough information from secondary sources to
do a good job on her report on attribution. From the CIOS

(Communication Institute Online Scholarship) search, she decides to look further at one article in the communication literature that sounds intriguing:

Berger, C. R. (1975). Proactive and retroactive attribution processes in interpersonal communications. *Human Communication Research, 2,* 33–50.

Jason has amassed about 30 references on parasocial interaction. Many of these are articles from scholarly journals like *Journal of Broadcasting & Electronic Media, Communication Research,* and *Human Communication Research.* Now is the time to apply good reading and note-taking skills to them. Instead of photocopying them all, Jason uses a notebook computer and takes notes on each article while reading it.

Kat, Rocky, and **Michelle** found too much academic information on conflict in organizations and groups. They decide to split up the references and read those that might provide guidance on how to train people to manage conflict. They've found some good references in trade and professional periodicals. They decide to visit the American Society for Training and Development website **<www.astd.org>** and look at the contents of its *Training and Development* magazine. The site allows visitors to read summaries of articles in each issue, and they find a feature in each issue that helps them become better trainers.

Eric, Gregory, Anthony, and **Scott** found many references in their search of indexes. By looking at the articles, they notice that other articles are referenced in them. So they add to their reference list by finding and reading some of the references in the articles that they had already found. They also noted that some of the articles were in special issues, in which several articles on the same topic are included in a particular journal issue. This helped the group become as thorough as possible in their search.

EXERCISES

1. During a literature search for a paper for your communication theory and research class, you've examined bibliographies and indexes and found references to several scholarly journal articles. The abstracts suggest that these articles are pertinent to your topic, *deception*, so you search for these articles. You want to read them thoroughly to determine whether they lend insight to the paper and whether their references and footnotes can offer further help in your literature search.

a. The first abstract leads you to:

> *Human Communication Research*: Brandt, D. R., Miller, G. R., & Hocking, J. E. (1980). The truth-deception attribution: Effects of familiarity on the ability of observers to detect deception. *Human Communication Research, 6*, 99–110.

How was *judgmental accuracy* measured in this study?

b. The second article is found in:

> *Communication Monographs*: Burgoon, J. K., Buller, D. B., Ebesu, A. S., & Rockwell, P. (1994). Interpersonal deception: V. Accuracy in deception detection. *Communication Monographs, 61*, 303–325.

What three hypotheses were tested in this study?

c. The third article is in:

> *Communication Research*: Stiff, J. B., Kim, H. J., & Ramesh, C. N. (1992). Truth biases and aroused suspicion in relational deception. *Communication Research, 19*, 326–345.

What two procedures have researchers typically used to investigate detection of deception?

2. You are now working on a class report for your Media Law class and want to find recent developments in broadcast regulations. Starting with the most recent online issue, you check the Washington Department in *Broadcasting & Cable* magazine for the most recent issue you can find. In one sentence, summarize the subject of the first news item. Be sure to give the date of this issue.

3. In your journalism class, your instructor suggests you can find out about innovations in the field by examining the *Columbia Journalism Review*. You pick up a recent issue in a journalism library on campus or at a newsstand and scan the table of contents for interesting articles. What is the title of the feature article in that issue? Be sure to give the date of the issue you're reading.

4. Identify journals that might have articles on your topic. Look at the tables of contents to be sure the topic is related. Examine recently published issues of these journals in your library's current periodicals section. Be sure to look at reference lists of articles on your topic.

5. Form topic-related discussion groups and talk about interesting articles found or sources valuable in searching the literature. Identify different facets of the topic so all of you will not be attempting to find the same sources.

chapter 8

Information Compilations

W e often need to find recent facts to use in research reports, speeches, news stories, and presentations on current topics. For example, you might be preparing a public relations campaign and need information on the cost of advertising in specific newspapers or magazines. Or the status of recent broadcast regulations is required for a paper or television script on trends in broadcast law. Or you may have to lead a group discussion and want to consult a source about parliamentary procedure.

Several factual, quick-reference research sources can help with these and other related needs. In addition, there are several collections and official publications of primary documents that are sometimes essential factual sources. In this chapter we focus on methods of finding facts to support viewpoints, finding sources of information outside the library, and locating current online information related to communication.

Collections and archives lead you to the text of speeches, editorials, television programs, communication regulations, and so on, which may be the focus of your analysis or may be used as supporting information for research reports or other projects. Indexes provide a means to search for specific media reports. Statistical sources identify reference works and websites where census and other government and media statistics are reported. Because the statistical data cited in books and in journal articles are often not the most current, you should know where to turn to update such information.

Government documents are helpful when searching for up-to-date information on what is happening in Congress, the Supreme Court, or federal agencies such as the Federal Communications Commission. The U.S. government publishes so much information that a first-time user of government documents can be overwhelmed with the amount of material available. Many smaller libraries do not house all these documents, so you must find out how to request specific materials that you need or how to find them online.

Yearbooks, directories, dictionaries, and manuals are also usually current. Yearbooks and directories are generally revised each year so that information is up to date. These sources provide names, addresses, and factual information about people, businesses, and clients and are vital tools for many types of communication professionals. They can be especially useful when you do not find needed information within library resources. These reference works can point the way to other information sources, such as trade and professional organizations. If contacted directly, these organizations might be able to supply useful information to meet your particular needs. Dictionaries and manuals are desktop and online reference sources, helpful when you need quick, practical information.

COLLECTIONS AND ARCHIVES

Collections are compilations of similar documents that are gathered together in one location (an **archive**) or published in periodical, book, microform, CD-ROM or DVD format, or on the web. Materials such as speeches, editorials, historical documents, and media transcripts are often not easily accessible for the typical researcher, even though they may have appeared in book, periodical, or original form. Thus published collections allow you to examine important original materials to learn more about the subject. They also enable you to use the materials as examples of communication events for supporting arguments in a position paper, research investigation, or other project. One somewhat dated reference source that allows us to determine where collections and archives are located is Ash and Miller's (1993) *Subject Collections*.

Speech Collections

If you are conducting critical or historical research, you may be interested in locating speeches given by important people or on newsworthy topics. The text of these addresses might help clarify the timeline of events or prove a point you're making about your topic. Segments can also be useful as evidence in your own speeches. Imagine the impact a video clip of a speech has in the middle of a PowerPoint presentation! Speeches are recorded in text or video format and stored in collections that specialize in particular subjects or topics (e.g., political or presidential speeches).

Major newspapers such as the *New York Times* publish many newsworthy speeches shortly after they're given, but published collections make it easier to consult the original text of the speech without searching through back issues of these newspapers. They are especially helpful when the speech is old or when the newspaper account of the speech is not the original text but an edited version.

Collections also contain speeches that are not published elsewhere. The collection of speeches used most often is the following:

> *Vital Speeches of the Day.* (1934–). New York: City News.
>
> ■ This collection of important recent speeches by government, industry, and other societal leaders usually includes the complete texts, but occasionally edited versions are presented. The many sides of issues are represented in the speeches selected for publication. *Vital Speeches* is published semimonthly. Annual author and subject indexes appear in the November issue. Speeches in this collection are referenced in the *Readers' Guide to Periodical Literature* and in comprehensive indexes such as *Academic Search,* which often includes the full text of speeches indexed. *Vital Speeches* is available through EBSCOhost Research Databases. You can read speech texts or send them to your e-mail address for downloading to your personal computer.

A new archive of recorded interviews and speeches is being compiled at Michigan State University library. *The National Gallery of the Spoken Word* <**http://www.ngsw.org/**> will contain more than 50,000 hours of speeches, dating back to Thomas Alva Edison's original recordings. Demonstrations are available, along with other relevant collections, at <**http://www.historicalvoices.org/**>. Political speeches are also available in the MetaLab Internet archive at the University of North Carolina in Chapel Hill, which is available at <**http://metalab.unc.edu/metalab.shtml**>.

Speeches of the president of the United States are published in the *Weekly Compilation of Presidential Documents* (1965–). This source makes speeches and other presidential documents accessible in a relatively short period of time. It is available online from 1993 onward via *GPO Access* <**http://www.access.gpo.gov**>. An article by K. J. Turner (in the July 1986 issue of *Communication Education,* pp. 243–253) explains how to use presidential libraries to do archival research.

Collections of past presidential speeches are found in the following presidential libraries:

George H. Bush Presidential Library, College Station, Texas
Jimmy Carter Library, Atlanta, Georgia
William J. Clinton Presidential Center, Little Rock, Arkansas
Dwight D. Eisenhower Library, Abilene, Kansas
Gerald R. Ford Museum, Grand Rapids, Michigan
Herbert Hoover Library, West Branch, Iowa
Lyndon B. Johnson Library, Austin, Texas
John F. Kennedy Library, Boston, Massachusetts
Richard M. Nixon Library, Yorba Linda, California
Ronald Reagan Library, Simi Valley, California
Franklin D. Roosevelt Library, Hyde Park, New York
Harry S Truman Library, Independence, Missouri

These libraries contain speeches, text documents, and media accounts of events that occurred during each presidency. Most require you to visit the library to use the materials. A list of library websites with current contact information is available through the National Archives and Records Administration <**http://www.nara.gov**>. State of the Union addresses for Presidents Washington through Jackson are available on the White House webpage **<http://www.whitehouse.gov>**. Information about the National First Ladies' Library can be found at **<http://www.firstladies.org/index.htm>**. Located in Canton, Ohio, users can borrow audiovisual materials and search the collection.

Collections of speeches are often published in books. To find these in your library, try searching the library catalog using the subject heading *Speeches, addresses, etc.* For speeches published through 1980, it is often possible to locate in which book the text of a speech appears by using the fourth (cumulative) edition of the *Speech Index* and its supplement. Other collections of speeches are listed at the end of this chapter. Many speeches are also available in an online collection of American public speeches:

> *Douglass: Archives of American public address.* (1995). (Available: **http://douglass archives.org/**)
>
> ■ This repository of American rhetoric and resources is searchable by title, date, speaker, or issue. Complete speech text and information about the speaker and occasion are provided. In addition, the Douglass site provides links to websites that contain additional speeches. For instance, Franklin D. Roosevelt's fireside chats are accessible through the *New Deal and WWII* section. Ratings provide information about off-site usefulness.

Media Collections

Print

Daily and weekly newspapers publish up-to-date information on current issues of local, national, and international scope. They also contain opinion columns, editorials, and media reviews that can be useful in the research process. For example, newspaper reports of Supreme Court decisions or regulatory agency actions can have a direct bearing on research about freedom of speech, broadcast programming, advertising, media law and regulation, and the like. These are useful when you are interested in learning what journalists have said about a topic. *Editorials on File,* for example, is composed of newspaper editorials.

> *Editorials on File.* (1969–). New York: Facts on File.
>
> ■ Editorials for this collection are selected from more than 140 newspapers in the United States and Canada. Published twice per month, each issue includes the text of about 200 editorials chosen to represent newspaper positions on current issues. A cumulative subject index appears at the end of each annual volume.

Viewpoint (1976–), a similar type of periodical, brings together the work of newspaper and radio columnists with that of political cartoonists. A more complete microform edition is also available. *Facts on File* (1940–) differs from these works in that it is a weekly digest of national and foreign news prepared from accounts published in selected major newspapers, periodicals, and other standard news sources. It is available via *FACTS.com Reference Suite.*

Newspapers have historically been difficult to research. In the past, only major papers were indexed, and newspaper archives were difficult to access. This situation has changed drastically in recent years with the advent, first, of **microform** (microfiche or microfilm) and, more recently, of CD-ROMs and the web. Virtually all major newspapers and most regional ones now have websites, and many archive at least some of their articles, so the web can be thought of as a virtual collection of newspaper archives. Note, however, that many newspapers offer only a selected version of the print newspaper, and the archives may be incomplete and available only for a fee. To find a particular title on the web, search for its title through *Google* or another search engine.

NewsDirectory.com **<http://www.newsdirectory.com/>** is one of many websites that furnish links to hundreds of online newspapers. It performs the important additional service of providing a listing of newspaper websites that includes searchable archives. Another useful site that lists newspaper archives is maintained by the Special Libraries Association. Called *U.S. News Archives on the Web,* it can be accessed through the News Division of the Ibiblio website **<http://www.ibiblio.org/slanews>**.

Most libraries now provide access to national, international, and regional newspaper collections through commercially available databases, such as *NewsBank, Global Newsbank, ProQuest Newstand,* EBSCOhost's *Newspaper Source, LexisNexis Academic,* and *EthnicNewsWatch.* Many libraries are also likely to provide online access to one or more historical collections. The *New York Times Historical Collection* (1851–1999) and the *Times Digital Archive* (1785–1985) are examples of those now becoming available.

In addition, coverage of selected topics in specialized print media is provided by two microform collections, *Underground Newspaper Microfilm Collection* (Alternative Press Syndicate, 1963–1977) and *Herstory: Microfilm Collection* (Women's History Research Center, 1972–). The *Alternative Press Index* provides limited information on tapping these two sources. Several historical collections of U.S. and British newspapers and periodicals are also available in microform. Many libraries are likely to own one or more of these collections. Because they may not be listed in library catalogs or periodical lists, and their contents are reviewed only by using special indexes, you'll need to ask a reference librarian about their availability.

Like periodical indexes, **newspaper indexes** help you identify and find pertinent articles. Many online newspaper indexes are now available, some of which include the full text of newspapers indexed. Newspaper indexes are often distributed by many of the same vendors that distribute indexes of magazines and journals. In fact, most of the comprehensive periodical indexes discussed include indexing for a few national newspapers, such as the *New York Times,* the *Wall Street Journal,* and the *Christian Science Monitor.* Likewise, major business periodical indexes usually include indexing for the *Wall Street Journal* and a variety of regional business newspapers. Most college and university libraries make available one or more of the following newspaper indexes:

New York Times Index. (1913–). New York: New York Times.

- This index provides subject access to and abstracts of news stories, editorials, letters to the editor, obituaries, and other features. Material from the four wire services used by the *New York Times*—Associated Press, Bloomberg, Dow Jones, and Reuters—also is included.

The *Prior Series* section of the print index provides coverage of the period 1851–1912. The full text of recent years is available online through several vendors, including *Newspaper Abstracts, LexisNexis Academic,* and *ProQuest Newspapers.* Full image and full text of the newspaper from its inception (1851) until 3 years before the current date are available through *ProQuest Historical Newspapers: New York Times.*

ProQuest Newspaper Abstracts [Online]. (1989–). Ann Arbor, MI: ProQuest Information and Learning.

■ *Newspaper Abstracts* contains indexing and abstracting of significant articles appearing in 27 national and regional newspapers. National publications indexed include the *New York Times, Wall Street Journal, American Banker, Christian Science Monitor, Washington Post,* and *USA Today.* Coverage for most papers begins in 1986.

Additional databases that provide comprehensive coverage of newspapers include the *National Newspaper Index* and *NewsBank.* In addition, comprehensive databases such as *LexisNexis Academic* and *Factiva* provide the full text of many newspapers. There are many options, but the situation will vary widely from library to library. Ask the reference staff at your library what access to newspaper indexing the library provides.

The web provides another approach. Most newspapers now have websites, and several provide searchable archives. Several comprehensive online directories to newspaper websites are available, including those maintained by the *American Journalism Review*'s *AJR NewsLink* **<http://www.newslink.org/menu.html>**. NewsVoyager at the Newspaper Association of America website provides links to local papers throughout the country **<http://www.newspaperlinks.com/voyager.cfm>**. These sites do not necessarily indicate whether a newspaper's site includes archives, however. For a comprehensive approach to searching more than 200 newspapers and their archives individually, regionally, or on the national level, try **<http://www.newslibrary.com>**. This website, maintained by NewsBank, allows you to search its database free of charge to retrieve substantial article abstracts. Complete articles are available online for a fee.

A print directory, *Fulltext Sources Online* (semiannual), provides comprehensive coverage of the full-text offerings of 29 major vendors, including DIALOG, LexisNexis, Westlaw, Dow Jones, EBSCO, and Burrelle's. This source also indicates newspapers (and journals) that offer free Internet archives.

Retrospective newspaper indexing has typically been limited. Few of the 1,500 daily newspapers in this country were indexed until fairly recently. Fortunately, indexing for many local newspapers is now available in the sources described. For example, NewsBank's *America's Newspapers* provides full-text access to approximately 270 national, regional, and local newspapers. A printed index may be available for earlier periods. *Newspaper Indexes: A Location and Subject Guide for Researchers,* Vols. 1 through 3 (1977–1982), provides a comprehensive list of newspaper indexes for a short time period. Newspapers that are not indexed sometimes have extensive library files you can search on-site.

Newspapers with smaller circulations, covering city, local, and regional news, can be located by using the *Gale Directory of Publications and Broadcast Media*. Occasionally, public libraries will index their own hometown newspapers, but college and university libraries seldom have time to do this.

If you are interested in investigating nonestablishment opinions on topics such as social movements, you might find articles in some newspapers to be important. Some publications with smaller circulations and specialized audiences are indexed in the following sources:

> *Alternative Press Index.* (1969–). Baltimore: Alternative Press Center. (Available: **http://www.altpress.org/api.html**)
>
> ■ This index covers most of the alternative and radical publications available in the United States. News of social issues and movements and opinions on issues published in these magazines, journals, and newspapers are accessible by combined author-subject listings. The print index is issued biannually. Direct links to the websites of indexed publications are maintained in the online directory of the Alternatives Press Center's website <**http://www.altpress.org**>, which features a directory of more than 400 *alternative online resources.*
>
> *Alt-Press Watch.* (2001–). Ann Arbor, MI: ProQuest Information and Learning/Softline. (Available: **http://www.proquest.com**)
>
> ■ This interdisciplinary, full-text database attempts to cover the alternative and independent press. It includes more than 170 newspapers, magazines, and journals. Retrospective coverage varies by publication, although coverage of many publications begins in 1988.
>
> *Ethnic NewsWatch.* (1991–). Ann Arbor, MI: ProQuest Information and Learning/Softline. (Available: **http://www.proquest.com**)
>
> ■ *Ethnic NewsWatch* is a full-text collection from 200 publications of the ethnic, minority, and native press. It includes newspapers, magazines, and journals published in the United States, United Kingdom, Africa, and Canada. English- and Spanish-language search options are available.

Broadcast and Electronic Media

Even though most of the collections just described consist of print media, electronic media collections are also available. Researchers often need to examine original broadcasts or their scripts, for example, to analyze their content or to conduct historical or critical research. Media professionals also consult archival materials when preparing news programs or documentaries.

Transcripts of national news broadcasts are available through several online databases, including *LexisNexis Academic, Newspaper Source, Factiva,* and *Global Newsbank.* For earlier years, the text of productions from CBS News through 1991 is available on microfiche for student use in libraries that have subscribed to the *CBS News Index.* Similar services are available for ABC News and public television.

Broadcast indexes are useful for ascertaining perspectives on current events and for conducting content analyses of news programs. The *CBS News Index* provides guidance on where in the microfiche collection the desired transcript can be found. It remains useful for historical retrospective research.

> *CBS News Index.* (1975–1991). Ann Arbor, MI: University Microfilms International.
>
> ■ This index catalogs all daily news broadcasts, public affairs broadcasts, and programs (such as *60 Minutes* and *Face the Nation*) produced by CBS News from 1975 to 1991. Subject headings lead to descriptive phrases of the pertinent broadcasts, and locator information is given for the verbatim transcripts found in an accompanying microfiche collection. The National Archives will lend (for a fee) the CBS videotapes through interlibrary loan; these videotapes are also available for use at 13 regional archives.

Full-text news transcripts of many major networks, including CBS, dating from 1990 to the present, are also available on *LexisNexis Academic*. As with the CBS broadcasts, actual collections of electronic media programs are generally available only in a few archives in the United States, such as the Museum of Television and Radio in New York City and Los Angeles and the Museum of Broadcast Communications in Chicago. Some are open to the general public. If they are, you'll still need to visit the archive to view or listen to the materials.

Two exceptions are the Vanderbilt Television News Archive at Vanderbilt University (Nashville, Tennessee) and the Public Affairs Video Archives at Purdue University (West Lafayette, Indiana); both rent videotapes and audiotapes. Vanderbilt lists its holdings in the *Television News Index and Abstracts* (1972–); it is searchable online at its website **<http://tvnews.vanderbilt.edu>** for those affiliated with institutions that subscribe. This collection and others are described in the Television News Study Center's (1981) *Television News Resources: A Guide to Collections.*

C-SPAN (Cable-Satellite Public Affairs Network) programs are archived in the C-SPAN Archives. C-SPAN airs programs on Washington politics, proceedings of Congress, national events, world legislatures, conferences, and special topics that deal with communication, such as talk radio and political campaign commercials. These programs are cataloged, indexed, and distributed on videotape or DVD or through printed transcript. Transcripts of Federal News Service materials (presidential speeches, daily briefings, congressional news conferences, Supreme Court decisions) are also available. For information, contact the C-SPAN Archives at **<http://www.c-spanarchives.org/>**, where many programs also can be viewed online.

The Julian P. Kanter Political Commercial Archive at the University of Oklahoma archives radio and television political advertisements. The archive includes commercials of candidates for political office as well as those sponsored by political action committees, corporations, and special interest groups. Presidential debates, conventions, and significant televised speeches are also archived. You can use *WorldCat* to locate these materials, but archive staff must retrieve materials for users. More information is available on the archive website **<http://www.ou.edu/pccenter/aboutthearchive.htm>**, where an online catalog to the collection can be searched.

Although dated, other archives are identified in the *Review and Criticism* section of the March 1984 issue of *Critical Studies in Mass Communication* (see Chapter 7), where archives in mass communication, film, television, photography, and newspapers are described. Other indexes and directories of archive collections, including Godfrey's (1983) *A Directory of Broadcast Archives,* are listed at the end of this chapter. Note that these sources are useful in a historical sense but are now dated. Sterling, Bracken, and Hill's (1998) guide to the literature, *Mass Communications Research Resources* (see Chapter 6), identifies more electronic media archives. Other useful source materials are primary documents relating to the regulation of the electronic media industries. A useful but older compilation of such documents for those working in the area of broadcast law and freedom of expression is the following:

> Kahn, F. J. (Ed.). (1984). *Documents of American broadcasting* (4th ed.). Englewood Cliffs, NJ: Prentice Hall.
>
> ■ This sourcebook collects 43 primary documents about public policy, history, and issues in U.S. broadcasting. Documents include federal laws, commission regulations, congressional reports and actions, court decisions, speeches, letters, and other documents from parts of the U.S. Constitution to cable access and radio deregulation. The broad subject areas of these documents are broadcast regulation development, freedom of expression, competition regulation, public broadcasting, and public interest. Brief commentaries provide background, explanation, and interpretation. A few related readings follow each document. There is a glossary of legal terms, a brief identification of legal citations, an index to legal decisions, and a general index.

Thus many new access tools have become available with the advent of CD-ROM and online technology. Printed abstracts and indexes are becoming less useful now that searching electronic databases is possible in most libraries and remote locations. If proper search techniques are used, searches should result in more valid citations for the researcher. In many cases, full-text documents are accessible (sometimes for a fee), and this saves researchers time and effort. Look through the list of additional access tools at the end of this chapter for more specialized tools.

Measurement Collections

One other type of collection is a compilation of measures of communication attitudes and personality. Researchers find these collections useful when planning descriptive and experimental research studies. Robinson, Shaver, Wrightsman, and Andrews' (1991) *Measures of Personality and Social Psychological Attitudes* and Rosen and McReynolds' (1968–1992) series of books, *Advances in Psychological Assessment,* are often helpful to students conducting their own research projects. One additional work, Chun, Cobb, and French's (1975) *Measures for Psychological Assessment* indexes by author and subject the original sources and applications of 3,000 psychological measures. For communication, consult the following:

> Rubin, R. B., Palmgreen, P., & Sypher, H. E. (Eds.). (1994). *Communication research measures: A sourcebook.* New York: Guilford.
>
> ■ This volume profiles more than 60 often-used research measures in instructional, interpersonal, mass, and organizational communication. Besides presenting the actual measure and pertinent references to its use, each profile highlights the purpose, development, reliability, and validity of the measure. In addition, the editors and associate editors discuss measurement trends and issues within the four areas of communication research. A table of contents and an index provide ready access to each measure that is profiled.

A second volume (Rubin, Rubin, Graham, Perse, & Seibold, 2009), published by Routledge, identifies additional measures in these areas plus covers health, family, intercultural, and group communication as well as often-used measures from other disciplines.

Collections of measures are helpful for researchers conducting investigations because these provide not only the scale items but information on the validity and reliability of the instrument. Often they furnish additional references to articles in which the instrument is used, so they can help broaden your search for a particular concept.

Legal Collections

Loose-leaf reporting services assemble, organize, and digest topical legal reports on a single subject. These materials are collected in a binder, and regular supplements are distributed, often weekly. The major goal of these services is to keep the legal profession abreast of continually evolving areas of law. These services are valuable for communication students interested in studying questions about policy, regulation, and freedom of speech. Two of these services provide the text of legislative actions and court decisions that are significant for the mass media.

Pike & Fischer Radio Regulation. (1946–). Bethesda, MD: Pike & Fischer.

■ This service consists of *Current Service, Digest,* and *Decision (Cases)* volumes. The *Current Service* volumes contain the text of current laws and regulations that affect broadcasting, including statutes, congressional committee reports, treatises, and international agreements as well as rules and regulations of the Federal Communications Commission (FCC) for radio, television, and cable television.

The *Digest* volumes contain all FCC decisions, as well as selected Federal Radio Commission and federal and state court decisions, through July 1963. The *Decision* volumes contain FCC decisions and reports and court decisions prior to July 1963 in the first series and after that date in the second series. There also is a volume that provides a master index, finding aids, and FCC forms.

Media Law Reporter. (1977–). Washington, DC: Bureau of National Affairs.

■ This weekly service provides indexed coverage of all decisions of the U.S. Supreme Court and selected decisions of federal and state courts and administrative agencies that affect the electronic and print media. The full text is published for most opinions, including concurrences and dissents. Summary opinions are presented for some cases.

Decisions are classified in four major divisions: Regulation of Media Content, Regulation of Media Distribution, Newsgathering, and Media Ownership. There is a topical index arranged alphabetically by major subjects (such as broadcast media or commercial speech) and subheads (such as regulation of advertising content). Also provided are tables of cases by plaintiff and defendant and by jurisprudence (such as U.S. Supreme Court or First Circuit Court of Appeals) and an index digest. There is an annual accumulation.

Besides the official report of the U.S. Supreme Court decisions, *United States Supreme Court Reports* (1790–), there are two useful and privately published editions of the court's decisions, *United States Supreme Court Reports: Lawyers'*

Edition, Second Series (1956–) and the *Supreme Court Reporter* (1882–). These unofficial reporting services reproduce the same text of the decisions as the official reports and include their own summary of cases and annotations written by the publishers' editorial staffs.

A new website, the *Findlaw Constitutional Law Center* <**http://supreme.lp. findlaw.com**> is an educational resource site dedicated to the U.S. Constitution and Supreme Court. It includes historical documents from 1893 to the present, biographies of Supreme Court justices and Supreme Court decisions, and current and upcoming cases.

These official and unofficial reports of court decisions can be useful when studying communication law, debate, or freedom of speech. They are available in law libraries and many university libraries. The *United States Supreme Court Reports: Lawyers' Edition* is available in many libraries through *LexisNexis*. West Publishing also produces a *National Reporter System* of seven regional and two state *Reporters* that includes most of the decisions issued by the appellate courts of the 50 states each year. These are also available in law libraries.

STATISTICAL SOURCES

You will often need to locate statistical data to document research for a wide variety of projects, such as finding facts to support a debate case on social welfare, developing background material for a newspaper article on unemployment in a local area, doing research for a term paper on the history of broadcasting, and preparing for a speech or group discussion on trends in American television. Or, when you are conducting research on a topic, you may find that the author of a book or article has cited data that are germane to your research but are now several years out of date. Thus an important step in the research process is attempting to update such references by using **statistical sources**, collections of numerical data compiled into comprehensive tables.

A major activity of governments at all levels is the collection, compilation, and publication of a wide variety of statistical data. The following statistical yearbook is often a good first place to check for data about the United States:

> U.S. Department of Commerce, Bureau of the Census. (1879–). *Statistical Abstract of the United States*. Washington, DC: Government Printing Office.
>
> ■ This annual compendium contains summaries of social, economic, and political statistics for the United States. Communications and Information Technology is one section of the *Abstract*. Population, Vital Statistics, Education, and Elections are also included among the *Abstract*'s 30 sections. The source notes given for each table and the bibliography of sources at the end of the volume make this a handy guide to many statistics published by the U.S. government as well as by trade associations and other organizations. A detailed subject index helps locate statistics on a specific topic. The table of contents is useful for researching broad subjects. This source is also available on CD-ROM and on the web at the U.S. Census Bureau's website <**http://www.census.gov/**>. The CD-ROM version includes additional data and direct links to all cited federal statistical sources. Data can be exported to a spreadsheet. The web version consists of PDF files that can be read with Adobe Acrobat Reader.

The U.S. Census Bureau's home page will also lead you to *American Factfinder* **<http://factfinder.census.gov/>**, which serves as the Bureau's interface for distributing the 1990 and 2000 *Census of Population & Housing,* the *1997 Economic Census,* and the *American Community Survey.* It's an easy-to-use source of fast facts. In addition to the Census Bureau, other government agencies provide online access to many of the statistics they collect. *FedStats* **<http://www.fedstats.gov/>** serves as a gateway to the statistical collections of more than 100 of these agencies.

A commercially produced index, the *American Statistics Index (ASI)*, indexes statistical publications produced by all departments and agencies of the U.S. government, including the FCC and the Census Bureau. It can be quite helpful when conducting statistical research.

> *American Statistics Index: A Comprehensive Guide and Index to the Statistical Publications of the U.S. Government.* (1973–). Bethesda, MD: Congressional Information Service.
>
> ■   This commercially produced indexing and abstracting service provides comprehensive coverage of statistical publications of the federal government. It is issued monthly in two sections (indexes and abstracts) and is cumulated annually. Besides the index by subjects and names, the source contains indexes by title, by agency report numbers, and by geographic, economic, and demographic categories. The latter index is useful for researchers who are interested in statistics that are broken down in a particular way, such as by age, city, and so forth. Documents abstracted in *ASI* are available on microfiche in some libraries. *ASI* is available online as part of *LexisNexisStatistical* and on CD-ROM as part of *Statistical Masterfile. LexisNexisStatistical* provides links to the full text of many documents.

If you're looking for statistics collected by states, other countries, international agencies, and many other sources, the *Statistical Resources on the Web* website, compiled and maintained by the Documents Center at the University of Michigan Library, is an excellent starting place **<http://www.lib.umich.edu/govdocs/stats.html>**. Links are comprehensive and kept current. This is a great site to bookmark.

Because the websites mentioned in this chapter and *ASI* provide excellent access to nearly all statistical information published by the federal government, we won't cite all statistical publications that might be of interest to communication researchers. Some selected publications are listed at the end of this chapter, along with several statistical sources on the international level that are published by the United Nations. Later in this chapter, we discuss other U.S. government publications.

Governments and agencies are not, of course, the only sources of useful statistics. Many of the publications described or identified in this chapter—in particular, the *Gale Directory of Publications and Broadcast Media* and the *Broadcasting & Cable Yearbook*—include substantial amounts of statistical data drawn from a variety of sources.

Other important sources of statistical data include trade and professional associations such as the American Association of Advertising Agencies, the American Newspaper Publishers Association, the Association of American Publishers, the Electronic Industries Association, the National Association of Broadcasters, the Radio Advertising Bureau, and the Television Bureau of Advertising. These associations gather and report a variety of statistical data and materials about their respective industries. For example, the research department of the National Association of Broadcasters has produced various booklets and reports about trends and developments in broadcasting. Statistical publications of many associations are indexed and abstracted in *Statistical Reference Index (SRI)*, published by Congressional Information Service. It is available online as part of *LexisNexis Statistical*.

Sources for some subject areas include several companies whose business it is to gather and market data, such as the Arbitron Ratings Company, the A. C. Nielsen Company, Standard Rate and Data, and the Gallup, Harris, and Roper polling organizations. These data are often summarized in separate publications, a few of which are listed at the end of this chapter. The Arbitron and Nielsen organizations produce a variety of materials, such as detailed ratings reports for their client stations in radio and television markets, studies of the reliability of broadcast ratings, and pamphlets that detail trends in the electronic media or report specialty studies like investigations of cable television.

One reference work that has compiled data from many of these sources provides a historical perspective on trends in the electronic media:

Sterling, C. H. (1984). *Electronic media: A guide to trends in broadcasting and newer technologies 1920–1983*. New York: Praeger.

■ Data about quantitative trends in the electronic media industry from 1920 to 1984 are included. About 150 tables are in the book's eight sections: Electronic Media Growth, Ownership, Economics, Employment, Content Trends, Audience, International Aspects, and Regulation. Each set of tables is accompanied by a narrative interpretation and by a discussion of the sources, reliability, and validity of the data. These features, as well as the additional references listed for each topic, make this a useful historical reference.

GOVERNMENT DOCUMENTS

Besides statistics, the U.S. government publishes periodicals, directories, handbooks, and bibliographies. You are probably already familiar with many of these documents. However, you might be less familiar with other common types of **government documents**, such as federal statutes, congressional hearings and reports, census materials, and government agency regulations and reports. In this section we describe some of these publications and special finding tools that can be used to identify and locate them. Many are listed in the *Selected Sources* section of this chapter.

Several government sources detail the laws, rules, and regulations of the United States. These sources help us keep abreast of changes in the law. For example, this information is important for preparing debate cases, analyzing media policy, understanding political campaign regulations, comparing the demographic composition of a sample, and the like. These materials are generally available in the government documents section of many libraries. Most are available on the web through *GPO Access* **<http://www.access.gpo.gov/>** and *LexisNexis Congressional*. The general and permanent laws of the United States are codified in the *United States Code*. The U.S. Code is available full text through *Lexis/Nexis Academic*.

U.S. Congress, House of Representatives. (2000). *United States code* (2000 ed.). Washington, DC: Government Printing Office.

■ The code includes the federal laws of this country. The text of the multitude of laws that existed in this country as of January 2001 is provided in the 50 titles or content areas of this 13th edition of the code. For example, selected chapters of Title 17, Copyrights, include Subject Matter and Scope of Copyrights, Copyright Ownership and Transfer, Duration of Copyrights, and the Copyright Office. Title 47 of the code, Telegraphs, Telephones, and Radiotelegraphs, includes the Communications Act of 1934, as amended. Other titles include Census, Commerce and Trade, Education, Labor, and Money and Finance. A new edition of the code has been published every 6 years since 1926 by the Law Revision Counsel of the House of Representatives. A supplement is issued after each session of Congress. The code is also available online through *GPO Access* and *LexisNexis Congressional*.

The *Federal Register* publishes daily, on weekdays, regulations and legal notices issued by the executive branch and federal agencies.

U.S. General Services Administration, Office of the Federal Register. (1936–). *Federal Register*. Washington, DC: Government Printing Office.

■ The purpose of the *Federal Register* is to make regulations and notices, including presidential proclamations, executive orders, and federal agency documents and activities, available to the public. It is divided into several sections: rules and regulations, proposed rules, notices, and Sunshine Act meetings. For each of the rules or proposed rules, the agency, action, rule summary, effective dates, addresses, and supplementary information are included. Each notice announces hearings and investigations, committee meetings, delegations of authority, agency decisions and rulings, and agency statements of organization and function. For example, rule-making proceedings and hearings of the FCC and the Federal Trade Commission (FTC) are announced in the *Register*. The regulatory documents contained in the *Federal Register* are keyed to and codified in the *Code of Federal Regulations*. This publication of the U.S. General Services Administration contains the general and permanent rules of executive departments and federal agencies that are published in the *Federal Register*. The *Code of Federal Regulations* is indexed in the *Code of Federal Regulations: CFR Index and Finding Aids*. Both the *Federal Register* and the *Code of Federal Regulations* are available through *GPO Access, LexisNexis Academic,* and *LexisNexis Congressional*.

The FCC can be a particularly useful source of information if you are researching communication policy and regulation. Three of its publications are especially helpful. *FCC Rules and Regulations* contains the text of FCC rules in such matters as commission operation, frequency allocations, broadcast services, satellite communications, and cable television services. The biweekly *FCC Record* incorporates the FCC's current decisions, orders, policy statements, and public notices of hearings and rule-making proceedings. The *Record* issues are cumulated yearly, and these volumes have a list of commission actions and documents. They also contain a subject digest that summarizes pertinent information on such topics as fairness, issues and program lists, and cellular communication systems. *The Annual Report of the Federal Communications Commission* provides a yearly comprehensive review of significant events in all areas of communication regulation, including broadcasting, cable television, common carriers (e.g., satellites), spectrum management, and frequency allocations. These sources are also available through the FCC website **<http://www.fcc.gov/>**.

Also useful are the various reports of congressional committees, executive agencies, and other regulatory commissions such as the FTC. For example, if you are researching the topic of television violence, you might find references to the report of the Surgeon General's Advisory Committee (1972), *Television and Social Behavior*, to the congressional report of the House Committee on Interstate and Foreign Commerce (1977), *Violence on Television*, or to the report by the National Institutes of Mental Health (1982), *Television and Behavior*. These reports are widely cited, and because they sometimes contain the testimony of expert witnesses in addition to well-researched background material, they are useful resources for a research project.

One problem with locating government publications is that they are not included in some library catalogs. Many libraries shelve government publications in a special section, so these publications might be overlooked. You will need to investigate how such documents are handled in the library you are using. If they have not been included in the library catalog, discover which local access tools are available and how they are shelved and arranged. A reference librarian can help you with this.

Another difficulty in locating government publications is that they are also not included in most periodical indexes. The Public Affairs Information Service (PAIS) *Bulletin* (listed in the *Periodical Indexes and Abstracts* section at the end of Chapter 6) indexes some government publications. But even this source lists only about 1 percent of the federal documents published. Another source, though, the *U.S. Government Periodicals Index*, does index the publications of more than 100 agencies of the U.S. government. This source is also available online and on CD-ROM in some libraries as *LexisNexis Government Periodicals Index (1988)*.

In any library setting, the basic all-around tool used to identify the availability of U.S. government publications on a given topic, by a given author, or published by a given agency is the following:

> U.S. Superintendent of Documents. (1895–). *Monthly Catalog of United States Government Publications*. Washington, DC: Government Printing Office.
>
> ■ The *Monthly Catalog* is the most complete catalog of publications of all branches of the federal government. It has semiannual and annual cumulative indexes by title, author or agency, and subject. Documents are listed only in the year they are published, so it is often necessary to search through several volumes to find information about a particular document.
>
> Library of Congress subject headings have been used in the subject index since July 1976. The catalog is arranged alphabetically by issuing agency, with each entry assigned a number. It is to this number that the index refers. Information given in entries is similar to that found in most library catalog records, with the addition of the Superintendent of Documents number. This number is a classification number similar in function to a Library of Congress or Dewey Decimal call number, and it is used in many libraries to arrange government documents on the shelf. Refer to the user's guide at the front of each volume to help identify the elements of each entry and decipher the abbreviations. The Cumulative Subject Index to the *Monthly Catalog of U.S. Government Publications, 1900–1971*, should be used for retrospective searches.
>
> The *Monthly Catalog* is available online from 1994 through *GPO Access* as the *Catalog of U.S. Government Publications* <**http://www.access.gpo.gov**>. This web version includes direct links to electronic documents issued by many government agencies. Many libraries with government document collections subscribe to a CD-ROM version of this database.

One disadvantage of the *Monthly Catalog* as a tool for identifying relevant materials is that it does not include annotations or abstracts. However, such abstracts for two important types of government publications are available. For those published by Congress, consult the *CIS/Index to Publications of the United States Congress* (available online as *LexisNexis Congressional*; see below), and, as you recall, for those that are statistical in nature, the *American Statistics Index* (online as *LexisNexis Statistical*) is helpful.

The various committees of the U.S. Congress and their staffs investigate many current social, economic, and political issues and publish the results of these investigations either as hearings, committee prints, or reports. A hearing is simply a transcript of the testimony of witnesses before a committee or subcommittee. Because many of these witnesses are experts in their fields and collectively represent a broad range of views, hearings are often excellent resource materials for researching controversial topics, such as the effects of television on children. Committee prints are reports of background research done either by committee staffs or by the Congressional Research Service of the Library of Congress. House and Senate reports are the official committee reports to the entire House or Senate, summarizing the results of investigations or hearings and making recommendations. Those published in 1995 and after are available online on *Thomas,* a Library of Congress website that provides legislative information **<http://thomas.loc.gov/home/thomas.html>**.

All of these publications, as well as the legislation that results from committee hearings and the like, are indexed and abstracted in the following:

> *CIS/Index to Publications of the United States Congress.* (1970–). Washington, DC: Congressional Information Service.
>
> ■   This service provides complete indexing and abstracting for all the working papers of Congress, including committee hearings, prints, and reports. *CIS* appears monthly and is cumulated quarterly and annually. It is published in two parts, an index section and an abstract section. Entries in the index volume refer users to relevant abstracts by means of an entry number. Included in both the index and abstracts are entries for individual witnesses at hearings. The history of individual pieces of legislation is covered in annual accumulations. Some libraries own the complete microfiche collection of all documents that are abstracted. Access to this collection is by entry number of the abstract.
>
> This index is also available as part of *LexisNexis Congressional* and on CD-ROM in some libraries. *LexisNexis Congressional* provides access to the full text of many documents, including most congressional hearings.

Other useful publications for following current congressional deliberations are the Congressional Record (available through *Thomas, GPO Access,* and *LexisNexis Congressional*), the *Index to Daily Proceedings* (available via *Thomas*), *Congressional Index* (a loose-leaf service published by Commerce Clearing House), and two works published by Congressional Quarterly: *Congressional Quarterly Almanac* and *Congressional Quarterly Weekly Report*. Congressional Quarterly also produces useful guides for understanding the history and workings of Congress, the Supreme Court, and U.S. elections. These are listed at the end of this chapter.

The tools just described are useful only for finding publications of the U.S. government and only for a relatively recent time period. If you need to identify earlier documents or those at local, state, or international levels, consult one or more of the finding aids for government materials listed at the end of this chapter, such as

Shepard's Acts and Cases by Popular Names: Federal and State (1992). As mentioned earlier, the Documents Center at the University of Michigan maintains a comprehensive listing of sources of documents published on the web by state, federal, and international governments **<http://www.lib.umich.edu/govdocs/>**.

The U.S. government helps the public navigate the web by providing a search engine for its 100 million pages of information. Called *FirstGov* **<http://www.firstgov.gov>**, the site's search engine indexes only government sites and has separate directories for federal and state or local government. *Google*'s *UncleSam* **<http://www.google.com/unclesam>** provides somewhat more relevant searches.

YEARBOOKS

Yearbooks and **annuals** contain current information on yearly developments in a specific field. They also provide excellent background information, statistics, narrative explanations, and listings, much like that found in directories and manuals. An excellent research tool for students in mass communication is the following:

> *Broadcasting & Cable Yearbook* (2 vols.). (1935–). New Providence, NJ: Bowker.
>
> ■   This comprehensive reference tool contains detailed information about various elements of the radio, television, and cable industries. Volume 1 contains a brief history of broadcasting and cable; overviews of broadcasting and cable ownership and station transactions; directories and summaries of television, radio, and cable stations and markets in the U.S. and Canada; descriptions of satellite operators and other carriers; overviews of television, radio, and cable programming, and equipment, broker, and professional services; listings of associations, events, and education programs; and a summary of law, regulation, and government agencies relevant to broadcasting and cable in these countries. Volume 2 includes a brief year-in-review summary and the *Yellow Pages* of radio, television, and cable, containing an alphabetical listing of stations, companies, and industry personnel.
>
> The *Yearbook* was originally issued as an annual supplement to *Broadcasting* magazine and then produced in two separate publications, *Broadcasting Yearbook* (1944–1979) and *Cable Sourcebook* (1972–1979). In 1980 the two were combined in the *Broadcasting/Cable Yearbook* (from 1982 to 1988 it was titled *Broadcasting/Cablecasting Yearbook*) and later called *Broadcasting Yearbook* until 1992, when the R. R. Bowker Company began publishing it as *Broadcasting & Cable Marketplace* until 1993.

Other useful yearbooks, such as *Editor & Publisher International Year Book* (1959–), are listed at the end of this chapter.

DIRECTORIES

Directories provide basic information about people, companies, organizations, and publications. One directory that students in journalism and communication find helpful is the following:.

> *Gale Directory of Publications and Broadcast Media* (5 vols., 137th ed.). (1869–). Detroit: Gale Research.

■ This directory covers over 57,000 publications and media outlets in the U.S. and Canada. Volumes 1 and 2 list newspapers, magazines, other periodicals, and cable, radio, and television stations. Also included are economic descriptions of the states, provinces, cities, and towns of these media. The main section lists media by location. The descriptions include format of the medium, starting date, frequency of publication or operating hours for electronic media, key personnel, ownership, service area, subscription rates, and advertising rates.

Volume 3 provides summary information of industry activity (start-ups and cessations), industry statistics, broadcast and cable networks, news and feature syndicates, publisher and subject indexes, newspaper feature editors, and a master name and keyword index. Volume 4 provides maps of the United States, Puerto Rico, and Canada and regional market indexes for the different media. Volume 5 contains the international index and maps. Before 1987 this directory was known as the *Ayer Directory of Publications* and from 1987 to 1989 as *Gale Directory of Publications*. This source is available online through *GaleNet* as the *Gale Database of Publications and Broadcast Media*.

Aside from the need to locate materials from newspapers and news programs, communication researchers occasionally need to find educational media when pursuing research projects dealing with the media—for example, historical or critical studies of film.

Educational or instructional media, including films, filmstrips, audiotapes, and videotapes, can be located in several reference sources. *The Video Source Book* is a handy way to find videotapes:

The Video Source Book (2 vols.). (1979–). Syosset, NY: National Video Clearinghouse.

■ This comprehensive annual lists videotapes available for purchase, rent or lease, off-air taping, free loan, or duplication. Coverage includes business and industry, entertainment, and instruction. Each entry contains a short description, credits, producer, audience or purpose, permissible uses (e.g., broadcast television, in-home viewing), terms of availability (e.g, loan, purchase, off-air record), television standards (e.g., NTSC, PAL), distributor, and often, price. This source provides subject and credit indexes and a section on distributors.

A useful source for locating reviews assessing the content and quality of educational media is the following:

Media Review Digest. (1974–). Ann Arbor, MI: Pierian.

■ This annual publication indexes reviews of feature films and educational media such as educational films, videotapes, filmstrips, records, audiotapes, and miscellaneous productions. Items are arranged alphabetically by title within sections devoted to each form of media (for example, *Films and Videotapes*). Entries include a brief description of the item, followed by a listing of reviews that have appeared in periodicals. Among the indexes are a subject index by Library of Congress subject headings and an index of reviewers. The *Digest* also includes lists of film awards and prizes, bibliographies of media materials, and book reviews. From 1970 to 1972 this index was known as *Multi Media Reviews Index*. It is available online via *FirstSearch*.

Another type of media directory compiles facts about and synopses of television and radio programs. These are helpful when doing research about programming trends and the antecedents of contemporary programming. Descriptions usually include dates of airing, cast members, and brief summaries of program content. One such directory is:

> Brooks, T., & Marsh, E. (Eds.). (2003). *The complete directory to prime time network and cable TV shows, 1946–present* (8th ed.). New York: Ballantine.

> ■ This volume lists and describes every regular television series (lasting 4 or more weeks) aired by the commercial networks during the 6 P.M. to sign-off period, as well as the top syndicated evening programs from 1946. News, sports, and movies are also included. Each entry provides dates of the first and last telecasts along with a history of the series, a list of cast members, and a synopsis of the program. Appendixes include season ratings, season network schedules, major television awards, and other information. There is also a comprehensive index of cast members.

A general directory useful to students of organizational or mass communication is the following:

> *Standard & Poor's Register of Corporations, Directors & Executives* (3 vols.). (1928–). New York: Standard & Poor's.

> ■ This work is issued annually and contains information on location, telephone number, offices, products, sales, and number of employees of more than 37,000 U.S. and Canadian corporations.

A more specialized directory of corporations is *Working Press of the Nation* (1945).

Some other directories of interest to communication students are at the end of this chapter. *Directories in Print* can help you find directories not given here. It lists more than 10,000 industrial, trade, and professional directories. It is available online as part of the *Gale Database of Publications and Broadcast Media,* offered through *GaleNet*.

DICTIONARIES

Academic disciplines use language and jargon that might confuse readers. The words can seem familiar, but often the meanings are not what we expect. There are sources that can help clarify your understanding of new or unique terms.

Dictionaries are usually thought of simply as alphabetic arrangements of words and their meanings. Although the denotative meaning of a word is typically sought when a dictionary is consulted, other information is available. This information often includes pronunciation, spelling, hyphenation, word etymology, syllabication, and synonyms.

There are four basic types of dictionaries. General dictionaries are the abridged and unabridged versions with which you are most familiar. You consult these when you need to find out the meaning of a word, how to pronounce a word, or where to divide a word into syllables. Language dictionaries give more attention to slang terms, the root and history of a word, and synonyms and antonyms. Foreign language dictionaries translate words from one language to another and often provide a guide to pronunciation. Subject dictionaries, which are much more specialized, concentrate on one specific topic or discipline and are our focus here.

Subject dictionaries list and define basic and specialized terms in a particular field. They also provide meanings for abbreviations, jargon, and slang. At times subject dictionaries resemble encyclopedias in that they give lengthy descriptions of and bibliographic references for terms. Less inclusive and more specialized dictionaries can be helpful when you encounter unfamiliar terms in communication and related areas. The dictionaries listed at the end of this chapter will help you find precise meanings of communication and research terms. The law dictionaries we list help when you need to know the legal sense or use of words. They are handy, quick-reference books, helpful in learning the language of a discipline.

MANUALS

A **manual**, or fact book, is a quick-reference handbook about a broad subject area. Usually, manuals present generally accepted data rather than the most recent information as do yearbooks and directories. They often provide statistical tables, bibliographies, glossaries, and limited directories. We list some examples of useful manuals in various facets of communication at the end of this chapter.

Students interested in publishing, writing, and editing also have several manuals and directories available for their use. The manuals provide tips on writing style and selling one's work. The directories reference publishing companies and other markets where work can be submitted. We also cite a few of these works in the list of *Selected Sources* that follows.

SUMMARY

In this chapter we identified many different types of quick-reference research sources used to find factual information. Collections and archives can be searched for supporting primary documents. Many of these are online collections, whereas others must be visited to take full advantage of their collections. For instance, transcripts of speeches can easily be accessed online, but some videos might have to be accessed at the archive. Most statistical sources and government documents today are online as well. Because there is so much published U.S. government information, smaller libraries might not house all the documents, but it may be possible to access them online. Yearbooks, directories, dictionaries, and manuals contain up-to-date information about people, businesses, meanings of words, and how-to information. All of this is helpful when you need quick, practical information.

References

Ash, L., & Miller, W. G. (Comps.). (1993). *Subject collections* (7th ed., Rev. & enl., 2 vols.). New Providence, NJ: Bowker.

House Committee on Interstate and Foreign Commerce. (1977). *Violence on television.* Washington, DC: U.S. Government Printing Office.

National Institutes of Mental Health. (1982). *Television and behavior* (2 vols.). Rockville, MD: U.S. Department of Health and Human Services.

Rosen, J. C., & McReynolds, P. (Eds.). (1968–1992). *Advances in psychological assessment* (8 vols.). New York: Plenum.

Sterling, C. H., & Bracken, J. K. (1998). *Mass communications research resources: An annotated guide*. Mahwah, NJ: Erlbaum.

Surgeon General's Advisory Committee. (1972). *Television and social behavior* (5 vols.). Rockville, MD: National Institutes of Mental Health.

Turner, K. J. (1986). The presidential libraries as research facilities: An analysis of resource for rhetorical scholarship. *Communication Education, 35*, 243–253.

SELECTED SOURCES

*Available Online

Collections

Speech

Campbell, K. K. (Ed.). (1993). *Women public speakers in the United States, 1800–1925: A bio-critical sourcebook*. Westport, CT: Greenwood Press.

Campbell, K. K. (Ed.). (1994). *Women public speakers in the United States, 1925–1993: A bio-critical sourcebook*. Westport, CT: Greenwood Press.

Executive Speeches. (1986–). Dayton, OH: Executive Speaker.

Lucas, S. E., & Medhurst, M. J. (Eds.). (2008). *Words of a century: The top 100 American speeches, 1900–1999*. Oxford, UK: Oxford University Press.

Podell, J., & Anzovin, S. (2001). *Speeches of the American presidents* (2nd ed.). Bronx, NY: H. W. Wilson.

Representative American Speeches. (1938–). New York: H. W. Wilson.

Vital Speeches of the Day. (1934–). New York: City News.

Voices of multicultural America: Notable speeches delivered by African, Asian, Hispanic, and Native Americans, 1790–1995. (1996). Detroit: Gale Research.

What They Said. (1969–1995). Palm Springs, CA: Monitor.

Finding Tools

Mitchell, C. (1982). *Speech index: An index to collections of world famous orations and speeches for various occasions. Fourth edition supplement, 1966–1980*. Metuchen, NJ: Scarecrow.

Oral History Index: An International Directory of Oral History Interviews. (1990–). Westport, CT: Meckler.

Oral History Sources. (1988–). Alexandria, VA: Chadwyck-Healey.

Sutton, R. B. (1966). *Speech index: An index to 259 collections of world famous orations and speeches for various occasions* (4th ed., Rev. and enl.). New York: Scarecrow.

Media

Alternative Press Center. (1963–). *Underground Press Collection*. Ann Arbor, MI: University Microfilms International.

*Alternative Press Center. (1969–1990). *Alternative Press Center Archive*. Baltimore: Author. (Coverage from 1991: http://www.altpress.org/)

CBS News Daily News Broadcasts. (1900–). Sanford, NC: Microfilming Corp. of America.

Early American Newspapers. (1984–). New York: Readex Microprint.

Editorials on File. (1970–). New York: Facts on File. (Available online via FACTS.com)

Facts on File: Weekly World News Digest with Cumulative Index. (1940–). New York: Facts on File.

NewsBank. (1970–). Stamford, CT: NewsBank.

NewsBank Full-text Newspapers. (1990–). New Canaan, CT: NewsBank.

NewsBank InfoWeb. (1996–). New Canaan, CT: NewsBank. (Available: http://www.newsbank.com)

NewsBank Retrospective. (2000–). Naples, FL: NewsBank. (Coverage: 1970–1991)

NewsLibrary.com. (2003–). Naples, FL: NewsBank. (Available: http://nl.newsbank.com)

*Newspaper Source (1990–). Ipswitch, MA: EBSCO.

Public Affairs Video Archives: The Education and Research Archives of C-SPAN Programming. (1987–). West Lafayette, IN: Purdue University.

Salem, J. M. (1971). *A guide to critical reviews*. Metuchen, NJ: Scarecrow.

Shapiro, M. E. (1989). *Television network prime-time programming, 1948–1988*. Jefferson, NC: McFarland.

Shapiro, M. E. (1990). *Television network daytime and late-night programming, 1959–1989*. Jefferson, NC: McFarland.

Signorielli, N. (Ed.). (1996). *Women in communication: A biographical sourcebook*. Westport, CT: Greenwood Press.

Television & Cable Factbook (3 vols.). (1983–). Washington, DC: Warren.

TV Facts, Figures & Film. (1986–). Syosset, NY: Broadcast Information Bureau.

Viewpoint. (1976–). Glen Rock, NJ: Microfilming Corporation of America.

Women's History Research Center. (1956–). *Herstory*. Berkeley, CA: Author.

Finding Tools

Black, S. (1990). *Thesaurus of subject headings for television: A vocabulary for indexing script collections*. Phoenix: Oryx Press.

Black, S., & Moersh, E. S. (Eds.). (1990). *Index to the Annenberg Television Script Archive*. Phoenix: Oryx Press.

Indexes to American Periodicals. (1990–). Indianapolis: Computer Indexed Systems.

Library of Congress, Copyright Office. (1891–). *Catalog of Copyright Entries*. Washington, DC: Author.

Rouse, S., & Loughney, K. (Comps.). (1989). *3 decades of television: A catalog of television programs acquired by the Library of Congress 1949–1979*. Washington, DC: Library of Congress, Motion Picture, Broadcasting, & Recorded Sound Division.

Rowan, B. G., & Wood, C. J. (1994). *Scholars' guide to Washington, D.C., media collections*. Baltimore: Johns Hopkins University Press.

Shamley, S. L. (Comp.). (1991). *Television interviews, 1951–1955: A catalog of Longine's chronoscope interviews in the National Archives*. Washington, DC: U.S. National Archives and Records Administration.

Smart, J. R. (Comp.). (1982). *Radio broadcasts in the Library of Congress, 1924–1941: A catalog of recordings*. Washington, DC: Library of Congress.

University of Oklahoma, Political Commercial Archive. (1996). *Political communication center: A catalog and guide to the archival collections*. Norman: University of Oklahoma.

Media Indexes

*Alternative Press Center. *Alternative Press Index*. (1969–). Baltimore: Author. (Coverage from 1991: http://www.altpress.org/)

Alt-press Watch. (2001–). Ann Arbor, MI: ProQuest Information and Learning/ Softline.

*American Journalism Review. (1999). *AJR NewsLink*. (Available: http:// www.newslink.org/menu.html)

America's Newspapers. (1981–). Naples, FL: Newsbank. (Available: http:// www.newsbank.com)

Black Newspapers Index. (1987–). Ann Arbor, MI: University Microfilms International. (Continues *Index to Black Newspapers*, 1977–1986)

British Film Institute. (2003–). *Film Index International*. Ann Arbor, MI: Chadwyck-Healey. (Coverage begins in 1900)

Cable News Network (CNN). (1991–). Oklahoma City: Data Times. (Available: http://www.cnn.com/)

CBS News Index. (1975–1991). Ann Arbor, MI: University Microfilms International.

Chicago Tribune Index. (1972–). Ann Arbor, MI: University Microfilms International.

Chicago Tribune Index. (1982–). New York: New York Times. (Continues *Chicago Tribune Newspaper Index*, 1972–1978, and *Bell & Howell Newspaper Index to the Chicago Tribune*, 1979–1981)

Christian Science Monitor Index. (1945–). Boston: Christian Science Monitor.

Christian Science Monitor Index. (1987–). Ann Arbor, MI: University Microfilms International. (Continues *Index to the Christian Science Monitor*, 1970–1978, and *Bell & Howell Newspaper Index to the Christian Science Monitor*, 1979–1986)

DataTimes. (1994–). Ann Arbor, MI: ProQuest Information and Learning. (Available through *ProQuest Direct*)

Dintrone, C. V. (2003). *Television program master index: Access to critical and historical information on 1927 shows in 925 books, dissertations, and journal articles*. Jefferson, NC: McFarland.

Disinformation. (No date). (Available: http://www.disinfo.com)

*Editor & Publisher Interactive. (1999). *MediaINFO links: Online media directory*. VNU Business. (Available: http://www.editorandpublisher.com/editorandpubl-isher/business_resources/medialinks.jsp)

Ethnic NewsWatch. (1991–). Ann Arbor, MI: ProQuest Information and Learning/ Softline. (Coverage from 1969; Available through ProQuest)

* *Factiva*. (2001–). New York: Dow Jones. (Coverage varies; Wall Street Journal from 1979; Continues *Dow Jones Interactive*; Available: http://www.factiva. com)

Film and Television: Index. (1975–). New Canaan, CT: NewsBank.

*Foreign Broadcast Information Service. (1995–). *World News Connection*. Springfield, VA: NTIS. (Available: http://wnc.fedworld.gov)

Fulltext Sources Online: For Periodicals, Newspapers, Newswires & TV/radio Transcripts. (1989–). Needham, MA: BiblioData. (Available: http://www.infotoday.com)

Gale Database of Publications and Broadcast Media. (1996–). Farmington Hills, MI: Gale Group.

Global NewsBank. (1996–). New Canaan, CT: NewsBank. (Coverage: 1985)

Hanson, P. K., & Hanson, S. L. (Eds.). (1986). *Film review index, volume 1: 1882– 1949*. Phoenix: Oryx Press.

Hanson, P. K., & Hanson, S. L. (Eds.). (1987). *Film review index, volume 2: 1950– 1985*. Phoenix: Oryx Press.

LexisNexis Academic. (1998–). Miamisburg, OH: LexisNexis.

*Library of Congress. (1999). *Newspaper indexes*. (Available: http://lcweb.loc.gov/ rr/news/oltitles.html)

Los Angeles Times Index. (1984–). Ann Arbor, MI: University Microfilms International. (Continues *Los Angeles Times Newspaper Index*, 1972–1978, and *Bell & Howell Newspaper Index to the Los Angeles Times*, 1980–1985)

Media Review Digest. (1989–). Ann Arbor, MI: Pierian.

Milner, A. C. (Ed.). (1977–1982). *Newspaper Indexes: A Location and Subject Guide for Researchers* (3 vols.). Metuchen, NJ: Scarecrow.

National Information Center for Educational Media. (1996–2000). *NICEM Thesaurus*. Albuquerque: Author.

National Newspaper Index. (1977–). Farmington Hills, MI: Gale Group/InfoTrac.

New York Times Index. (1851–). New York: New York Times.

NewsBank Electronic Index. (1986–). New Canaan, CT: NewsBank.

Newspaper Abstracts. (1989–). Ann Arbor, MI: ProQuest Information and Learning/University Microfilms International.

Newspaper Source. (1995–). Ipswich, MA: EBSCO.

NICEM AV Database. (1995–). Albuquerque: National Information Center for Educational Media. (Coverage: Materials date from 1900)

Official Index to the Times, 1906–1980. (1998–). Ann Arbor, MI: ProQuest Information and Learning/Chadwyck-Healey.

Palmer's Index to the Times, 1790–1905. (1998–). Cambridge, UK: Chadwyck-Healey.

ProQuest Historical Newspapers. (2002–). Ann Arbor, MI: University Microfilms International. (Includes the *New York Times*, 1851–2001; *Wall Street Journal*, 1889–1987; *Washington Post*, 1877–1988; *Christian Science Monitor*, 1908– 1991; *Los Angeles Times*, 1881–1984)

ProQuest Newspapers. (2000–). Ann Arbor, MI: ProQuest Information and Learning. (Coverage varies; Indexing for most national newspapers begins in 1989 and have full text since 1995)

*Special Libraries Association, News Division. (2003). *International news archives on the Web*. (Available: http://www.ibiblio.org/slanews/internet/intarchives.htm)

*Special Libraries Association, News Division. (2003). *U.S. news archives on the Web*. (Available: http://www.ibiblio.org/slanews/internet/archives.html)

Television News Index and Abstracts: Annual Index. (1968–). Nashville, TN: Vanderbilt Television News Archive. (Available: http://tvnews.vanderbilt.edu)

TV News Index and Abstracts. (1980–). (Available: http://tvnews.vanderbilt.edu)

Wall Street Journal Index. (1955–). Ann Arbor, MI: University Microfilms International.

Washington Post Index. (1989–). Ann Arbor, MI: University Microfilms International. (Continues *Official Washington Post Index,* 1979–1988, and *Bell & Howell Newspaper Index to the Washington Post,* 1979–1981)

Measurement

Bearden, W. O., & Netemeyer, R. G. (1999). *Handbook of marketing scales: Multi-item measures for marketing and consumer behavior research* (2nd ed.). Thousand Oaks, CA: Sage.

Robinson, J. P., Shaver, P. R., Wrightsman, L. S., & Andrews, F. M. (1991). *Measures of personality and social psychological attitudes: Vol. 1: Measures of social psychological attitudes*. San Diego: Academic Press.

Rubin, R. B., Palmgreen, P., & Sypher, H. E. (Eds.). (1994). *Communication research measures: A sourcebook*. New York: Guilford Press.

Rubin, R. B., Rubin, A. M., Graham, E. E., Perse, E. M., & Seibold, D. R. (2009). *Communication research measures: A sourcebook, Volume II*. New York: Routledge.

Finding Tools

Chun, K., Cobb, S., & French, J. R. P., Jr. (1975). *Measures for psychological assessment: A guide to 3,000 original sources and their applications*. Ann Arbor: University of Michigan.

Mental Measurements Yearbook (1990–). Ipswitch, MA: EBSCO.

Rosen, J. C., & McReynolds, P. (Eds.). (1968–1992). *Advances in psychological assessment* (8 vols.). New York: Plenum.

Sterling, C. H., & Bracken, J. K. (1998). *Mass communications research resources: An annotated guide*. Mahwah, NJ: Erlbaum.

Tests in Print. (2007–). Ipswitch, MA: EBSCO.

Legal/Government

Federal Reporter. (1880–). St. Paul: West.

Media Law Reporter. (1977–). Washington, DC: Bureau of National Affairs.

National Reporter System. (1879–). St. Paul: West. (Includes the *New York Supplement* and the following *Reporters*: *Atlantic, California, North Eastern, North Western, Pacific, South Eastern, Southern,* and *South Western*)

Pike & Fischer Radio Regulation, Second Series. (1963–). Washington, DC: Pike & Fischer.

Shepard's United States citations (8th ed.). (1994). Colorado Springs, CO: Shepard's/McGraw-Hill.

Supreme Court Reporter. (1882–). St. Paul: West.

*U.S. Administrative Office of the United States Courts. (1993–). *Judicial Business of the United States Courts*. (Available: http://www.uscourts.gov)

*U.S. Congress, House of Representatives. (2000). *United States code* (2000 ed.). (Available: http://www.house.gov, http://www.law.cornell.edu/uscode, and through *LexisNexis Congressional*)

United States Supreme Court Reports: Lawyers' Edition, Second Series. (1956–). Rochester, NY: Lawyers Co-operative.

Weekly Compilation of Presidential Documents. (1965–). Washington, DC: Government Printing Office.

West's General Digest: A Digest of All Current Decisions of the American Courts as Reported in the National Reporter System and Other Standard Reports. (1936–). St. Paul: West.

West's Supreme Court Reporter. (1984–). St. Paul: West.

Finding Tools

FindLaw. (2008). Mountain View, CA: FindLaw. (Available: http://www.findlaw. com/)

Historic Documents: Cumulative Index. (1973–). Washington, DC: Congressional Quarterly.

Martindale-Hubbell lawyer locator. *(1999)*. (Available: http://www.martindale. com/Home.aspx)

Shepard's Acts and Cases by Popular Names: Federal and State. (1968–). Colorado Springs, CO: Shepard's/McGraw-Hill.

Shepard's United States Citations: United States Supreme Court Reports (Lawyer's ed.). (1996–). Colorado Springs, CO: Shepard's/McGraw-Hill.

Statistical Sources

A. C. Nielsen Company. (1954–). *The Pocketpiece: Nielsen Television Index National TV Ratings*. New York: Author.

A. C. Nielsen Company. (1979–). *Nielsen Report on Television*. Northbrook, IL: Author.

American public opinion cumulative index, 1981–1985. (1987). Louisville: Opinion Research Service.

American Statistics Index: A Comprehensive Guide and Index to the Statistical Publications of the U.S. Government (1973–). Bethesda, MD: Congressional Information Service. (Available as part of *LexisNexis Statistical*)

Arbitron Radio. (1996). *Arbitron Radio market report reference guide: A guide to understanding and using radio audience estimates*. New York: Author.

Armstrong, C. J., & Fenton, R. R. (Eds.). (1996). *World databases in social sciences*. New Providence, NJ: Bowker-Saur.

Axiom Market Research Bureau. (1979–). *Target Group Index*. New York: Author.

FACTS.com Reference Suite. (1999–). New York: Facts on File. (Available: http://factsonfile.infobasepublishing.com/newsservices.asp)

FactSearch. (1984–). Ann Arbor, MI: Pierian. (Available through *FirstSearch*)

Index to International Statistics (1983–). Washington, DC: Congressional Information Service. (Available through *LexisNexis Statistical*)

*Kurian, G. (2001). *Datapedia of the United States, 1790–2005: America year by year* (2nd ed.). Lanham, MD: Bernan.

Polling the Nations. (1998–). Bethesda, MD: SilverPlatter. (Available through *FirstSearch*)

LexisNexis Statistical. (2002). Dayton, OH: LexisNexis. (Available: http://www.lexisnexis.com/academic/universe/statistical)

Radio Advertising Bureau. (1989–). *Radio Marketing Guide and Fact Book for Advertisers*. New York: Author.

Roper Organization. (1995). *America's watching: Public attitudes toward television*. New York: Network Television Association.

Schick, F. L., & Schick, R. (1994). *Statistical handbook on aging Americans: 1994 edition*. Phoenix: Oryx Press.

Standard Rate & Data Service. (1993–). *SRDS Consumer Magazine Advertising Source*. Des Plaines, IL: Author.

Standard Rate & Data Service. (1995–). *SRDS Newspaper Advertising Source*. Des Plaines, IL: Author.

Standard Rate & Data Service. (1995–). *SRDS Radio Advertising Source*. Des Plaines, IL: Author.

Standard Rate & Data Service. (1994–). *SRDS TV and Cable Source*. Des Plaines, IL: Author.

Stanley, H. W., & Niemei, R. G. (2003). *Vital statistics on American politics 2003–2004*. Washington, DC: CQ Press.

Statistical Reference Index. (1980–). Washington, DC: Congressional Information Service. (Available through *LexisNexis Statistical*)

UNESCO Institute for Statistics. (2002). (Available: http://www.uis.unesco.org/ev.php?ID=2867_201&ID2=DO_TOPIC)

United Nations Statistical Division. (2008). (Available: http://unstats.un.org/unsd/)

*U.S. Department of Commerce, U.S. Census Bureau. (1985–1998). *Census Catalog & Guide*. Washington, DC: Government Printing Office. (Available: http://www.census.gov/prod/www/abs/catalogs.html; formerly *Bureau of the Census Catalog*; continued by a page on the U.S. Census Bureau's website called *Product catalog*)

U.S. Department of Commerce, U.S. Census Bureau. (1949–). *County and City Data Book*. Washington, DC: Government Printing Office.

U.S. Department of Commerce, Bureau of the Census. (1974–). *Population Profile of the United States*. Washington, DC: Government Printing Office.

U.S. Department of Commerce, Bureau of the Census. (1980). *Social indicators III*. Washington, DC: Government Printing Office.

U.S. Department of Commerce, U.S. Census Bureau. (1879–). *Statistical Abstract of the United States*. Washington, DC: Government Printing Office.

*Wall, C. E. (Ed.). *A Matter of Fact: A Digest of Current Facts, with Citations to Sources*. (1984–). Ann Arbor: Pierian. (Available online as *FactSearch*)

*York, G. (2003). *Statistical resources on the Web*. Ann Arbor, MI: University of Michigan Library Documents Center. (Available: http://www.lib.umich.edu/ govdocs/stats.html)

Finding Tools

American statistics index: User guide. (1991). Washington, DC: Congressional Information Service.

Barrett, R. E. (1994). *Using the 1990 U.S. census for research*. Thousand Oaks, CA: Sage.

Government Documents

CQ Library. (1998–). Washington, DC: Congressional Quarterly. (Available: http:// library.cqpress.com)

*Federal Communications Commission. (1934/1935–1998). *Annual Report of the Federal Communications Commission*. Washington, DC: Government Printing Office. (Available: http://www.fcc.gov/omd/strategicplan/)

Federal Communications Commission. (1982–1999). *FCC Rules and Regulations* (Rev. ed.). Washington, DC: Government Printing Office.

Federal Communications Commission. (1934/1935). *Federal Communications Commission reports*. Washington, DC: Government Printing Office.

Historic Documents. (1972–). Washington, DC: Congressional Quarterly.

*U.S. Administrative Office of the United States Courts. (1994–). *Judicial Business of the United States courts*. Washington, DC: Government Printing Office.

*U.S. Congress. (1873–). *Congressional Record: Proceedings and debates of the Congress*. Washington, DC: Government Printing Office. (Available: http:// www.access.gpo.gov and through *LexisNexis Congressional*)

*U.S. Congress, House of Representatives. (2000). *United States code* (2000 ed.). Washington, DC: Government Printing Office.

U.S. General Services Administration, Office of the Federal Register. (1936–). *Federal Register*. Washington, DC: Government Printing Office.

U.S. General Services Administration, Office of the Federal Register. (1938–). *Code of Federal Regulations*. Washington, DC: Government Printing Office.

U.S. Supreme Court. (1790–). *United States Supreme Court Reports*. Rochester, NY: Lawyers Co-operative.

Finding Tools

AccessUN. (1997). Chester, VT: NewsBank. (Available online through NewsBank)

Biskupic, J., & Witt, E. (1997). *Congressional Quarterly's guide to the U.S. Supreme Court* (3rd ed.). Washington, DC: Congressional Quarterly.

CIS Index to Publications of the United States Congress. (1970–). Washington, DC: Congressional Information Service. (Available through *LexisNexis Congressional*)

Congressional Index. (1938–). Chicago: Commerce Clearing House.

Congressional Quarterly Almanac. (1945–). Washington, DC: Congressional Quarterly.

Congressional Quarterly's guide to Congress (5th ed.). (2000). Washington, DC: CQ Press.

CQ Weekly (*Congressional Quarterly weekly report*). (1943–). Washington, DC: Congressional Quarterly. (Available through CQ at http://www.cq.com)

Declassified Documents Catalog. (1975–). Woodbridge, CT: Research Publications.

Federal data base finder index. (1990). Potomac, MD: Information USA.

GPOAccess. (2003–). Washington, DC: Government Printing Office. (Available: http://www.gpoaccess.gov/index.html)

Guide to United States Supreme Court reports, lawyers' edition. (1994). Rochester, NY: Lawyers Co-operative.

Hardy, G. J., & Robinson, J. S. (1996). *Subject guide to U.S. government reference sources* (2nd ed.). Englewood, CO: Libraries Unlimited.

Index to the Code of Federal Regulations. (1997). Bethesda, MD: Congressional Information Service. (Available through *LexisNexis Congressional*)

Index to United Nations Documents and Publications. (1992–). New Canaan, CT: NewsBank/Readex. (Available through Newsbank)

LexisNexis Congressional. (1997–). Bethesda, MD: LexisNexis/Congressional Information Service. (Available: http://academic.lexisnexis.com/online-services/congressional-overview.aspx)

Moore, J. L., Preimesberger, J. P., & Tarr, D. R. (2001). *Congressional Quarterly's guide to U.S. elections* (4th ed.). Washington, DC: CQ Press.

Sears, J. L., & Moody, M. K. (1994). *Using government information sources: Print and electronic* (2nd ed., 2 vols.). Phoenix: Oryx Press.

United States Government Manual. (1995–). (Available: http://www.gpoaccess.gov/gmanual/index.html)

U.S. Congress. (1981–). *Congressional Record, Index to Daily Proceedings*. Washington, DC: Government Printing Office.

U.S. General Services Administration, Office of the Federal Register. (1977–). *Code of Federal Regulations: CFR Index and Finding Aids*. Washington, DC: Government Printing Office.

U.S. Government Information: Publications, Periodicals, Electronic Products. (1984–). Washington, DC: Government Printing Office.

U.S. Government Information, New and Popular Titles: Publications, Periodicals, Electronic Products. (1994–2001). Washington, DC: Government Printing Office.

U.S. Government Periodicals Index. (1993–1999). Bethesda, MD: LexisNexis/Congressional Information Service. (Available through *LexisNexis Government Periodicals Online Index* from 1988)

U.S. Library of Congress. (1984). *Popular names of U.S. government reports* (4th ed.). Washington, DC: Government Printing Office.

U.S. Superintendent of Documents. (1895–). *Monthly Catalog of United States Government Publications*. Washington, DC: Government Printing Office. (Available: http://www.gpoaccess.gov)

Yearbooks

Barone, M., & Ujifusa, G. (1972–). *The Almanac of American Politics*. Washington, DC: National Journal.

Broadcasting & Cable Yearbook (2 vols.). (1935–). New Providence, NJ: Bowker.

Cook, C., & Walker, W. (Comps.). (2001). *Facts on File world political almanac: From 1945 to the present* (4th ed., Rev.). New York: Facts on File.

Editor & Publisher International Year Book. (1959–). New York: Editor & Publisher.

Educational Media and Technology Yearbook. (1973–). Littleton, CO: Libraries Unlimited.

Facts on File World News Digest Yearbook. (2000–). New York: Facts on File.

Facts on File Yearbook. (1941–1999). New York: Facts on File.

Information Please Almanac, Atlas and Yearbook. (1947–). New York: Simon and Schuster.

International Motion Picture Almanac. (1929–). New York: Quigley.

International television & video almanac. (1956). New York: Quigley.

Senecah, S. (Ed.). (2003). *The environmental communication yearbook*. Mahwah, NJ: Erlbaum.

World Almanac and Book of Facts. (1868–). New York: Newspaper Enterprise Association.

Directories

Media

Audio Video Review Digest: A Guide to Reviews of Audio and Video Materials Appearing in General and Specialized Periodicals. (1989–). Detroit: Gale Research.

AV Market Place. (1984–). New Providence, NJ: Bowker. (Formerly *Audiovisual market place*, 1969–1983, and *Audio video market place*, 1984–1988)

Brooks, T., & Marsh, E. (Eds.). (2007). *The complete directory to prime time network and cable TV shows 1946–present* (9th ed.). New York: Ballantine.

Cable Advertising Directory. (1980–). Washington, DC: National Cable Television Association.

Directory of Scholarly Electronic Journals, Newsletters, and Academic Discussion Lists. (1991–2000). Washington, DC: Association of Research Libraries.

DWM: A Directory of Women's Media. (1988–). Washington, DC: Women's Institute for Freedom of the Press.

Gale Directory of Publications and Broadcast Media (4 vols.). (1869–). Detroit: Gale Research.

*Gale Database of Publications and Broadcast Media. (1996–). Detroit: Gale Research. (Available through *GaleNet*)

Gale's guide to the media. (2000). Detroit: Gale Research.

Gianakos, L. J. (1947–). *Television Drama Series Programming: A Comprehensive Chronicle*. Metuchen, NJ: Scarecrow.

Hammond, C. M. (1981). *The image decade: Television documentary, 1965–1975*. New York: Hastings House.

*Literary Market Place: The Directory of the American Book Publishing Industry with Industry Yellow Pages. (1940–). New Providence, NJ: Bowker. (Available: http://www.literarymarketplace.com)

MacNeil/Lehrer News Hour: Broadcast Review and Index. (1983–). New York: WNET/13.

McNeil, A. (1997). Total television: A comprehensive guide to programming from 1948 to the present (4th ed.). New York: Penguin.

*Media Review Digest. (1973/1974–). Ann Arbor, MI: Pierian. (Formerly Multi Media Reviews Index, 1970–1972; Available through FirstSearch)

News Media Yellow Book: Who's Who among Reporters, Writers, Editors, and Producers in the Leading National News Media. (1989–). New York: Leadership Directories.

PBS Video: Program Catalogue. (1974–). Washington, DC: Public Broadcasting Service.

Reed, M. K., & Reed, R. M. (1999). Career opportunities in television, cable, video, and multimedia (4th ed.). New York: Facts on File.

Terrace, V. (1981). Radio's golden years: The encyclopedia of radio programs, 1930–1960. San Diego: Barnes.

Terrace, V. (1991). Fifty years of television: A guide to series and pilots, 1937–1988. New York: Cornwall.

United Nations Department of Public Information. (1990). World media handbook. New York: Author.

Video Source Book (3 vols.). (1979–). Detroit: Gale Research.

Woolery, G. W. (1983). Children's television: The first thirty-five years, 1946–1981: Part I. Animated cartoon series. Metuchen, NJ: Scarecrow.

Woolery, G. W. (1985). Children's television: The first thirty-five years, 1946–1981: Part II. Live, film, and tape series. Metuchen, NJ: Scarecrow.

Working Press of the Nation (3 vols.). (1945–). New York: Farrell.

World Guide to Television. (1994–). Philadelphia, PA: North American.

World Radio TV Handbook. (1947–). New York: Billboard.

Writer's and Artist's Yearbook: A Directory for Writers, Artists, Playwrights, Writers for Film, Radio and Television, Designers, Illustrators and Photographers. (1906–). London: Black.

Writer's Market. (1922–). Cincinnati: F & W Publications.

General

*Directories in Print. (1989–). Detroit: Gale Research. (Formerly Directory of Directories; Available as Gale Database of Publications and Broadcast Media through GaleNet)

Directory of Research Grants. (1975–). Phoenix: Oryx Press.

Federal Regulatory Directory. (1956–). Washington, DC: Congressional Quarterly.

Guide to American Directories. (1954–). Rye, NY: B. Klein Publications.

Information Industry Directory: An International Guide to Organizations, Systems, andSservices Involved in the Production and Distribution of Information in Electronic Form (2 vols.). (1971–). Detroit: Gale Research.

International Who's Who. (1935–). London: Europa.

Martindale-Hubbell Law Directory (20 vols.). (1869–). New Providence, NJ: Martindale-Hubbell.

*Ruffner, F. G., & Fisk, M. (Eds.). *Encyclopedia of Associations* (4 vols.). (1961–). Detroit: Gale Research. (Available online as *Associations Unlimited* through *GaleNet*)

Standard & Poor's Register of Corporations, Directors & Executives. (1928–). New York: Standard & Poor's.

United States Government Manual. (1974–). Washington, DC: Government Printing Office.

Washington Information Directory. (1975–). Washington, DC: Congressional Quarterly.

Who's Who in Advertising. (1990/1991–). Wilmette, IL: Marquis Who's Who.

Who's Who in America (3 vols.). (1899/1900–). New Providence, NJ: Marquis Who's Who.

Worldbook of IABC Communicators. (1900–). San Francisco: International Association of Business Communicators.

Dictionaries

Appiah, K. A., Gates, H. L., & Vazquez, M. C. (Eds.). (1997). *The dictionary of global culture*. New York: Knopf.

Audi, R. (1999). *The Cambridge dictionary of philosophy* (2nd ed.). New York: Cambridge University Press.

Bauml, B. J., & Bauml, F. H. (1997). *Dictionary of worldwide gestures* (2nd ed.). Lanham, MD: Scarecrow.

Bealey, F., & Johnson, A. G. (1999). *Blackwell dictionary of political science*. Oxford, UK: Blackwell.

Black, H. C. (Ed.). (1933–). *Black's Law Dictionary*. St. Paul: West.

Blandford, S., Grant, B. K., & Hillier, J. (2001). *The film studies dictionary*. London: Arnold.

Bryant, D. C., Smith, R. W., Arnott, P. D., Holtsmark, E. B., & Rowe, G. O. (1968). *Ancient Greek and Roman rhetoricians: A bibliographical dictionary*. Columbia, MO: Artcraft.

Collin, P. H. (1998). *Dictionary of government and politics* (2nd ed.). Chicago: Fitzroy Dearborn.

Cross, W. (1995). *Prentice Hall encyclopedic dictionary of business terms*. Englewood Cliff, NJ: Prentice Hall.

Demers, D. P. (2005). *Dictionary of mass communication & media research: A guide for students, scholars, and professionals*. Spokane, WA: Marquette Books.

Dictionary of computing and communications. (2003). New York: McGraw-Hill.

Dodge, Y., & Marriott, F. H. C. (2003). *The Oxford dictionary of statistical terms* (6th ed.). Oxford: Oxford University Press.

Everett, B. (2002). *Cambridge dictionary of statistics* (2nd ed.). Cambridge, UK: Cambridge University Press.

Fox, R. W., & Kloppenberg, J. T. (1995). *A companion to American thought*. Cambridge, MA: Blackwell.

Godfrey, D. G., & Leigh, F. A. (1998). *Historical dictionary of American radio*. Westport, CT: Greenwood Press.

Gregory, R. L., & Zangwill, O. L. (1998). *The Oxford companion to the mind* (2nd ed.). New York: Oxford University Press.

Honderick, T. (Ed.). (1995). *The Oxford companion to philosophy*. New York: Oxford University Press.

Hurwitz, L. (1985). *Historical dictionary of censorship in the United States*. Westport, CT: Greenwood Press.

Jary, D., & Jary, J. (Eds.). (2000). *Collins dictionary of sociology* (3rd ed.). New York: HarperCollins.

Koocher, G. P., Norcross, J. C., & Hill, S. S. (Eds.). (1998). *Psychologists' desk reference*. New York: Oxford University Press.

Marshall, G. (2003). *Dictionary of sociology*. Oxford: Oxford University Press.

McBrien, J. L., & Brandt, R. S. (1997). *The language of learning: A guide to education terms*. Alexandria, VA: Association for Supervision and Curriculum Development.

Muller, N. J. (1998). *Desktop encyclopedia of telecommunications*. New York: McGraw-Hill.

Penney, E. F. (1991). *The Facts on File dictionary of film and broadcast terms*. New York: Facts on File.

Plano, J. C., & Greenberg, M. (2002). *The American political dictionary* (11th ed.). Fort Worth, TX: Harcourt College.

Reed, R. M., & Reed, M. K. (1994). *The Facts on File dictionary of television, cable, and video*. New York: Facts on File.

Ritzer, G. (2003). *Blackwell companion to major social theorists*. Malden, MA: Blackwell.

Schwandt, T. A. (2001). *Qualitative inquiry: A dictionary of terms* (2nd ed.). Thousand Oaks, CA: Sage.

Slide, A. (1998). *The new historical dictionary of the American film industry*. Chicago: Fitzroy Dearborn.

Stempel, G. H. (Ed.). (1999). *Historical dictionary of political communication in the United States*. Westport, CT: Greenwood Press.

Stuart-Hamilton, I. (Ed.). (1996). *Dictionary of cognitive psychology* (Rev. ed.). London: Kingsley.

Sutherland, S. (1996). *The international dictionary of psychology*. New York: Crossroad.

Thussu, D. K. (2006). *International media and communication: A dictionary*. London: Hodder Arnold.

Vogt, W. P. (1999). *Dictionary of statistics and methodology* (2nd ed.). Thousand Oaks, CA: Sage.

Watson, J., & Hill, A. (2006). *Dictionary of media and communication* (7th ed.). London: Hodder Arnold.

Weik, M. H. (1996). *Communications standard dictionary* (3rd ed.). New York: Chapman & Hall.

Weiner, R. (1996). *Webster's New World dictionary of media and communications* (Rev. ed.). New York: Macmillan.

Wolman, B. B. (1989). *Dictionary of behavioral science* (2nd ed.). San Diego: Academic Press.

Words and Phrases: All Judicial Constructions and Definitions of Words and Phrases by the State and Federal Courts from the Earliest Times (90 vols.). (1940–). St. Paul: West.

Manuals

Balnaves, M., Donald, J., & Donald, S. H. (2001). *The Penguin atlas of media and information*. New York: Penguin.

Berring, R. C., & Edinger, E. A. (2002). *Legal research survival manual*. St. Paul: West.

Block, M. (1994). *Broadcast newswriting: The RTNDA reference guide*. Chicago: RTNDA/Bonus Books.

Christ, W. G. (1999). *Leadership in a time of change: A handbook for communication and media administrators*. Mahwah, NJ: Erlbaum.

Crawford, M. G. (2002). *The journalist's legal guide* (4th ed.). Scarborough, Ontario: Carswell.

Dwyer, J. (2003). *The business communication handbook* (6th ed.). Frenchs Forest, N.S. W.: Pearson Education.

Goldstein, N. (2002). *The Associated Press stylebook and briefing on media law*. Cambridge, MA: Perseus.

Kalbfeld, B., & Hood, J. R. (2001). *The Associated Press broadcast news handbook*. New York: McGraw-Hill.

Katz, H. (2003). *The media handbook: A complete guide to advertising media selection, planning, research, and buying* (2nd ed.). Mahwah, NJ: Erlbaum.

Keller, B. P., & Cunard, J. P. (2001). *Copyright law: A practitioner's guide*. New York: Practising Law Institute.

Kessler, L., & MacDonald, D. (2004). *When words collide: A media writer's guide to grammar and style* (6th ed.). Belmont, CA: Wadsworth.

MacDonald, R. H. (1994). *A broadcast news manual of style* (2nd ed.). New York: Longman.

Macnamara, J. R. (1996). *Public relations handbook for managers and executives* (Rev. ed.). New York: Prentice Hall.

Nash, C. (1993). *The screenwriter's handbook*. New York: HarperPerennial.

O'Hair, D., Stewart, R., & Rubenstein, H. (2001). *A speaker's guidebook: Text and reference*. New York: Bedford/St. Martin's.

Price, S. (1997). *The complete a-z media & communication handbook*. London: Hodder & Stoughton.

Remocker, A. J. (1999). *Action speaks louder: A handbook of structured group techniques* (6th ed.). Edinburgh: Churchill Livingstone.

Robert, H. M., & Robert, S. C. (2000). *Robert's rules of order newly revised* (10th ed.). Reading, MA: Perseus.

Stein, M. L., & Paterno, S. F. (1998). *The newswriter's handbook: An introduction to journalism*. Ames: Iowa State University Press.

Weinberg, S., Houston, B., & Bruzzese, L. (2002). *The reporter's handbook: An investigator's guide to documents and techniques* (4th ed.). New York: St. Martin's Press.

West's Law Finder: A Legal Research Manual. (1959–). St. Paul: West.

Willis, E., & D'Arienzo, C. (1993). *Writing scripts for television, radio, and film* (3rd ed.). Fort Worth, TX: Harcourt Brace Jovanovich.

Wood, D. N. (1999). *Media writing handbook: Guidelines for radio, television, and film scripts and academic papers*. Dubuque, IA: Kendall Hunt.

EXAMPLES

Jack decides to check out some additional speech collections to see whether speech authors are identified. At the *Douglass* site, they didn't seem to be given. Now it's time to check out the University of North Carolina site.

Valerie's initial investigation of voice mail has led to statistical sources. Just how many businesses out there have voice mail systems? Valerie checks *A Matter of Fact* for an answer. Eleven records are found for *voice mail*. One of these articles is a press release about the University of Michigan's voice mail system and provides good comparative data for the piece.

Robin has now read several summary articles about attribution, and the term seems to be used consistently in the literature. Just to be sure, she checks the *Dictionary of Behavioral Science* to see how the term is defined. A one-sentence definition adds nothing new, but a look at *Heider* revealed an entry for *Heider's theory of attribution*. This paragraph presented the core of the theory in a nutshell.

Jason's paper on parasocial interaction is just about done. Throughout the journal articles there have been references to measurement techniques to measure the degree of parasocial interaction. Jason decides to examine a measurement collection, *Communication Research Measures: A Sourcebook,* to see whether the Parasocial Interaction Scale is profiled. It is! This source provides a double check on sources as well.

Kat and **Rocky** have teamed up to find an audiovisual aid for the group project on conflict management. They decide to check *Media Review Digest*. In the alphabetical subject index under *conflict management,* they are led to *mediation*. The only film they find is *Breakthrough... Choosing a New Road,* a film meant for grades 4 to 9. Nothing is listed under *group conflict* or *interpersonal relations* either. **Michelle**, however, looks at *The Video Source Book* and finds a film called *Conflicts, Conflicts!,* a 1985 management-training film that presents techniques for avoiding conflict geared to the adult viewer. She also finds out that it can be rented from the University of Washington Educational Media Collection, so she asks the interlibrary loan staff for help in securing it for the project.

Eric, Gregory, Anthony, and **Scott** dig into additional measurement collections for their research project. They've been looking for measures of relationship maintenance and Internet use. The

> new volume of *Communication Research Measures: A Source-book, Volume II*. (Rubin, Rubin, Graham, Perse, & Seibold, 2009) contains several that can be used. They read about them to see how reliable and valid they are before choosing one for each construct.

EXERCISES

1. In your political communication course, you have been studying the rhetoric of President Bill Clinton. To find verbatim texts of important speeches by national newsmakers, you consult *Vital Speeches of the Day*. Use the annual index (printed in November) to locate Clinton's first Inaugural Address (called *American Renewal*) delivered between October 15, 1992, and October 1, 1993. When was this speech delivered?

2. For your term paper in mass media management, you will be using an article written in 1985 that cites statistical data, giving the Federal Communications Commission as its source. To see whether the FCC has updated these data, you use the online version of *American Statistics Index, LexisNexis Statistical*. You find a reference under this agency to a publication that includes data on *TV station channel allocation*. It sounds like this might be what you are looking for.
   a. What is the accession number for this item?
   b. Find the abstract for this publication. What is its title?

3. In your seminar on issues in the press, you will be giving a presentation on newspaper publishing. Although you have compiled a rather comprehensive bibliography on the topic, you find that you need additional facts and figures on circulation trends. You turn to *LexisNexis Statistical* to access the *Statistical Abstract of the United States*, where you find an entire section of the volume devoted to communications. Find the 1998 publishing section.
   a. Find a table in this section giving data on the number and circulation of daily and Sunday newspapers by states. What is the newspaper circulation per capita for the state of Hawaii?
   b. How does this figure compare with that given for the District of Columbia?
   c. What is the number of this table?
   d. These data are useful, but you would like to find a more comprehensive source. What is the title of the publication given as the source of these data?

4. You are studying the early development of radio in your media history class. You come across a reference to an early radio station in Cleveland, Ohio, but the reference fails to mention the call letters of the station and when the station began. You consult the index of the most recent edition of the *Broadcasting & Cable Yearbook* and find a listing for a directory of U.S. and Canadian radio stations. Turning to this section, you discover that Cleveland has several radio stations.
   a. What are the call letters of the oldest radio station in Cleveland?
   b. In what year did that station go on the air?
   c. To whom is the station licensed?

5. You are interning as a communication training specialist in a large company and have been asked to help develop an in-service human relations training

program. You've been given the task of identifying commercially available audiovisual materials that might be of use in this program. To identify existing videotapes and to determine their availability, you turn to the most recent edition of *The Video Source Book*. Looking in the subject index under the heading *personnel management*, you find a video with the title *Managing Diversity*. Find the full description of this video.

a. Is this video's level suitable for your audience?

b. Can the video be rented or leased?

c. What is the purchase price?

6. Identify projects or assignments that would require use of the sources listed in this chapter. Which sources would you keep near your desk? Why?

7. Meet in the library reference area and examine a selection of these sources. What interesting new things did you learn? How might you as a communication professional use these sources?

part three

Communication Research Processes

N ow that we've identified the basic search strategies and sources important for communication research, we discuss the two processes next undertaken by researchers: research and writing. Through the literature review, we determine questions that still need answers and formulate research strategies to uncover those answers. When conducting primary research, we seek to answer those questions. In writing, we determine the best way to present information found during the literature search and, perhaps, the research investigation.

In Chapter 9, we focus on systematic procedures for conducting a research study. Our purpose in this chapter is to present an overview of the major procedures used in communication research. In Chapter 10, we identify the main quantitative and qualitative methods we use to conduct original research. We also provide several useful sources you can consult when planning your own research project. Even if you will not be doing your own research, the information in the chapter will help you become an effective consumer of the research literature you encounter.

Writing is just as systematic as searching and researching in that specific and rigorous conventions must be followed. In Chapter 11, we discuss basic writing projects: abstracts, literature reviews, critical papers, research prospectuses, and research reports. In Chapter 12, we focus on basic writing principles, formatting styles, and copyediting.

Part 3, then, identifies important processes in researching and writing about communication topics. We hope this final part of the book will whet your appetite for doing communication research.

chapter 9

The Process of Communication Research

S ometimes a literature review summary and a critical evaluation of past research is the end product of our research efforts. In many instances, though, the literature review is only a beginning. We often need to go further—to investigate new questions or problems we've uncovered. We need to conduct original research to answer questions not answered by past studies. Research is the process by which we seek answers to our questions about how and why people communicate.

All researchers realize that many facets of communication are not fully understood. Because there are many questions that have yet to be answered adequately, the literature on a specific research topic is seldom complete. When this is the case, we must conduct our own investigations to answer the questions. By conducting research, we seek to understand and improve how communication works in different settings, such as between people, inside organizations, or via the media. In this chapter we provide an overview of the process of communication research, which helps bridge these gaps in our knowledge.

Our goal in this chapter is to introduce you to important elements in the process of doing research. In Chapter 10, we explore several different methods used for conducting communication research. These two chapters will help you understand much of the literature you encounter and, if needed, help you design your own research project. In either case, when reading research or doing research it is important that you consult additional books on research methods, measurement, and analysis. We identify many useful sources at the ends of Chapters 9 and 10.

THE RESEARCH PROCESS

Research is an objective, systematic, empirical, and cumulative process by which we seek to solve theoretical and applied problems. Such problems present obstacles to our understanding of communication. Research is *objective* because we try to be impartial when seeking the best solutions to the research problem. It is *systematic* because we move through a series of planned stages when conducting an investigation. It is *empirical* because we look beyond ourselves to observe and to gather evidence. And, it is *cumulative* because it builds upon past knowledge. Research does not stand isolated from what others have done before.

If a question has already been answered in the literature, there is little need to duplicate the effort. However, many questions are unanswered, and duplicating or replicating research is warranted if (a) there is reason to suspect the validity of earlier studies, (b) another view would add to the diversity of knowledge about the problem, or (c) new information might bolster or alter previous findings in light of a changing communication environment. For example, the growth of DVDs, cable and satellite television, and personal computers in people's homes might change earlier findings about how television is used by the family. The expanding use of e-mail, cell phones, and other electronic digital devices alters the nature of interpersonal communication.

We also should note that, traditionally, research in the social and behavioral sciences is approached objectively. Others, however, especially qualitative and critical researchers, approach research as value-driven and open to one's subjective interpretation of the empirical world. For example, they might seek to inform society about the negative impact of mass media ownership by fewer and fewer corporations. Their purpose would be to raise awareness so that policymakers will alter the rules of media ownership. We summarize some of these more qualitative and critical methods in the next chapter, alongside more traditional social and behavioral research methods in communication.

DESCRIPTIVE AND EXPLANATORY RESEARCH

Researchers observe, describe, and often explain the relationships between different factors or events. Research can be descriptive or explanatory. The research question guides the choice of research method (see Chapter 10). When doing **descriptive research**, we try to identify or describe events or conditions. We would conduct descriptive research if we were asking, "What is the present or past state of events?" To do this, we need a representative sampling of the people or messages we are studying. When doing **explanatory research**, we look for underlying causes and explanations of events. Explanatory research encompasses what is referred to as *interpretive research*, as a way of making sense of events. We would conduct explanatory research if we were asking, "Why have these events happened in the manner they did?" Or, "What are the implications of these events occurring as they have?"

Let's consider our example of media-related training programs for executives. If our research question is, "How have training programs in organizations changed during the past 3 decades?," our focus is descriptive. We would want to describe how training programs have evolved over the years. If we ask, "Why is the information contained in these instructional methods effective?," our focus is explanatory. We would want to evaluate the content of past training programs on the basis of how we define *effective*—that is, in terms of our criteria for evaluating effectiveness (e.g., the ability to field questions or the credibility of response). Here, we would arrive at an informed judgment about *why* an instructional training method produces positive or negative, or expected or unexpected, results. The overall purpose of the study, then, would guide the research process.

Research Stages

The process of conducting original empirical research consists of several stages:

1. Posing and developing a problem in need of a solution
2. Reviewing past research and writings about this problem
3. Identifying worthy questions that investigators have not yet answered
4. Devising the best method to seek answers to these questions
5. Sampling the population to gather the necessary information to answer these questions
6. Analyzing that information in a valid and reliable manner
7. Presenting the results of the inquiry
8. Considering the meaning and implications of these results to expand our knowledge of the problem or the underlying theory

Problem and Literature

We need to define and to describe our research problem precisely. Once we select and define the problem we need to solve, we must go to the appropriate literature to see whether others have already addressed similar issues. The literature will help clarify the current state of knowledge about our topic. It will also help us identify precise research questions about the problem we need to solve or question we need to answer. For example, suppose our problem concerns the role of nonverbal communication in the classroom, the use of nonverbal cues by newscasters, or how nonverbal cues influence perceptions during job interviews. By reading what other researchers have written about the subject, we learn what they have discovered before us. This helps us focus on the precise questions we need to answer—in other words, on exactly what we still need to know about the problem.

Research Question and Hypothesis

We might narrow our focus to "How does nonverbal immediacy affect learning in the classroom?" Or, "How does nonverbal immediacy affect perceptions during the job interview?" Or, "How does nonverbal immediacy affect the credibility of the television newscaster?" Sometimes, if there's no theory or prior research to guide the study, the research question will suggest an *inductive* approach to the problem. We make our observations and then try to understand what we've observed and to develop a theory about the role of, in our example, immediacy and learning.

Or, if the research literature suggests, we might want to test a hypothesis. For example, we might predict a positive relationship between nonverbal immediacy and learning. Perhaps the literature suggests that, as we increase nonverbal immediacy in the classroom, learning will increase. Or, as we increase nonverbal immediacy, the chances of a successful job interview will increase. Or, as the television newscaster increases her nonverbal immediacy, her credibility will increase. A **hypothesis**, then, is an educated guess or prediction about the relationship between two or more **variables**. One of these variables is the **independent variable**. It is the antecedent, or the presumed cause, in the relationship. The other variable is the **dependent variable**. It is the consequent, or the presumed effect, in the relationship. Here, the independent variable is *nonverbal immediacy*, and the dependent variable is *learning*, in the first example (and *success* and *credibility*, in the second and third examples, respectively).

If our hypothesis is, "Communication training will improve a manager's media interview performance," training is our independent variable, and interview performance is our dependent variable. Or, we might *predict* (in other words, hypothesize) that "higher degrees of communication competence will result in better academic performance." Communication competence is our independent variable, and academic performance is our dependent variable. What we are predicting is that academic performance (the consequent) will vary *as a result* of a person's level of communication competence (the antecedent).

Whether we seek to answer a research question or to test a hypothesis, we must be sure all elements, such as nonverbal immediacy and learning, are clearly defined, so that we know precisely which answers we are seeking or what it is that we are testing. There are two types of these definitions.

First, a **conceptual definition** refers to terms used to describe the variable. For example, a conceptual definition of communication competence might be "being an effective communicator." A conceptual definition of academic performance might be "showing knowledge in the classroom." A conceptual definition of newscaster credibility might be "how believable the newscaster is." Conceptual definitions, then, are similar to dictionary definitions in language and style.

Second, an **operational definition**, describes the procedures we follow to observe or to measure the variables. For example, an operational definition of communication competence might be "the score obtained on the Communication Competency Assessment Instrument." An operational definition of academic performance might be "cumulative grade point average." An operational definition of a successful job interview might be whether one is "hired for the job." And, an operational definition of newscaster credibility might be "the score received on a source credibility scale." Operational definitions consist of the procedures we follow to observe or measure our variables.

It is important that an operational definition matches the conceptual definition. If you were to define a student's academic performance conceptually as "sharing knowledge in the classroom" and measure it as "score on the Graduate Record Exam," the measure doesn't necessarily match the *classroom* element inherent in the concept, whereas "grades received on group exercises" better reflects the sharing of knowledge in the classroom environment. The method of inquiry will reflect basic premises of the conceptual and operational definitions.

Method of Inquiry

Our method of inquiry is how we go about trying to answer the question or to test the hypothesis. Researchers have a wealth of possible methods available to them, and we discuss several of these methods in the next chapter. We might choose, for example, to conduct an experiment or a survey, or we might want to use observational methods or to do a critical analysis.

Sometimes the question itself suggests the most suitable approach. Often, though, past research, as described in the literature, suggests the best approach. In addition, different researchers are more comfortable working with one of the different **quantitative** (i.e., deductive and statistical) or **qualitative** (i.e., inductive and interpretive) research methods we discuss in Chapter 10. So, several factors determine the choice of research method.

Sampling and Data Gathering

Once we select the most appropriate method, we need to gather our data. If we use observational methods, for example, we'll conduct our observations of nonverbal immediacy—in selected classrooms or in job interview settings—in a systematic manner. If we use critical methods, we'll collect and examine written or visual examples or artifacts. For example, we might examine fan mail received by the newscaster. If we use experimental methods, we'll set up a controlled environment in which we manipulate the amount of nonverbal immediacy and then measure the amount of learning.

Data collection typically involves selecting a sample of people to talk with, messages to analyze, events to observe, or artifacts to examine. There are standard methods of selecting a valid **sample** of people from a **population**. Samples are chosen because it is too costly, time-consuming, or unnecessary to conduct a census of the entire population. Sometimes, in fact, a sample is better than a census of the whole population. For example, a sample allows more in-depth analysis of content or artifacts. In addition, if chosen randomly and care is taken to achieve a high rate of return, a sample can better represent the population than could a census with a poor rate of return. We use probability (random) and nonprobability (nonrandom) techniques to select samples.

Probability sampling allows us to generalize from the sample being observed to the entire population from which that sample is chosen. It uses random sampling techniques and assures that the sample is representative of the population. These techniques include simple random, systematic, stratified, and cluster sampling.

- In a **simple random sample**, each person has an equal or known chance of being chosen. We might use a list of names to select a sample randomly and a table of random numbers to identify those who are chosen. This is not very efficient, though, when we have a large population. However, in some studies (i.e., experiments) there may not be a large population, and participants might be assigned *at random* to different experimental or treatment groups (see Chapter 10).
- In a **systematic sample** we select every *n*th person from a current and complete list, or *sampling frame*. For example, we might choose every 10th name from a student directory.
- A **stratified sample** allows us to compare certain subgroups in the population. For example, to compare their responses, we randomly select men and women for our sample in relation to how many of each group are in the campus

population. For example, we would select 55 women and 45 men if women comprise 55 percent and men 45 percent of the campus population.

■ We could use a **cluster sample** if we find it impractical or impossible to compile a list of everyone in a population but can obtain lists of, say, housing units on campus. We could then draw a random or systematic sample of dorm residents from a random sample of dormitories.

All of these probability sampling techniques assure the sample is representative of the population from which it is selected, so we can generalize our findings from the sample to the population.

Sometimes, though, a probability sample isn't necessary. For example, we might be doing an exploratory pilot study or assessing relationships between two variables to test a hypothesis. Or we might need to be intentional in what or whom we select, whether it be media, messages, or people.

Nonprobability sampling does not permit us to generalize to other groups or situations, but it is valuable for studying particular groups of people. It also allows us to explore certain relevant and accessible artifacts for more in-depth analysis. Nonprobability sampling techniques include purposive, quota, and accidental sampling.

■ With a **purposive sample**, we select a sample that contains either a variety of people (i.e., to pretest a questionnaire before distributing it to our actual sample), people who have a certain characteristic in which we're interested (i.e, student leaders, reticent communicators, Internet users), or media or other sources of messages or content of interest.

■ A **quota sample** requires us to identify people with certain traits or who are members of known demographic groups (such as different college classes). If class standing is important to our research of a college population, we might want to sample 25 members of each undergraduate class (first-year to fourth-year students) for our 100-person sample. Quota sampling does *not* require random sampling among the different groups, as does stratified sampling.

■ An **accidental sample**, or a **convenience sample**, is based on sampling participants who happen to be available. Surveys done in college classes or by intercepting shoppers in malls are examples of this sampling technique.

Nonprobability sampling can lead to conclusions that differ from those we would have reached by using probability sampling. But nonprobability methods are still useful when investigating many research questions.

These various techniques of locating participants, content, or artifacts are necessary for using many of the methods discussed in Chapter 10. Among the many relevant methods are survey research, experimental research, and content analysis.

Analysis, Validity, and Reliability

After we select our sample and collect our data, we need to analyze the data to determine the answer to our research question. We might, for example, look for common themes in classroom discussions, job interviews, or fan mail, or submit the data to statistical analysis. We also need to consider whether our measurement and analysis are valid and reliable.

Measurement of variables must be valid. In general, **validity** means measuring what we intend to measure. If an index, test, or scale is used to measure a particular construct, such as credibility, the measure should include items or questions about all aspects of the construct (*content validity*)—for example, authoritativeness, believability, and the like. It also should relate to other similar measures or predict future behavior or attitudes (*criterion-related validity*), and it should measure the construct it purports to measure (*construct validity*). The operational definition, then, requires the researcher to choose and use a method, procedure, or instrument that provides valid data.

Measures also must be reliable. **Reliability** refers to how dependable, stable, consistent, and repeatable measures are in a study and across several studies. If we use a measure twice and the results are about the same both times, the measure has *test-retest reliability*. If all items in a measurement scale seem to measure the same thing, we say the measure has *internal consistency*. If there are two forms of the same measure (say, a test) and people score the same on both, we say the forms are *parallel*. And, if two or more raters, observers, or coders agree when using some sort of scale for their observations, we have *interrater reliability*. Researchers try to choose measures that have a good track record of reliability, but they often assess it again during their own research to make sure the reliability holds for their study as well.

Valid and reliable instruments increase the **internal validity** of a research study. They ensure that no one can derive other possible interpretations of the results. We also want our research to have **external validity**, meaning the results are generalizable to people and contexts beyond the group and situation being studied.

Writing and Discussing

After completing our analysis in a valid and reliable manner, we need to write up our results and consider the meaning and implications of our findings. Does our analysis support our hypothesis? What does it mean if nonverbal immediacy leads to better learning in the classroom? Do other factors also contribute to learning? Could we have improved our study in any manner? What does this suggest for future researchers to consider?

Let's return to our earlier investigation into the use of media-related training programs for company executives. That study might have left several questions unanswered. For example:

1. How long have these training programs been in existence?
2. How widespread are such media-training programs in this country or other countries today?
3. Are these training programs effective in improving an executive's ability to deal with the media?
4. Do training programs simply maintain the power structure of the organization?
5. Do training programs maintain male dominance in corporate decision making?

After defining our problem and reading the literature, we will refine and seek to answer our research questions. We can probably find answers to questions 1 and 2 in the literature. The literature should also offer tentative but incomplete answers to questions 3, 4, and 5, as well as disagreements among researchers. We might, therefore, need to design our own study or analysis to answer those questions. How we go about answering the questions reflects our method of approach to the investigation. We discuss various methods of communication research in Chapter 10.

RESEARCH ETHICS

No discussion of the research process is complete without considering how researchers meet their ethical obligations to the participants in their investigations and to their discipline. Researchers need to be responsible to their discipline and to the participants in their research projects. They must conform to professional standards of conduct. **Research ethics** concerns what is right and wrong in the conduct of research.

Research involves a series of choices about how to answer research questions, test hypotheses, and conduct such inquiries. Empirical researchers need to remain systematic and objective in the many choices they make when designing measures, selecting and observing participants, analyzing their data, and reporting the results of their studies. It should go without saying that researchers need to be *accurate*, *honest*, and *precise* when conducting research and when discussing the meaning of their data.

In addition, especially because we involve people in so much of our research in communication, researchers must constantly respect the rights of research participants. Researchers need to adhere to a basic rule: *Do no harm*. If you would not be willing to be a participant in your research project, you probably shouldn't be asking others to participate in that project. Researchers need to take steps to reduce or to eliminate the risk of physical or psychological discomfort. Toward this end, universities and many other organizations have Internal Review Boards (IRBs), or Human Subjects Review Boards, whose purpose is to balance the needs of the researcher and the rights of research participants. Researchers who use people as participants need to obtain approval from this board before conducting their research. Primarily, IRBs consider whether proposed research projects are of sufficient benefit to offset any potential costs or discomfort to participants.

Researchers also consider several other ethical concerns. First, subjects or respondents should be voluntary participants in any research project. They should provide their *informed consent* and should not be coerced to participate. We should engage participants in research with their knowledge and consent. This, of course, is difficult for research that takes place in the field and in public places by observing people's behavior. This task is easier for research that involves the completion of questionnaires or that takes place in laboratory settings.

Second, researchers must consider possible *deception* in their research. Often, researchers withhold the true nature of the research project from participants (this is referred to as *omission*) because knowing the purpose of the project may influence how participants act and answer questions, so it's best to leave the true purpose of the study unexplained. Sometimes, intentional dishonesty or trickery (*commission*) is even a necessary part of an experimental research project. In that case, researchers are obliged to inform participants about the goals or dishonesty within the project at the project's conclusion. This is typically referred to as *debriefing*.

Third, researchers need to protect the *privacy* of their participants by promising them anonymity or confidentiality. *Anonymity* means that participants take part in the research project without the researcher's knowledge of their identity (e.g., no names are written on questionnaires). However, there are times when researchers need to be able to identify their participants, especially when they need to do follow-up questionnaires or interviews with the same people. In such instances, research participation might be confidential. *Confidentiality* means that researchers will protect and not reveal the names of participants.

We've just touched upon several important ethical concerns: honesty, harm, informed consent, deception, and privacy. In general, research participants must be treated fairly and shown courtesy and respect. Researchers must meet these standards when they plan and conduct communication investigations.

SUMMARY

Research is an objective and systematic process for solving theoretical and applied problems. It can be descriptive or explanatory. It seeks to answer research questions not already answered by past research or to test hypotheses, which specify relationships among independent and dependent variables. The research process moves through several stages, from developing a research problem to discussing implications of the findings of a study. Decisions about sampling procedure are critical to the method of data collection. However research is done, the manner of study and the measurement of variables must be valid and reliable. Researchers must also address several ethical issues when planning and conducting their studies.

SELECTED SOURCES

Comprehensive Research Texts

Babbie, E. (2007). *The practice of social research* (11th ed.). Belmont, CA: Thomson/Wadsworth.

Barzun, J., & Graff, H. F. (2004). *The modern researcher* (6th ed.). Belmont, CA: Thomson/Wadsworth.

Baxter, L. A., & Babbie, E. R. (2004). *The basics of communication research*. Belmont, CA: Thomson/Wadsworth.

Berger, A. A. (2000). *Media and communication research methods: An introduction to qualitative and quantitative approaches*. Thousand Oaks, CA: Sage.

Booth, W. C., Colomb, G. G., & Williams, J. M. (2008). *The craft of research* (3rd ed.). Chicago: University of Chicago Press.

Frankfort-Nachmias, C., & Nachmias, D. (2008). *Research methods in the social sciences* (7th ed.). New York: Worth.

Frey, L. R., Botan, C. H., & Kreps, G. L. (2007). *Investigating communication: An introduction to research methods* (3rd ed.). Boston: Pearson/Allyn & Bacon.

Hocking, J. E., McDermott, S. T., & Stacks, D. W. (2003). *Communication research* (3rd ed.). Boston: Pearson/Allyn & Bacon.

Hoyle, R. H. (2007). *Research methods in social relations*. Belmont, CA: Wadsworth/ Cengage.

Kerlinger, F. N., & Lee, H. B. (2000). *Foundations of behavioral research* (4th ed.). Fort Worth, TX: Harcourt.

Keyton, J. (2006). *Communication research: Asking questions, finding answers* (2nd ed.). Boston: McGraw-Hill.

Merrigan, G., & Huston, C. (2004). *Communication research methods*. Belmont, CA: Thomson/Wadsworth.

Reinard, J. C. (2008). *Introduction to communication research* (4th ed.). Boston: McGraw-Hill.

Schutt, R. K. (2006). *Making sense of the social world: Methods of investigation* (2nd ed.). Thousand Oaks, CA: Pine Forge.

Sumser, J. (2001). *A guide to empirical research in communication: Rules for looking*. Thousand Oaks, CA: Sage.

Measurement

Camilli, G., & Shepard, L. A. (1994). *Methods for identifying biased test items*. Thousand Oaks, CA: Sage.

Carmines, E. G., & Zeller, R. A. (1979). *Reliability and validity assessment*. Beverly Hills, CA: Sage.

Hopkins, K. D. (1998). *Educational and psychological measurement and evaluation* (8th ed.). Boston: Allyn & Bacon.

Rubin, R. B., Palmgreen, P., & Sypher, H. E. (Eds.). (1994). *Communication research measures: A sourcebook*. New York: Guilford Press.

Rubin, R. B., Rubin, A. M., Graham, E. E., Perse, E. M., & Seibold, D. R. (2009). *Communication research measures: A sourcebook, Volume II*. New York: Routledge.

Sax, G. (2005). *Principles of educational and psychological measurement and evaluation* (5th ed.). Belmont, CA: Wadsworth.

Traub, R. E. (1994). *Reliability for the social sciences: Theory and application*. Thousand Oaks, CA: Sage.

Media Research

Berger, A. A. (1998). *Media research techniques* (2nd ed.). Thousand Oaks, CA: Sage.

Dochartaigh, N. O. (2002). *The Internet research handbook*. London: Sage.

Gunter, B. (2000). *Media research methods*. London: Sage.

Jones, S. (1999). *Doing Internet research*. Thousand Oaks, CA: Sage.

Lang, A. (Ed.). (1994). *Measuring psychological responses to media*. Hillsdale, NJ: Erlbaum.

Meyer, P. (2002). *Precision journalism*. Lanham, MD: Rowman & Littlefield.

Poindexter, P. M., & McCombs, M. E. (2000). *Research in mass communication: A practical guide*. Boston: Bedford/St. Martin's.

Sparks, G. G. (2006). *Media effects research: A basic overview* (2nd ed.). Belmont, CA: Thomson/Wadsworth.

Stacks, D. W. (2002). *Primer of public relations research*. New York: Guilford Press.

Startt, J. D., & Sloan, W. D. (2003). *Historical methods in mass communication* (Rev. ed.). Northport, AL: Vision.

Van Leeuwen, T., & Jewitt, C. (Eds.). (2001). *The handbook of visual analysis*. London: Sage.

Webster, J. G., Phalen, P. F., & Lichty, L. W. (2006). *Ratings analysis: The theory and practice of audience research* (3rd ed.). Mahwah, NJ: Erlbaum.

Wimmer, R. D., & Dominick, J. R. (2006). *Mass media research: An introduction* (8th ed.). Belmont, CA: Thomson/Wadsworth.

Qualitative and Applied Research

Applied Social Research Methods. (1984–). Thousand Oaks, CA: Sage. (A series of more than 50 monographs)

Banks, M. (2001). *Visual methods in social research*. London: Sage.

Berg, B. L. (2007). *Qualitative research methods for the social sciences* (6th ed.). Boston: Pearson/Allyn & Bacon.

Blakesley, A., & Fleischer, C. (2007). *Becoming a writing researcher*. Mahwah, NJ: Erlbaum.

Boje, D. M. (2001). *Narrative methods for organizational communication research*. Thousand Oaks, CA: Sage.

Buddenbaum, J., & Novak, K. B. (2001). *Applied communication research*. Ames: Iowa State Press.

Corbin, J. M., & Strauss, A. L. (2008). *Basics of qualitative research* (3rd ed.). Los Angeles: Sage.

Creswell, J. W. (2007). *Qualitative inquiry and research design* (2nd ed.). Thousand Oaks, CA: Sage.

Denzin, N. K., & Lincoln, Y. S. (Eds.). (2005). *SAGE handbook of qualitative research* (3rd ed.). Thousand Oaks, CA: Sage.

Denzin, N. K., & Lincoln, Y. S. (Eds.). (2008). *Collecting and interpreting qualitative materials* (3rd ed.). Thousand Oaks, CA: Sage.

Denzin, N. K., & Lincoln, Y. S. (Eds.). (2008). *Strategies of qualitative inquiry* (3rd ed.). Thousand Oaks, CA: Sage.

Fetterman, D. M. (2007). *Ethnography: Step by step* (3rd ed.). Thousand Oaks, CA: Sage.

Flick, U. (2006). *An introduction to qualitative research* (3rd ed.). Thousand Oaks, CA: Sage.

Hammersley, M., & Atkinson, P. (2007). *Ethnography: Principles in practice* (2nd ed.). London: Routledge.

Hansen, A. (2008). *Mass communication research methods*. London: Sage.

Herndon, S. L., & Kreps, G. L. (2001). *Qualitative research: Applications in organizational life* (2nd ed.). Cresskill, NJ: Hampton.

Huberman, M., & Miles, M. B. (2002). *The qualitative researcher's companion*. Thousand Oaks, CA: Sage.

Iorio, S. H. (Ed.). (2004). *Qualitative research in journalism*. Mahwah, NJ: Erlbaum.

Jensen, K., & Jankowski, N. (Eds.) (2006). *Handbook of qualitative methodologies for mass communication research*. London: Routledge.

Krueger, R. A., & Casey, M. A. (2009). *Focus groups: A practical guide for applied research* (4th ed.). Thousand Oaks, CA: Sage.

Lindlof, T. R., & Taylor, B. C. (2002). *Qualitative communication research methods* (2nd ed.). Thousand Oaks, CA: Sage.

Lofland, J. (2006). *Analyzing social settings: A guide to qualitative observation and analysis* (4th ed.). Belmont, CA: Wadsworth/Thomson Learning.

Marshall, C., & Rossman, G. B. (2006). *Designing qualitative research* (4th ed.). Thousand Oaks, CA: Sage.

Maxwell, J. A. (1996). *Qualitative research design: An interactive approach*. Thousand Oaks, CA: Sage.

McKee, A. (2003). *Textual analysis: A beginner's guide*. Thousand Oaks, CA: Sage.

Morgan, D. L., & Krueger, R. A. (1998). *The focus group kit* (6 vols.). Thousand Oaks, CA: Sage.

Qualitative Research Methods. (1986–). Thousand Oaks, CA: Sage. (A series of more than 50 monographs).

Rossman, G. B., & Rallis, S. F. (2003). *Learning in the field* (2nd ed.). Thousand Oaks, CA: Sage.

Stake, R. E. (2006). *Multiple case study analysis*. New York: Guilford.

Stewart, A. (1998). *The ethnographer's method*. Thousand Oaks, CA: Sage.

Stewart, D. W., Shamdasani, P. N., & Rook, D. W. (Eds.). (2007). *Focus groups: Theory and practice* (2nd ed.). Newbury Park, CA: Sage.

Wolcott, H. F. (2001). *Writing up qualitative research* (2nd ed.). Thousand Oaks, CA: Sage.

Yin, R. K. (2009). *Case study research: Design and method* (4th ed.). Thousand Oaks, CA: Sage.

Statistics

Bruning, J. L., & Kintz, B. L. (1997). *Computational handbook of statistics* (4th ed.). New York: Longman.

Cohen, J. (1988). *Statistical power analysis for the behavioral sciences* (2nd ed.). Hillsdale, NJ: Erlbaum.

Hair, J. F. (2006). *Multivariate data analysis* (6th ed.). Upper Saddle River, NJ: Pearson/Prentice Hall.

Healey, J. F. (2009). *Statistics: A tool for social research* (8th ed.). Belmont, CA: Thomson/Wadsworth.

Levin, J., & Fox, J. A. (2006). *Elementary statistics in social research* (10th ed.). Boston: Pearson/Allyn & Bacon.

Mendenhall, W., Beaver, R. J., & Beaver, B. M. (2006). *Introduction to probability and statistics* (12th ed.). Belmont, CA: Thomson/Brooks/Cole.

Quantitative Applications in the Social Sciences. (1976–). Thousand Oaks, CA: Sage. (A series of more than 140 monographs on statistics and research methodology).

Salkind, N. J. (2008). *Statistics for people who (think they) hate statistics* (3rd ed.). Thousand Oaks, CA: Sage.

Sirkin, R. M. (2006). *Statistics for the social sciences* (3rd ed.). Thousand Oaks, CA: Sage.

Stevens, J. (2002). *Applied multivariate statistics for the social sciences* (4th ed.). Mahwah, NJ: Erlbaum.

Walsh, A., & Ollenburger, J. C. (2001). *Essential statistics for the social and behavioral sciences*. Upper Saddle River, NJ: Prentice Hall.

Williams, F., & Monge, P. (2001). *Reasoning with statistics* (5th ed.). Fort Worth, TX: Harcourt Brace Jovanovich.

EXERCISES

1. Identify three problems in communication of interest to you and that you feel are in need of answers.
    a. For each problem, write a precise research question.
    b. Indicate whether each research question is descriptive or explanatory in nature.
    c. Explain why each question is important to study.
    d. Rephrase one of the questions in the form of a hypothesis.
2. For one of the above questions, consider when a nonprobability sample might be better than a probability sample when conducting research to answer that question.
3. When might a communication researcher use deception in conducting a research study? What concerns about research ethics might this raise?
4. Find out the guidelines for using humans in research at your college or university. Does an IRB oversee this process? Does it have specific guidelines for student research projects?

chapter 10

Designing the Communication Research Project

A s we saw in Chapter 9, research presents students and professionals with many choices. Among these choices is how to go about seeking answers to our research questions and testing our hypotheses. In this chapter, we examine several methods for conducting research to explore a variety of descriptive and explanatory research topics and to find answers to our communication research questions. We classify the method of communication research into two broad approaches.

APPROACHES TO COMMUNICATION RESEARCH

First, *message-* or *artifact-oriented research* looks at communication messages and the underlying values associated with messages. Researchers classify the words or images that people use, examine the motives for creating such discourse, look at the historical and environmental factors that contribute to understanding the messages' impact at the time they were communicated, and explore the surrounding culture. Sometimes they examine archives of objects or recorded events, already collected data, or statistical results of published studies. We have grouped these methods into two main subcategories: archival/documentary and textual.

Second, *people-* or *behavior-oriented* research looks at human behavior, attitudes, and opinions rather than the text, content, or context of the message. Researchers ask people to recall or report on their communication attitudes and behaviors, develop reliable methods of observing communication behavior, and put people in situations to see whether a change in an independent variable produces different results. This research category includes survey, observational, and experimental research.

We discuss these two approaches in the remainder of this chapter. Having this preliminary information, you should consult other research books to determine the best procedures for a particular investigation. We list several such sources at the end of this chapter and at the end of Chapter 9.

Message- or Artifact-Oriented Research

Message- or **artifact-oriented research** focuses on examining and interpreting messages and related ideas, such as people's underlying values. There are two principal types of message- or artifact-oriented research methods: archival/documentary and textual.

Archival/Documentary Research

Archival/documentary research centers on finding, examining, and interpreting messages that were communicated in the past. These are messages that others have created at different points in time that can tell us about communication during a particular period, policies that affect how we communicate, and the content of various communication messages. For example, Richardson (2003) conducted an archival case study of why people visited an online discussion group about agnosticism. He examined the online postings and noted six motives for visiting the discussion group: wrangling, service, fulmination, understanding, tourism, and sanctuary. Richardson suggested that visitors sought similar benefits from the online forum as they would seek from traditional religious participation.

Common forms of qualitative archival/documentary research include library/documentary, historical, and legal/policy research. Common forms of quantitative archival research include secondary data analysis and meta-analysis. We briefly describe these archival/documentary research forms and provide some examples of scholarly research using this method.

Library/Documentary Research

When conducting **library/documentary research**, we examine all relevant published materials about our research topic. These include printed materials such as published and collected documents (for example, chapters, articles, papers, speeches) and, perhaps, media materials such as films, audiotapes, and videotapes. In other words, when we do library/documentary research, we use many of the materials described in Chapters 5 through 8. We might use general sources, access tools, periodicals, and information compilations to examine a research problem or to answer a research question.

All original research begins with library/documentary research. That is, as we develop and adjust our research questions to conduct a study, we must first find out what others have learned about a subject. Of course, the Internet now connects us to many of these sources from remote locations.

Historical Research

Historical research entails drawing conclusions and presenting new explanations about past communication events or communicators. Historical researchers work with *primary* documents, records, and artifacts, such as original speeches, letters, and recordings found in archives and libraries like a presidential library, broadcast museum, or archives. Researchers prefer original works to *secondary* sources, which provide another person's summary or explanation of original sources. It's always best to go to the original source.

Historical researchers also seek to collect testimony from authorities or others who can support or disconfirm written and media materials. Interviews and oral histories are useful for gathering such testimony. Historical researchers need to be as thorough as possible, examining all relevant and available records and artifacts. They seek to record accurately what transpired and to clarify relationships among societal institutions, conditions, people, and events.

An example of an early historical study is one by Aly (1943). Aly looked at the history of speechmaking in the United States as a research area and considered the links between education and speechmaking. In a more recent historical study, Mizuno (2003) examined newspaper censorship in Japanese-American internment camps in the United States during the Second World War. By examining two camp newspapers, diaries, personal correspondence, memoirs, and government reports, Mizuno concluded that censorship and control of those newspapers reflected considerable abridgements of personal civil liberties of Japanese-Americans and of the First Amendment rights of the press.

Historical studies can be biographical, movement- or idea-oriented, regional, institutional, case history, or editorial in nature (Phifer, 1961). A biographical study, for example, might focus on the career of a government leader, business executive, or other personality. A movement study might examine women's rights, civil rights, or antiwar movements during certain periods. An institutional study might consider the societal forces that influenced the development of a news organization during the early twentieth century.

Legal/Policy Research

Legal/policy research is both historical and critical in nature. It seeks to clarify and to understand how law operates in society. It focuses on the evolution and application of legal doctrine such as First Amendment law and Federal Communications Commission (FCC) policy.

Legal research centers on issues and cases in several areas: defamation, privacy, restraint of expression (such as censorship and obscenity), freedom of information and news access, newsperson privilege, free press and fair trial, and media regulation. It often considers the origin and evolution of legal precedent, debate over such doctrine, and the role of societal agencies, government bodies, groups, and media in the status of the legal or policy issue. It relies heavily on primary documentation from legal codes, court cases, judicial opinions, and administrative rulings. For example, Haridakis (1999) addressed the value of legal commentary in the U.S. media and the moral and ethical principles for establishing a code of conduct for legal commentators.

Secondary Data Analysis

Researchers sometimes work with previously gathered or archived data. Their purpose is to reconsider and to reinterpret the data in light of different ways of thinking. The goal of such **secondary data analysis** is to shed new light on the prior data, interpretations, and conclusions.

Researchers conducting a secondary analysis usually ask different questions than the original investigators—for example, about factors influencing how people vote—and use the same set of data previously used to answer those new questions. The Inter-University Consortium for Political and Social Research (ICPSR) is an archive of statistical social science data that students and faculty in member institutions can use for secondary data analysis; check with your library to see whether you have access.

Researchers might also want to reorder the data. For example, they might collapse continuous data, such as ages ranging from 18 to 90 years, into discrete categories such as younger, middle age, and older. By using several data sets, they might want to see whether trends are discernable over time. Or, they might use different statistical techniques to reanalyze relationships. In short, secondary research seeks new answers to new questions using not-so-new data.

In one recent study, for example, Guzman, Schlehofer-Sutton, and Villanueuva (2003) addressed how discussions about sex affect the behavior of Latino teenagers. In their secondary analysis, the researchers found that having comfortable communication about sex predicted reduced likelihood of adolescent sexual activity.

Meta-Analysis

A recent trend in communication research is analyzing published studies to examine trends in the literature or in the results of research studies, such as the impact of a certain independent variable with multiple samples. By combining statistical results found in scholarly journals and chapters, for instance, researchers can tell how much of an effect a particular variable has had over time. The availability of electronic databases containing the results of published studies is a substantial benefit for researchers conducting meta-analyses.

One type of **meta-analysis** looks at research trends or themes in published literature. An example is a study by Kim and Weaver (2002) that identified theoretical, topical, and methodological trends in research on the Internet. Another type of meta-analysis draws conclusions about the strength or consistency of communication effects across studies. Benoit, Glenn, and Verser (2003), for instance, considered research on the effects of viewing televised presidential debates in the United States. Among their conclusions drawn from analyzing results of previous studies are that viewing debates enhances knowledge of candidates' positions on issues, sets the agenda of important issues, influences perceptions of candidates' personalities but not of their competence or leadership abilities, and affects voter preferences.

Textual Research

Several forms of **textual research** are found in communication. **Critical/cultural** approaches involve examining events, messages, and structures from a particular perspective. **Textual analysis** focuses on media or other content and meanings generated from the content. **Conversation** and **interaction analysis** focus on everyday interpersonal interactions and result in interpretations of relationships using qualitative and quantitative methods, respectively. **Content analysis** is a procedure that helps researchers identify themes and relevant issues often contained in media messages.

Critical/Cultural Approaches

Critics interpret and evaluate communication events and their consequences. There are many examples of this mode of research in communication, such as: a **rhetorical criticism** that applies Aristotle's concepts of invention (argument), disposition (arrangement), style, delivery, and effects on the audience to analyzing political debate; a **fantasy-theme analysis** of organizational behavior that looks at language and other symbols used to create shared realities; a **dramatistic analysis** of a political campaign that concentrates on how politicians use tactics of division and identification of the electorate; a **cultural criticism** that examines the social and economic reasons for the decline in numbers of daily newspapers; a **feminist criticism** that analyzes corporate glass ceilings and their influence on the domination of female employees; and a **Marxist criticism** that explores how media help foster hegemony and maintain societal power structures.

In a recent essay, Hunt (2003) identified three standards of a worthy rhetorical criticism: (a) it focuses on a significant rhetorical text, (b) it delineates appropriate criteria by which to evaluate the text, and (c) it is "well written and argued" (p. 378). The same can be said about the application of any critical method to events, strategies, structures, and the like in a variety of social and cultural contexts. The criticism must focus on a significant topic, apply appropriate criteria to evaluate the topic, and be well-reasoned and well-presented.

Critical/cultural researchers rely on thorough historical gathering of facts. In a manner similar to rhetorical critics, they rely on choosing and applying appropriate criteria or standards of judgment to interpret and to evaluate communication events. Events, then, are understood through a certain lens of observation and the application of appropriate criteria.

For example, a president's televised news conferences might be evaluated according to several criteria, such as effective use of the medium, directness of response to reporters' questions, degree of control over the ground rules, rapport with members of the press, and the amount and quality of information disclosed. Which criteria would be used, of course, evolves from the research topic and question. For example, a critical research project might evaluate how news media affected government policy during the past 25 years or how government policy has restricted the flow of information from the media in a society.

A few other examples should help illustrate some rhetorical and critical approaches. For instance, Benson (1996) used rhetorical criticism to examine political debate on computer bulletin boards. He wanted to learn whether the political debate that took place on these bulletin boards contributed to a sense of civility and democratic community. Benson noted that such political debate was characterized by anger and an attempt to humiliate opponents but also by free speech and political participation.

Using fantasy-theme analysis of news coverage of Fred Rogers, Bishop (2003) argued that journalists framed Mr. Rogers as a respected, tolerant, and calming influence who embodied the positive potential of television. According to this vision, Rogers was presented as the Pied Piper or Dalai Lama of children's television and offered hope for parents struggling to raise their children. And, conducting a critical case study, Morgan (2001) looked at how managers in a department store chain used metaphors such as *get out of the box* as a call to action to implement changes wanted by corporate headquarters.

As noted before, Marxism and cultural approaches are two types of critical theory in mass communication. In Marxist theories, the media are seen as powerful agents to restrain change, for either ideological or economic reasons. According to the approach, the media are owned by a capitalist class and are organized to serve the interests of that class. Media messages depend on the underlying economic and ideological interests of media owners. Marxist approaches direct us to examine critically the structure of media ownership, the operation of media market forces, and how ideological media messages intentionally influence culture by presenting distorted views of reality and class relationships.

Cultural approaches focus our attention on understanding the meaning and role of popular culture for societal groups. They direct us to consider, for example, how mass culture subordinates deviant societal groups to mainstream groups, minority groups to majority groups, one gender to the other gender, or a class of people to other classes of people.

Textual Analysis

Textual analysis, or reception analysis, is derived from literary criticism. It focuses on *reading* media content, or *text*. It is interested in relationships between text and audience. Audience interpretations are compared to the media text to explain how meaning is socially constructed and variable. Researchers suggest that audience members *rework* the content.

Researchers generally use ethnography, including in-depth interviews and participant observation, to gather audience interpretations of discourse. They systematically record and categorize these audience reports of experiences with selected media content, seeking explanations of how the meaning of such content is socially or culturally constructed. Such analyses have been done with television dramas, news, print media such as magazines and romance novels, and the like.

Paek and Shah (2003), for instance, reinforced a quantitative analysis of stereotyping of Asian Americans in U.S. magazine advertising with a textual analysis. Their textual analysis supported depictions of racial stereotypes in the advertising, a view of advertising as conveying a *dominant racial ideology*, and conclusions about gender, conflict, and relationships among minority groups.

Conversation/Interaction Analysis

Also termed relational and interactional analysis in the 1960s and 1970s, conversation analysis uses qualitative methods to examine the structure, messages, function, rules, and content of people's conversations. Researchers aim to discover whether and how people accomplish their interactive goals by looking for themes in dyadic conversation transcribed into text. Some researchers gather their data by surreptitiously eavesdropping on conversations. Others design experimental settings to record talk. Most, however, prefer to record interaction in the natural environment. Interpersonal and small group communication researchers often use this latter method.

Some have compared different theoretical and methodological approaches to interpreting conversation and discourse. Stubbe et al. (2003), for instance, compared five approaches to discourse analysis—conversation analysis, interactional socio-linguistics, politeness theory, critical discourse analysis, and discursive psychology—in seeking to understand and interpret the same 9-minute audio recording of a spontaneous interaction in the workplace.

Interaction analysis is mainly quantitative. Researchers gather samples of conversation, transcribe these samples into written text, and use a selected coding scheme to categorize messages and analyze message content and category structure. These researchers then draw conclusions about participants' goals, rules, and impact on the interaction.

There are two well-known types of interaction analysis. Rogers and Farace's (1975) Relational Control Coding Scheme is used to analyze the power and effect of talk on interpersonal relationships. Bales' (1950) Interaction Process Analysis is used to trace the stages of small group interaction. More recently, researchers have been interested in the beginnings and endings of conversations and in the rules people develop and use in everyday conversation.

Content Analysis

Those who perform a content analysis look at the characteristics of communication messages. Their purpose is to learn something about message content and about those who produce the messages. Their eventual interest might lie with the effects the content has on those who receive the message, that is, on the audience. However, researchers would need to link content analysis with another method, such as survey or experimental research, to address these effects. Researchers often subject speeches, news stories, and television programs to content analysis to learn about underlying attitudes, biases, and repeating themes. The same can now happen with websites, such as those of politicians.

If we were to perform a content analysis on the memos superiors send to subordinates, we might decide to code each sentence according to whether its topic is a directive, helpful suggestion, reprimand, request for information, friendly reminder, compliment, and so on. This would let us determine the nature of the nonpersonal communication process between superiors and subordinates. The type of topic could affect the communication process without the superiors' awareness of this effect. Content analysis can thus provide important information about human interaction.

A couple of examples should illustrate some applications of content analysis. Hoffman-Goetz, Shannon, and Clarke (2003), for example, sought to describe the coverage of chronic diseases in Canadian aboriginal (CA) newspapers. They randomly selected 14 of 31 English-language CA newspapers published between 1996 and 2000. They then searched selected disease terms appearing in headlines or in the first or last paragraphs of selected stories. Of the 400 identified articles about chronic disease, there were more articles about HIV/AIDS and diabetes than there were about cancer and cardiovascular disease. Just over one-third of the articles provided information that allowed readers to pursue health action. The researchers concluded that these ethnic newspapers are "a missed opportunity" for health promotion.

In another content analysis, this time in political communication, Prior (2001) content-analyzed 1996 presidential campaign ads aired in Columbus, Ohio. Prior compared the tone of the 132 ads produced by the two candidates with the 2,522 ads actually aired by three television network affiliates in Columbus. The weighted analysis used by the researcher showed that Republican advertising was more negative than Democratic advertising during the campaign.

Doing such a content analysis is a systematic, multistage process. Let's consider another research problem: sex-role stereotyping on television. Here's the way the process might proceed.

1. We first select the titles we want to sample (e.g., television comedy programs).
2. We then select the dates to sample these programs (e.g., comedy programs aired on prime-time television in 2008). We can form two **composite weeks** that represent the entire year by randomly selecting two Mondays, Tuesdays, Wednesdays, and so on throughout the year.
3. Next we select our units of analysis, that is, what we will examine on these programs to discover whether there is sex-role stereotyping on television (e.g., the major characters on the TV programs).
4. We then assign these units of analysis to predetermined categories that are mutually exclusive and exhaustive (such as lawyer, physician, teacher, police officer, and so on). By *mutually exclusive* we mean that all categories differ from one another. By *exhaustive* we mean that all possible categories (of occupations depicted on television, in this instance) are included in our analysis.
5. We then compare whether more men or more women are presented in these different roles. We also might compare our results to population statistics to see whether television presents an unfair or unflattering bias against women or men.

As you can see, doing a content analysis should be an objective and systematic process. We assign the content to certain categories according to our predetermined rules. Content analysis is a frequently used method in communication research. Next, we turn our attention to two other widely used communication research techniques: surveys and interviews.

People- or Behavior-Oriented Research

People- or **behavior-oriented research** focuses on actions and reactions of people. This approach to communication research includes self-reports of attitudes and behaviors via survey questionnaires, observations of other people's behavior, and experimental research.

Survey Research

Survey researchers seek to describe or to explain people's current attitudes, opinions, thoughts, and, perhaps, reports of behavior (such as whether they voted or what news programs they viewed) surrounding an issue or event (such as an election). Because survey research has been the most widely used method of communication research, we explain it in more depth. We also briefly identify other survey or interview forms, including polls, ratings, interviews, and focus groups.

In our example research study we asked, "How widespread are media-training programs in this country today?" We can use survey research to answer the question by sampling corporate leaders. **Survey research** is an efficient means of gathering data from large numbers of people. Survey researchers try to obtain the needed information systematically and efficiently (i.e., in the shortest period of time and as inexpensively as possible). Hao (1994), for example, used data gathered through national surveys of U.S. adults and found a trend in increased television viewing in the early 1990s. Hao also found differences in the amount of television viewing for different groups based on race, education, and occupation.

Before conducting a survey, we must first determine what it is we are trying to learn. Survey research can be used to measure attitudes, opinions, and reported behaviors or behavioral intentions. It can be used to discern trends in attitudes and behaviors. It often employs correlational designs, looking not for cause-and-effect connections but instead seeking to describe reported opinions or behaviors of people or relationships between two or more variables in hypotheses or research questions.

Before we can construct specific questions for our own surveys, though, we must (a) determine how best to get this information (i.e, our data-collection methods) and (b) choose a sample of participants or **respondents** (i.e., our form of sampling). We discussed sampling in Chapter 9. We discuss data-collection methods next.

Data Collection and Interviews

There are four basic *data-collection methods* used in survey research: personal interviews, telephone interviews, mail questionnaires, and self-administered surveys. *Personal interviews* are face-to-face interactions between an interviewer and selected participants. *Telephone interviews* also require an interviewer but are conducted over the phone. *Mail questionnaires* are self-administered; a participant receives a survey in the mail and is asked to respond to it and return it. Besides mail questionnaires, respondents complete other *self-administered surveys* without prompting from interviewers, such as in a classroom or work setting or via e-mail or on a website. Web-based surveys are becoming more common nowadays because they're easy to administer and involve less cost.

Each data-collection technique has its advantages and disadvantages. For example, self-administered questionnaires are best for gathering personal or sensitive information. Consult one of the sources at the end of this chapter for additional information. The sources contain detailed descriptions of questionnaire design and methods of getting a high rate of return for completed questionnaires.

Similar to content analysis, survey research is a multistage process. Imagine, for example, that we want to learn about student attitudes toward parking on campus. Here's what we can do:

1. Identify our population of interest—say, the 10,000 students who attend the university.
2. Select a sample of that population to answer our questions. If our print or online student directory is inclusive and up-to-date, we can systematically sample, say, 500 people from that directory. Or we might use random-digit dialing or draw a

web-based sample. Because we know we won't reach everyone, we might hope to end up with about 300 or more completed questionnaires.

3. Choose our method to collect the information. Here we can use telephone interviewing because the survey is brief and we are working from a good phone directory.
4. Write the survey questions to gather the information. Our questions will be brief and focus on attitudes toward parking and other relevant information, such as times of classes, work schedules, and so on.
5. Collect the information and analyze the responses.

Questionnaires

How we present the questions is crucial for getting the information we seek. Effective questionnaire development is necessary for getting appropriate responses from the sample. Here are some suggestions for constructing questionnaires.

■ Instructions at the beginning of the questionnaire should relay the importance and voluntary nature of the survey.
■ Instructions for completing or skipping questions should be easily understood by participants and interviewers.
■ The questions asked must be clear, precise, easily understood, logically arranged, and easily answered.
■ Each question should ask for only one piece of information at a time. Double-barreled questions must be avoided. Don't ask in a single question whether participants favor a new parking garage on campus *and* think it will help relieve traffic congestion.
■ There should be effective transitions connecting different questions and parts of the questionnaire.
■ If participants are given possible options to respond to, make sure those choices are exhaustive (i.e., include all possible responses) and mutually exclusive (i.e., the answers do not overlap and will fit only one response option).
■ The questionnaire itself must be printed clearly (or presented clearly, if online) and look professional. It should contain sufficient space in margins and between questions. Avoid clutter.

We can use surveys for descriptive or explanatory purposes (see Chapter 9). As a descriptive technique, we can use survey research to identify current attitudes or opinions about issues or persons, such as political candidates. Here we need probability samples so that we can generalize from the smaller sample to the larger population.

As an explanatory technique, we can use survey research to examine relationships between variables. We often use nonprobability samples when using surveys for explanation because we are interested in conceptual questions of how variables relate to each other rather than in describing or generalizing to a population. We can, for example, devise and use measures of nonverbal immediacy and of learning in an explanatory survey and see whether learning actually relates to nonverbal immediacy. Of course, it's best if our sample reflects the population.

When doing survey research, we need to consider, among other decisions, our sampling procedure, method of data collection, and questionnaire construction. Regardless of whether we use surveys for description or explanation, the choices for effective conduct of survey research, as you can see, are many. Be sure to consult some of the sources at the end of this chapter for more complete information about these various survey research techniques.

Polls and Ratings

We use probability sampling techniques when conducting polls and doing ratings research. Polls fit nicely with our discussion of surveys.

Polls are a descriptive form of survey research whereby we try to learn about the attitudes or opinions of certain groups. Because these groups are usually large (e.g., U.S. voters), we draw smaller, representative samples of the population and question those members of the sample about our topic of interest (e.g., which candidate they prefer). Typically, this has to do with attitudes about issues of importance or toward politicians. We constantly see results of such polls conducted by media organizations and polling organizations (e.g., the *CBS News/New York Times* poll, the *NBC News/ Wall Street Journal* poll, the *USA Today/Gallup* poll, and the *Roper* poll).

Ratings are measures of reported behaviors of viewers or listeners of television or radio programs. They express the percentage of viewers or listeners who tune to a given program at a certain time. For example, a *rating* of 14 for *60 Minutes* means that 14 percent of all possible television households watched *60 Minutes* at that time. A *share* of 20 for the same program means that 20 percent of the television sets actually turned on at that time were tuned to that program. Ratings research is often conducted by companies such as A. C. Nielsen and Arbitron, although other organizations and individuals also do ratings research. These organizations use probability sampling procedures and, generally, either electronic data gathering (e.g., *people meters*) or viewer/listener diaries.

Intensive Interviews

Besides their use in survey research, **interviews** can be in-depth. Such intensive interviews are used as qualitative techniques (i.e., answering *why* and *how come* questions) by which we can gather information for several research methods, such as oral histories and case studies. In such interviews, for example, we might explore techniques of film directors or communicative behaviors of personnel directors in organizations. We can use intensive interviews to probe communication attitudes and behaviors, such as views of television programs or reasons for interacting with others.

Interviews allow one-on-one contact between the researcher and the research participant for longer periods of time than survey questionnaires (e.g., 1 or more hours). The interviews are usually structured. That is, an interviewer uses a prepared schedule of questions, which are presented in a planned and predetermined order. Interviews do, though, allow the flexibility to follow up and probe reasons for certain attitudes and responses.

Interviews also can be combined with other research techniques to confirm or explain research results. Rodgers and Thorson (2003), for instance, found gender differences in a content analysis of news coverage by male and female reporters at three daily newspapers in the United States. They found that women reporters were more positive in their stories, stereotyped less, and used a greater diversity of sources compared with men reporters. They used follow-up interviews with the women reporters at the three newspapers to learn that socialization, or the training the women received, explained the differences observed in the content analysis of the reporting practices.

Focus Groups

The **focus group** is another qualitative technique widely used in marketing research but also gaining favor in communication research. Essentially, it is intensive group interviewing that seeks to understand consumer attitudes and behavior. Groups usually contain 6 to 12 participants, and researchers generally conduct at least two focus groups on a topic. A moderator or facilitator leads the group through a planned discussion of a topic, such as attitudes about an organization, its programs, or policies. Such groups are popular for testing advertised product and broadcast programming ideas. They require careful planning and recruiting of participants. Controlled group discussion is the key to successful focus groups, so that all present get a chance to be heard.

Focus groups are used to study several realms of communication. For instance, Oates, Blades, Gunter, and Don (2003) used focus groups to explore whether 6-, 8-, and 10-year-old children could explain the persuasive intent of television advertising. They concluded that the children did not have a well-established understanding of the persuasive nature of advertising, challenging broadcasting and legislative practices in the U.K.

We include some sources at the end of Chapters 9 and 10 that provide more detail about survey research, polls and ratings research, and interviews and focus groups.

Observational Research

Those who conduct **observational research** look and see how people act in different situations. Here we don't rely on the self-reports of those surveyed or interviewed (although we might want to interview people to check on the accuracy of our observations). Instead, we observe people in their typical or natural social settings and describe the actions (i.e., behaviors) or messages of the individuals, groups, or media studied.

Suppose we are interested in studying communication between superiors and subordinates in organizations. We could devise a survey and interview selected people to get answers to our questions. But we might find that our questions are not answered sufficiently or that the response rate is low. The workers might feel that their employers have access to their answers, or they do not respond in enough detail to offer insight into superior-subordinate communication. Or perhaps we aren't able to frame the questions adequately to get at the interactive behaviors displayed between superiors and subordinates.

Observational techniques might be more effective for gathering this information. There are at least five forms of observational research: ethnography, participant observation, unobtrusive observation, network analysis, and verbal and nonverbal coding.

Ethnography

Ethnography is used to form objective descriptions of social norms and events as they occur. When attending to the physical and social ecology of the communication setting, ethnographers try to explain the regularities of how people behave in social situations. In our superior-subordinate study, for example, a researcher might try to describe the social rules of interaction (for example, who can initiate an interaction, who can request a response of the other) by observing different participants in the organization. These would include the patterns of behavior and use of communication channels in that organization. For example, is it appropriate in the organization for a subordinate to send e-mail requests to superiors? The ethnographer also might interview employees or examine documents and artifacts to verify these observations.

This observational technique often results in a *case study*, such as a description of the culture among fans in a stadium at sporting events, the language used by police officers performing their jobs, conversations among patrons at a bar, or a family's social rules for television viewing. For instance, Bury (2003) conducted a 1-year ethnographic case study of three private e-mail lists to consider the meaning women fans derived from the television series *The X-Files*. Bury sought to learn how these fans shared their enjoyment of texts that were mostly written by men for men.

Public relations campaigns are also suited to this case study format. Here a problem has already been identified. Looking for behavioral norms and regularities, the researcher would observe and describe what the public relations practitioner did to solve the problem and then describe the consequences of this action. Ethnographies should include testimony from participants and examine available records and materials related to the case. Participant observation—whereby the researcher both participates in the activities of the group and observes the behaviors—is often used in ethnographic research.

Participant Observation

Participant observation is used to study social situations or organizations from an insider's perspective. Researchers participate in the social environment they are observing. They systematically record and classify their observations. The end result of the research is an analytic description of the social situation or organization, moving from specific observations to generalizations about the situation or organization (for example, the rules and norms of social interaction). Participant observers rely on their own observations, on information from group members, and on whatever records and materials are available and pertinent. Tracy (2002), for instance, used a combination of techniques including participant observation, interviews, and analysis of transcripts of 911 calls to look at conflict occurring in an emergency communication context.

A participant observer might secure a job in an organization, observe superior-subordinate interactions, talk to colleagues who have worked there more than 2 years, examine memos, plaques, and documents, overhear conversations, and, perhaps, examine personnel files. From all these observations, the researcher would form conclusions about effective and ineffective communication patterns in that organization.

Unobtrusive Observation

Unobtrusive observation is used when researchers want to study communication in a natural setting yet choose not to become participants in the group or organization. They might want to remain objective observers because they feel their participation would contaminate the research setting they are studying, bias their objectivity, or present ethical concerns about becoming a participant. They also feel that if those whom they're observing know they're being observed, they might behave differently. Kuhn and Corman (2003) used such observations, along with interviews and discourse analysis, to study the convergence and divergence of knowledge during a planned change in a municipal government organization.

Unobtrusive field observers also examine social situations or organizations in a systematic manner, similar to participant observation, without becoming a group or social participant. For example, we might observe the use of persuasive sales tactics, the creative advertising process at an ad agency, gatekeeping in the newsroom, or the social climate of viewing television in public places.

Network Analysis

Network analysis is the study of behavioral interactions among large numbers of people. If, for example, we are interested in communication among all members of an organization, we can ask workers to keep a log of the people with whom they communicate, the length of these conversations, and the channels used (speech, memo, meetings, electronic mail, teleconferencing, fax, and so on). Then we can analyze the data to find out whether key individuals have open channels to those with whom they must communicate, what the directional flow of information through the various channels is, and what social or task roles different people fulfill in the organization.

Two studies illustrate different applications of network analysis. First, in a network analysis of group structures in computer-mediated communication (CMC), Postmes, Spears, and Lea (2000) looked at the formation of group norms in the CMC context. They found that group norms defined how CMC group members communicated, conformity to group norms increased over time, and different social norms affected communication outside the group. Second, in a different application, Doerfel and Marsh (2003) used semantic network analysis to examine how the three candidates positioned themselves during the 1992 U.S. presidential debates. They uncovered the issues emphasized the most by the different candidates in the debate (for example, domestic and fiscal concerns by Clinton and Perot). They also found that, based on specific issues, the candidates teamed up on different issues to use a two-against-one strategy.

Verbal and Nonverbal Coding

Researchers have devised a variety of schemes to code verbal behavior (such as self-disclosure) and nonverbal behavior (for example, kinesics and facial expression). Others have developed systems to code marital, family, and group interaction. **Verbal and nonverbal coding** schemes seek to identify patterns of behavior found in the interaction. In a somewhat atypical study of verbal and nonverbal coding, Sharples, Davison, Thomas, and Rudman (2003) analyzed the photographic behavior and intentions of 7-, 11-, and 15-year-old children and adolescents in five European countries. The researchers developed a coding scheme for the content of images and the intentions of the photographers. Among their findings, they noted that older adolescents valued informality and authenticity more than technical proficiency in their photography.

Experimental Research

Like observational research, **experimental research** focuses on people and behavior. It is, however, more concerned with manipulating an aspect of behavior and controlling the environment in order to view reactions better. Experimental research, then, is markedly different from observational research in that observations are made under *controlled conditions*. Experimental research is causal. It is based on the premise that one event—let's say Z—will follow another event—let's say Y. If other factors are present (such as A, B, or C), then we could not be certain that Y produces Z.

Thus, experimental researchers must **control** all relevant factors other than the one being studied. Laboratory settings provide the most control. The researcher designs experiments to test hypotheses about the events. That is, if the researcher is examining the effect of variable Y on variable Z, she or he will form a hypothesis about the relationship.

In a fairly typical pretest–posttest experimental design, Harrington et al. (2003) considered whether individual differences in need for cognition and sensation-seeking influenced responses to antidrug messages. Participants were randomly assigned to different conditions in a laboratory setting over a 4-week period. They were exposed to antidrug public service announcements containing different message strategies. The findings suggested that message manipulation, rather than personality differences, led to more negative attitudes toward marijuana and lower frequency of use.

We can use experimental research to answer the question, "Is a training program effective in improving executives' abilities to deal with the media?" How can we design an experiment to give us an idea of the program's effectiveness? Experimental research employs several **experimental designs**, or blueprints, for the study.

Preexperimental Designs

We could design an experiment in which executives are given a training program, which we label **X**. We will measure an executive's ability to deal with the media through a simple test, which we label **O**. We have the test consist of a question-and-answer session in which we rate the executives on various factors (for example, keeping cool when questioned intently, the speed of answering after a question is asked, perceived honesty). We use the resulting scores to measure the executives' abilities. This research design can be diagrammed like this:

$$X \quad O$$

This design is known as a *One-Shot Case Study Design*. It closely resembles descriptive survey or observational research. It is not, however, a controlled observation because many other variables can enter the situation. For example, we don't know what abilities these executives had before undergoing the training program. We also don't know their communication skills or their past history in dealing with the media.

If we modify our original design and measure the executives' abilities before and after training, we would be controlling for prior abilities and have a *One-Group Pretest-Posttest Design*:

$$O \quad X \quad O$$

This design allows us to say more about the effectiveness of the training program, **X**, although other variables still might be present. The executives might have improved their abilities on their own time, ability might be increased normally each time any executive deals with media questions, or the first measure of their abilities might cause the executives to become more receptive to training in this area.

Experimental Designs

What we need, then, is a group of executives who do not receive the training program so that we can be more certain that it is the program that influences the executives' abilities. The design that controls for these factors is known as the *Pretest-Posttest Control-Group Design*:

R O X O
R O   O

We also need to use the principles of probability sampling to assign participants randomly to different experimental and control groups in the experiment. In the diagram, **R** refers to the fact that we randomly assign individuals to one of the two groups, so that some with higher and lower initial ability are presumably in each group.

We give both groups an ability test but have only one group undergo the training program. The group that does not undergo the training is called the **control group**. We then give the ability test again after the training to both groups. We assume that any natural increase in ability from test 1 to test 2 would (because of random assignment to groups) occur in both groups. If ability improves more in the trained group, we can say that the training program had some effect.

What we still have not controlled, however, is the possibility that the group receiving the training might be more sensitized and influenced by the training as a result of the first test of a participant's ability. We can see whether the initial ability test was influential in increasing sensitivity by dividing the executives into four groups instead of two. We would then give two of the groups the initial ability test and not give it to the other two groups. This is the *Solomon Four-Group Design*:

This design can help determine whether the first test of ability increased executives' sensitivity to the training program. However, it does make our experimental research unnecessarily complicated. For one thing, it requires twice as many participants as the other designs.

An adaptation of this design, the *Posttest-Only Control-Group Design*, might serve our initial purposes sufficiently:

In this design, we assign executives randomly to one of two groups. One group undergoes the training program; the other group does not. At the end, we measure the abilities of individuals in both groups. Now we have controlled for everything we could think of that would provide alternative explanations of our findings. Although we lack a pretest, we have also avoided the potential complications of sensitizing a group to the test and the unnecessary additional demands of the Solomon Four-Group Design. See the sources listed under *Research Design* at the end of this chapter for more information about experimental designs.

Control groups do not receive the experimental treatment that **experimental groups** do. Control groups are crucial for experimental designs. In these experimental designs, we randomly assign **subjects** (i.e., participants in an experiment) to either the experimental group or the control group. Only those in the experimental group receive the experimental treatment (the independent variable) before we observe or measure the behavior (the dependent variable) of subjects in both groups.

In our media training example, only those participants assigned to the experimental group would undergo communication training. We would measure the be havior or performance in media interviews for members of both the experimental and control groups. This enables us to see whether differences on the dependent measure (i.e., performance in media interviews) result from the experimental treatment (i.e., communication training) because only one of the two groups received that treatment.

Laboratory and Nonlaboratory Research

Experimental research is often subdivided into two main types: laboratory and non-laboratory. In **laboratory research**, people are taken out of their natural surroundings so that more variables can be controlled (for example, noise, the presence of other people, or the surroundings themselves). Sometimes, however, unrealistic results are achieved when people are moved from their normal social surroundings and when they perceive they are being observed. That is, they might communicate differently in a laboratory setting.

In **nonlaboratory** (or **field**) **research** settings (which are similar to those used in participant observation and case study research), people are studied in their natural settings. The researcher, though, has less control over potentially influential variables in the environment.

For example, let's imagine you want to study the effects of violent cartoons on children's interactions with one another. In a laboratory study, you would randomly assign children to play groups where half the children view violent cartoons and the other half view nonviolent ones. You would then measure their aggression toward each other. However, moving these children into foreign surroundings might in some way influence their behavior. They could realize they're being watched and curtail their aggression. But if you were to study them in a natural (or nonlaboratory) environment such as a day care center, other factors might influence their behavior, such as already existing personality conflicts between certain children or the teacher's rules for proper behavior in the day care center.

Obviously, the decision about where to study communication must take into account other factors (or **intervening variables**) that could affect research results. We must make choices about which elements of control can be sacrificed. This refers to questions of validity, as discussed in Chapter 9.

The various research methods described in this chapter are used to seek answers to research questions or to test hypotheses. Original research, then, is an important means of adding to our knowledge about communication. The sources listed at the end of this chapter, as well as some at the end of Chapter 9, describe more fully the types of communication research discussed here.

SUMMARY

How we seek to answer questions reflects our method of inquiry. One communication research approach is message- or artifact-oriented research, which includes archival/documentary and textual research. Forms of archival/documentary research are library/documentary, historical, legal/policy, secondary analysis, and meta-analysis. Forms of textual research are critical/cultural approaches, textual analysis, conversation/interaction analysis, and content analysis.

Another communication research approach is people- or behavior-oriented research, which includes survey, observational, and experimental research. Survey researchers primarily seek to describe or to explain attitudes, opinions, and reported or intended behaviors. Decisions about method of data collection, sampling, and questionnaire construction are crucial. Other survey forms include polls, ratings, interviews, and focus groups. Forms of observational research are ethnography, participant observation, unobtrusive observation, network analysis, and verbal and nonverbal coding. Experimental research is conducted under controlled conditions and employs several designs. It can be done in the laboratory and in the field.

References

Aly, B. (1943). The history of American public address as a research field. *Quarterly Journal of Speech, 29,* 308–314.

Bales, R. F. (1950). *Interaction process analysis.* Reading MA : Addison-Wesley.

Benoit, W. L., Glenn, J. H., & Verser, R. M. (2003). A meta-analysis of the effects of viewing U.S. presidential debates. *Communication Monographs, 70,* 335–350.

Benson, T. W. (1996). Rhetoric, civility, and community: Political debate on computer bulletin boards. *Communication Quarterly, 44,* 359–378.

Bishop, R. (2003). The world's nicest grown-up: A fantasy theme analysis of news media coverage of Fred Rogers. *Journal of Communication, 53*(1), 16–31.

Bury, R. (2003). Stories for [boys] girls: Female fans read the X-Files. *Popular Communication, 1,* 217–242.

Doerfel, M. L., & Marsh, P. S. (2003). Candidate-issue positioning in the context of presidential debates. *Journal of Applied Communication Research, 31,* 212–237.

Guzman, B. L., Schlehofer-Sutton, M. M., & Villanueva, C. M. (2003). Let's talk about sex: How comfortable discussions about sex impact teen sexual behavior. *Journal of Health Communication, 8,* 583–598.

Hao, X. (1994). Television viewing among American adults in the 1990s. *Journal of Broadcasting & Electronic Media, 38*, 353–360.

Haridakis, P. (1999). Commentator ethics: A policy. *Journal of Mass Media Ethics, 14*, 231–246.

Harrington, N. G. et al. (2003). Persuasive strategies for effective anti-drug messages. *Communication Monographs, 70*, 16–38.

Hoffman-Goetz, L., Shannon, C., & Clarke, J. (2003). Chronic disease coverage in Canadian aboriginal newspapers. *Journal of Health Communication, 8*, 475–488.

Hunt, S. B. (2003). An essay on publishing standards for rhetorical criticism. *Communication Studies, 54*, 378–384.

Kim, S. T., & Weaver, D. H. (2002). Communication research about the Internet: A thematic meta-analysis. *New Media & Society, 4*, 518–539.

Kuhn, T., & Corman, S. R. (2003). The emergence of homogeneity and heterogeneity in knowledge structures during a planned organizational change. *Communication Monographs, 70*, 198–229.

Mizuno, T. (2003). Journalism under military guards and searchlights. *Journalism History, 29*(3), 98–106.

Morgan, J. M. (2001). Are we "out of the box" yet? A case study and critique of managerial metaphors of change. *Communication Studies, 52*, 85–102.

Oates, C., Blades, M., Gunter, B., & Don, J. (2003). Children's understanding of television advertising: A qualitative approach. *Journal of Marketing Communications, 9*(2), 59–71.

Paek, H. J., & Shah, H. (2003). Racial ideology, model minorities, and the "not-so-silent partner": Stereotyping of Asian Americans in U.S. magazine advertising. *Howard Journal of Communications, 14*, 225–243.

Phifer, G. (1961). The historical approach. In C. W. Dow (Ed.), *An introduction to graduate study in speech and theatre* (pp. 52–80). East Lansing: Michigan State University Press.

Postmes, T., Spears, R., & Lea, M. (2000). The formation of group norms in computer-mediated communication. *Human Communication Research, 26*, 341–371.

Prior, M. (2001). Weighted content analysis of political advertisements. *Political Communication, 18*, 335–345.

Richardson, J. D. (2003). Uses and gratifications of agnostic refuge: Case study of a skeptical online congregation. *Journal of Media & Religion, 2*, 237–250.

Rodgers, S., & Thorson, E. (2003). A socialization perspective on male and female reporting. *Journal of Communication, 53*, 658–675.

Rogers, E., & Farace, R. (1975). Analysis of relational communication in dyads: New measurement procedures. *Human Communication Research, 1*, 222–239.

Sharples, M., Davison, L., Thomas, G. V., & Rudman, P. D. (2003). Children as photographers: An analysis of children's photographic behaviour and intentions at three age levels. *Visual Communication, 2*, 303–340.

Stubbe, M., Lane, C., Hilder, J., Vine, E., Vine, B., Marra, M., et al. (2003). Multiple discourse analyses of a workplace interaction. *Discourse Studies, 5*, 351–388.

Tracy, S. J. (2002). When questioning turns to face threat: An interactional sensitivity in 911 call-taking. *Western Journal of Communication, 66*, 129–157.

SELECTED SOURCES
Content Analysis

Krippendorff, K. (2004). *Content analysis: An introduction to its methodology* (2nd ed.). Thousand Oaks, CA: Sage.

Krippendorff, K., & Bock, M. A. (Eds.). (2009). *The content analysis reader*. Thousand Oaks, CA: Sage.

Neuendorf, K. A. (2002). *The content analysis guidebook*. Thousand Oaks, CA: Sage.

Riffe, D., Lacy, S., & Fico, F. G. (2005). *Analyzing media messages: Using quantitative content analysis in research* (2nd ed.). Mahwah, NJ: Erlbaum.

Weber, R. P. (2000). *Basic content analysis* (2nd ed.). Newbury Park, CA: Sage.

Research Design

Creswell, J. W. (2009). *Research design: Qualitative, quantitative, and mixed methods approaches* (3rd ed.). Thousand Oaks, CA: Sage.

Miller, D. C., & Salkind, N. J. (2002). *Handbook of research design and social measurement* (6th ed.). Thousand Oaks, CA: Sage.

Shadish, W. R., Cook, T. D., & Campbell, D. T. (2002). *Experimental and quasi-experimental designs for generalized causal inference*. Boston: Houghton Mifflin.

Spector, P. E. (1999). *Research designs*. Beverly Hills, CA: Sage.

de Vaus, D. (2009). *Research design in social research* (3rd ed., 4 vols.). Thousand Oaks, CA: Sage.

Rhetorical and Media Criticism

Brunsdon, C., & Spigel, L. (2008). *Feminist television criticism: A reader*. New York: Open University Press.

Chesebro, J. W., Brock, B. L., Bertelsen, D. A., & Messerschmidt, J. (2007). *Methods of rhetorical criticism*. Cary, NC: Oxford University Press.

Foss, S. K. (2004). *Rhetorical criticism: Exploration & practice* (3rd ed.). Long Grove, IL: Waveland Press.

Hart, R. P., & Daughton, S. M. (2005). *Modern rhetorical criticism* (3rd ed.). Boston: Pearson/Allyn & Bacon.

O'Donnell, V. (2007). *Television criticism*. Los Angeles: Sage.

Orlik, P. B. (2008). *Electronic media criticism: Applied perspectives* (3rd ed.). New York: Routledge/Taylor and Francis.

Rybacki, K. C., & Rybacki, D. J. (2002). *Communication criticism: Approaches and genres* (2nd ed.). Boston: Pearson Custom.

Survey Research

Czaja, R., & Blau, J. (2005). *Designing surveys: A guide to decisions and procedures* (2nd ed.). Thousand Oaks, CA: Sage.

Dillman, D. A. (2007). *Mail and Internet surveys: The tailored design method* (2nd ed.). Hoboken, NJ: Wiley.

Fielding, N., Lee, R. M., & Blank, G. (2008). *The SAGE handbook of Internet and online research methods*. London: Sage.

Fink, A. (2006). *How to conduct surveys: A step-by-step guide* (3rd ed.). Thousand Oaks, CA: Sage.

Fowler, F. J., Jr. (2009). *Survey research methods* (4th ed.). Thousand Oaks, CA: Sage.

Gubrium, J. F., & Holstein, J. A. (2002). *Handbook of interview research: Context and method*. Thousand Oaks, CA: Sage.

Lavrakas, P. J. (Ed.). (2008). *Encyclopedia of survey research methods*. Thousand Oaks, CA: Sage.

Maloy, T. K. (1999). *The Internet research guide* (2nd ed.). New York: Allworth.

Reynolds, R. A., & Woods, R. (2007). *Handbook of research on electronic surveys and measurements*. Hershey, PA: Idea Group Reference.

EXERCISES

1. Choose a research topic and identify one historical research question and one critical research question that are as yet unanswered by previous research.
2. Identify a research question for that topic that can be answered by content analysis. Describe the procedure you would use to conduct that content analysis.
3. How could you use participant observation to answer such a question on this topic? How would you function as a researcher in that environment, and what artifacts would you need to examine?
4. What research question relating to this topic could be answered by survey research? Explain the strengths and limitations of survey research to examine that question. Which observational technique would best lend itself to this project? Explain why.
5. Describe a possible experiment that could be conducted to provide more information on your topic. Develop two specific research questions about this topic and present an appropriate experimental design for each.
6. Choose one of the studies used as examples in this chapter and read the method section. What have you learned about this research technique?

chapter 11

Preparing Research Projects

S tudents of communication become involved in different types of research projects during their careers. Many of these projects are theoretical and involve research to increase our knowledge about a topic. Other projects are applied and are geared to solving a problem or answering a practical question. Often professional organizations have their own format and style for writing and presenting reports. Here we focus on the basic elements of preparing a written project. Communication professionals also use these basics when they prepare reports, reviews, and critiques.

TYPES OF WRITING PROJECTS

Research papers have a variety of names, but most can be classified as one of two main types: analytical or argumentative. In **analytical papers**, writers use evidence to examine various sides of an issue. In **argumentative papers**, writers use evidence to support a particular position.

Analytical papers are mainly descriptive. They begin with a research question. Writers of analytical papers need to examine this question thoroughly, finding all possible evidence for its answer. To do so, they examine and evaluate scholarly journal articles, books, and chapters, summarize findings, and develop new conclusions or propositions. In the case of historical or descriptive essays, writers might examine original documents or artifacts and develop conclusions about them, their meaning, and the society of which they are a part. Literature reviews, research prospectuses, and original research reports usually are analytical in nature, although they also contain a thesis or argument that germinates during the research process.

Argumentative papers are mainly persuasive in nature. They begin with a position, or thesis, which is one side of a debatable issue. Then the writer supports the thesis with evidence gleaned from research reports, opinions, events reported in the media, and other credible sources. Critical or interpretive research papers (sometimes called *essays*) and review essays are examples of argumentative projects.

We focus in this chapter on five academic projects students commonly undertake: abstracts, literature reviews, critical papers, research prospectuses, and original research reports. For each project, we define what it is, identify different types, explain the format for preparing it, and outline steps involved in completing the project. Some examples of these kinds of projects can be found on this book's website.

As you'll learn, abstracts are not typically considered writing projects. Most writers create abstracts of their sources as they collect materials for their analytic or argumentative projects. So, we'll focus on these first, because mastering the art of abstracting helps writers condense and organize their materials.

ABSTRACTS

An **abstract** is an abbreviated version or condensation of a written work. There are three main types of abstracts, each identifiable by its internal purpose.

Indicative abstracts are used for screening, so readers can see whether a document is pertinent to their interests. These abstracts describe the scope of the study, the main sections, and other relevant information found in the document. They are short paragraphs (usually 100 to 150 words) that give the purpose and results of research. They guide the reader rather than inform substantially. Indicative abstracts might precede journal articles or be included in the journal's table of contents in order to give the reader a flavor of the piece. Many journals, however, prefer shorter versions of informative abstracts.

Informative abstracts provide sufficient information so that readers can identify main findings and data in a document without having to reread the article. They are fairly detailed in nature, usually 150 to 400 words, and include information on the purpose and scope of research, methods, results, and conclusions. They should not contain references to previous literature or to unreported results. Informative abstracts allow readers to identify basic research concepts and findings and to determine whether the study is relevant to their interests. This is the type of abstract to use when preparing bibliography cards. *Communication Abstracts*, *Psychological Abstracts*, and *Dissertation Abstracts*, for example, publish informative abstracts.

Critical abstracts provide, in addition to main findings and information, a judgment or comment about the study's validity, reliability, or completeness. If a critical abstract becomes too critical, the abstract turns into a *review*. Critical abstracts are usually 400 to 500 words long.

Students and researchers should use abstracts only for their intended purposes. Indicative abstracts allow the reader to confirm whether or not the article contains the main features he or she seeks in the study. Informative abstracts provide an overview of the study, making the reading of the technical report much easier, but they do not contain all findings; often the abstract hints at something important found but doesn't really tell you what. And critical abstracts contain an opinion about the study, which often is useful in sorting out which articles to emphasize in one's review. When you write your own abstracts about articles you read, often you intend to incorporate some of the writing in a longer paper or project. Be sure to use your own words in writing the abstract so that in future uses you avoid plagiarism. When you consider the reason the abstract was created, you can be sure you're using it to its fullest capability.

Format

Abstracts, especially of empirical research articles, typically have four sections. The first is an orientation to the nature of the study and what the researcher is investigating (e.g., hypotheses and research questions). The second section describes the method, procedures, sample, and other specific information about how the study was done. The third section contains the results of the study. Those unfamiliar with statistics can have a difficult time understanding the elaborate statistical procedures used in many scholarly journal articles. It is important, however, that you read and note these results, especially as they relate to the study's hypotheses and research questions. The last section of the abstract is typically the shortest. It greatly condenses the author's discussion of the results, the relationship of the results to previous research findings, and proposed directions for further research.

Steps

Cleveland and Cleveland (2000) and Collison (1971) have outlined the main steps in writing an abstract.

1. Ideally, read the article two or three times before writing the abstract.
2. Identify the main sections of the document and highlight, mark, or note important passages.
3. Write a draft of the narrative, using complete sentences and your own words. Include the following:
   a. Objectives and scope: Why was the study done? What does the study include?
   b. Methodology: How was the study done? What procedures, participants, instruments, and data analyses were used or performed?
   c. Results: What was found?
   d. Conclusions: What do we now know? What implications does this have?
   e. Additional information: What interesting information doesn't fit in the categories listed? Which findings are incidental?
4. Edit and rewrite the draft.
   a. Check for brevity, reduce redundancy, and avoid repetition whenever possible.
   b. Use your own words.
   c. Clarify the lead sentence, or *thesis*. It contains vital information about the purpose of the study and should be clear, concise, and thorough.

5. Prepare and proofread the final abstract.
   a. Record the complete citation or reference, accurately and completely, at the top of the abstract.
   b. Provide your name at the bottom.

Keep in mind that informative and critical abstracts will be more detailed than indicative abstracts.

LITERATURE REVIEWS

You might be asked to find specific information in the communication literature, to review research on a specific topic, and to write a literature review about that research. A **literature review** has two main purposes: (a) to summarize the research, and (b) to evaluate the research. Pure summary is akin to objective and descriptive journalism, whereas evaluation contributes original ideas to our understanding and results in scholarship. Evaluation addresses the validity of research findings.

A literature review is a crucial part of the research process. It enables us to understand the current state of knowledge about a topic. Before conducting original research, we must know what scholarship already exists on the topic and evaluate the findings. This enables us to formulate new or revised research questions about the research problem to guide the study. As you begin to read original reports of communication scholarship, you will see that researchers explain to the reader how the literature was examined before the research question was formed. The literature review, then, acts as a guide for developing questions not yet answered by the published research literature.

There are two basic types of literature reviews: exemplary and exhaustive. An **exemplary literature review** is representative of the published literature. It is similar to a preface in a research study. In the exemplary review, the writer assumes the reader knows about the subject and so presents only key references to reacquaint the reader with representative works that relate to the research study.

Key references are those that have directly influenced the study being proposed or conducted. Writers cite these key references and describe how they relate to the research topic. Key references provide the reader with a starting point for building further information. However, the reader should understand that other, perhaps more general, articles and books exist that also relate to the subject. Missing key references is a sign of poor scholarship.

Most scholarly journal articles begin with exemplary literature reviews. Consult journal articles for examples of this type of literature review.

An **exhaustive literature review** is comprehensive. The writer attempts to find all information pertinent to a topic (usually scholarly journal articles, book chapters, and books) and summarizes and evaluates major findings. This type of review is typical of review essays in scholarly handbooks or yearbooks, theses and dissertations, and research papers required for communication classes. In an exhaustive review, the writer assumes the reader has less knowledge of the area than is assumed with an exemplary review. The writer's goal is to summarize major conclusions, to emphasize pertinent findings, to review methodological issues, and to evaluate the status of research on the topic. The reader of this type of review assumes the writer has examined all theory and research in the area and that most works on the topic are referenced in the review.

To demonstrate the difference between an exemplary review and an exhaustive review, consider the following two pieces of scholarship by the same author. The first piece is the prelude to a study about technology in the classroom. The second piece is a review article. Note that there are nine authors of the second piece, so we use APA (American Psychological Association, 2001) reference list style here to show how nine authors are treated. Had this appeared in the text, only the first author would have been listed, followed by *et al.* (Lievrouw et al., 2001).

Haythornthwaite, C. (2000). Online personal networks: Size, composition and media use among distance learners. *New Media & Society, 2*, 195–228.

Lievrouw, L. A., Bucy, E. P., Finn, T. A., Firndte, W., Gershon, R. A., Haythornthwaite, C., et al. (2001). Bridging the subdisciplines: An overview of communication and technology research. *Communication Yearbook, 24*, 271–295.

A literature review differs from a **literary review**, both in title and in purpose. Professional literary reviews publish poetry and fiction, articles about authors and poets, and critiques of their creative work. In an academic literary review, one that students might be asked to write for a class, you'll find a critique of a piece of literature (usually a book, poem, or short story) and comments on its style, form, and worth. Although both a literature review and a literary review result in a critique, the former focuses on how well the research was done and the latter proffers an opinion on the style of the author or poet.

Format

You are probably familiar with writing *term papers*. The goal of a term paper is usually to summarize information from secondary sources and to draw a conclusion about a particular topic. That is why instructors emphasize the need for creating a thesis statement and supporting it throughout the paper. Literature reviews are similar in this respect. A review of pertinent literature should also be cohesive (in other words, not choppy). Sources examined in the literature review, however, are usually primary rather than secondary ones. In each section of the literature review, the reader should see how the research helps clarify a specific aspect of the problem. The writer of such a review, consequently, must know exactly what that problem is before beginning the writing process.

The *thesis statement* is a clear assertion of a position on the subject you plan to support. It is not a personal opinion or belief. You must demonstrate the proposition with evidence from the research literature. Most often, an understanding of the problem emerges from the literature search process and discussions with others. Then, by organizing, integrating, and evaluating the published materials, you consider how adequately the research has clarified the problem. In short, you develop the thesis statement and support various arguments by summarizing and synthesizing those pertinent writings you found during the literature search. An example of a thesis statement is:

> Research has not supported axioms 3 and 5 of uncertainty reduction theory, but it has substantially supported axioms 1, 2, and 4.

Introduction

This first part of a literature review orients the reader to the subject and indicates what is to follow. It is sometimes better to write the introduction after you have completed the paper because you might change your outline slightly during the writing process.

General Statement of the Problem

This second section describes the topic and explains its significance. Answer these questions: What do you mean by the topic? Why is it interesting? How is this a significant communication topic? Are there controversies that need to be resolved? Is this research area of special interest to a particular group of people?

You can establish the significance of the topic by arguing (a) that this research fills a gap in the literature (in other words, no one else has adequately summarized this necessary or essential material), (b) that it provides the possibility for fruitful exploration in the future, and (c) that it relates to a problem that needs to be solved to make communication theory and practice more meaningful. By the end of this second section, then, you should clearly define and clarify the problem for the reader.

Summary of Literature

The third section is the meat of the literature review. Here you summarize previous research, theory, and writings to inform the reader of the state of current knowledge in this area. You also should identify relationships, gaps, contradictions, and inconsistencies in the literature reviewed.

You can use several organizational strategies for this summary. Which pattern works best depends on the problem being examined. Therefore, it is important to understand the problem before you begin to summarize the literature. The pattern of organization depends on knowing what the end of the paper will look like. Here are several ways to organize the summary of literature.

- *Problem-cause-solution order.* One way to organize this section is to move from the problem to a solution. You begin by fully describing the problem (e.g., what is the influence of friends on decisions to purchase magazine subscriptions?). Then you identify and discuss the cause of the problem (e.g., although the impact of opinion leaders on newspaper reading has been examined, the influence of friends on magazine subscriptions has not been investigated). Finally, you propose a solution— what type of research is needed to fill this gap in our knowledge?
- *General-to-specific order.* Another organizational scheme is, first, to examine broad-based research and, then, to focus on specific studies that relate to the topic. For example, you might first look at writings that address general issues

about media effects, then review studies that look specifically at the influence of television viewing on children's aggressive behavior.

- *Known-to-unknown order.* Yet another way to organize this summary is to examine current literature about the problem and then identify, at the end, what is still not known.
- *Comparison-and-contrast order.* Another organizational structure is to show how research studies and findings are similar to and different from each other.
- *Specific-to-general order.* In this scheme you attempt to make general sense out of specific studies so that you can draw conclusions. For instance, you might describe three studies that have tried to measure interpersonal communication competence and then draw conclusions about how competence should be defined or measured.
- *Topical order.* According to this organizational pattern, you present the main topics or issues, one by one, and emphasize the relationship of the issues to the main problem. For example, a topical order for a literature review on approaches to group leadership would include the trait approach, the situational approach, and the functional approach. Obviously, without transitions, the topics would appear as a sequence of mini-papers and would not seem connected. Thus you must keep the reader aware of the direction of this organizational scheme and the connections among the topics.
- *Chronological order.* One further structure is most useful for historical research papers. It doesn't make much sense to describe, chronologically, research studies of group communication if you are emphasizing the need for more research on group cohesion. Research developments do not typically happen in a neat sequence over time. However, if you are arguing that group research proceeds from an early emphasis on individual variables to a later emphasis on process variables, a chronological order is consistent with the problem being discussed.

Critical Evaluation

A literature review typically ends with a critical evaluation of the literature. This section of the review carefully examines the research done to date by (a) critiquing the conduct and validity of the research on the topic, and (b) posing research directions by proposing questions that are still unanswered in the literature. Through this critical evaluation, the review becomes a piece of scholarship. It creates knowledge by adding new information to the already existing literature on the topic. Your research questions or hypotheses will probably evolve from this evaluation. The questions you ask set forth an agenda for other researchers to follow. By learning about research methodology, students can understand and evaluate the communication literature and add to the body of knowledge through their own scholarship.

Steps

1. Choose and then narrow (i.e., focus) the topic. How narrow the topic becomes depends on the purpose, scope, and type of project (see Chapter 2).
2. Formulate a working statement of the problem. According to Hubbuch (1996), the statement should begin with, "What are the basic trends and developments in _____?"

3. Search the literature, employing either a general-to-specific or specific-to-general search strategy (see Chapter 2).
4. Once all sources have been abstracted, examine the bibliography records for themes, topics, issues, patterns, and developments.
5. Write a thesis that summarizes these trends.
6. Refine the statement of the problem.
7. Choose an organizational strategy for the review and create an outline for the summary section.
8. Write each part of the summary section by focusing on the trends, themes, or ideas, citing studies you've read as illustrations or examples. Use the literature to develop your thesis or argument for each section. Do not just give abstracts of your studies. Show how the studies are connected and how they relate to the themes. Critique, where possible, the validity of the research.
9. Form conclusions about each main section and about the topic in general.
10. Identify gaps in the literature and propose questions for further study.
11. Write the introduction to the paper, orienting the reader to the subject, what will follow, and the significance of the topic. Make sure you define all terms needing clarification.
12. Refine the summary section. Write transitions between the sections by pointing out common elements or referring to the thesis and mini-thesis statements.
13. Put the review aside for a few days and prepare the reference list, citing only those sources that actually appear in the review.
14. Reread the review, refine the grammar, and edit carefully for clarity. Sometimes reading it aloud will help uncover mistakes.
15. Check the review carefully for spelling, typographic, and punctuation errors. Make necessary corrections.
16. Examine the review one last time with an APA manual in hand (or whatever manual you are following) to be sure all stylistic conventions are followed. Make necessary corrections.
17. Print the final version of the literature review. Proofread it carefully.

CRITICAL PAPERS

As we have explained, a critical evaluation is often considered a part of any literature review. Sometimes, however, your goal may be to conduct an exemplary literature review rather than an exhaustive one and to draw conclusions about the subject based on pertinent evidence. This, then, is a critical paper. **Critical papers** can range from a few pages to **monograph** length. Their size depends on how narrowly defined the topic is and how much pertinent literature exists on it. Article-length critical papers can be found in journals such as *Critical Studies in Media Communication* and *Quarterly Journal of Speech*.

A key feature of a critical paper is a strong thesis statement. You test the thesis by gathering facts and other evidence and analyzing these materials for authenticity, validity, and relevance. You can change the thesis as you proceed because you want to let the facts guide the paper rather than to select only those facts that support a predetermined opinion. This thesis statement of a critical paper is more argumentative than that of a literature review. That is, it expresses a position, conclusion, or opinion that has already been formed through the research process. An example of a thesis for a critical paper is:

> Uncertainty Reduction Theory (Berger & Calabrese, 1975) provides a better explanation of initial interaction development than does Predicted Outcome Value Theory (Sunnafrank, 1986).

Historical, rhetorical, and cultural critical reviews or essays naturally will follow conventions for each of these research styles. For examples of studies using these methods, see the examples we provide in Chapters 9 and 10. Because of the wide variety of styles you will find, no set format exists for critical papers. The topic, data, and author's perspective determine the format and structure.

Steps

1. Choose and then narrow the topic. Consult with those who have written critical papers to adjust the topic to the size appropriate for your specific purpose or goal.
2. Search the literature and archives for relevant data or facts, transcripts, opinions, recordings, research reports, and so on. Primary sources are better than secondary sources (see Chapter 10).
3. Develop a working thesis statement. Post it in a prominent place in your writing area so you can keep focused. Remember to change it as it develops.
4. Test the thesis with previously gathered data. Adjust as necessary.
5. Search for and gather additional data. Adjust the thesis as the data suggest.
6. Check for appropriate grammar and sentence structure.
7. Critically evaluate the clarity of the paper's ideas.
8. Carefully check for spelling, typographic, punctuation, and stylistic errors. Make necessary corrections.
9. Print the final version of the critical paper. Proofread it carefully.

RESEARCH PROSPECTUSES

Some assignments (such as an independent study project, senior thesis, master's thesis, or doctoral dissertation) require you to move beyond a summary and critical evaluation of the literature to suggest the next step or steps that should be taken to solve the problem. At this point, statements of hypotheses or research questions should clearly and logically emanate from the literature review. Proposed research methods to answer these questions (see Chapter 10) also must be consistent with those used and critically discussed earlier in the paper. These are the basic elements of a research **prospectus**.

Typically, the type of research project proposed will influence which type of literature review we write. Some institutions, for example, require that the literature review be exhaustive for thesis and dissertation prospectuses, whereas others require only exemplary reviews. A prospectus for an independent study project might include only several paragraphs or a couple of pages of literature review. So the purpose of the project and the guidelines of the institution influence the extent of the prospectus. Be sure to ask before proceeding.

Format

Many formats exist for organizing research prospectuses. Most often the format depends on the project proposed. Many times the format for people- or behavior-oriented studies differs slightly from that used for artifact- or message-oriented studies. The outline on pages 242–244 contains basic elements of the prospectus and questions that research prospectuses should answer.

Depending on the nature of the proposed project, you may not need to include answers to all these questions. Note that some entries in the outline are more relevant for some forms of research (i.e., message or behavior) than for others. The main difference among these is in the *Method* section. Also, you might want to shift the order of some sections to reflect your own project. In any case, this outline will guide you in providing a complete prospectus for an adviser or a committee to examine. The questions in the last section suggest that planning is vital to any research project. You must have a clear plan of action and stick to it throughout the project. Remember, research is systematic, and objective methodological conventions must be followed.

OUTLINE FOR A RESEARCH PROSPECTUS

  I. COVER PAGE
    A. Title
    B. Author
    C. Date
    D. Purpose of Submission
 II. ONE-PAGE ABSTRACT
III. RESEARCH PROBLEM (Introduction, Questions, and Overview)
    A. What is the goal of the research project?
    B. What is the problem, issue, or critical focus to be researched?
    C. What are the important terms to be defined?
    D. What is the significance of the problem?
      1. Do you want to test a theory?
      2. Do you want to extend a theory?
      3. Do you want to test competing theories?
      4. Do you want to replicate a previous study?
      5. Do you want to correct previous research that was conducted inadequately?
      6. Do you want to resolve inconsistent results from earlier studies?
      7. Do you want to solve a practical problem?
      8. Do you want to test a methodology?
    E. What are the limitations and delimitations of such a study?

IV. REVIEW OF LITERATURE
    A. What is the theoretical framework for the investigation?
    B. Are there complementary or competing theoretical frameworks?
    C. What does previous research reveal about the different aspects of the problem?
    D. What research questions and hypotheses have emerged from the literature review?

V. METHOD
    A. What will constitute the data for the research?
    B. What materials and information are needed to conduct the research?
       1. How will they be obtained?
       2. What special problems can be anticipated in acquiring needed materials and information?
       3. What are the limitations in the availability and reporting of materials and information?
    C. Who will provide the data or materials for the research?
       1. What is the population being studied?
       2. Who will be the participants (i.e., subjects or respondents) for the research, or what materials will be examined?
          a. What is the sample size?
          b. What are the characteristics of the sample?
       3. Which sampling technique will be used?
    D. What questionnaire or measures will be used (if any)?
       1. If previously developed:
          a. How reliable and valid are the measures?
          b. Why use these measures rather than others?
       2. If developing a measure for the research:
          a. Why develop a new measure?
          b. How will items be developed?
          c. What format will be used for the items?
          d. How will reliability and validity be assessed?
    E. What methods or techniques will be used to collect the data or materials?
       1. What are the variables?
       2. How will the variables be manipulated, controlled, measured, and/or observed?
    F. What procedures will be used to apply the methods or techniques?
       1. What are the limitations of this methodology?
       2. What factors will affect the study's internal and external validity?
       3. How will plausible rival hypotheses be minimized?
       4. What sources of bias will exist? How will they be controlled?
    G. Will any ethical principles be jeopardized? How will subjects be debriefed?

VI. DATA ANALYSIS
    A. How will the data or materials be analyzed?

B. What criteria will be used to determine whether the hypotheses are supported?

C. What was discovered (about the goal, data, method, and data analysis) as a result of doing a pilot study (if conducted)?

D. What statistics will be used, if any?

VII. **CONCLUDING INFORMATION**

A. How will the final research report be organized? (Outline)

B. What sources have you examined thus far that pertain to your study? (Reference List)

C. What measures, questions, credentials, or data must be made available? (Appendixes of Materials and Instruments)

D. What timeframe (deadlines) have you established for collecting and analyzing the data and for writing the report? (Timetable/Schedule)

Steps

Here are the main steps to follow in constructing a research prospectus. We do not repeat here the steps involved in conducting a literature review or critical essay. They are, however, pertinent to preparing a research prospectus. Review the steps for preparing a literature review or a critical essay when you arrive at the second step below.

1. Determine what it is you want to study. Discuss the topic with an adviser who is interested in this topic and is willing and able to advise your research.

2. Review the literature and develop specific research questions you want to answer or hypotheses you want to test.

3. Consult with your adviser on the feasibility of conducting such research. Your adviser might want to see your literature review before this meeting. If you need to have a prospectus committee, now is the time to begin to set it up.

4. Construct the *research problem* section and orient the literature review to your particular problem area.

5. Determine which procedures or methods will best answer your questions or test your hypotheses. Explain these thoroughly and review other research that has used these procedures or methods.

6. Submit the plan to your adviser and discuss the wisdom of proceeding as planned.

7. Polish (rewrite, edit, proofread) the prospectus and submit it.

ORIGINAL RESEARCH REPORTS

Original **research reports** are comprehensive summaries of what happened when a research project was carried out. Besides the literature review, research reports include information on what was planned and what was discovered.

Reports differ slightly depending on the type of research conducted. Archival and documentary research reports emphasize support for arguments and procedures for analyzing the contents of documents. Survey research reports focus on sampling procedures, questions asked, and statistical analysis of results. Observational research reports detail methods for observing behavior and the findings of the observations. Experimental reports emphasize controlled procedures and statistical analysis of results. Examples of these reports are given in Chapters 9 and 10 and on this text's website **<http://academic.cengage.com/communication/rubin/7e>**. Be sure to take a look at these and note their similarities and differences.

Format

As previously stated, the research process involves careful planning and execution. You should follow a specific convention for reporting research results. Although reports vary depending on the type of research project conducted, some elements are common to all research reports.

In the first section, the *introduction*, develop the problem and its significance and provide background information on the study. Include the purpose of the investigation, the rationale for the study, and a review of the most pertinent literature. If you will be submitting the report to a journal or editor for publication, the review should be exemplary (briefer than that required for a classroom literature review). If the report will be a thesis or dissertation, the review should be more exhaustive.

In the second section, detail the *method* and materials used in the study. Include in this section the sample you studied, the research design, the measures you used, and the specific procedures you followed in conducting the study. In other words, how did you examine, observe, or measure your data? These details should be precise so that another researcher could reproduce or replicate your study.

In the third section, present your *results*. This might be the shortest section of an experimental research report because you are limited to just the results of your investigation. It could, however, be the longest section of a report if the study is archival or documentary in nature. You might find tables and figures helpful for relating complicated or summary data here, especially for survey and experimental research. For historical or critical research, this section might not even be labeled *Results* because the entire article would contain findings and supporting data.

The last section of the report is the *discussion*. In this section *discuss* (don't just recapitulate) the results you found. Show how your results agree or disagree with previous research. Point out where unexpected results were found. Why might you not have found the expected results? Discuss the theoretical meaning, implications, and/or practical applications of your results. Identify the limitations of your study and point to future directions for investigation. Make sure that the meaning of the results and the significance of the study are clear.

Steps

We outlined the basic steps in conducting research in Chapters 9 and 10. Later in this chapter we summarize some basic concerns of reviewers when they read a submitted manuscript. Keep these concerns in mind as you prepare to conduct a research study and as you write the research report about that project. Earlier, in the literature review and prospectus sections of this chapter, we detailed the steps for writing research reports. Here we take you through the steps that follow a completed prospectus.

1. Conduct the research.
2. Analyze the data and summarize the results.
3. Review the findings in relation to what you expected to find and what has been found before. Generate important ideas that need further explanation or elaboration in the discussion section.
4. Write the discussion section, pulling together the main themes or issues that are important and the new findings from your study. Also include ideas for new research projects that emerged from your findings.
5. Check the research report for coherence and clarity.
6. Submit the report to your professor or committee, for convention presentation, or for publication.

SUBMITTING YOUR WORK

Writing Papers for Classes

As you will see in Chapter 12, a wide variety of writing projects are common in different classes. Collaborative writing projects should detail team members' contributions. If papers are submitted electronically, this detail is available to the instructor. Perhaps the instructor would like to see both electronic and paper copies. With *WebCT* and *Blackboard* class-management programs available on many campuses, papers can be uploaded as an assignment and read and graded electronically as well. Be sure to ask your instructors about their submission preferences.

Sometimes students submit their work to several instructors or a panel of reviewers, such as a thesis committee or academic review committee. These are mainly faculty members (but occasionally professionals and alumni might sit on these committees, too) who are looking for certain standards of quality. If there is a *defense* meeting where a thesis proposal is presented, the student's role is to argue that this project is worthy and significant and to explain and defend various choices made. This is not unlike real-life professional situations in which communication professionals pitch advertising campaigns, business operating procedures, sales plans, new curricula, or motivational suggestions. Knowledge of effective public speaking is critical in these situations.

Occasionally instructors will suggest that you submit your papers or research studies to be considered for publication or for presentation at a meeting of a professional association or conference. There are also undergraduate conferences where students can present their work. This means that you must pay special attention to the writing style and to the guidelines for contributors that each journal or association publishes. Not only must the paper be flawless in writing, typing, and word choice, but it must be appropriate for the particular journal or association to which it will be submitted.

Submitting Manuscripts: The Process

Where to submit a manuscript is the first important step in the process. Students submit projects to their instructors, and researchers often consider submitting literature reviews and research reports to professional associations for convention presentation and for publication in scholarly journals. Each year the professional associations issue a *Call for Papers* for the next year's convention. Contact the organization for further information (see Chapter 1).

The choice of where to submit a completed research report to be considered for publication largely depends on the nature of the work. To find the right place for your manuscript, scan *Current Contents* or go to *Ingenta.com* (see Chapter 7) and examine the contents of recent issues of a variety of journals. Look at the prefaces and the *Instructions to Authors* or *Manuscript Submission Guidelines* in the journals to see which one is most likely to consider your paper for publication.

Three other publications offer detailed descriptions of communication journals and can help you decide where to submit your articles:

Alexander, A., & Potter, W. J. (Eds.). (2001). *How to publish your communication research: An insider's guide*. Thousand Oaks, CA: Sage.

Dyer, C. (2004). *The Iowa guide: Scholarly journals in mass communications and related fields*. (Available: http://fm.iowa.uiowa.edu/fmi/xsl/iowaguide/search.xsl)

Knapp, M. L., & Daly, J. A. (2004). *A guide to publishing in scholarly communication journals* (3rd ed.). Mahwah, NJ: Erlbaum.

It is, of course, important to consider the prestige of publishing in a quality journal, but you also must consider where the article will have the most impact for the audience you have in mind. A small-scale study, a study focused on a state or regional issue, or a study looking at links between two or three variables might be more appropriate in a state or regional journal, whereas a study having wider implications or seeking to add to our theoretical knowledge would be better placed in a national or international journal. Discussions with colleagues and professors can help you decide on the best market for your paper. Sometimes departments have rankings of journals that can help you determine the degree of rigor and expertise.

Each journal details its policies and procedures for submitting manuscripts for consideration within each issue and also on the journal's webpage. These guidelines explain the journal's review policy, the appropriate manuscript style (such as APA or MLA), and the number of copies of the manuscript to send. Most journals do not ask you to send the original printed copy and do not return copies if the manuscript is not accepted for publication. So be sure to keep a copy for yourself before you send the paper out for review. Electronic journals and some other publications accept submissions online, as do some professional associations.

To send a manuscript or to address inquiries about specific journal policies and procedures, contact the editor, whose name is listed on the inside cover or on the first pages of each journal. Because most editors change every 3 or so years, be sure to consult the most recent issue of the journal. Typically, you would send three or four copies of a manuscript (depending on the journal's requirements) to the editor of the selected journal. It is important that the paper be written in the style acceptable to that journal. You will often have to provide an abstract with your manuscript. Examine the journal to decide whether to send an indicative or an informative abstract.

The editor will decide whether the manuscript is within the purview of the journal and of sufficient quality to consider for publication. If it is not, you will receive a letter saying so. If it is, the editor will acknowledge receipt and send the manuscript, usually with author identity removed, to two or three reviewers chosen for their expertise in the paper's content or methodology (this is referred to as *blind review*). These reviewers will send their recommendations to the editor. After receiving all recommendations, the editor will evaluate the manuscript and the reviews and send you a letter. The letter will advise you whether the editor has accepted the paper for publication. He or she will usually include copies of the reviews. The review process typically takes 3 or 4 months (sometimes longer). To be publishable, a study has to investigate significant research questions in a rigorous and methodologically sound manner. It should extend knowledge in one's field. Most seminar papers and many convention papers do not meet these criteria.

The editor's decision letter may accept (which is rare) or reject the paper or ask you to resubmit a revision after you have incorporated the editor's and reviewers' suggestions. Don't be disheartened by a less-than-enthusiastic review. A vast majority of manuscripts (often 85 to 90 percent in the best journals) are either rejected or in need of revision. Very few initial submissions are accepted. If you're asked for a revision, follow the specific editor and reviewer suggestions and rewrite. The process may be time consuming and demanding, but often the results are rewarding. If a paper is rejected and you feel the manuscript really does have merit, use the editor and reviewer comments to revise the paper and submit it to a different journal. Most journal editors will tell you that they want to see only your best work, and reviewer comments help you make the manuscript better.

Achieving Success

We offer the following suggestions about what to avoid when submitting manuscripts. These are the sorts of things that guarantee failure:

■ *Inadequate rationale.* The purpose of the study is not clear. A topic is not important to study just because you are interested in it or others have or haven't studied it before. Perhaps others haven't studied the topic or problem before because it isn't important. You need to explain a rationale or guiding force for the study and support the importance of the investigation. Authors have this burden of proof. Authors have an obligation to present clearly (a) the purpose of the study and (b) a solid rationale for the significance or importance of the study.

- *Uninteresting questions*. Authors must ask good and interesting questions. You must show that you are familiar with what others have written about your topic or problem in the literature. You need to present these questions in a compelling manner and build on the work that others have done before.

- *Sloppy procedures*. Whether the method is quantitative or qualitative in nature, sloppiness is not tolerated. Using questionable scales and measures, coders who cannot agree on their observations, and biased raters will result in measurement that is not valid or reliable. These can be fatal flaws in that the procedure does not allow you to address the research problem adequately.

- *Inappropriate sample*. The sample must be chosen with the study's purpose in mind. Convenience samples instead of probability samples need to be justified. The sample must sufficiently represent the population being studied. The size of the sample must be adequate. The number and kind of artifacts or primary documents examined must be appropriate for qualitative and historical research.

- *Inadequate analyses*. Once you have asked good and interesting questions, established the significance of the study, and used sound methods, you also need to analyze your observations appropriately. If all else is right, computing or reporting the wrong statistics or conclusions or not providing a complete analysis will not end the manuscript's future. Reviewers might suggest a different path for analysis. Following the sensible suggestions of reviewers and revising and resubmitting the work can put the manuscript back on track.

- *Lack of contribution*. Overall, does the manuscript make an important contribution to current knowledge? As you discuss the meaning of your findings, you need to convince reviewers about the significance of the study and how its publication is essential to furthering current understanding of the topic or problem. Often this comes out in the *theory-development* and *discussion* sections of the manuscript.

- *Inappropriate place of submission*. Occasionally, the manuscript is simply sent to the wrong place. Highly quantitative studies should not be submitted to *Quarterly Journal of Speech* or *Critical Studies in Media Communication*. Oral interpretation studies should not be sent to the *Journal of Broadcasting & Electronic Media*. And, generally, mass communication papers should not be sent to the Organizational Communication Division of the NCA or ICA. Opinion essays would be more appropriate for a trade or professional periodical than for a scholarly journal. Discussing the paper with professors, perusing the journals, and reading contributor submission guidelines in the journals can help place the manuscript in the right place.

SUMMARY

Abstracts condense research reports. They indicate what can be found in a document or what the major findings are; sometimes, critical comments are added. Taking notes by abstracting articles on bibliography cards or in electronic records saves researchers time and energy.

Literature reviews are the bases of most research projects. They have standard patterns of organization: introduction to the subject, statement of the problem, summary of previous research, and critical review of the literature. An exemplary, or representative, literature review is similar to the introductory section of a research report. An exhaustive literature summarizes all major writings on a topic. Both types of review require the writer to select and narrow a topic and to search the relevant literature for appropriate sources.

Critical papers include a literature review but focus on developing new understanding of the literature. The thesis of such papers is supported by the literature and information reviewed.

A literature review also is part of a research prospectus. After identifying the problem, reviewing the literature, and posing research questions, the writer describes the method, sample, and procedures for the study in a prospectus. The prospectus also includes a list of references, appendixes of instruments (i.e., the scales, coding system, or questionnaire) used in the study, and a timetable for the project.

A research report also must be systematically organized. The first section is an introduction that provides the purpose, rationale, and background of the investigation and a review of pertinent literature. The second section contains the study's method and procedures. The third section describes the results. The final section is a discussion of the meaning and significance of the findings.

Research reports submitted for presentation or publication must follow the association's or the journal's guidelines. Journals follow systematic procedures for reviewing manuscripts. Manuscripts must address important questions, advance knowledge, and be methodologically and stylistically sound.

References

Alexander, A., & Potter, W. J. (Eds.). (2001). *How to publish your communication research: An insider's guide*. Thousand Oaks, CA: Sage.

American Psychological Association. (2001). *Publication manual of the American Psychological Association* (5th ed.). Washington, DC: Author.

Berger, C. R., & Calabrese, R. J. (1975). Some explorations in initial interaction and beyond: Toward a developmental theory of interpersonal communication. *Human Communication Research, 1*, 99–112.

Cleveland, D. B., & Cleveland, A. D. (2000). *Introduction to indexing and abstracting* (3rd ed.). Englewood, CO: Libraries Unlimited.

Collison, R. L. (1971). *Abstracts and abstracting services*. Santa Barbara, CA: ABC-CLIO.

Dyer, C. (2004). *The Iowa guide: Scholarly journals in mass communications and related fields*. (Available: http://fm.iowa.uiowa.edu/fmi/xsl/iowaguide/search.xsl)

Knapp, M. L., & Daly, J. A. (2004). *A guide to publishing in scholarly communication journals* (3rd ed.). Mahwah, NJ: Erlbaum.

Sunnafrank, M. (1986). Predicted outcome value during initial interactions: A reformulation of uncertainty reduction theory. *Human Communication Research, 13*, 3–33.

SELECTED SOURCES

Barzun, J., & Graff, H. F. (2004). *The modern researcher* (6th ed.). Belmont, CA: Thomson/Wadsworth.

Brooks, B. S. (2007). *Telling the story: The convergence of print, broadcast, and online media* (3rd ed.). Boston: Bedford/St. Martin's.

Day, R. A., & Gastel, B. (2006). *How to write & publish a scientific paper* (6th ed.). Westport, CT: Greenwood Press.

Galvan, J. L. (2006). *Writing literature reviews*. Glendale, CA: Pyrczak.

Glatthorn, A. A., & Joyner, R. L. (2005). *Writing the winning thesis or dissertation: A step-by-step guide* (2nd ed.). Thousand Oaks, CA: Corwin Press.

Henson, K. T. (2005). *The art of writing for publication: Road to academic advancement.* Boston: Pearson/Allyn & Bacon.

Hubbuch, S. M. (2004). *Writing research papers across the curriculum* (5th ed.). Belmont, CA: Wadsworth.

Kasdorf, W. E. (2003). *The Columbia guide to digital publishing*. New York: Columbia University Press.

Locke, L. F., Spirduso, W. W., & Silverman, S. J. (2007). *Proposals that work: A guide for planning dissertations and grant proposals* (5th ed.). Thousand Oaks, CA: Sage.

Meloy, J. M. (2002). *Writing the qualitative dissertation: Understanding by doing* (2nd ed.). Mahwah, NJ: Erlbaum.

Purdue University Online Writing Lab. (n.d.). *Genres of writing*. Retrieved June 8, 2008, from http://owl.english.purdue.edu/internet/resources/genre.html#tut.

Pyrczak, F., & Bruce, R. R. (2007). *Writing empirical research reports* (6th ed.). Glendale, CA: Pyrczak.

Roth, A. J. (1999). *The research paper: Process, form, and content* (8th ed.). Belmont, CA: Wadsworth.

EXERCISES

1. Choose a scholarly journal article and write informative, indicative, and critical abstracts of it. After writing these, compare them with one about that same article in *Communication Abstracts*.

2. Prepare an outline of a research article that you have found interesting.

3. Examine a thesis or dissertation and an article that has been written and published based on that work. Look at the scope of the literature covered and depth of coverage. When comparing the two, identify what was omitted, condensed, changed, or added.

4. Compare the publication submission guidelines for three different journals. What do they have in common? What elements differ?

5. Prepare a critical review of a research article that you read this semester.

6. Examine the articles provided as examples in Chapters 9 and 10. Choose one, find and read the article, and identify the thesis.

chapter 12

Writing Research Papers

Writing is an important part of any research endeavor. Without clear writing, readers would not be able to understand a writer's research ideas and findings. In this chapter we present basic elements of good writing style, writing and bibliographic formats, and copyediting and proofreading techniques. In general, writers must use a clear, lucid style, adhere to rules of grammar and spelling, and present reports in an acceptable format.

BASIC ELEMENTS OF GOOD WRITING

Clear writing is smooth and consistent. That is, it has no shifts in topic or person and maintains consistent verb tense. A shift in topic or thought means the writer begins writing about one subject and ends the paragraph or section with a different theme or idea. A shift in person means the writer begins a sentence using, for example, a singular noun or pronoun but finishes the sentence with the plural form. Shift in verb tense means sentences vacillate among past, present, and future tenses. Writers must read over their drafts to avoid these errors.

Tense and Agreement

Most literature reviews and research reports use a standard formula for *verb tense*. The *Publication Manual of the American Psychological Association* (APA, 2001), for example, advocates using past tense (Miller [1983] showed) or present perfect tense (Miller [1983] has shown…) when reviewing the literature. Writers should also use past tense to describe the procedures and results of an already completed study. Thus, writers should use past tense for any research finding, idea, or opinion already published. This makes sense because, in these instances, you're writing about something in the past, that is, about something that has already been said or done.

When they express their own conclusions or ideas about those results or past ideas, writers should shift to present tense to show the reader the difference between results and conclusions. Use present tense to discuss the meaning and implications of study results and to present interpretations and conclusions. Writers should use future tense in the *Method* section of the research prospectus, before the study is actually done, and when presenting future research ideas. Using this standard format helps ensure clear and consistent verb tense and smooth reading.

One mistake writers make when adopting APA rules is to sometimes put everything in past tense. But as the following sentences show, the writer uses past tense in the first sentence to indicate the study was conducted in the past. In the second sentence, however, the writer uses present tense to discuss these results:

> Brown (1990) found that students who like their instructors asked more questions. Her results suggest that students learn more when teachers use immediacy behaviors in the classroom.

A *shift in person* means there are inconsistencies in person and number (i.e., between a noun and a singular or plural pronoun). One common mistake is to begin a sentence with a singular noun but shift to a plural pronoun, as in the following sentence:

> A person who has high communication satisfaction finds they like conversing with other people.

The *they* in this example is incorrect because *person* is a singular noun. Writers often shift pronouns to plural to avoid mistakes with noun-pronoun agreement or to avoid using the awkward he/she construction. They must remember to shift the subject also:

> People who have high communication satisfaction find they like talking with other people.

Actually, a more concise way of writing this sentence is to say:

> People with high communication satisfaction like talking with others.

How much simpler it is!

Voice

We sometimes confuse *past tense* with *passive voice*. Writers should use *active*, not passive, *voice* in their writing whenever possible. When using active voice, writers present the subject of the sentence first and avoid using prepositions. Active voice makes the text more interesting and readable. Consider the following two pairs of sentences. In each pair, the first sentence is in passive voice and the second is in active voice.

> In a study by Livingstone (1989), it was found that people had a clear understanding of the characters in *Coronation Street*.

> Livingstone (1989) found that *Coronation Street* viewers clearly understood the program's characters.

It was found by Sterling (2002) that female anchors were underpaid by broadcast stations.

Sterling (2002) found that broadcast stations underpaid female anchors.

Grammar checkers in many word processing programs (e.g., those in Word and WordPerfect) can point out passive voice. If you need to turn on the grammar checker, set it to highlight passive voice phrases. These programs can also identify spelling and grammatical errors.

Grammar

Writers must follow standard rules of grammar throughout their writing projects. Most scholars routinely consult a basic writing or grammar guide. Keep one handy for your writing projects. Three good books to have on your desk are by Hacker, Sommers, Jehn, Rosenzweig, and Van Horn (2007), O'Conner (2003), and Strunk and White (2005) (see the references at the end of this chapter for titles and publishers). The reason why writers keep these guides handy is that everyone makes grammatical mistakes. Day and Gastel (2006) aptly illustrate common grammatical errors in "The Ten Commandments of Good Writing"

1. Each pronoun should agree with their antecedent.
2. Just between you and I, case is important.
3. A preposition is a poor word to end a sentence with.
4. Verbs has to agree with their subject.
5. Don't use no double negatives.
6. Remember to never split an infinitive.
7. Avoid clichés like the plague.
8. Join clauses good, like a conjunction should.
9. Do not use hyperbole; not one writer in a million can use it effectively.
10. About sentence fragments. (p. 188)

Now, if you view these ten commandments in Word, most of the errors above are underlined in green. However, this word processing program is not able to catch the disagreement between a singular subject and a plural possessive pronoun (item 1), does not pick up on the split infinitive (item 6), and doesn't recognize hyperbole (item 9). Relying on such programs, then, might help you find some grammatical errors, but you should aim for better results by using your handy grammar manual. These manuals also can help with paragraph structure and organization of ideas.

Paragraph Structure

Good writing also features strong paragraphs with clear thesis statements and complete sentences that develop the thesis in the paragraph. A strong paragraph focuses on only one idea. It begins with a *thesis* (i.e., a brief statement or overview of the paragraph) and uses explanation, elaboration, and supporting material to develop the thesis. Each sentence supports and develops that main idea (i.e., the thesis). Often the paragraph ends with a transition to the next main idea.

Paragraphs can be too long or too short. Lengthy paragraphs (e.g., a page long) often have more than one main idea. They should be split into separate single-idea paragraphs. On the other hand, one- or two-sentence paragraphs usually fail to develop the thesis or main idea adequately.

Transitions

If you present your ideas in an orderly progression, you will achieve continuity and smoothness. You should identify relationships between ideas and use transitions to maintain the progression of ideas. Transitions provide (a) a time link (*then, next, after, while, since*); (b) a cause-effect link (*therefore, so, thus, as a result*); (c) an addition link (*besides, in addition, moreover, furthermore, similarly*); or (d) a contrast link (*however, but, conversely, nevertheless, although, whereas*) (APA, 2001, p. 32). Transitions are useful within paragraphs and between paragraphs and sections of a paper.

Transitions between paragraphs provide a flow between two ideas. Just as each paragraph should develop one main idea, paragraphs about similar topics within a section of the paper should be linked via transitions. As you've seen in the previous paragraph, the last sentence ends with a transition to this paragraph, which deals with transitions between paragraphs. This paragraph will end with a transition to the next section. If you find it difficult to present a transition to the next section, you might want to look at your outline to see whether another part of the paper would work better at that juncture. Also, you should aim for consistency in your writing by using a uniform style.

Style

Writing style has many important elements. The following "Tips for Effective Writing" can help you improve your writing style.

1. Research papers are typically written in a formal style, often in third person. Some scholarly journal editors, however, have relaxed this guideline and allow first-person writing. With a first-person style, you see a lot of *I* or *we* used in the manuscript. It is easier to write in active voice when using first-person style, but sometimes this style makes a document sound too informal and diary-like. Third-person style appears to increase objectivity and to be detached from personal opinion. Note the difference between these two examples:

    I chose to test three axioms from uncertainty-reduction theory in this study.

    Three axioms from uncertainty-reduction theory provided the foundation for this study.

2. Avoid an overly descriptive writing style, as in, "The subjects cowered nervously as the thought of spilling their souls to a stranger filled their busy minds." That style may be appropriate for a creative writing assignment, but it is not appropriate for a scholarly research project. Also, avoid slang terms and colloquialisms.
3. Use active voice: "Johnson (1992) studied the effects of watching television on adolescents." Avoid passive voice: "The effects of television viewing on adolescents were studied by Johnson (1992)." Although you'll often encounter

passive voice in many published research articles, readers find the style tiresome and unexciting. Writing in third person sometimes encourages use of passive voice.

4. Avoid jargon in place of common terminology. Be precise. You might be familiar with certain terms, but your readers may not be. Kessler and McDonald (2008) provided a good example of scientific jargon: "Despite rigid reexamination of all experimental variables, this protocol continued to produce data at variance with our subsequently proven hypothesis" (p. 144). All the authors needed to say was, "The experiment didn't work."

5. Language should be gender-neutral. Avoid using sexist language, sexist style, and ambiguous referents—for example, *his* (when you intend *his* or *her*) and *men* (when you are referring to *people*). Also avoid language that stereotypes people—for example, "the physician saw *his* patient," "the *female* psychiatrist," or "the police*man*." In many instances, you can avoid sexist language by using plural forms and being sensitive to stereotypes.

6. Be economical in expression. Say only what needs to be said. Wordiness does not improve comprehension and can interfere with getting the main idea across. Yet, be sure to say enough so the reader can understand the point.

7. Clarify conclusions as well as contradictions you find in the literature. Don't assume readers know your subject because you know it. It is often wiser to assume the reader knows little about the topic.

8. Use pronouns (*its, this, that, these, those*) that have clear references to their antecedents. Also, use pronouns to focus nouns—for example, *this* test, *that* concept, *these* subjects, *those* results.

9. Use short rather than elongated sentences. Avoid run-on expressions that lose the reader's attention, interest, and understanding.

10. Move smoothly from section to section. Avoid abruptness. Use transition sentences to help shift the reader's attention from one section to another. Provide appropriate headings and logical organization.

11. Use correct punctuation to support your meaning.

12. Use proper grammar and spelling. In addition to the grammatical errors identified earlier in the chapter, dangling modifiers are often a problem. Sentences that begin with clauses often fall prey to this. The first sentence below contains a dangling modifier, and the second one corrects it.

After considering the errors in the first study, a second study was conducted.

After considering the errors in the first study, the research team conducted a second study.

13. Never submit a paper you haven't carefully checked for spelling and typographical errors. *Proofread your work!*

14. Use consistent tense, topic, and person.

15. *Never plagiarize.* When you use another person's words or ideas in your writing, give credit to the original author. It is *never* acceptable to copy anything from someone else's materials without using quotation marks and citing the original source. Paraphrasing also requires proper citation of the original work.

16. Do not quote from an abstract. Either summarize the original source (not the abstract) in your own words or quote the original author.

17. Pay attention to the structure and form of published articles. Such articles are usually effective examples of how literature reviews should look.

WRITING FORMATS

There are several different acceptable writing and bibliographic formats. These formats help users cite sources within a paper and format a list of references at the end. Style manuals or guides also provide tips on writing and suggest the best way to construct a manuscript. They mandate the writer be consistent in style (i.e., in the style presented in the manual) and show how to cite sources and attribute others' ideas and words consistently.

You might have become familiar with one style in high school and a different style in college. Commonly used formats in the humanities and social sciences are those of the Modern Language Association (MLA) and the University of Chicago (which is abstracted in Turabian, referenced below):

> Gibaldi, J. (2003). *MLA handbook for writers of research papers* (6th ed.). New York: Modern Language Association. (For high school and undergraduate college students)
>
> Gibaldi, J. (2008). *MLA style manual and guide to scholarly publishing* (3rd ed.). New York: Modern Language Association. (For graduate students, scholars, and professional writers)
>
> Turabian, K. L. (2007). *A manual for writers of research papers, theses, and dissertations: Chicago style for students and researchers* (7th ed.). Chicago: University of Chicago Press.
>
> University of Chicago Press. (2003). *The Chicago manual of style* (15th ed.). Chicago: Author.

Only a few main communication journals require **MLA style** (for instance, *Quarterly Journal of Speech, Text and Performance Quarterly, Communication and Critical/Cultural Studies*) or *Chicago Manual of Style* (for instance, *Journalism & Mass Communication Quarterly, Journalism & Mass Communication Educator*). The vast majority allow or require submission of articles using the style of the American Psychological Association (APA). Most communication journals have adopted *APA style*:

> American Psychological Association. (2001). *Publication manual of the American Psychological Association* (5th ed.). Washington, DC: Author.

Because almost all our journals accept or require manuscripts in this style, we have used **APA style** throughout this book. We hope that, as you have read the various chapters, you have become familiar and adept with this style. We give an overview of the basics of APA style in Appendix A. This is not a substitute for the APA *Publication Manual* (APA, 2001), which presents much more information than we can here. In our overview, we summarize some technical aspects of APA style that are helpful in constructing literature reviews and research reports. Several websites help sort through the rules explained in the 439-page manual. Because the URLs for these change quite frequently, we list and link to these on this book's home page.

You should note that MLA style has become similar to APA style in recent years. For instance, in-text footnotes, prevalent in MLA and in Turabian (an easy-to-follow guide to the *Chicago Manual of Style*), are now sometimes replaced by endnotes or endnote numbers (enclosed in parentheses), which refer to numbered *Works Cited* listed in the bibliography at the end of a manuscript. The MLA and Chicago (Turabian) footnote styles, however, are similar. For example, to refer a reader to page 55 of this textbook or to page 260 of an article on symbolic convergence theory, the MLA footnotes and the Turabian endnotes would look like this (remember, APA style does not use footnotes for references):

MLA

[1] Rebecca B. Rubin, Alan M. Rubin, Paul M. Haridakis, and Linda J. Piele, *Communication Research: Strategies and Sources*, 7th ed. (Boston: Wadsworth/Cengage Learning, 2010) 55.

[2] Ernest G. Bormann, John F. Cragan, and Donald C. Shields, "In Defense of Symbolic Convergence Theory: A Look at the Theory and Its Criticisms after Two Decades," *Communication Theory* 4 (1994): 260.

Chicago

1 Rebecca B. Rubin, Alan M. Rubin, Paul M. Haridakis, and Linda J. Piele, *Communication Research: Strategies and Sources*, 7th ed. (Boston: Wadsworth/Cengage Learning, 2010), 55.

2 Ernest G. Bormann, John F. Cragan, and Donald C. Shields, "In Defense of Symbolic Convergence Theory: A Look at the Theory and Its Criticisms after Two Decades," *Communication Theory* 4 (November 1994): 260.

Chicago style permits references within the text (Rubin, Rubin, Haridakis, and Piele 2010, 55). MLA also allows citations in the text (Rubin, Rubin, Haridakis, Piele 55). As mentioned, both MLA and Turabian use a *Works Cited* section for the bibliography, whereas the APA-style bibliography is simply called *References*. Additional information on the *Chicago Manual of Style* can be found at the manual's website, and members can search the manual online for guidelines (**<http://www.chicagomanualofstyle.org>**).

Chicago actually has two style formats: humanities and author-date. We present the author-date style here. To show how the three **bibliographic styles** differ, we present one book and one article in each of the three styles:

MLA

Rubin, Rebecca B., Alan M. Rubin, Paul M. Haridakis, and Linda J. Piele. *Communication Research: Strategies and Sources*. 7th ed. Boston: Wadsworth/Cengage Learning, 2010.

Bormann, Ernest G., John F. Cragan, and Donald C. Shields. "In Defense of Symbolic Convergence Theory: A Look at the Theory and Its Criticisms after Two Decades." *Communication Theory* 4 (1994): 259–294.

Chicago

Rubin, Rebecca B., Alan M. Rubin, Paul M. Haridakis, and Linda J. Piele. 2010. *Communication research: Strategies and sources*. 7th ed. Boston: Wadsworth/Cengage Learning.

Bormann, Ernest G., John F. Cragan, and Donald C. Shields. 1994. In defense of symbolic convergence theory: A look at the theory and its criticisms after two decades. *Communication Theory* 4: 259–94.

APA   Rubin, R. B., Rubin, A. M., Haridakis, P. M., & Piele, L. J. (2010).
Communication research: Strategies and sources (7th ed.).
Boston: Wadsworth/Cengage Learning.

Bormann, E. G., Cragan, J. F., & Shields, D. C. (1994). In defense
of symbolic convergence theory: A look at the theory and its
criticisms after two decades. *Communication Theory, 4*, 259–294.

Consult the manuals for more details on these styles. The manuals also contain important information on how to cite sources and how to present quotations used from these sources. Using the appropriate standard style for quoting another's work prevents plagiarism.

Quoting and Paraphrasing

Plagiarism means using an author's words or ideas without giving proper credit. Giving credit for ideas usually takes the form of citing the author and year of publication in the text and reference list. Credit for actual words goes beyond simple citation to giving the page number in the text and using quotation marks around the quoted material. All U.S. college handbooks (and most from other countries) require that students be aware of how to cite sources properly, and all publishers and professional associations adhere to strict rules forbidding plagiarism. If you're not sure what plagiarism is, this is the time to learn!

Babbie (2007) devised a system to help students see the difference between acceptable and unacceptable *citations*, and we've adapted it here (note that we're giving Babbie credit for his idea and showing where you can go to find his version of this system). First, here is a paragraph from Rubin and McHugh's (1987) article on parasocial interaction:

> As Horton and Wohl (1956) hypothesized, parasocial interaction is similar to the establishment of social relationship with others. In this investigation, parasocial interaction was related strongly to social and task attraction towards the media personality, and to importance of relationship development with the personality. This supports previous contentions that media relationships can be seen as functional alternatives to interpersonal relationships (Rosengren & Windahl, 1972; Rubin & Rubin, 1985). Interpersonal and mediated relationships appear to follow a similar process of development. (p. 288)

Second, here are three acceptable citation methods:

Quotation	As Rubin and McHugh (1987) concluded, "interpersonal and mediated relationships appear to follow a similar process of development" (p. 288).
Paraphrase	Rubin and McHugh (1987) argued that interpersonal and media relationships follow a similar developmental pattern.
Idea	The way people develop relationships with others is very much like the way they develop relationships with television characters (Rubin & McHugh, 1987).

Note that all three methods give credit to the source. When you use a string of actual words, you must surround them with quotation marks and give the page number. Terms, variables, or constructs that authors use in their text need not be quoted because they are likely terms that others would use. The key here is a *string of words*. Only use quotations if someone says something that is particularly articulate or if the reader would find interesting or important *who* said it.

Third, here are three *unacceptable* citations. We would term them *plagiarism*.

Direct quotation, no citation	Interpersonal and mediated relationships appear to follow a similar process of development.
Edited quotation, presented as one's own	Media relationships can be seen as functional alternatives to interpersonal relationships and follow a similar process of development.
Paraphrased, but ideas presented as one's own	Media and interpersonal relationships follow similar developmental processes.

It is unethical to use another person's words or ideas and present them as your own.

Universities and other organizations have specific rules about plagiarism which they expect people to follow. Breaking these rules can result in dire consequences. College instructors often use one of several available websites or software programs to detect plagiarism, but they usually consult these only after suspecting plagiarism when reading a paper. Often there is a shift in writing style (from a student's normal style to a very professional one) or a shift in grammatical correctness (from lots of errors to no errors). Using your own consistent style and vocabulary helps you avoid inadvertent plagiarism.

Verb Choice

Often, when introducing quoted material or paraphrasing authors, we need a verb to tell the reader what the authors said, found, and so on. Many verbs are appropriate for scholarly reports, but choosing one to use depends on the context of the paraphrase or quotation. For example, the following sentence shows an active way of referring to a particular study (because the authors are listed as the subject instead of in a prepositional phrase):

Bell and Daly (1984) _____ four components of affinity seeking.

Now, which verb to use? Here are some verbs commonly found in sentences in journal articles. Each has a specific meaning. Which one would be appropriate here?

argued	extended	proposed
assumed	explained	questioned
believed	found	reasoned
concluded	identified	replied
contended	investigated	reported
declared	maintained	showed
defined	noted	suggested
described	observed	thought
developed	presented	viewed

Many of these verbs would fit our sentence, depending on the meaning we want to convey. For example, we could use *proposed* to show there was some controversy in the past about the number of components, and Bell and Daly's opinion is that there are four. We could use *presented* to introduce the four components. Or we could use *identified* to suggest Bell and Daly were among the first to see the four-part system; they may also have *described* and *found* it, but using *identified* in the thesis sentence helps us structure a paragraph about what the components of affinity seeking are and how the authors discovered them. Which verb to use depends on the paragraph's purpose.

Thus, a standard style for presenting a report or review is essential. (The APA and MLA manuals are helpful because they contain rules for writing.) The other important element is a suitable and consistent physical appearance. Rules for headings, margins, use of numerals, table and figure formats, and reference formatting help keep style consistent. Some of these rules are described in Appendix A. Anything that attracts negative attention—such as misspellings, typographic errors, tense shifts, nonparallel headings—will diminish a paper's effect. In short, the ideas will be lost in a maze of stylistic miscues.

Proofreading

Proofread all work before submitting it. Careless errors diminish its positive impact for the reader, whether the reader be an employer, a professor, a thesis committee, or an editor. When readers trip over careless word choices or blatant errors, they often lose sight of important points in the manuscript and instead start looking for other errors. When this happens, they miss important thoughts and ideas. Use the following checklist to proofread your writing.

Proofreading Checklist

1. Are all words spelled correctly? (Remember that word processing spelling checkers cannot tell the difference in usage between correctly spelled homonyms or out-of-context typographic errors, such as *that* instead of *than* or *not* instead of *note*.)
2. Is the writing grammatically correct? Do subjects and verbs agree, is the form parallel, is the writing voice active, and is past verb tense used when appropriate?
3. Are there any punctuation errors? Are all quotation marks outside the punctuation (except for semicolons and colons)? Question marks and exclamation marks go inside quotation marks only if they're part of the original quote.
4. Is one writing format used consistently throughout? Choose APA or MLA style and stick with it religiously.
5. Are any paragraphs overly long? If so, determine how many main thesis statements appear in the paragraph and divide the paragraph accordingly.
6. Do all sentences flow together? If not, check the thesis sentence and be sure all other sentences support or illustrate the thesis.
7. Do all words have precise meanings? Is there any slang or casual language? Work on using short, clear, and standard words rather than slang or technical jargon.
8. Are all quotations in proper form? Is proper credit given to other authors for their ideas and quoted material?

Proofreading Symbols

Many researchers write at a computer. They can read and correct errors as they view their writing on the monitor. However, it is a good idea to print a copy of your work to edit before printing the final version. Students and instructors find standard proofreading and copyediting symbols useful when proofreading and copyediting manuscripts. We identify main ones here:

Awk	Awkward
Cap	Use a capital letter
CF	Comma fault
Gr	Error in grammar
Ital, underlining	Italics
Mng	Meaning not clear
Org	Faulty organization
Par	Paragraph problem (development, length, continuity)
//	Parallel-form problem
Pn	Punctuation problem
Pron	Error in pronoun form
Sp	Spelling error
T	Error in use of tense
Trans	Needs better transition
Wdy	Wordy
WW	Wrong word

Many other symbols are also used by journal and book editors when they edit manuscripts for publication. These are also useful for editing your own work before submitting the final copy.

Most instructors use similar symbols or develop their own proofreading and copyediting systems. It's a good idea to ask if you don't understand the notations. Some journal editors and book publishers send information about their systems to authors during the proofreading stage. This involves authors in the process so they can be sure that what appears in print is how they want the text to appear. Visit this book's website for a sample paper proofread using the marks explained here.

Getting Help With Your Writing

Most colleges have developed systems to help you improve your writing. Most large schools have writing centers where students can take their papers for feedback from well-informed peers. Staff members will not rewrite or edit the paper but will point out where extra attention is required. If writing is a struggle for you, you might want to look into refresher books and remedial classes, which are designed to help students recall or relearn basic grammar. Gelfand and Walker (2002, 2005) have produced manuals to train students and instructors in proper APA style. Today, however, many websites provide the same help. Go to this book's website for links to helpful grammar sites.

Another difficulty some students have is writing apprehension. Some writing centers have developed programs to help the apprehensive student overcome fear or anxiety. Apprehension is much more debilitating than writer's block. For instance, a writer can often unblock by getting fresh air, taking a short walk, or exercising. Writers who suffer from apprehension fear the act of writing as well as evaluation of their work. They might want to seek help for this problem.

Collaborative writing projects are becoming increasingly common, both in colleges and in professions. Work teams often produce reports or proposals and handle conceptual and written elements collaboratively, either in person (for example, via team meetings) or electronically (via e-mail, discussion lists, or shared documents). Most students work on group projects at one or more points in their college careers, but the writing of the final report often falls on one or two people. Today, however, with greater electronic access to a report, all group members can contribute to the final product. Students should be concerned that classmates know how to cite sources properly. Tracking changes in a document via a word-processing program can help document who contributed which part of a manuscript. Group members can also provide each other with feedback on their writing.

SUMMARY

In this chapter we have highlighted basic elements of good writing. We distinguish between tense and voice, emphasizing the need for consistent writing and agreement between subject and verb and between noun and pronoun. We also list important grammatical rules. Good writing is characterized by clear, coherent paragraphs that contain thesis sentences and transitions between paragraphs and topics.

In this chapter we also introduced writing formats (APA, Chicago, and MLA) commonly used in writing projects. These styles have specific guidelines for citing references in the text and at the end of a work, for paraphrasing, and for proofreading. Writing centers, manuals, and online sources can help a writer conform to standards and present the best product possible.

References

American Psychological Association. (2001). *Publication manual of the American Psychological Association* (5th ed.). Washington, DC: Author.

Babbie, E. R. (2007). *The practice of social research* (11th ed.). Belmont, CA: Cengage Learning/Wadsworth.

Day, R. A., & Gastel, B. (2006). *How to write & publish a scientific paper* (6th ed.). Westport, CT: Greenwood Press.

Gelfand, H., & Walker, C. J. (2002). *Mastering APA style: Instructor's resource guide* (4th ed.). Washington, DC: American Psychological Association.

Gelfand, H., & Walker, C. J. (2005). *Mastering APA style: Student's workbook and training guide* (5th ed.). Washington, DC: American Psychological Association.

Gibaldi, J. (2003). *MLA handbook for writers of research papers* (6th ed.). New York: Modern Language Association.

Gibaldi, J. (2008). *MLA style manual and guide to scholarly publishing* (3rd ed.). New York: Modern Language Association.

Hacker, D., Sommers, N., Jehn, T. R., Rosenzweig, J., & Van Horn, C. (2007). *A writer's reference* (6th ed.). Boston: Bedford/St. Martin's.

Kessler, L., & McDonald, D. (2008). *When words collide: A media writer's guide to grammar and style* (7th ed.). Boston: Cengage Learning/Wadsworth.

O'Conner, P. T. (2003). *Woe is I: The grammarphobe's guide to better English in plain English*. New York: Riverhead.

Strunk, W., Jr., & White, E. B. (2005). *The elements of style* (4th ed.). New York: Longman.

Turabian, K. L. (2007). *A manual for writers of research papers, theses, and dissertations: Chicago style for students and researchers* (7th ed.). Chicago: University of Chicago Press.

University of Chicago Press. (2003). *The Chicago manual of style* (15th ed.). Chicago: Author.

SELECTED SOURCES

Brooks, B. S., Pinson, J. L., & Wilson, J. G. (2006). *Working with words: A handbook for media writers and editors* (6th ed.). Boston: Bedford/St. Martin's.

Harvard Law Review Association. (2005). *The bluebook: A uniform system of citation* (18th ed.). Cambridge, MA: Author.

Kessler, L., & McDonald, D. (2008). *When words collide: A media writer's guide to grammar and style* (7th ed.). Boston: Cengage Learning/Wadsworth.

Knapp, M. L., & Daly, J. A. (2004). *A guide to publishing in scholarly communication journals* (3rd ed.). Mahwah, NJ: Erlbaum.

Slade, C., & Perrin, R. (2008). *Form and style: Research papers, reports, theses* (13th ed.). Boston: Houghton Mifflin.

EXERCISES

1. Check a paper you have written for effective writing style. Use the "Tips for Effective Writing" and "The Ten Commandments of Good Writing" as guidelines for this examination.

2. Select one recent single-authored communication book, one multi-authored communication book, one essay in an edited communication book, and one single-authored and one multi-authored article in scholarly communication journals. Construct the citations for each of these five sources using correct APA style (see Appendix A).

3. Choose two or three verbs (from page 260) for the following sentences. Compare and contrast the different meanings for those selected.
   a. Smith (1990) _____ verbal qualifiers as terms that connote a great degree of uncertainty.
   b. Smith (1990) _____ a method of measuring verbal qualifiers in speech.
   c. Smith (1990) _____ that women who use more verbal qualifiers are more likely to be perceived as weak.

d. When Jones (1992) criticized Smith's (1990) new method of measuring verbal qualifiers, Smith _____ that the validity and reliability data were within the bounds of acceptability.

e. Although Smith (1990) _____ that the method was acceptable, more current research (Jones, 1996; Miller, 1994; Williams, 1998) _____ that Smith's claim was premature.

f. Smith (1990) _____ that future research should compare perceptions of both men and women as a result of qualifier use.

4. Another finding from page 287 of the Rubin and McHugh (1987) article discussed in this chapter follows. Write a paraphrased summary of this finding in one sentence.

The fifth hypothesis predicted a positive significant relationship between perceived relationship development importance and parasocial interaction. The correlation between these two variables was significant ($r = .52$, $p < .001$), supporting the fifth hypothesis.

5. Rewrite the following passive sentences in the active voice. Remember to use past tense when necessary.
   a. It was found by Graham (1986) that humor is used by people to get others to like them.
   b. When questionnaires were completed, subjects were allowed to leave the laboratory.
   c. Demographic characteristics of East Liverpool residents have been consistently found by researchers to be representative of the general population (Barbato, 1987; Offutt, 1990; Perse, 1986).
   d. The scale was submitted to factor analysis to discover how many dimensions were contained in it.

6. Use proofreading and copyediting symbols to edit the following passage. Compare your editing with that of others and with that of your instructor.

We find that the notion of controlalso is very important when we think about and hypothesize about communication bheavior. Rubin (1986) argued that: "we need to consider whether locus of control, alone or in combination with other factors, produces variations in motives for and consequences of using personal and mediated information channels." (p. 135) Locus of control affects behavior (Rotter, 1954). "Internals" feel tehy control events in their lives, "externals" viewing life outcomes as dependent on luck, chance or powerful others. pointing to the reaserch of Williams, Phillips and Lum (1985) and Schoenbach and Hackforth (1987), Levy asked whether consumers use VCRs for control.

7. Find a copy of your college's or university's rules about writing and plagiarism. Read it carefully. What penalties are specified? Can you suggest any tips to avoid inadvertent plagiarism?

APA Style Basics

T he *Publication Manual of the American Psychological Association* (APA, 2001) contains nine main sections: Content and Organization of a Manuscript, Expressing Ideas and Reducing Bias in Language, APA Editorial Style, Reference List, Manuscript Preparation and Sample Papers to Be Submitted for Publication, Materials Other Than Journal Articles, Manuscript Acceptance and Production, Journals Program of the American Psychological Association, and Bibliography. Here we highlight some principles of APA style that are important to consider when writing literature reviews, prospectuses, and research papers. First, we explain bibliographic format used for **references**. Then we present basic elements of editorial style used in the text of a paper. As an experienced researcher, you will find that the more you consistently use any style, the easier it is to organize your findings for a final product, be it a research or seminar paper, speech, editorial, newspaper article, debate, or report.

BIBLIOGRAPHIC FORMAT

A **bibliography** is a list of sources compiled on a specific topic. It is not just the end product of communication research; it is a necessary component of any research project. Bibliographies sometimes include citations for additional sources beyond those sources actually cited in a paper. However, the reference list attached to research reports, literature reviews, review articles, term papers, and the like includes only those works that have been consulted (i.e., actually read) during research and that are cited in the paper. No other sources should be included. The purpose of a reference list is not to show all the works you've found but to give necessary information so that readers can identify and retrieve those sources that have been used. In APA style, the reference list is given the heading *References*.

The APA *Publication Manual* (APA, 2001) suggests that reference lists be double-spaced when prepared. However, to save paper, your instructor may allow you to single-space entries and double-space between them. As you might have noticed by now, the second and succeeding lines of each citation are indented three spaces when they are typeset. This allows a reader to distinguish more easily between entries when looking for a specific source. When you prepare references, type each entry with a *hanging indent*, with the second and successive lines indented half an inch. If you have a lot of references, you can format these (in Microsoft Word, e.g.) after you enter them by specifying a hanging indent for each as a paragraph.

Books

Learning APA style for books is not difficult. For a single-authored book (see Example 1), the first element in a citation is the author's last name, followed by a comma, and then the author's initial(s). Next, place the year the book was published in parentheses followed by a period. Then give the title of the book. Capitalize only the first letter of the first word (and the first letter of proper nouns), and italicize the entire title. End the title with a period. The final elements in the citation are the city (and state postal abbreviations for smaller cities) where the book was published, followed by a colon and the name of the publisher. End the citation with a period. Note that only single spaces are used to separate each element in all citations. For example:

Example 1: Single-Authored Book

Perloff, R. M. (1995). *The dynamics of persuasion*. Hillsdale, NJ: Erlbaum.

If only a specific part of a source, such as a chapter, is used, this is indicated in the text citation itself. For example: (Perloff, 1995, chap. 3). If a book has been reissued since its first edition, specify that in the citation, as in Example 2.

Example 2: Reissued Book

Newcomb, H. (Ed.). (1995). *Television: The critical view* (5th ed.). New York: Oxford University Press.

Note the abbreviations used. The lowercase *(ed.)* is an abbreviation of *edition*. When this term is capitalized (*Ed.* or *Eds.*), it is an abbreviation of *editor* or *editors*. If the book has two authors, use a comma and an ampersand between the names (see Example 3). If the reference is an essay or chapter in an edited book, the essay's title is not italicized, but the book's title is (see Example 4). Specify in the reference the inclusive page numbers of an essay in an edited book. Doctoral dissertations (Example 5), films (Example 6), and television programs (Example 7) are stylistically similar.

Example 3: Dual-Authored Book

Baran, S. J., & Davis, D. K. (1995). *Mass communication theory: Foundations, ferment and future*. Belmont, CA: Wadsworth.

Note the use of an ampersand before the name of the last author in a series of authors. Also use the ampersand in the text of the paper, but only when the names appear as a citation in parentheses—for example: (Baran & Davis, 1995). We could have eliminated the state in this reference if it were a one-of-a-kind city (such as Chicago or Boston; see Example 2). Had this been an edited book, *(Eds.)* would have been inserted between the last editor's name and the year of publication, as in Example 4.

Example 4: Essay in an Edited Book

Bryant, J. (1989). Message features and entertainment effects. In J. J. Bradac (Ed.),
    Message effects in communication science (pp. 231–262). Newbury Park, CA:
    Sage.

As you can see, the page numbers of the essay are included in parentheses following the book's title. If an edited book has two editors, use an ampersand between the two names. If there are three or more editors, separate all names with commas and use an ampersand before the last name.

Example 5: Doctoral Dissertation

Rodgers, R. V. P. (1991). *An analysis of rhetorical strategies in the recruitment*
    literature directed to prospective black student populations at The Pennsylvania
    State University (Doctoral dissertation, The Pennsylvania State University,
    1991). *Dissertation Abstracts International, 52,* 4147A.

If you read the dissertation on microfilm, you would also include the University Microfilms number in parentheses at the end of the entry. When an unpublished doctoral dissertation does not appear in *Dissertation Abstracts International,* italicize the title. Follow the title with the words *Unpublished doctoral dissertation,* a comma, the name of the university where it was completed, another comma, the city where the university is located, and the state or country if the city is not well known. The year when the dissertation was completed sometimes is 1year earlier than when the abstract appears in *Dissertation Abstracts International.* If that is the case, both dates are slashed (for example, 1991/1992) when the dissertation is cited in the text. Also note that the first letters in *The Pennsylvania State University* are capitalized because it is a proper noun.

Nonprint Media

The style for audiovisual and electronic media is explained in the APA *Publication Manual* (APA, 2001, pp. 266–281). For motion pictures and television, the producer is the first author (see Example 6); sometimes the director is listed as second author. Example 7 also shows the producer as the first author for a series in the first citation, and a writer as the author for an episode in that series for the second citation.

Example 6: Motion Picture

Lehman, E. (Producer), & Nichols, M. (Director). (1966). *Who's afraid of Virginia Woolf?* [Motion Picture]. United States: Warner Brothers.

Example 7: Telecast (Series and Episode)

Lasiewicz, C. (Producer). (1995). *48 hours* [Television series]. New York: CBS.

Kandra, G. (Writer), & Shapir, E. (Director). (1995). Stopping the clock [Television series episode]. In C. Lasiewicz (Producer), *48 hours*. New York: CBS.

The APA *Publication Manual* (APA, 2001, pp. 266–268) provides other examples for broadcast programs, music recordings, and audio recordings. As with any referencing style, it is most important to be accurate, complete, and consistent.

Government Publications

The style used for government publications is explained in the APA *Publication Manual*'s (APA, 2001) Technical and Research Reports section. If the report is available from the National Technical Information Service (NTIS) or from the U.S. Government Printing Office (GPO), use the style shown in Example 8. If the report is not available from these agencies, do not include it in the bibliography but treat it as a footnote along with other not widely or easily accessible material.

Example 8: Government Document

U.S. Senate, Special Committee on Aging. (1980). *How old is "old"? The effects of aging on learning and working* (DHHS Publication No. NIH 78-1446). Washington, DC: Government Printing Office.

Technical reports of nongovernment organizations that are available to the public are treated like books (see Example 9).

Example 9: Technical Report

Balkema, J. B. (Ed.). (1972). *A general bibliography on aging*. Washington, DC: National Council on the Aging.

Note that in Example 8 the primary government body is identified as the document's author, followed by the subsidiary agency (in this case, a committee). The reference also includes the issuing department's report number. This report is issued by the National Institutes of Health (NIH) of the Department of Health and Human Services (DHHS). It can be purchased by the public from the U.S. Government Printing Office. Example 9 is very much like a single-authored book reference (Example 1), except that the author is an editor—(Ed.)—of the work and the publisher of the report is an agency. Consult the *Publication Manual* for assistance when the preceding examples do not fully apply.

Periodicals

The format for periodicals is slightly different from that used for books. Capitalize only the first letter of the first word of an article's title and the first letter of any proper nouns in the article title. In the name of the periodical, capitalize the first letter of each word (except prepositions that are three letters or less, conjunctions, and articles). Italicize the name of the periodical (but not the title of the article) and the volume number of the journal in which the article appears. The page numbers of the article come after the periodical's volume number. The standard format for a journal article with one author is shown in Example 10; that for a coauthored article is given in Example 11.

Example 10: Single-Authored Article

Garramone, G. M. (1985). Effects of negative political advertising: The roles of sponsor and rebuttal. *Journal of Broadcasting & Electronic Media, 29,* 149-159.

Example 11: Dual-Authored Article

Suzuki, S., & Rancer, A. S. (1994). Argumentativeness and verbal aggressiveness: Testing for conceptual and measurement equivalence across cultures. *Communication Monographs, 61,* 256–279.

If each issue of a particular journal starts with a page 1, include the issue number in parentheses after the volume number to make locating the article easier, as in Example 12.

Example 12: Issues Beginning With Page 1

Turow, J. (1994). Hidden conflicts and journalistic norms: The case of self-coverage. *Journal of Communication, 44*(2), 12-31.

In Example 12, the number 2 in parentheses indicates the article appears in Volume 44's second issue. The volume number is italicized, but the issue number is not.

Example 13: Book Review

Benjamin, L. (1994). [Review of *Telecommunications, mass media, and democracy: The battle for the control of U.S. broadcasting, 1928-1935*]. *Journal of Broadcasting & Electronic Media, 38,* 241-242.

Similar to a journal article title, a book review title follows the date if the review has its own title. The information in the brackets indicates the title of the book being reviewed.

Articles appearing in general-interest or trade periodicals and magazines, such as *Advertising Age* or *Time,* are identified by date and by volume number (see Example 14). If an article begins in one place and is continued elsewhere, give all page numbers but use a comma to separate page numbers. Similar to journal articles, do not use *Vol.* before a volume number or *p.* before a page number.

Example 14: Magazine Article

Bell, N., & Amdur, M. (1994, January 24). NBC Super Channel looks to make mark in Europe. *Broadcasting & Cable, 124*(4), 112.

When an author is unknown, begin a citation with the article's title and alphabetize it according to the first significant word in the title (not *a, an, the,* or other articles of grammar). Bibliographic format for titles of newspaper articles is similar to that of general-interest periodicals but omits the volume number and uses *p.* or *pp.* before the page numbers. Consult the APA *Publication Manual* (APA, 2001, pp. 239-247) for other examples of periodical citations.

Unpublished Papers, Reports, Personal Communications, and Speeches

Professional convention papers or other reports are often available though the ERIC Document Reproduction Service. Example 16 shows how these are referenced. However, not all convention papers are submitted to or accepted by ERIC. When unpublished papers and reports are available for use in a research project, they are cited as in Examples 16 and 17.

Example 15: ERIC Report/Paper

Feeser, T., & Thompson, T. L. (1990). *A test of a method of increasing patient question asking in physician-patient interactions.* Paper presented at the annual meeting of the Speech Communication Association, Chicago. (ERIC Document Reproduction Service No. ED 325 887)

Example 16: Unpublished Convention Paper

Thomas, S., & Gitlin, T. (1993, May). *Who says there's a dominant ideology and what happens if that concept is falsified?* Paper presented at the annual meeting of the International Communication Association, Washington, DC.

Example 17: Unpublished Convention Poster Session

Sharkey, W. F., & Kim, M. (1994, November). *The effect of embarrassability on perceived importance of conversational constraints.* Poster session presented at the meeting of the Speech Communication Association, New Orleans.

Do not enter oral interviews, personal conversations, memos, letters, and unpublished speeches in the list of references because the text of these is not permanently stored for others to examine. They are, however, referenced in the text. Be sure to include the name, type of communication, and date. An example is: (R. Jacobs, personal communication, March 27, 2003).

Electronic Sources

Citations to works on the Internet or on CD-ROM are treated similarly, but there are a few differences. A new APA guide details these differences (APA, 2007). Generally, the citation begins with the author of the work (if known), the title of the work, the medium [in brackets], year of creation, title of the work, and publisher and location. Example 18 shows the style used for an electronic version of an article from a printed source, and Example 19 shows citation style for an article in an online journal (note that issue numbers are provided following the volume number in all articles retrieved electronically). Note in Examples 19, 20, and 21 that you need to cite the date you visited the site. The style for electronic sources is still evolving. Check the APA website for additional information on electronic media citations <http://www.apastyle.org/elecref.html>.

Example 18: Internet Article Based on a Print Source

Rubin, A. M., & Rubin, R. B. (1985). Interface of personal and mediated communi-
    cation: A research agenda [Electronic version]. *Critical Studies in Mass
    Communication, 2*(1), 36–53.

Normally, you need not provide a retrieval date for books or journal articles, but if it appears that the article contains additional information or has been changed from its original form, you'll need to provide the URL for the electronic version and the date you visited the site at the end of the citation.

Example 19: Article in an Internet Journal

Rubin, A. M., & Rubin, R. B. (2001). Interface of personal and mediated
    communication: Fifteen years later. *Electronic Journal of Communication, 11*(1).
    Retrieved January 20, 2004, from http://www.cios.org/getfile\Rubin_V11n101

Example 20: Government Document on a Website

U.S. Congress, House of Representatives. (1995). *United States code* (1994 ed.).
    Retrieved June 8, 2008, from http://www.law.cornell.edu/uscode

Example 21: Website With Author

Dyer, C. (2004). *The Iowa guide: Scholarly journals in mass communications and
    related fields.* Retrieved June 8, 2008, from http://fm.iowa.uiowa.edu/fmi/xsl/
    iowaguide/search.xsl

If the author of a site is not given, start with the website's name before the date.
    Format also exists for e-mail messages, postings to newsgroups, and online discussions. E-mail is treated as *personal communication* and is handled in the text as such. It does not get cited in references. But a message posted to a news group,

discussion group, or electronic mailing list does have formats, such as in the created Examples 22, 23, and 24.

Example 22: Message Posted to a Newsgroup

Walther, J. B. (2001, October 31). Theories, boundaries, and all of the above [Msg 1]. Message posted to http://groups.google.com/group/HCTD?Ink=

Example 23: Message Posted to a Discussion Group

Simon, D. J. (2000, July 14). Three new resources for visual communication [Msg 1]. Message posted to http://groups.yahoo.com/group/visualcognition/message/31

Example 24: Message Posted to an Electronic Mailing List

Rubin, R. B. (2004, January 13). New communication measures. Message posted to CRTNET electronic mailing list, archived at http://lists.psu.edu/cgi-bin/wa? A2=ind0401&L=crtnet&P=R7562

Legal References

The field of law has its own conventions for citing work in legal periodicals. In most legal periodicals, citations of court cases, statutes, and such are placed in footnotes. In the APA style, legal references are placed in the reference list along with other references.

In the text of a manuscript, cite legal materials the same way as other references. Begin with the first few words of the reference list entry, then give the date. This information will help a reader identify the citation in the references. Italicize the names of court cases, but not statutes. The APA *Publication Manual* (APA, 2001, pp. 397–410) offers examples of typical citations of legal materials but refers users to *The Bluebook: A Uniform System of Citation* (Harvard Law Review Association, 2005) for more information.

CITING SOURCES IN THE PAPER

You have probably seen APA style used in many sources you've already examined. It is easily recognizable. First, books or other publications are generally not cited in footnotes or notes. There are usually only a few, if any, notes (or footnotes) in an article. When the work of an author is referred to in the text of a paper, it is cited by using the author's last name and year the source was published. For example:

Scott (1992) identified …
Several researchers (Abel, 1990; Baker & Charley, 1985; Delta et al., 1980) reported …
Douglass (1986) concluded: "The research findings clearly indicate support for the hypotheses" (p. 55).

These sources are then fully listed in the *References* at the end of the article or chapter. This eliminates the need for most footnotes in the text.

As these examples of text citations suggest, there are rules governing where in the sentence a citation occurs. As the first example [Scott (1992) identified ...] shows, if an author's (or authors') name is used in the sentence, the year of publication directly follows the name. If an author (or authors) has two or more works published in the same year cited in the reference list, the works are alphabetized in the list by the first significant word in the title of the article or book. The first receives an *a* after the year, the second a *b*, and so on. The *a* and *b* are also used in the text reference so a reader can find the exact source being referenced. For examples, see page 212 of the APA (2001) *Publication Manual* for how to cite this in the text and page 221 of the APA *Publication Manual* for the reference format.

In the second example of a text citation, several researchers are identified, so their names (alphabetically arranged by first author) and years are enclosed in parentheses; the individual works are separated by semicolons. When a source has two authors, always give both names (joined by an ampersand). When there are three to five authors, list all names the first time the reference is mentioned in the text—for example (Polk, Erickson, Adams, & Johnson, 1980)—and abbreviate for the next and subsequent mentions (Polk et al., 1980). Whenever a source has six or more authors, always use this abbreviated convention—et al.—in the text, even the first time the reference is mentioned.

The third example shows how sources of quotations are cited. Note that the page number of the quotation is given at the end of the sentence, before the period. Had the author's name not been integrated into the sentence, as it was here, it would be placed along with the year and page number, as follows:

"The research findings clearly indicate support for the hypotheses" (Douglass, 1986, p. 55).

When citing parts of sources retrieved electronically, also use the page or chapter number, if provided. If it is not, use a paragraph number (you might have to count these if they're not provided in the text) with a paragraph symbol (¶) or the name of the section and paragraph number within the section (e.g., Jacobs, 2006, Conclusion section, ¶4).

MANUSCRIPT STYLE

Typing

Using standard 8½-inch by 11-inch paper, create margins of at least 1 inch on the top, bottom, and sides. This allows a maximum 6½-inch typed line: 65 characters in pica (10 pitch) and 78 characters in elite (12 pitch). Do *not* justify the right margin or hyphenate words, even if your software program wants to do it automatically for you. Double-space everything. Just set your paragraph style to double space and everything should conform to APA style. Put no more than 27 lines of text on a page. Check with your instructor, adviser, or graduate school for possible alterations to these standard typing instructions.

Format

APA style suggests a standard system of setting up and ordering the pages of a manuscript. See pages 3–30 and the sample paper on pages 306–320 of the APA *Publication Manual* (APA, 2001).

Title Page

Papers begin with a title page. Type a *page header* (the first few words of the title) in the upper right-hand corner, with the page number several spaces to its right. Page headers should be consistent on every page of the manuscript.

Then, starting flush left across the top of the page (but below the page header), type *Running head*: and insert a shortened title in the space. This is the abbreviated title appearing at the top of published pages (50 characters or less, all in capital letters). Then, center in the middle of the page the paper's complete title (in uppercase and lowercase letters) and type the author's name and institutional affiliation below. Double space between lines of the title as well as between title, author, and author's affiliation.

Abstract

The abstract is on the next page (page 2). In one double-spaced paragraph, concisely summarize what the paper or study is about (for example, the problem, method, findings, and conclusions). Do not indent the first line of the abstract as you would normally indent paragraphs. The abstract should be 100 to 120 words for empirical research papers and 75 to 100 words for review or conceptual papers.

Text

The text begins on the next page (page 3). Most research reports are broken into sections, and headings help a reader see where different sections begin and end. Headings and subheadings also help readers see the flow of text and orient them to the thesis of each area.

Most journal articles have two or three levels of headings. Longer manuscripts might use more than three levels. The headings should be precise and clearly worded and their format standardized throughout the paper. The form of the heading depends on how many levels you need throughout the paper.

For example, if you need three levels of headings beyond the title, center the first level and type in both uppercase and lowercase letters. Position the second level flush left, type in both uppercase and lowercase letters, and italicize.

Indent (as you would a normal paragraph) and italicize the third-level heading. Type the third-level heading in lowercase letters (with the first letter of the first word capitalized) and end the heading with a period. The text of the paragraph begins one space after the period. This format is as follows:

Second-Level Heading

    Third-level heading. Begin the text of the paragraph …

Because the entire manuscript is double spaced when typed, the text is double spaced before and after the first- and second-level headings (extra space is not used above and below headings). Page 113 of the APA *Publication Manual* (APA, 2001) contains examples of headings when more than or fewer than three levels are needed.

References

References begin on a new page following the end of the manuscript's text. Center the heading—References—at the top of the page and begin entering reference entries, after a normal double space. Check with others to see whether there might be a different style at your university.

Appendix

If you have appendixes, they come next. Center the heading—Appendix A—at the top of the first appendix and center the appendix title in uppercase and lowercase under it. Remember to double space before the title. Appendix B would follow on a separate page or pages, and so on.

Notes

Author notes and content footnotes, if any, follow any appendixes. Content footnotes are used sparingly in APA style. They are occasionally used to add important information to points made in the text. Use footnotes only when the flow of the discussion would be broken by incorporating this information directly into the text.

    Center the heading—Footnotes—at the top of the page, and then sequentially number and enter each note, using a 5- to 7-space paragraph indentation for the first line of each. Place the footnote number slightly above and to the left of the first word of each note. In the text, number all notes consecutively and enter the numbers (called *superscripts*) slightly above the end of the line of text (following any punctuation marks except a dash).

Tables, Figure Captions, and Figures

Place tables, figure captions, and figures at the end of the manuscript. Tables and figures require a very specific format. Quantitative tables contain exact values of data (usually statistics) in columns and rows. Qualitative tables contain words instead of numbers. Figures are charts, graphs, pictures, or drawings that extend and clarify the content of the paper.

    APA style suggests you use tables and figures sparingly. If you have only a few statistics to report, incorporate them in the text of the paper. For a large number of statistics, use a quantitative table, and do not duplicate numbers in the text. Tables need descriptive headings and clear labels for variables in columns and rows. Headings for both tables and figures should clearly identify the content. Table 1 is an example of how to present a table. Again, the APA *Publication Manual* (APA, 2001) provides specific information on how to format tables (pp. 147–176) and to present figures (pp. 176–201).

Table 1 Percentage of Employed U.S. College Students

Work Hours per Week	Region			
	Southeast	Northeast	Midwest	West[a]
0	25	20	21	22
1–10	35	39	40	37
11–20	19	20	30	30
21–30	10	12	6	9
31–40	8	8	3	2
Over 40	3	1	0	0

Note: These are fictitious data created for this book.
[a]Includes Alaska and Hawaii.

References

American Psychological Association. (2007). *APA style guide to electronic references.* Washington, DC: Author.

American Psychological Association. (2001). *Publication manual of the American Psychological Association* (5th ed.). Washington, DC: Author.

Harvard Law Review Association. (2005). *The bluebook: A uniform system of citation* (18th ed.). Cambridge, MA: Author.

appendix B

Glossary

Note. Terms appearing in *italics* within glossary entries are also defined in this glossary.

abstract   (a) A paragraph-length or longer summary, or condensation of an *article,* book, or other work. (b) A *periodical* composed of summaries of scholarly *research reports* and theoretical articles that have been published in *journals* and books. Some abstracts also include summary descriptions of books and dissertations.

abstracting service   (a) An organization that produces *abstracts.* (b) Abstracts supplied to subscribers by an organization.

access point   Any searchable field in a record in a *computerized database.* Access points in most *bibliographic databases* include author, article title, journal title, *subject headings* or *descriptors,* and *keywords* in each of these fields as well as in the abstract field. Access points in searchable full-text documents include, in addition, all words in the text.

access tool   A bibliographic work or *computerized database* that can be used to locate sources of information on a topic. Examples include *periodical index, abstracting service, bibliography, catalog,* online or *computerized database,* and *directory.*

accidental sample   A *nonprobability sampling* technique in which those people who happen to be available are chosen for the *sample.*

accumulation   Contents of successive volumes of a title incorporated in one volume. Current issues of *periodical indexes,* for example, are usually accumulated in volumes covering a longer time period.

almanac   A yearly compendium of factual information.

analytical paper   A manuscript in which the author uses evidence to examine various sides of an issue.

annotated bibliography   A list of writings or other materials that includes short descriptions or evaluations in addition to citations.

annotation   A short description of a published work. Critical annotations also evaluate the works described.

annual   A publication that appears once a year.

annual review   An *annual* that provides summaries of scholarly research activities in a particular content area.

APA style (format)   The style recommended by the American Psychological Association (APA) for referencing information in research publications and presentations, and for arranging information in *citations* and *bibliographies.*

appended bibliography   A list of writings or other materials that appears at the end of a book, *article,* or other work.

archival/documentary research   An inquiry that centers on finding, examining, and interpreting messages. Common forms include *library/documentary research, historical research,* and *legal/policy research,* as well as *secondary data analysis* and *meta-analysis.*

archive   (a) An organized body of public records or historical documents. (b) An institution that collects, preserves, and provides services related to using stored materials.

argumentative paper   An essay that begins with a point of view, which the writer supports with facts and opinion.

article   A manuscript published in a *journal,* other *periodical,* or an *encyclopedia.*

artifact-oriented research   See *message-* or *artifact-oriented research.*

audience   The target of a class project: class members, the general public, an instructor, or a specific societal group.

behavior-oriented research   See *people-* or *behavior-oriented research.*

bibliographic database   A *computerized database* that consists primarily of *citations* to publications and often includes *abstracts.*

bibliographic style   A style used for arranging information in a *citation* or a *bibliography.* Examples: *APA style* and *MLA style.*

bibliography   A list of writings or other materials, usually compiled on the basis of topic, author, or other element common to the entries and systematically arranged. Types of bibliographies include *annotated, appended, current, general, retrospective,* and *selective topical.*

bibliography record   A record in which the complete *citation* for a publication is entered by a researcher. It includes a brief summary of the contents of the publication.

bibliography-management program   Software program that facilitates the development and maintenance of personal *bibliographic databases.* Examples include EndNote, RefWorks, Reference Manager, and ProCite. These programs allow a user to create records or to download them directly from bibliographic databases, to add notes and *keywords,* and to format the output in a variety of *bibliographic styles,* including APA and MLA. Some can be integrated into standard word-processing programs.

bimonthly   A publication that appears every other month.

blog   A shortened form of weblog, a blog refers to a diary or log of thoughts, opinions, actions, or photos posted on the web by an individual, representing either himself/herself or an organization.

book stacks   Library book shelves or floors of a library containing retrievable books.

Boolean operator   See *logical (Boolean) operator.*

bound periodical   Older *periodicals* in a library collection. Recent issues of periodicals normally accumulate until an entire volume can be collected for binding.

broadcast index   A list of programs archived via audiotape or videotape that can be searched by title or subject.

browse   A feature of search systems that allows a user to review, or scan through, the database *index* to identify variations of a name or term.

browser   Software that provides an interface to the *World Wide Web* (web). Examples include Windows Internet Explorer and Mozilla Firefox.

catalog   A systematic list of books and other materials that records, describes, and indexes the resources of one or more libraries or *collections.* Some library catalogs are still available on cards; some are published in book format or on *microfilm* or *microfiche.* Most library catalogs are now accessed *online.*

CD-ROM   An abbreviation for "compact disk-read only memory," this usually refers to a small laser disk that stores electronic *data.*

citation   A reference note on the source of facts, quotations, or opinions. A complete citation contains sufficient bibliographic information to enable a researcher to locate an item.

citation index   A published listing of works that have been cited by subsequently published works. The listing is usually arranged by cited author, enabling one to locate later works that have cited that author's *research.* Searching carried out using these tools is often called "cited reference searching."

cited references   A list of articles that authors include in their reference list. These are articles that the authors consulted and referenced in the paper.

cluster sample   A *probability sampling* technique in which subgroups of a *population* are identified in stages, and then the *sample* is drawn randomly from the final subgroup.

collection   A compilation of documents or media of a similar type that are gathered and published as *periodicals,* books, or in *microform.*

communications software   A software program that enables a computer to communicate with another computer electronically.

composite week   In *content analysis,* when a week is created by randomly selecting one Monday, one Tuesday, one Wednesday, and so on from all possible Mondays, Tuesdays, Wednesdays, and so on for the year.

computerized database   A *database* stored on a magnetic or optical medium so that it can be accessed by computer. Types of computerized databases include *bibliographic, directory, full-text, image, source,* and *statistical.*

Comserve   An electronic information service for the communication field available through the CIOS (Communication Institute for Online Scholarship) *website.*

conceptual definition   Terms used to describe the true meaning of a *variable.*

content analysis   An examination of the structure and content of messages, particularly those in the media.

control   (a) One aim of science (in addition to theory, explanation, understanding, and prediction). (b) To test or verify by means of conducting an experiment in a contained environment.

control group   A group of individuals that does not receive an experimental treatment.

controlled vocabulary   A set of *subject headings* or *descriptors* used by a particular *abstracting service, catalog, computerized database,* or *index* to describe listed works.

convenience sample   A nonrandom collection of participants in survey research; people who just happen to be available.

conversation analysis   An examination of the structure, messages, function, rules, and content of everyday talk.

critical abstract   A summary of the main findings of an article plus commentary on the study's validity, reliability, or completeness.

critical paper   A treatise that analyzes and evaluates literature and draws conclusions about a subject.

critical/cultural   A research approach in which a critic selects and applies appropriate criteria to interpret and to evaluate a communication event and its consequences. Types include *cultural criticism, dramatistic analysis, fantasy theme analysis, feminist criticism, Marxist criticism,* and *rhetorical criticism.*

cultural criticism   A *critical/cultural* textual approach in which a critic identifies social and economic reasons for a communication event.

current bibliography   A list of writings or other materials that is updated on a regular basis.

data   Information that is observed or gathered in the conduct of *research.*

database   A collection of information organized in such a way that specific items can be retrieved.

database producer   An organization that compiles and publishes *computerized databases.*

dependent variable   A consequent or presumed effect in a relationship between two or more *variables.*

descriptive research   An identification and account of events or conditions.

descriptor   A word or phrase under which publications dealing with a particular subject are listed in a *periodical index.* See also *subject headings.*

dictionary   A book or *computerized database* containing a collection of words, together with their meanings, equivalents, derivation, syllabication, and other useful information. See also *subject dictionaries.*

directory   A systematically arranged list of individuals, institutions, or organizations, giving addresses, activities, publications, and other information.

directory database   A *computerized database* that contains references to organizations, people, grants, research projects, contracts, and so forth. See also *web directory.*

discipline   A branch of knowledge and the individuals who teach and *research* in it.

document delivery service   A service offered by database *vendors,* allowing users to order publications *online* for delivery through the mail.

documentary research   See *archival/documentary research.*

domain   A subsection of an *Internet* address that specifies a computer or set of computers being addressed; it typically includes logical or geographical designations such as ".com", ".org", ".gov", ".ca", and ".fr". Example: "kent.edu".

downloading   The practice of transferring *data* from a larger computer to a smaller one.

dramatistic analysis   A *critical/cultural* textual approach in which researchers examine a communication event as though it were theatrically staged and acted.

e-book   A book in which text is downloaded to an electronic display and readers page through it, just as they do with a printed book.

edited book   A volume that contains original research reports, original essays, or review essays written by different authors.

e-mail   Electronic mail or messages that are sent via computer networks.

encyclopedia   A comprehensive compilation of information, usually arranged alphabetically by topic in essays and providing overviews that might include definitions, descriptions, background, and bibliographic references. General encyclopedias attempt to encompass all branches of knowledge, whereas subject encyclopedias limit coverage to a specific *discipline.*

ethnography   An *observational research* method used to describe social norms and events as they occur.

exemplary literature review   An examination and description of only those materials that pertain most closely to a topic.

exhaustive literature review   An examination and description of all materials on a topic.

experimental design   A plan or blueprint for the conduct of *experimental research.*

experimental group   A group in an experiment that receives an experimental treatment or manipulation.

experimental research   An investigation of communication events under controlled conditions. Usually, the goals are to explain and to predict relationships among *variables.*

explanatory research   An inquiry that looks for underlying causes and explanations of events.

external validity   Results of an empirical *research* study that are generalizable to other people, situations, times, and so forth.

fantasy theme analysis   A *critical/cultural* textual technique in which an image or vision is created and examined.

feminist criticism   A *critical/cultural* textual technique that examines events as a result of oppression of women in society.

field   A part of a *record* used in a *database* to hold information about each document. *Bibliographic databases* include such fields as title, author, journal name, publication year, *abstract,* and *subject heading* or *descriptor.*

field research   See *nonlaboratory research.*

finding tool   See *access tool.*

focus group   A type of intensive group interviewing used to understand consumer attitudes and behaviors.

free-text searching   A method of searching *computerized databases* in which all words in a *record* or *citation* can be searched. Free-text searching uses *natural language* rather than a *controlled vocabulary.* It is often called *keyword searching.*

full-image database   See *image database.*

full-text database   A *computerized database* that contains a complete text of publications, such as *journals,* newspapers, and books. Every word of the entire text of these publications can be searched.

full-text periodical   A journal, magazine, or other publication that provides an entire text electronically.

general bibliography   A list of writings or other materials that includes *citations* of materials on a variety of topics.

goal   The aim of a project: to inform and/or persuade.

government document   Any printed matter originating from or printed at the expense or with the authority of an office of a government. Types include hearings, committee prints, and reports.

guide to the literature   A type of reference that lists and annotates available sources (e.g., *directories, indexes,* and *journals*) for a *discipline* or subject area. Guides might offer descriptions of the literature in a field, recommend effective *search strategies,* and identify organizations that provide additional information to researchers.

handbook   A compact book of facts, sometimes called a *manual.* Scholarly or subject handbooks organize, summarize, and make readily accessible a body of information about a field of study.

historical research   An examination of past observations to understand events that occurred.

hit   A record that a computer has found containing the *descriptor* or *keyword* used with a *computerized database* search. It is sometimes termed a "posting."

home page   A default document that *World Wide Web* (web) users see when connecting to a particular web *server.* From a home page, a user goes to other *webpages* on the *website.*

html (hypertext markup language)   A language used to write *hypertext* documents for the *World Wide Web.*

http (hypertext transport protocol)   A program that establishes connections between *hypertext* documents on the *World Wide Web.*

hyperlink   A connection on *World Wide Web* documents to another web resource that can be activated by clicking. A textual hyperlink is usually underlined and/or highlighted in color. It can also be an icon, image, or button.

hypertext   A document that includes links to other documents.

hypertext markup language   See *html.*

hypertext transport protocol   See *http.*

hypothesis   An educated guess or prediction about the relationship between two or more *variables.*

identifier   A type of *controlled vocabulary* used by ERIC for subject retrieval.

image database   A *computerized database* that contains graphic images such as photographs, reproductions of artworks, and textual material.

implied Boolean symbol   A symbol used in a search *query* to designate *records* to be included (+) or excluded (−).

independent variable   An antecedent or presumed cause in a relationship between two or more *variables.*

index   (a) A list (usually alphabetical) giving the location of materials, topics, names, and so forth in a work or group of specified works. (b) A shortened form of *periodical index.* (c) A feature of search systems that allows a user to *browse* an alphabetical list of words and names in a particular *field.*

indicative abstract   A short paragraph that describes a study and gives the purpose and results.

informative abstract   A brief summary of the purpose, method, results, and conclusions of a research article.

interaction analysis   A *textual research* technique in which samples of conversation are transcribed, coded, and analyzed to draw conclusions about the communicators' goals, rules, and interaction.

interface   A screen design and features used by a search system to facilitate communication between a user and a *computerized database.*

interlibrary loan system   A cooperative arrangement between libraries and groups of libraries by which one library borrows material for its patrons from another library.

internal validity   Indicates that results of a study cannot be explained in any other way. That is, little or no fault can be found with a study's sampling method, measuring instruments, and *research* design.

Internet   An international network of computer networks used to access *computerized databases,* communicate with others, and retrieve document files.

Internet protocol (IP) address   An *Internet* address expressed numerically.

intervening variable   A factor other than an *independent variable* that can affect a *dependent variable.*

interview   A qualitative technique used to probe *respondents'* attitudes and behaviors.

journal   A *periodical* containing *research reports* and *review articles* in a scholarly field or *discipline.*

keyword   Any word in a *database record* that can be searched. In most *bibliographic databases,* any word in the title, *abstract,* and subject heading *fields* is a keyword. In a *full-text database,* any word in the body of the text can be a keyword. Keywords are not part of a *controlled vocabulary,* so searching that does not rely on *subject headings* or *descriptors* is often called *keyword searching.*

keyword searching   A method of searching *computerized databases* in which the words in most or all *fields* in a *record* can be searched. Keyword searching uses *natural language* rather than a *controlled vocabulary.*

laboratory research   Investigations conducted in surroundings that are new to the individuals being studied. Usually, laboratory research is conducted to *control* extraneous *variables.*

LC   Abbreviation for the Library of Congress. *Library of Congress subject headings* are often called LC subject headings.

legal encyclopedia   A type of subject encyclopedia that contains narratives about legal cases and indexes. It is most useful when researching communication law, freedom of speech, and debate topics.

legal/policy research   An inquiry into how law operates in society.

legal research   An examination of primary sources (legislative statutes, court decisions, executive orders, administrative agency decisions and rules, and treaties), secondary sources (legal textbooks, dictionaries, encyclopedias, commentaries, periodicals, restatements, and document sourcebooks), and finding tools (bibliographies, citators, computerized search services, indexes, law digests, loose-leaf services, and legal research guides).

Library of Congress classification   A system of subject classification of materials developed by the Library of Congress for its *collection.* It is widely used by college and university libraries in the United States to arrange and locate materials on shelves. Call numbers are composed of letters and numbers.

Library of Congress subject headings   *Subject headings* developed by the U.S. Library of Congress. These are used in the *catalogs* of most academic and public libraries in the United States.

library/documentary research   A review of existing documents or written, printed materials such as those found in a library.

listserv   An electronic discussion group on a particular topic, which uses a mailing list software program to distribute messages to all members' *e-mail* boxes.

literary review   A publication that prints poetry, fiction, and articles about authors and poets.

literature review   A summary, synthesis, and evaluation of previous *research* about a topic. Two types are *exemplary* and *exhaustive.*

literature search   The process of systematically seeking published material on a specific subject.

logical (Boolean) operators   A word such as AND, OR, or NOT, which is used in *database* searching to combine words and concepts.

magazine   A type of *periodical* intended for general reading or for a particular profession.

manual   A compact book of facts. Manuals are similar to *handbooks,* but the term "manual" more specifically denotes how-to guides for accomplishing specific tasks.

Marxist criticism   A *critical/cultural* textual approach that examines events as a result of equality or inequality of power.

media index   A finding tool for newspaper materials, films, television videotapes, and reviews of the same.

message- or artifact-oriented research   Scientific inquiry that examines messages and related issues, such as underlying values. Types include *archival/documentary* and *textual research.*

meta-analysis   A re-analysis of statistics contained in published studies to examine trends in the literature or trends in the results of research studies.

metasearch engine   A *search engine* that automatically submits a search *query* to several other search engines.

microfiche   Positive or negative sheet film (usually 4 x 6 inches) for compact storage of information.

microfilm   Positive or negative roll film, loose or in a cartridge, used for compact storage of information.

microform   A general term for either *microfiche* or *microfilm.*

MLA style (format)   The style recommended by the Modern Language Association (MLA) for referencing information in scholarly publications and for arranging information in *citations* or *bibliographies.*

modem   A device used with a computer to translate digital computer signals into analog signals, making it possible to transmit *data* between computers over telephone or fiberoptic lines or via cable or satellite technologies.

monograph   A book that treats a single subject within a single volume.

multimedia database   A collection of *data* that includes media such as audio, graphic images, and video.

natural language (a) Words and phrases, in no particular order or arrangement, used to conduct *natural language searches*. (b) A term used in *computerized database* searching to distinguish vocabulary available for *keyword searching* from a *controlled vocabulary* and consisting of *descriptors* or *subject headings* listed in a *thesaurus*.

natural language searching system A search system that allows *queries* to be entered informally, using *natural language* terms, phrases, and syntax. Queries can be stated in the form of a question. This type of search system contrasts with Boolean search systems.

nesting Using parentheses to combine terms into logical sets when constructing search *queries*. Example: (television OR radio) AND censorship.

network analysis The study of behavioral interactions among organizational members.

newsgroup An electronic discussion group on *Usenet*.

newspaper index A list of articles, editorials, and reviews that have been published in a newspaper.

newsreader A program that allows a user to access and participate in *Usenet* newsgroups.

noncirculating collection A *collection* of library materials that cannot be checked out for use outside the library. The *reference collection* of a library is usually noncirculating.

nonlaboratory research An investigation conducted in naturalistic surroundings. The subjects may or may not be aware that *research* is being done.

nonprobability sampling The nonrandom selection of members of a *population* for a *sample*.

observational research A *nonlaboratory research* procedure in which trained observers describe behaviors or messages of people or media being studied. Observational research includes *ethnography, network analysis, participant observation, unobtrusive observation,* and *verbal and nonverbal coding*.

online A term used in online database searching designating the direct, interactive process of retrieving computer *data* when a search is in progress.

online catalog A *bibliographic database* consisting of the holdings of a library.

Online Computer Library Center (OCLC) This service is used by many libraries to automate their cataloging and *interlibrary loan* procedures. OCLC makes the resulting *WorldCat* database available through the FirstSearch service. *WorldCat* includes the holdings of most U.S. academic and public libraries.

online search service A service offering access to online databases using search protocols usually specific to the service *vendor*.

operational definition A procedure followed to observe or to measure a *variable*.

operator A word or symbol used to create logical sets that can then retrieve terms in various combinations. *Boolean operators* include AND, OR, and NOT. *Implied Boolean symbols* (operators) include "+" and "−".

participant observation An *observational research* technique used to study social interaction in a natural environment.

PDF (Portable Document Format) Adobe Acrobat was the first to develop PDF files—documents that can contain both text and graphics—which can be sent or retrieved without losing the original formatting.

peer-reviewed   The practice of asking reviewers about the worth of a manuscript submitted for publication.

people- or behavior-oriented research   Scientific inquiry that examines people's behavior. Types include *survey, observational,* and *experimental research.*

periodical   A publication with a distinctive title intended to appear at some specified interval (e.g., weekly or *quarterly*). See also *journal* and *magazine.*

periodical index   An *index* to *articles* published in many different *periodicals,* often including *abstracts* of articles. This term is often shortened to *index.*

plagiarism   Using an author's published words or ideas without giving credit.

poll   *Survey research* used to describe the attitudes or opinions of a *sample.*

population   People or objects that have some common characteristic. Researchers often draw a *sample* of this group to investigate for the purpose of generalizing to the larger population.

primary source   A document, manuscript, record, recording, or an original published report of *research.* Primary sources are often written about or reworked, resulting in *secondary sources.* Legal primary sources include statutes, court decisions, executive orders, and treaties.

probability sampling   The random selection of members of a *population* for a *sample.* The purpose is to generalize observations from that sample to the population.

professional magazine   See *magazine.*

prospectus   A proposal for a research study in which an author thoroughly reviews the supporting literature, creates *hypotheses* or research questions, and details the methods that will be followed to answer the questions or test the hypotheses.

proximity operator   A word or symbol used to specify the closeness of *natural language* terms in *free-text* or *keyword searching* of *computerized databases.*

purposive sample   A *nonprobability sampling* technique in which a *sample* is chosen to represent *respondents* who possess a certain trait.

qualitative research   Inductive, interpretive methods of scientific inquiry.

quantitative research   Deductive, statistical methods of scientific inquiry.

quarterly   A publication that appears four times a year.

query   A request for information entered by a user of *computerized databases* that instructs a search system to retrieve a specified *set* of documents. This is also termed a *search statement.*

quota sample   A *nonprobability sampling* technique in which members of a *sample* are chosen because they have a certain characteristic.

ratings   A measure of the size of broadcast audiences.

record   An entry in a *computerized database* that provides sufficient information about a publication or other information source to permit its identification and retrieval. Records include standardized *fields,* such as title, author, journal name, publisher, and *subject headings* or *descriptors.*

reference   See *citation.*

reference book   A book that forms part of a *reference collection* in a library. Reference books are generally meant to be consulted rather than read in their entirety. Examples include *encyclopedias, dictionaries, almanacs, yearbooks,* and *directories.* They are normally *noncirculating.*

reference collection   A library collection that houses *reference books*. This is normally a *noncirculating collection*.

reference librarian   A librarian who staffs a reference desk and can assist library patrons in locating suitable materials.

relevance or relevancy   An order used to list results of a *database* search in which the most pertinent results are listed first and the least applicable are listed last. Relevance is determined automatically by a ranking algorithm that takes into account such factors as the number of search terms that appear in each document and where they appear. *Search engines* and *natural language search systems* often rank results by relevance.

reliability   A measure's stability, consistency, and repeatability.

research   The objective, systematic, empirical, and cumulative inquiry into a subject.

research ethics   What is right and wrong in the conduct of *research*. Issues include honesty, harm, deception, informed consent, and privacy.

research report   A summary of an original *research* study typically consisting of four main sections: introduction, method, results, and discussion.

respondent   A participant in *survey research*.

retrospective bibliography   A list of writings or other materials that appears at a particular point in time and is not updated.

review article   A published manuscript that thoroughly examines the literature on a particular topic and presents original conclusions about the strength, sufficiency, or consistency of the information.

rhetorical criticism   A *critical/cultural textual research* approach in which a critic identifies a communication event and uses appropriate criteria to evaluate it.

sample   A subgroup of a *population* that is examined in a *research* study. Two methods of sampling are *probability* and *nonprobability*.

scholarly journal   See *journal*.

scope   The breadth of a project: narrow, moderate, or broad. This is determined by amount of time allowed (for oral projects) or length of final copy (for written projects).

search engine   A *keyword searching* system that creates its own *database* of *World Wide Web* resources and facilitates searches of this database through its own search interface. Most search engines allow the use of *Boolean, implied Boolean,* and adjacency *operators*. Some also allow *natural language searching*.

search statement   A request for information entered by a user of *computerized databases* that instructs a search system to retrieve a specified *set* of documents. Often called a search *query*.

search strategy   An organized plan by which a person conducts a *literature search*. In *computerized database* searching, it refers to a set of planned search statements entered into a search system to retrieve desired records.

secondary data analysis   Examining previously gathered or archived *data*.

secondary source   A work that consists of information compiled from *primary*, or original, sources. Examples include *annual reviews, encyclopedias,* and *textbooks*.

selective topical bibliography   A list of writings or other materials that includes *citations* only to those materials judged most pertinent or valuable to a topic. It is not comprehensive.

semiannual   Published twice each year at 6-month intervals.

series   Separate works usually related by subject, author, or format that are assigned a collective series title and issued successively by a publisher.

server   A computer whose software allows it to store *data* and make it available to network users. Users employ client software on their workstations to access the *data*.

set   A group of *records* retrieved from a *computerized database* as a result of a particular *search statement*.

simple random sample   A *probability sampling* technique in which each person has an equal or known chance of being chosen for a *sample*.

source database   A *computerized database* that includes sufficiently complete information to satisfy an information need. *Full-text, statistical,* and *image databases* are examples.

statistical database   A *computerized database* that consists primarily of numerical or other statistical *data*.

statistical source   A reference work that reports census and other government or media statistics.

stratified sample   A *probability sampling* technique in which a *sample* is selected from certain subgroups of a *population* to ensure adequate representation.

subject   A participant in *experimental research*.

subject dictionary   A *dictionary* that resembles an *encyclopedia* in that it contains meanings of one subject area or discipline's terminology.

subject heading   A word or group of words under which publications dealing with a subject are listed in a *abstracting service, bibliography, catalog, computerized database,* or *periodical index*. Subject headings are usually arranged alphabetically. See also *descriptor*.

survey research   A *research* procedure used to collect information about conditions, events, opinions, people, organizations, and so forth. Survey researchers question members of a *sample* often to describe a *population*.

systematic sample   A *probability sampling* technique in which every *n*th person or event is chosen for a *sample* from a list of persons or events.

table-of-contents service   A *periodical index* that delivers to subscribers a list of new article titles and authors.

textbook   An overview and explanation of one or more topics presented in an easy-to-understand manner.

textual analysis   A form of textual research that involves "reading" media content and audience interpretations of the meaning of messages. Also known as reception analysis.

textual research   Examining content or message text in relation to *audience* interpretation. Approaches include *conversation analysis, content analysis, critical/cultural analysis, interaction analysis,* and *textual analysis*.

thesaurus   (a) A list of *descriptors* or *subject headings* and their related terms that accompanies a *computerized* or printed *index, abstracting service,* or *catalog* to indicate specific indexing terms used in that source. (b) A book of synonyms and antonyms.

trade magazine   See *magazine*.

uniform resource locator (URL) A standardized way of representing the addresses of many types of resources on the *World Wide Web,* including *servers, documents, media, databases,* and network services.

union catalog A list of library contents for multiple libraries.

unobtrusive observation A method of *nonlaboratory research* in which a researcher observes participants without their awareness that they are being observed.

Usenet A worldwide network of electronic discussion groups, or *newsgroups,* that can be accessed on most college and university campuses through a *newsreader* program.

validity Measuring what one intends to measure.

variable Something that can assume different values. A concept to which numbers are assigned and that changes in value. For example, television viewing can be a variable with values that range from 0 to 24 hours each day; eye color can be a variable (blue = 1, green = 2, brown = 3, hazel = 4, and so forth).

vendor An organization supplying online databases to other organizations or individuals. Vendors are essentially retailers of online *databases.*

verbal and nonverbal coding A form of observational research in which a researcher applies schemes to describe messages systematically.

web directory A listing of web resources arranged hierarchically by subject or type of resource. Directories are searchable by *keyword.* Directories are called virtual libraries, meta websites, clearinghouses, and subject guides. Some directories are devoted to a single subject, whereas others evaluate, select, and list sites (and other directories) from many subjects.

webpage A single document, written in *html.* It can be thought of as a single computer screen, although a user might have to scroll to view an entire document.

website A collection of *webpages* that are linked to each other and focused on a single subject. A website consists of a *home page* and other *webpages* containing resources. The term more generally refers to any *World Wide Web* resource.

World Wide Web A system based on *hypertext* and other *hyperlinks* that allows a user to explore and connect to other *Internet* resources. Often abbreviated as "the web" or WWW.

yearbook An *annual* volume describing current developments in a specific field. Information is given in narrative or statistical form.

Subject Index

Broadening searches, 64–65
Browsers, World Wide Web, 75–76, 281

C

Call numbers, Library of Congress, 21
Canadian Communication Association, 10
Case history, 213
Catalogs, library, 25, 27, 28, 31–32, 281
CD-ROMs, 51, 281
Central States Communication Association
(CSCA), 11
Chicago format or style, 257–259
Chinese Communication Association, 10
Chronological order, 239
CIOS, 85
Citation indexes, 130–131, 281
Cited references, 130–131, 281
Citing sources, 274–275
Cluster sample, 202, 281
Coding, verbal and nonverbal, 224
Collections
defined, 157–158
legal, 166–167, 181–182
measurement, 165–166, 181
media, 160–165, 178–181
microform, 161
selected list, 177–182
speech, 158–160, 177
Committee print, Congressional, 169–173
Communication, professional pursuits, 14
Communication discipline, 3–8
Communication Institute for Online
Scholarship (CIOS), 85
Communication organizations
activities, 8–9
conventions, 9
divisions, 12–13
newsletters and publications, 9–10
professional, 11–12
regional scholarly, 11
Communication and technology, 5, 7
Comparison-and-contrast order, 239
Composite week, 218, 281
Comserve, 85, 281
Conceptual definition, 200, 281
Congressional Information
Service, 169
Consequent, 200
Content analysis
defined, 215, 217–218, 281
selected list, 230
Content footnotes, 277
Contexts, communication, 4
Control groups, 226, 281
Controlled conditions, 225
Controlled vocabulary, 53–55, 281
Convenience sample, 202, 282

Conversation analysis, 214–215, 282
Copy-editing symbols, 262
Critical abstracts, 234, 282
Critical papers, 240–241, 282
Critical/cultural approaches, 215–216, 282
Criticism, feminist, 215, 283
Criticism, Marxist, 215, 216, 286
Criticism, rhetorical, 215, 289
Criticism, rhetorical and media, selected list, 230
C-SPAN archives, 164
Cultural approaches, 215–216, 282
Cultural criticism, 215, 282
Current awareness services, 132

D

Data gathering and analysis, 201–202
Databases
bibliographic, 50–51, 280
defined, 49–50, 282
directory, 51, 282
evaluation, 124–125
full-text, 52, 283
image, 52, 122–131, 284
multimedia, 52, 286
producers, 123, 282
searching, 52–68
source, 51–52, 290
statistical, 51, 290
types, 50–52
vendors, 123–124
World Wide Web as source of, 80–81
Deep web, 80
Dependent variable, 200, 282
Descriptive research, 198, 282
Descriptors, 34, 53–55, 282
Design
experimental, 225–227, 283
one-grouppretest-posttest, 225–226
one-shot case study, 225
pretest-posttest control group, 225–226
Solomon four-group, 226–227
Designs, preexperimental, 225–226
Deutsche Gesellschaft fur Publiz und
Kommunikationswissenschaft, 10
DIALOG searches, 68
Dictionaries
selected list, 188–189
subject, 102, 175–176
Direct Marketing Association, 12
Directories
communication, 77–79
media, 173–175, 186–187
WWW, 77–79, 291
Directory databases, 51, 282
Discipline, communication, 3–8
Doctoral dissertations, bibliographic format, 269
Document delivery services, 35, 67, 282

Documentary research, 212, 282
Dramatistic analysis, 215, 282

E

Eastern Communication
    Association (ECA), 11
E-books, 100, 282
EBSCOHost, 60–61
Editorial studies, 213
Educational Resources Information Center
    (ERIC), 9, 128
Electronic discussion groups, 82–84
Electronic Industries Association, 168
Electronic journals, 154
Electronic media collections, 163–165
Electronic sources, bibliographic
    format, 273–274
Empirical research, 198–199
Encyclopedias
    defined, 101, 283
    selected list, 108–110
    subject, 101
    types, 101–102
ERIC, 9, 128
Ethics, research, 204–205
Ethnography, 216, 222–223, 283
European Communication Research and
    Education Association, 10
Evaluation of sources
    Internet, 85–89
    scholarly, 35–37
Exemplary literature reviews, 236–237, 283
Experimental design, 226, 283
Experimental groups, 227, 283
Experimental research, 225–228, 283
Explanatory research, 198, 283
External validity, 203, 283

F

Fantasy theme analysis, 215, 283
FCC, 166, 170
Federal Communications Commission (FCC),
    166, 170
Federal Radio Commission, 166
Feminist criticism, 215, 283
Field research, 227, 283
Field-specific online search techniques, 60–62
FirstSearch, 118
Focus groups, 222, 283
Footnotes, 257–259
Free-text searching, 53, 283
Full-image databases, 52, 283
Full-text databases, 33, 52, 123, 131, 283
Full-text periodicals, 131, 143, 154, 283

G

Gallup, 169
General search-record card, 42

General-to-specific order, 238
General-to-specific search strategy, 33
Google, 79–82, 84
Government publications/documents
    defined, 169–173, 284
    selected finding tools, 184–185
    selected list, 184
Grammar, 254
Group communication, 5, 7
Guides to the literature
    defined, 118–120, 284
    selected list, 133–134
    types, 118–120

H

Handbooks
    defined, 97–98, 284
    selected list, 104–106
    types, 97–100
Harris (poll), 169
Health and Sciences Communications
    Association, 12
Health communication, 5, 7
Hearings, congressional, 172–173
Historical research, 213, 284
HTML, 72, 284
HTTP, 74, 284
Hyperlinks, 72, 284
Hypertext, 72, 284
Hypertext markup language, 72, 284
Hypertext transport protocol, 284
Hypotheses, 14, 199–200, 284

I

Image databases, 52, 122–131, 284
Implied Boolean operators, 59, 82, 284
Independent variable, 200, 284
Indicative abstracts, 234, 284
Informative abstracts, 234, 284
Institutional study, 213
Instructional communication, 6, 7
Interaction analysis, 215, 216–217, 285
Interaction Process Analysis, 217
Intercultural/international
    communication, 6, 7
Interlibrary loan systems, 21–22, 35, 67, 285
Internal validity, 203, 285
International Advertising
    Association, 12
International Association for Media &
    Communication Research, 10
International Association of Business
    Communicators, 12
International Association of Language and Social
    Psychology, 10
International Communication
    Association (ICA), 9, 10
International Listening Association, 10

International Speech Communication
    Association, 10
International Telecommunications Union, 10
Internet
    access to, 73–74
    addresses, 74–75
    evaluating sources, 85–89
Interpersonal communication, 6, 7
Intervening variables, 227, 285
Interviews, 219, 285
Investigative Reporters and Editors, 11
Invisible Web, 80, 90

J

Jargon, 256
Journal alerting services, 132
Journals, scholarly
    advertising, business, marketing, and public
        relations, 150–151
    communication, 141–144, 146–147
    electronic, 143, 154
    history and political science, 152
    psychology, sociology, and social psychology,
        151–152
    speech and language, 149–150
    submitting manuscripts, 246–249

K

Keyword searching, 33–34, 53–55, 285
Known-to-unknown order, 239
Korean American Communication
    Association, 10

L

Laboratory research, 227, 285
Lambda Pi Eta, 12
Language and symbolic codes, 6, 7
Legal
    collections, 166–167
    encyclopedias, 102, 285
    research, 120–121, 285
    selected list, 181–182
Legal references, bibliographic format, 274
Legal/Government collections
    finding tools, 182
    loose-leaf reporting services, 166
    selected list, 181–182
Legal/policy research, 213, 285
Library of Congress
    catalog, 118
    classification system, 285
    subject headings, 25–26, 29–30, 286
Library procedures, 20–23
Library/documentary research, 212, 286
Listservs, 82–84, 286
Literary reviews, 237, 286
Literature reviews
    defined, 236–237, 286

exemplary, 236–237, 283
exhaustive, 236–237
non-linear search process, 19
organizing strategies, 238–239
outline, 43
parts, 237–239
research questions, 14, 24–25, 43, 198–200
search strategies, 23–44
steps, 239–240
tips, 42
topics, 23–25
writing, 43–44, 237–240
Literature search, 23–44, 286
Logical (Boolean) operators, 55–59, 82, 286
Loose-leaf reporting services, 166

M

Magazine Publishers of America, 11
Manuals
    defined, 176, 286
    selected list, 190
Manuscript style, APA, 262, 275–278
Marxist criticism, 215, 216, 286
Mass communication, 6, 8
Measurement collections
    defined, 165–166
    selected list, 181
Media
    collections, 160–165, 178–181
    directories, 173–175
    electronic collections, 163–165
    indexes, 160–163, 179–181, 286
    instructional, 183
Media Communications Association
    International, 12
Media Ecology Association, 10
Mediated online search services, 68
Message-oriented research, 211–218, 286
Meta-analysis, 214, 286
Meta-search engines, 80, 286
Microform collections, 163
MLA format or style, 257–259
Monographs, 100, 286
Movement study, 213
Multimedia databases, 52, 286
Museum of Broadcast Communications, 164
Museum of Television and Radio, 164

N

Narrowing a topic, 24–25, 29–30, 64–65
National Association of Broadcasters, 11, 168
National Association of Television Program
    Executives, 11
National Communication Association
    (NCA), 9, 10, 11
National Conference of Editorial Writers, 11
National Forensic Association, 10
National Press Club, 11

National Press Photographers Association, 11
National Speakers Association, 12
National union catalog, 118, 291
Natural language searching, 65–66, 287
Nesting, 57–59, 287
Network analysis, 224, 287
Newsgroups, Usenet, 84–85, 287
Newspaper Association of America, 11
Newsreaders, 84, 287
Non-laboratory research, 235, 287
Non-print media, bibliographic format, 269–270
Nonprobability sampling, 202, 287
Nonverbal coding, 224
Note taking, 38–41

O

Observational research, 222–224, 287
OCLC, 118, 287
One-grouppretest-posttest design, 225–226
One-shot case study design, 225
Online catalogs, 31–33, 287
Online Computer Library Center
    (OCLC), 118, 287
Online search techniques, 52–68
Operational definitions, 200, 287
Operators, logical, 55–59, 82, 287
Organizational communication, 5, 6, 8
Original research reports, 245–246
Outdoor Advertising Association of America, 12

P

Pacific and Asian Communication
    Association, 10
Paragraph structure, 254–255
Paraphrasing, 259–260
Participant observation, 223–224, 287
PDF (Portable Document Format), 52, 287
Peer-reviewed, 131, 287
People- or behavior-oriented
    research 218-228, 288
Periodical indexes
    abstracts, 122–123
    communication, 125–128
    defined, 122, 288
    full-text, 123–124,
    general and interdisciplinary, 128–129
    selected list, 134–136
    types, 122–123
Periodicals
    bibliographic format, 271–272
    defined, 139
    electronic, 143, 154
    full-text, 143, 154,
    professional and trade magazines, 144–145
    scholarly journals, 139–144
Phrase searching, 60
Pi Kappa Delta, 11
Plagiarism, 89–90, 259–260, 288

Political Commercial Archive, 164
Polls, 221, 288
Population, 201, 288
Posttest-only control-group design, 226
Preexperimental designs, 225–226
Presidential libraries, 159
Pretest-posttest control-group design, 226–227
Primary sources, 213, 288
Print media collections, 160–163
Probability sampling techniques, 201–202, 288
Problem-cause-solution order, 238
Professional and trade magazines
    selected list, 153–154
    types, 144–145
Proofreading
    checklist, 261
    symbols, 262
Prospectus, research, 241–242, 288
Proximity operators, 59–60, 288
Public Affairs Video Archives, 164
Public communication, 6, 7, 8
Public Relations Society of America, 12
Public Relations Student Society of America, 12
Publishers' series, 103, 290
Purposive sample, 202, 288

Q

Qualitative research methods, 201, 288
Quantitative research methods, 201, 288
Questionnaires, 220–221
Quota sample, 202, 288
Quoting, 259–260

R

Radio Advertising Bureau, 168
Radio-Television News Directors Association, 11
Ratings research, 221, 288
Reading research, 37–38
Reception analysis, 216
Regional studies, 213
Relational analysis, 216
Relational Control Coding Scheme, 217
Relevance ranking, 66, 289
Reliability, 203, 289
Religious Communication Association, 10
Reports, congressional, 172
Research
    approaches, 15, 211–228
    archival/documentary, 212–214, 280
    artifact-oriented, 211–218, 280
    behavior-oriented, 218–224, 280
    critical/cultural, 215–216, 282
    defined, 3
    descriptive, 198, 282
    empirical, 198–199
    ethics, 204–205
    ethnography, 216, 222–223, 283
    experimental, 225–228, 283

Research (*continued*)
explanatory, 198, 283
field, 227, 283
historical, 213, 284
laboratory, 227, 285
legal, 120–121, 166–167, 181–182, 285
legal/policy, 213, 285
library/documentary, 212, 286
message-oriented, 211–218, 286
non-laboratory, 227, 287
observational, 222–224, 287
people- or behavior-oriented, 218–228, 288
problem, 199
process, 197–204
projects, 13–14
prospectus, 241–244
qualitative, 201, 288
questions, 14, 24–25, 43, 199–200
ratings, 221, 288
stages, 199
survey/interview, 218–222, 290
systematic nature, 3
texts, selected list, 205–206
textual, 214, 290
writing reports, 245–246
Research designs
selected list, 230
types, 225–227
Research methods
quantitative, 201, 288
Respondents, 219, 289
Review, literary, 237, 286
Rhetoric, 4
Rhetoric Society of America, 10
Rhetorical criticism
defined, 215, 289
selected lists, 230
Roper, 169
Russian Communication Association, 10

S
Sample, purposive, 202, 288
Samples and sampling, 289
Sampling, nonprobability, 202, 287
Sampling and data gathering, 201–202
Satellite Broadcasting and Communications
Association, 11
Scholarly journals, 139–144
Search concepts/terms, 25–29
Search engines, 79–82, 289
Search procedures, online, 30–35, 52–68
Search records, 39–43
Search strategy, 23–44, 97, 115–116, 289
Search strategy sheet, 32
Search techniques, online
Boolean operators, 55–59, 82
controlled vocabulary, 53–55

field-specific searching, 60–62
keywords, 53–55
narrowing and broadening, 26–29, 64–65
natural language, 65–66
phrase searching, 60
proximity operators, 59–60
subject headings, 53–55
truncation, 62–63, 81
word/phrase indexes, 63
Secondary data analysis, 214, 289
Secondary sources, 213, 289
Series, 103, 110–111, 290
Servers, 74, 290
Sexist language, 256
Sigma Chi Eta, 12
Simple random sample, 201, 290
Society for New Communication Research, 10
Society of Broadcast Engineers, 11
Society of Environmental Journalists, 11
Society of Motion Picture and Television
Engineers, 11
Society of Professional Journalists, 11
Solomon four-group design, 225–227
Source databases, 51–52, 290
Southern States Communication
Association (SSCA), 11
Speakers Platform, 12
Specific-to-general order, 239
Specific-to-general search strategy, 33
Speech collections, 158–160, 177
Speech Communication Association (SCA), 12
Standard Rate and Data Service, 169
Statistical databases, 51, 290
Statistical sources, 167–169, 182–184
Statistical sources, finding tools, 184
Stratified sample, 201–202, 290
Student Clubs, 12
Subject
dictionaries, 102, 290
encyclopedias, 101–102
handbooks, 97–100
Subject headings
defined, 34, 290,
Library of Congress, 25–26, 29–30
lists, 26, 41–42
thesauri, 26–27, 290
Subjects
defined, 227, 290
ethical treatment, 204–205
random assignment, 226, 227
Submitting research papers, 246–249
SuDocs (Superintendent of Documents)
numbers, 21
Supreme Court decisions, 166–167
Survey research
defined, 226–230, 300
selected list, 238–239

Source Index